PROFESSIONAL PIANO TEACHING

Volume 1: Elementary Levels

A Comprehensive Piano Pedagogy Textbook

Second Edition

Jeanine M. Jacobson

Edited by E. L. Lancaster and Albert Mendoza

Alfred Music
Los Angeles

Dedication

*With humble thanks, this book is dedicated to my husband, Carl,
and my daughters Katherine and Rachel, who have provided love, patience,
understanding and the means to make this book a reality.*

Copyright © 2006, 2015 by Alfred Music
P.O. Box 10003, Van Nuys, CA 91410-0003

All rights reserved. First edition 2006
Second edition 2015

Printed in the United States of America

ISBN-10: 1-4706-2649-7
ISBN-13: 978-1-4706-2649-5

Library of Congress Cataloging-in-Publication Data

Jacobson, Jeanine Mae, 1940- author.
  Professional piano teaching : a comprehensive piano pedagogy textbook / Jeanine M.
Jacobson ; edited by E. L. Lancaster and Albert Mendoza.
    volume cm
  Includes bibliographical references and index.
  ISBN 978-0-7390-8169-3 (alk. paper)
  1. Piano--Instruction and study. 2. Music--Textbooks. I. Lancaster, E. L., 1948- editor. II.
Mendoza, Albert, 1979- editor. III. Title.
  MT220.J18 2015
  786.2'193071--dc23
                        2014049251

Preface

Now is an exciting time to be a professional piano teacher. New teaching materials, affordable instruments, and breakthrough technologies have made piano study more accessible than ever before. With this in mind, *Professional Piano Teaching* has been revised to accommodate the needs of today's piano teacher. This second edition has been expanded to include two additional chapters on special topics: teaching adult students (Chapter 11) and teaching popular, sacred, and other familiar music (Chapter 12). Links to websites and other information related to various resources have been updated.

Professional Piano Teaching, Book 1, is designed to serve as a basic text for a first-semester piano pedagogy course. It provides an introduction to the profession, an overview of learning principles, a thorough approach to all aspects of teaching beginners and elementary students, and a detailed analysis of the business aspects of independent teaching. Special topics related to group teaching, teaching preschool students, and evaluation of teaching also are included. Its thorough treatment of subject matter makes it useful for pedagogy students, new teachers, university graduates with little or no pedagogy coursework, and teachers who have had limited opportunity for advanced training. Due to its comprehensive approach, experienced teachers will also find it filled with helpful hints to enhance their skills.

The book deals not only with what to teach, but with how to teach and solve problems in teaching. Teachers will be able to apply the principles that are discussed to real situations that they encounter on a daily basis. Actual teaching problems are discussed and workable solutions are offered for them. Numerous musical examples are used to illustrate the discussions. For copyright reasons, most musical examples were chosen from materials published or distributed by Alfred Music. Because bibliographies quickly become outdated and new teaching materials appear with regularity, specific lists of materials are limited. Additionally, computer and keyboard technology has not been treated as a separate chapter in the book. Because of the rapidly changing technology, general applications are suggested throughout the text as appropriate.

For the beginning pedagogy class, it is recommended that students study Chapters 1 through 8 in order. By following this order, they explore the field in a systematic way, learning:

- what it means to become a professional piano teacher (Chapter 1)

- principles of learning applied to piano teaching (Chapter 2)

- how to choose a beginning piano method (Chapter 3)

- elementary teaching concepts and common problems of beginners (Chapter 4)

- specifics of teaching rhythm and reading (Chapter 5)

- specifics of teaching technique and musical sound development (Chapter 6)

- how to choose repertoire and present it (Chapter 7)

- how to develop musicality in students (Chapter 8)

The special topics in the book can be integrated into the class according to the preference of the teacher, the length of the term, and the needs of the student. These topics include:

- an exploration of group teaching (Chapter 9)

- a philosophical and practical discussion about teaching preschoolers (Chapter 10)

- teaching adult students (Chapter 11)

- teaching popular, sacred, and other familiar music (Chapter 12)

- the business aspects of teaching piano (Chapter 13)

- suggestions for observing and evaluating lessons (Chapter 14)

In Chapter 13 (Business Aspects of Teaching), samples of professional forms, studio policies, brochures, business cards, and ads are given. The publisher hereby grants the purchaser of this book permission to use and adapt these forms for personal and professional purposes.

Chapter 14 (Evaluation of Teaching) should be studied as soon as pedagogy students start to observe experienced teachers and begin their own student teaching.

Important points covered in each chapter are summarized at the end of the chapter. These summary points can be used in the pedagogy classroom for starting classroom discussions of key topics. Projects that build on the teaching principles introduced in the chapter are suggested for both new teachers and experienced teachers. Pedagogy teachers can assign or adapt those projects that are appropriate for students in their classes.

Additionally, *Professional Piano Teaching*, Book 2, is now available. Book 2 covers topics related to teaching students beyond the elementary levels. When used together, the two books offer a comprehensive and unparalleled approach to piano pedagogy instruction.

The quest for improvement of piano teaching skills never ends. Whether you are beginning the journey as a new teacher with this book or whether you are an experienced teacher refining your skills, the author wishes you continued success as you pursue your career in *professional piano teaching*.

Acknowledgments

The writing of a book like this represents the assimilation of a lifetime of information collected from influential mentors, colleagues, and personal experience. There are very few original teaching ideas within these pages, but rather, a compilation of what I have learned from others. This book would not have been possible without the love, wisdom, creativity, and expertise of the following persons. For all that, I give my heartfelt thanks.

It would not have been possible for me to take my first piano lessons at age five if it were not for my grandmother, May Grossman, who sent me, from Nebraska to Washington, her piano that she had purchased with her first school teaching money at the age of 15. My parents Erma and William Ahrens sacrificed so they could provide me with lessons. My first piano and music teachers, Borghild Anderson, Marybeth Fadden Gilbert, and Dorothy Gilmore, instilled in me a genuine love for music and the sound of the piano. They also taught me that teaching and performing music is about giving to others.

My teachers at the University of Washington, Berthe Poncy Jacobson, Eva Heinetz, and John Moore, taught me discipline and broadened my musical understanding. Subsequent piano and piano pedagogy teachers, Bernard Weiser, Martha Hilley, E. L. Lancaster, and Jane Magrath, helped refine my playing and teaching, and prepared me for my professional work. Over the years, the many workshops, seminars, conferences, conventions, and lessons yielded kernels of wisdom from Frances Clark, Jacqueline Csergi-Schmitt, Gail de Stwolinski, Louise Goss, Tinka Knopf, Barbara Lister-Sink, Susan McCleary, Steven McCurry, Daniel Pollack, Françoise Regnat, Nellie Tholan, and many others too numerous to name. But, it is Richard Chronister who stands out in his dedication to the piano pedagogy field, who provided knowledge, influence, opportunity, and friendship to a whole generation of piano pedagogues, including myself.

I have taught piano for over 50 years, first as an independent piano teacher, and later as a university professor of piano and piano pedagogy. It is my students, too numerous to list by name, who I want to especially thank for allowing me the opportunity to learn about piano teaching from them.

The *Professional Piano Teaching* books have gone through a long process of growth and development. If it were not for the faith of E. L. Lancaster, they would not exist. For this and his numerous edits, I am truly thankful. Editors and readers Mary Landroth and Linda Owen taught me about writing. A special thanks goes to Gary Muhlbach for his editorial assistance with the first edition. Additional thanks go to editor Albert Mendoza, graphic designer Patti McMahon, and engraver Jason Retana.

CONTENTS

CHAPTER 7:
ELEMENTARY PERFORMANCE AND STUDY REPERTOIRE

CHAPTER 8:
DEVELOPING MUSICALITY IN ELEMENTARY STUDENTS

Chapter 1

THE ART OF
PROFESSIONAL PIANO TEACHING

What does it mean to be a professional piano teacher? Is piano teaching even considered a profession? Some people think of piano teaching as a cottage industry. Many piano teachers teach in their homes—some charge small fees to supplement other family income, while others earn a living entirely from teaching. The educational background of teachers varies from those with little formal musical training to those with advanced degrees. This tradition has created a wide range in the quality of piano teaching. Anyone can teach piano since no minimal educational standards, no legal licensing and no mandatory certification processes exist. Consequently, some teaching is highly crafted, some marginally effective, with most falling in between. The lack of national- or state-mandated educational teaching standards often contributes to a public perception that piano teachers provide a service, but are not professionals.

Fortunately, with the growth of university music departments and piano pedagogy programs during the latter half of the twentieth century, talented young pianists majored in music and entered the teaching field with an extensive musical, pianistic and pedagogical education. This has not only provided guidance for teaching advanced or gifted students, but has helped prepare teachers to work with a wide range of ages, levels and abilities, particularly at elementary and intermediate levels. Furthermore, professional organizations, journals, workshops and conferences have increased awareness about this specialized body of knowledge. In the United States, Music Teachers National Association (MTNA) has a teacher certification program that encourages study, even for those without access to university programs. These trends have made piano teacher education more accessible and have increased respect for the profession.

Teaching a broad spectrum of students can be satisfying if the teacher has learned how to teach effectively. University pedagogy coursework addresses those needs, but is often limited and can only open the door for future teachers. It is each teacher's responsibility to refine the art of teaching through continuing education and thoughtful experience.

CHARACTERISTICS COMMON TO ALL PROFESSIONALS

Professional piano teachers possess characteristics that are common to all professionals. They also have specialized skills that are unique to piano teaching. They recognize the purposes and values of music study and have developed a personal teaching philosophy.

Piano teachers should strive to achieve the following characteristics common to all professionals:

- an advanced education gained through a lengthy period of rigorous training

- training that involves the study of the theory and practice of a specialized body of knowledge

- a commitment to continuing education to upgrade skills

- a professional code of conduct

- an alignment with others in their field through professional organizations that have networks of state and regional associations, annual conferences, mentoring programs and peer review of publications

- professional certification

- active participation and volunteer service in the activities of professional organizations in their field

- the belief that their work is a calling that provides emotional satisfaction as well as financial support

- a clear picture of the goals and objectives of the professional activity

CHARACTERISTICS OF PROFESSIONAL PIANO TEACHERS

"Teachers are born, not made."

This and similar statements suggest that one cannot learn to teach. It also suggests that some teachers are gifted and will teach well, regardless of training, and that others will only be mediocre despite their background or experience. If one were to believe this, one would also have to believe that pedagogy textbooks, journals, classes and workshops are ineffective. However, because pedagogy is the art of teaching, aspiring teachers can learn it with study and practice.

Success in piano teaching is a result of innate talent combined with refined skills. To play the piano well, one takes lessons and practices regularly. Preparing to teach piano also involves lessons, practice and a sustained time commitment. Yet, it is sometimes assumed that anyone who plays the piano at a minimal level also can teach piano. Furthermore, some pianists feel that the study of pedagogy and practice teaching are unnecessary if they are planning to teach only advanced students. It is rare, however, for a teacher to work exclusively with very gifted and/or advanced students. Successful teachers are those who prepare to teach a wide variety of students. They understand the value of teaching and the responsibility for nurturing young musicians. They share the following distinguishing qualities.[1]

Empathy and Concern

Teachers who have a genuine love for students and want to help them learn are positive and happy about their profession. They are open minded and responsive to students, establishing a supportive learning environment that promotes a positive attitude toward music. While the primary role of the teacher is to be a teacher, not a friend, students can sense a teacher's warmth and genuine concern and learn to trust that the teacher will listen to and address their needs in a caring manner.

---

[1] Before continuing this chapter, the reader may want to complete Project 1 and Project 2 for new teachers on p. 15.

Passion and Ability to Inspire

Teachers are inspiring when they have an insatiable desire for learning, express a love for the beauty of music, and are passionate about helping students communicate through music. Such teachers are happy to see students arrive for lessons and are able to instill a love for music and learning in them. Those who are teaching solely for financial reasons, or those who would rather perform instead of teach usually are not passionate or inspiring. Teachers often fulfill their own musical needs and stay inspired by regularly practicing and performing. In addition, playing for students during the lesson sets a positive example and displays a passion for music.

Knowledge

Knowledgeable teachers have a curiosity about music, teaching and learning. They are great students as well as teachers. They regularly practice not only to develop their own pianistic skill, but also to explore new ways to meet student needs. Successful piano teachers have the skills and knowledge to do the following:

- present musical concepts and skills
- develop technical skills and solve technical problems
- develop music reading and aural skills
- prevent problems from developing
- help students develop a full, rich piano sound
- teach the appropriate style and interpretation for a vast repertoire of piano music

Furthermore, successful teachers know how to instruct effectively. These teaching qualities include the following:

- interact comfortably with students
- give clear explanations and directions
- ask probing, focused questions
- help students find ways to express their ideas
- correctly diagnose problems and effectively prescribe solutions
- quickly and accurately assess student learning
- set realistic goals for students and help them realize these goals
- provide effective feedback

Teachers can increase their musical knowledge and teaching skills through continuing education opportunities, such as the following:

- piano lessons
- pedagogy classes

- guided practice teaching
- master classes
- books and professional journals
- teacher conferences and workshops

An undergraduate degree with emphasis on piano teaching usually provides the necessary training. When this is not practical, teachers can obtain equivalent training to help them meet the standards of their profession.

Dedication

Dedicated teachers are always prepared for students and provide them with opportunities beyond the lesson, such as the following:

- varied performance venues
- field trips to recitals and concerts
- diverse educational opportunities including group lessons, studio classes, or technology-assisted instruction

Encouraging Attitude

Encouraging teachers work with all students, regardless of level, interests and ability, to instill courage and confidence. Praise for hard work during lessons or for learning a difficult piece helps motivate students. Specific reinforcement is the key to encouragement. When students know what has or has not been done correctly, it is easier for them to know how to practice effectively. Students become discouraged when teachers are specific about what was incorrect without mentioning what was done well. Professional teachers make corrections in instructive and positive ways that help students learn from their mistakes.

Honesty

High but realistic and achievable goals produce students who develop and respect themselves for their accomplishments. It is unfair, out of misguided kindness, to lead students to believe that their work is fine when it isn't. Honest and forthright teachers are respected by students and parents. The teacher can promote their students' success by asking them to do the following:

- follow rules and procedures;
- attend to the task at hand and work diligently throughout the lesson;
- practice regularly and carefully;
- miss lessons only for emergencies.

When teachers set high standards, students are much more likely to reach their potential.

Patience

Patient teachers give students time to think about difficult tasks and master them. Some students may not be able to answer questions instantly, may not have the same abilities as others, or may be unable to progress in a steady manner. Prudent teachers recognize that a student is a work in progress, not a professional pianist. However, patience is not a substitute for high standards, nor does it imply that the teacher should avoid being stern when necessary.

Teachers who prepare lesson plans will find it easier to be patient. Without lesson plans, teachers often neglect important incremental learning steps. As a result, students can become confused, make mistakes or be unable to answer questions. This can cause teachers to become impatient. Lesson plans ensure that information is presented in a step-by-step fashion and that students learn incrementally and successfully.

Tolerance and Respect

Successful teachers are sensitive to the individuality of students; thinking of each as special, regardless of ability or interest. Students often come to lessons with little or no knowledge of music or the piano and undeveloped musical tastes. Seeing things from the students' point of view and respecting their opinions help create a positive learning environment. Diplomatically guiding students toward appropriate views, while treating them with respect, help build a trusting relationship. Teachers must also recognize their own mistakes. "That's my fault" or "I didn't make myself clear" show respect and build a trust that leads to learning. Students come from diverse and often complex family structures and may have physical or emotional problems that interfere with practice or learning. While teachers should not compromise their personal integrity, unrealistically high standards will result in excessive stress, frustration and discouragement for some students.

Enthusiasm and Energy

Students are more likely to be motivated to practice and will look forward to returning to the next lesson if the teacher is enthusiastic about the student and if lessons are full of energy. Such lessons pass quickly. Slow-moving teachers produce slow-moving students. Teachers whose personalities are more introspective, analytical and intellectual have to work harder to inject vitality into teaching. Speaking with exaggerated inflection (loudly, softly, faster, slower, or in a monotone) to make interpretive points stimulates the lesson and ignites musical expression.

Humor

A touch of humor (without sarcasm) lightens a difficult learning situation. Understanding that piano lessons are serious does not preclude finding ways to make learning fun. Dramatic teaching, of which humor is a part, might include feigning horror at a careless mistake. The student and teacher can enjoy laughing together, and unnecessary stress is reduced. A periodic, honest appraisal of whether both the student and teacher had a good time during the lesson goes a long way toward improving the lesson environment.

Adaptability and Spontaneity

Flexible teachers adapt their teaching to the demands of any given moment. When a student does not feel well, has not practiced, or does not understand explanations, the lesson should be restructured immediately. Spontaneously creating productive learning experiences that meet the student's needs might be achieved by varying the order of the lesson, concentrating on a single piece, or practicing with the student. Giving an occasional lesson or assignment that incorporates the student's choice of music demonstrates a teacher's flexibility. Devising special activities, using verbal imagery, or making up a story for a piece are all ways to turn lessons into exciting learning experiences. Furthermore, such lesson restructuring helps meet the needs of students with different learning styles.

Generosity

A generous teacher recognizes when a student would benefit from study with a different teacher. It may become necessary for a student to study a different instrument or even to stop taking lessons. Some students will study with one teacher for many years, but others may need a change. Some teachers work well with elementary students, while others are especially successful with teenagers. When a student has accomplished the desired goals of study, it may be time to encourage the student to move to another teacher or to pursue other interests. Teachers should not feel betrayed or blame themselves when a student stops lessons or changes teachers. A generous and gracious attitude in these situations is not easy, but it is a mark of a fine teacher.

Professionalism

Joining and participating in the activities of an organization for music teachers provides one of the best opportunities for professional growth. Such participation expresses a commitment to a high standard of musical instruction. Professional organizations require members to abide by a code of ethical behavior toward students and other teachers. Membership and participation in such organizations signifies respect and professionalism.

Organizational Skills

Teachers who are organized will be able to identify goals and keep track of progress toward those goals. Individualized curriculums, lesson plans and materials should be prepared and ready for use at the right moment. Lessons should begin and end promptly and be organized to cover a variety of learning tasks.

The physical environment of the teaching studio should be conducive to good learning, and the teacher should look and act professional. Business aspects of teaching, such as collecting tuition, should be executed in a professional and timely manner. Written policies for make-up lessons and a calendar of studio events will prevent conflicts. Telephone calls and personal matters should not interfere with the lesson time. Teachers who are organized and exhibit authoritative behavior are more likely to enlist parental cooperation in all aspects of study.

DEVELOPING A TEACHING PHILOSOPHY

Goals and objectives can be limiting if teachers devise a curriculum, conduct lessons and craft assignments based solely on their own learning experience. Awareness of good teaching characteristics and of the values of music study helps teachers define a personal teaching philosophy.

Some teachers are primarily interested in the product—the performance, while others believe the process of learning is more important. A great majority of piano teachers, whether product- or process-oriented, use the private lesson format exclusively. A smaller number of teachers use partner lessons or a group lesson format. The best teaching combines aspects of product- and process-oriented approaches and is enhanced by using some type of group lessons regularly as an adjunct to private lessons.

Teachers must also consider the expectations of parents and students when crafting their teaching philosophy. While some parents would like their children to win competitions, others want them to learn purely for enjoyment and personal satisfaction, and still others want their children to learn to sight-read and understand music fundamentals.

Many parents (and students) may not understand the time commitment and discipline required in learning to play the piano. Most students start piano lessons because they simply want to play the piano, learn to improvise, play by ear or play a particular popular piece. In some cases, they want to make their own sounds at the piano and do not understand the importance of learning to read music. They may not want to transpose, harmonize, practice ear training or learn theory. Teachers should recognize that students also gain musical enjoyment and understanding from "fooling around" at the keyboard.

Weekly study often ends when students and/or parents are unhappy. Teachers can avoid this by accommodating student and parent expectations, without compromising their own standards. Consider the following philosophical ideas:

Love of Music and Music-Making

One of the primary goals of a teacher is to promote a love of music and music-making. A love for music is enhanced by the teacher doing the following:

- performing for students

- listening to recordings with students

- assigning music that students enjoy learning

- helping students produce a musical sound and express themselves musically beyond mere notes and rhythm

Students who enjoy the aesthetics of music, experience the physical sensations of playing, and sense accomplishment in piano study are motivated to continue learning and further their love of music.

Love of the Process of Learning Music

Helping students enjoy the learning process sets the tone for successful piano study. When students learn how to solve technical and musical complexities, they will be motivated to continue practicing. Making music together with the teacher and experimenting at the keyboard are as much a part of the learning process as perfecting and performing pieces. Good teaching entices and enthralls students throughout the week and develops within them the desire, dedication and discipline to accomplish daily tasks. This sense of accomplishment will promote a love of learning.

Joy of Musical Communication

Teachers should choose expressive pieces that communicate to the audience—music that reflects stories, characters, moods and personalities. A learning environment that entices the student to understand the deeper meaning behind the music makes the learning process exciting and leads to dramatic performances. While it is important that pieces be played stylistically correct, performances can also reflect the joy of music-making. Teachers who allow students to express musical messages through improvisation will find that the students' performances of composed music will also be more meaningful.

Develop Desire to Lifelong Skills

A realistic goal is to teach concepts and skills that are necessary for students to continue playing as adults. Teaching in a way that promotes independent learning and musical self-reliance guarantees many things for students:

- usable skills to build on for the rest of their lives

- sufficient aural, reading and keyboard skills to teach themselves further

- the ability to think critically about their performances and music in general

- the path to becoming educated consumers of music

Respect for Student Individuality and Recognition of Student Potential

Caring for the individuality of each student is as important as the music itself. Since all students are different, their needs and desires change as they progress. Teaching can be tailored to individual strengths, limitations and potential. Understanding elements of developmental stages, learning styles, personality types and learning disabilities will further refine the teaching process. Effective teachers assess each learner's abilities and needs to assign appropriate materials and tasks. The vast amount of available methods and printed music allows teachers to choose materials that match student personalities and abilities, while devising learning tasks that accentuate strengths. By being aware of learning spurts and plateaus, teachers can adjust the curriculum to help students reach their potential.

Accomplishment in a Reasonable Time

Students should be able to accomplish musical goals in a reasonable length of time. Students become discouraged if they do not progress in a timely manner or perceive the music they are playing as unimportant or too simple. Instant gratification is neither wise nor possible, but a student should not be held back unnecessarily while perfecting minute details. Students progress and are motivated to practice when they feel successful. When an individual student seems unable to progress as expected, the teacher's role is to communicate to the student and parent that progress is lacking. The teacher may even need to suggest that lessons should stop. It is realistic and honest to tell a parent that learning to play the piano for long-term enjoyment takes a minimum of six to eight years.

The Teacher as a Role Model

Lastly, teachers will want to consider the importance of being a role model for their students. Most professional musicians remember at least one individual who inspired and guided them. Teachers have an opportunity and obligation to share the gift of music with others. One way teachers become role models is by giving clear messages that they enjoy teaching.

HELPFUL QUESTIONS FOR DEVELOPING A PERSONAL TEACHING PHILOSOPHY

Once teachers have considered teaching goals, they can refine their philosophy based on personal standards. Expectations of students and parents, as well as the goals of the teacher, should be incorporated into this philosophy of teaching. The following questions will encourage reflection on these important issues. A teacher's philosophy will include answers to the questions that follow.

* **Whom will the teacher teach?** Piano lessons are more productive when teachers decide what types of students they are willing to instruct. Realizing that every person has the right to study piano, are teachers willing to provide instruction to the following:

  * any student, regardless of background, ability and commitment
  * only the innately talented
  * students who prefer to play music other than classical styles
  * students who are involved in numerous other extracurricular activities
  * students who are ambivalent about lessons, but have parents who want them to study
  * students who are not disciplined in practice
  * students who do not have an acoustic piano on which to practice
  * students who will make only a short-term commitment to the study of piano
  * only advanced students
  * students with learning disabilities
  * preschoolers
  * teenagers
  * adults

✻ **Who makes the curricular decisions?** Students are more likely to be motivated if they have some role in deciding the content and direction of their learning experience. This sharing of decisions develops a positive alliance between student and teacher. Each teacher needs to decide what amount of student input is acceptable, for example:

- what music to play

- how much to practice

- whether to participate in group lessons, recitals, competitions and auditions

- the lesson activities

- long-term and short-term goals

✻ **Will there be variety in the teaching format?** Teaching modes should be structured to maximize each student's potential.

- Will students who are less motivated be placed on an "amateur track" of study?

- Will all students, regardless of ability, be given the opportunity to achieve their highest possible level?

- Will some form of group instruction be incorporated to enhance the learning?

✻ **What are the teaching standards?** Teachers can become discouraged when students are unable to meet unrealistically high standards. Standards that are achievable by most students in the studio can be considered realistic, but must allow for individual differences between students.

- Will students be expected to work on only one piece at a time until that piece is perfected?

- Will students be expected to study several pieces simultaneously, perfecting and memorizing selected ones?

- Will students be expected to study *all* pieces until they are stylistically and musically satisfying?

- Will students be allowed to drop pieces once they are note- and rhythm-perfect?

- Will students be allowed to discontinue pieces that are not perfected, after they have learned valuable concepts from them?

- Will students be allowed to study selected pieces for only a week or two as an introduction or review?

- Will students be expected to study all pieces until they are at a performance tempo?

- Will students be expected to keep their eyes on the page most of the time when playing a piece with the score?

- Will students be expected to be able to count aloud with every piece while playing?
- Will students be expected to achieve a specific level of musical and technical advancement each year?

✳ **How will materials and repertoire be chosen and studied?** Students should be able to learn as much music as possible from varying styles. Will students be allowed to play the following types of music:

- simplified versions of more difficult piano literature
- simplified versions of familiar classical works (non-piano) and arrangements of familiar tunes
- only original piano literature
- popular and jazz styles of music

✳ **What is the scope of the curriculum?** Independent music teachers frequently provide the student's total musical education.

- Will the curriculum consist solely of solo repertoire pieces and a healthy dose of technical exercises?
- Will the student's training be enhanced by carefully integrating music theory?
- Will the quality of the student's sound be enhanced through an aural development curriculum?
- Will students develop functional skills through harmonization, transposition and sight-reading?
- Will students regularly express themselves musically through creative activities such as improvisation?
- Will students be given instruction in music appreciation and music history?

✳ **What reading approach will be used?** Most teachers commit to a strong reading approach.

- Will the development of eye/hand coordination, through the development of reading skills, be a strong focus from the very beginning of piano instruction?
- Will a general approach to music development, in which students learn to "speak" music, precede note-reading?
- Will note-reading be delayed, preceded by a rote approach to initial learning?
- Will music literacy, through an emphasis on strong reading skills, be an important and ongoing part of the teaching curriculum?

✳ **What is the approach to technical development?** Strong physical skills are an aid to fluent reading, the learning of pieces and the development of a musical sound.

- Will technical exercises for the development of strong physical skills comprise the initial approach in piano study?

- Will technical mastery of pieces overshadow musical communication?

- Will technical facility be achieved primarily through the repertoire?

- Will exercises and etudes comprise an independent segment of the curriculum?

- Will technical exercises prepare students for the demands of the repertoire?

✳ **What are the memorization requirements?** The tradition of playing piano music by memory frequently causes conflicts.

- Will students be given short memory assignments every week?

- Will students be expected to memorize all pieces or not be expected to memorize at all?

- Will students be expected to memorize one or more recital pieces each year?

- Will students be expected to maintain a rotating body of memorized pieces that can be performed at all times?

✳ **What are the practice requirements?** Most successful teachers view practice requirements as a way to build tenacity and concentration in students.

- Will practice requirements be tailored to the age, level and natural ability of the student?

- Will students be allowed to practice only when they are motivated to do so?

- Will lesson continuation depend upon meeting minimal practice requirements?

✳ **What is the view concerning parental involvement?** Parental interest and involvement generally enhances the quality of piano instruction.

- Will parents be invited to monitor and/or encourage practice?

- Will parents be required to attend every lesson and practice daily with their children?

- Will parental involvement be tailored to the age and level of the student?

- Will parental involvement be discouraged?

✳ **Is the teacher willing to consider other roles with students?** Changes in society have given the piano teacher a larger role in the lives of students.

- ◆ Will the teacher adopt a holistic approach to the curriculum, encompassing all aspects of music and the arts?

- ◆ Will the teacher become a confidant for students who have limited input from other adults in their lives?

- ◆ Will the teacher view herself/himself as a friend, an authority figure, or balance the two roles?

- ◆ Will the teacher choose the singular role of piano teacher, without becoming involved in other aspects of students' lives?

PROFESSIONAL RESOURCES FOR PIANO TEACHERS

Teachers need help to enhance and refine their teaching. Professional teaching organizations provide syllabi for assistance in defining and developing goals and they offer opportunities for student evaluations, performances and competitions. Some of these organizations have local affiliations that meet regularly to discuss common teaching concerns and hear presentations from professional experts. Developing positive relationships with other local teachers is a positive by-product of these meetings. Furthermore, some of these organizations have state, regional and national conferences or conventions. These larger gatherings provide inspiration, contacts and resources.

Numerous professional journals include a variety of articles related to the piano and music teaching professions. These informative articles are good sources for continuing education. Journals also include music reviews, information about continuing education seminars and advertisements from businesses that sell music, software and piano-related products.

Some websites offer information similar to that found in journals. Others provide opportunities for teachers to interact with other professionals by asking questions, discussing issues and locating information. Such resources, at this time, include the following:

Professional Organizations
The Canadian Federation of Music Teachers' Association (CFMTA)
    cfmta.org
Early Childhood Music and Movement Association (ECMMA)
    ecmma.org
European Piano Teachers Association (EPTA)
    epta-uk.org
Music Teachers Association of California (MTAC)
    mtac.org
Music Teachers National Association (MTNA)
    mtna.org
National Association for Music Education (NAfME)
    nafme.org

National Federation of Music Clubs (NFMC)
>   nfmc-music.org

National Guild of Piano Teachers (NGPT)
>   pianoguild.com

National Piano Foundation (NPF)
>   pianonet.com

Journals

American Music Teacher (magazine of the Music Teachers National Association)
>   mtna.org/publications/american-music-teacher/

The Canadian Music Teacher
>   cfmta.org/html/cmten.html

Clavier Companion
>   claviercompanion.com

Music Educators Journal (magazine of the National Association for Music Education)
>   mej.sagepub.com

Teaching Music (magazine of the National Association for Music Education)
>   musiced.nafme.org/resources/periodicals/teaching-music-online-edition/

Beyond various websites, the internet offers numerous interactive possibilities for teachers. By using Internet search engines and other means, teachers can find new and exciting ways to connect with teachers and other professionals.

SUMMARY

Piano teachers become professional in the following ways:

- meeting a professional standard through education and professional alignment

- learning about and striving to develop the characteristics that are common to successful teachers

- teaching in ways that will benefit students beyond learning to play the piano

- developing, refining and modifying a teaching philosophy that reflects the needs, strengths and weaknesses of both the student and the teacher

PROJECTS FOR NEW TEACHERS

1. Think about the best teacher you have ever had, in any subject. List the characteristics that made that teacher outstanding and describe how those characteristics can be relevant to piano teaching.

2. Think about the least effective teacher you have had, in any subject. List the characteristics that made that teacher so unsatisfactory and describe how those characteristics can be relevant to piano teaching.

3. Using the questions on pages 9–13, conduct interviews with two or more independent piano teachers regarding their teaching philosophies and goals. Summarize their teaching philosophies.

PROJECTS FOR EXPERIENCED TEACHERS

1. Answer the following questions to rate yourself as a professional. For the questions to which you answered "no," summarize a plan that will help you improve in that area.

   - Do I have an education that included an extended period of training?
   - Do I upgrade my skills through continuing education?
   - Do I belong to, participate and volunteer in the activities of a professional organization?
   - Do I support the teacher certification program of professional organizations through my own certification?
   - Do I feel emotional satisfaction from my work?
   - Do I conduct the business aspects of teaching in an ethical, organized and businesslike manner?
   - Do I know my teaching goals and objectives?

2. For the following positive teaching characteristics, determine your professional profile by rating yourself from 1–5, with 5 being the highest rating. If there are characteristics at which you rate yourself 3 and below, develop a list of goals for improvement.

Passionate	1	2	3	4	5
Inspiring	1	2	3	4	5
Knowledgeable	1	2	3	4	5
Dedicated	1	2	3	4	5
Organized	1	2	3	4	5
Encouraging	1	2	3	4	5
Honest	1	2	3	4	5
Goal-oriented	1	2	3	4	5
Patient	1	2	3	4	5
Tolerant	1	2	3	4	5
Respectful	1	2	3	4	5
Energetic	1	2	3	4	5
Humorous	1	2	3	4	5
Generous	1	2	3	4	5
Adaptable	1	2	3	4	5

3. Review the questions posed in the section on developing a personal teaching philosophy on pages 9–13 and write your own teaching philosophy. Divide the philosophy into two sections: a section you can give to parents and students as a studio policy statement, and a section that is only for yourself.

Chapter 2
PRINCIPLES OF LEARNING

Learning to play the piano involves understanding concepts and acquiring skills in a logical progression. Concepts are the principles students must understand and skills are what they physically execute at the keyboard. For example, students should understand that half notes last twice as long as quarter notes (the concept), and they should also have the physical ability to hold half notes for the proper duration (the skill). The teacher functions as a facilitator, using principles of learning to guide students toward the correct observations, answers and physical motions.

FROM THE KNOWN TO THE UNKNOWN

Teachers must ascertain what students know before new information is introduced. Understanding musical sound and knowing how to produce it on the keyboard and discriminating between the right and left hands, high and low pitches, finger numbers, and black and white keys are all examples of some basic information that students may know before the first piano lesson. The information on a page of music that experienced musicians regard as routine—lines, spaces, clef signs, rhythm symbols, notes and finger numbers—is a confusing array of black marks to beginning students. Students might also be misinformed about basic musical concepts. For example, they may think that sharps and flats are only black keys, or that middle C is always played with the thumb.

A first lesson or interview should include activities that help the teacher find out what the student knows. Asking the student to "play three high pitches on the piano" will show whether the student understands high and low on the piano. If it is obvious there is confusion, the teacher can play a series of high pitches and ask the young student if they sound like a bird or a tiger. Once the student has identified that the sounds are "birdlike," the teacher can ask the student whether a bird spends most of its time high in the air or low on the ground. The student is then asked to determine whether the pitches were played on the right or left side of the keyboard. The student knows the sounds related to birds and tigers, knows that birds generally fly in the air and that tigers generally move on the ground, and knows that the bird sound was made on the right side of the keyboard. From known information, the student learns what was previously unknown—that high sounds are to the right on the keyboard.

Known information can also assist students in learning about the musical elements that help pieces become more than just notes and rhythm. For example, playing loud and soft can be related to marching and tiptoeing; staccato and legato can be compared to popcorn popping versus rolling on the floor.

A student's knowledge of various subjects can facilitate learning pieces that have imaginative titles. Students can be led to play a piece in a more expressive way by using articulation, dynamics and a tempo appropriate to the piece's title. For example, a title that includes the word "soldier," "marching" or "parade" might suggest an accented articulation, a louder dynamic (reflecting the action of marching) and a moderate tempo. Knowing that drums and trumpets are frequently used in parades can signal the use of crisp rhythmic figures and articulation.

DISCOVERY LEARNING AND ROTE LEARNING

Discovery learning and rote learning are two approaches to teaching. When teachers lead students to teach themselves, students learn through discovery. When teachers tell or show students what to do, students learn by rote. Both approaches are valid when used at the appropriate times.

Discovery Learning

In a discovery learning process, teachers give only a minimal amount of information, guiding the students to discover on their own. For example, when teachers guide students to recognize the pattern and contour (interval and direction) of notes on the staff, students learn to read notes by their relationship to one another. This guided discovery leads the student to know exactly how each piece or exercise should sound and feel before practicing at home. However, without guidance, students will be unable to find the information they need to succeed. Teachers can ask questions that will heighten awareness and help students observe important information about assigned pieces, scales or creative activities.

To become independent learners, students must make observations about the music, evaluate their performance, and decide how to improve it. Teachers can facilitate this independence by asking questions and having the student make observations, such as the following:

- What is the distance between these two notes?

- Find all the measures that are alike.

- Which measures look different?

- What makes this piece easy?

- Which part of this piece looks difficult?

- How does the key signature affect what you will do?

- Do you recognize any scales, five-finger patterns or chords in this piece?

- Which black keys will you play in this scale?

- Point to all the notes that will be played as sharps (or flats).

- Demonstrate how you will play "this measure."

- Will you hear loud (soft, fast, slow, long, short, smooth, disconnected) sounds in this piece?

- If your improvisation is about an elephant, where on the piano do you think it would sound best?

- Which of these sounds do you think the composer wanted in this section? (The teacher demonstrates two sounds and the student decides.)

- Try "this measure" these two ways and decide which feels more comfortable. (The teacher demonstrates two ways for the student to try.)

- Did you notice where the *f* sign is written?

- How would you bring out the melody?

- Do you think that your playing was better this time?

When students learn through discovery, they are likely to remember and use the information they have acquired when related material is encountered in the future. Similar experiences lead students to independently learn new concepts, develop technical skills, and make interpretive decisions.

Discovery learning is aided when teachers give precisely the right amount of information in the most direct manner. The following two questions will help teachers determine whether they are giving the appropriate information:

- Does the student need to know the information now?

- Is the information completely accurate?

Rote Learning

Students learn by rote when they copy something that has been verbalized or shown to them. Rote learning requires the memorization of many small bits of information without necessarily making connections between them. For example, during the initial note-reading process, students are using a rote approach when they memorize the placement of each note on the staff.

Rote learning can be useful in several situations. It is sometimes the most effective way to begin piano instruction. Some students come to their first lesson having already learned pieces such as "Chopsticks" by rote. These beginning students have developed a basic physical feel for playing the piano and will be able to make music immediately when teachers build on this knowledge. Students who begin their musical instruction with rote learning become familiar with the physical positions and motions of playing, feel the musical patterns, and are even able to apply dynamics, rhythms, and various tempos and touches to their playing. This type of teaching is used effectively in the approach developed by Shin'ichi Suzuki (1898–1998). In the Suzuki method, the teacher plays a small portion of a piece while the student watches and listens. The student then copies what the teacher has demonstrated, without first seeing the written music.

With students of all levels, the physical aspects of technique and the physical motions required to produce a desired sound can be taught easily using a rotelike approach that involves teacher demonstration. For example, even though students may be able to discover that a melody in one hand must be played slightly louder than the accompaniment in the other hand, or that an arpeggio should sound fluent and smooth, it is unlikely that they can discover how to physically achieve the desired sounds. An arpeggiated passage can be learned by following these steps:

1. The teacher demonstrates each hand separately with the correct hand position and arm motion for playing.

2. The student watches the motions as the teacher plays, listening to the tone and dynamic level or the smooth sounds that result from the correct motions.

3. The student places his/her hand and arm on the teacher's hand and arm, "riding along" and feeling the motion as the teacher plays.

4. The student plays the same passage alone, while the teacher offers guidance.

When beginning students learn a basic technical exercise (such as a five-finger pattern) by copying the teacher, their hand position and sound are improved. In contrast, when students learn the exercise by reading alone, physical and musical development are often delayed.

Another effective teaching technique that incorporates elements of rote learning is the use of *abstracts*. An abstract uses nonmusical notation (such as words or other familiar symbols) to guide students to the correct notes and/or rhythms. This approach is highly effective for teaching pieces that are beyond elementary students' reading ability, but still within their technical ability. By using an abstract with an intervallic note-reading approach, the piece that follows might be taught to a first-year student who is unable to read the notes on the staff easily or coordinate the hands while reading music (see examples 2.1 and 2.2).

Example 2.1 Türk's "March in C," p. 9 from *Everybody's Perfect Masterpieces*, Vol. 1, edited by Carole L. Bigler and Valery Lloyd-Watts

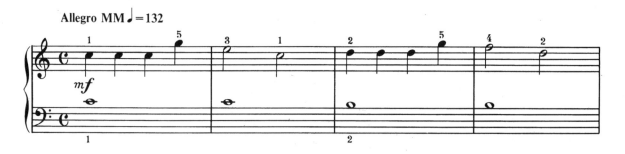

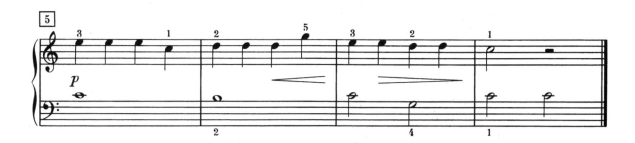

Example 2.2 Abstract version of Türk's "March in C"

The student would then use the following steps to learn the piece from the abstract:

1. Play the RH, starting on the C one octave above middle C, and follow the interval numbers and arrows for directions (using only white keys).

2. Play the LH, starting on middle C, and follow the interval numbers and arrows for directions (using only white keys).

3. Play the RH while counting aloud.

4. Play the LH while counting aloud.

5. Play both hands while counting aloud.

PREVENTION OF ERRORS

Errors can often be prevented by preparing students for a new concept or skill, beginning a few weeks before they encounter that concept or skill in a piece. Systematic presentation of new pieces will also help minimize errors.

Incremental Preparation

One of the most effective ways to teach is by using small, progressive steps in preparing for a final goal. Learning a difficult new concept or skill can be spread out over several weeks using a series of small steps, rather than a large step just before its use in a piece. As an example, one of the most difficult concepts to present to elementary students is the ♩. ♪ rhythm pattern. Students may have heard this rhythm in songs like "Silent Night" or "London Bridge," but that experience does not mean they can play this rhythm correctly in unfamiliar pieces.

Before students encounter this rhythmic pattern in music, they should be prepared incrementally, as follows:

1. Several weeks prior to presenting pieces with the ♩. ♪ rhythm, teachers can prepare students by clapping or playing it and having students clap or play back the rhythm by rote.

2. In a few more weeks, introduce five-finger pattern exercises using the rhythm, played by rote.

3. A week or two before learning pieces containing the rhythm, flash cards that include the rhythm can be clapped, tapped, played and counted.

4. Finally, assign easy pieces containing the rhythm.

All technical skills, especially difficult ones, should be prepared prior to use in a student's repertoire. For example, if a student will soon encounter blocked triads, the teacher must prepare the student for that task. Previously studied pieces will have developed the student's ability to play blocked intervals comfortably with the correct hand position. Exercises in which the student plays blocked 3rds with fingers 1 and 3 and fingers 3 and 5, and exercises in which the student plays a blocked 5th followed by adding the third finger while holding the 5th (see example 6.8 on page 158), should precede the playing of a complete blocked triad. When these skills are achieved with ease, the student will be ready to play all three notes of the triad simultaneously.

Systematic Presentation

Errors in new pieces can be prevented by systematic presentation and detailed assignments. Consider the following scenario. The teacher assigns pieces for home practice with little or no preparation. At the next lesson, note and rhythm errors are corrected and the pieces are reassigned for another week's practice. Hearing practiced pieces, correcting errors and reassigning the pieces consume a major portion of the lesson time. The teacher has to spend time dealing with problems, rather than refining the pieces and preparing new pieces. Subsequently, more new pieces are assigned with little or no preparation. The student returns home to *unlearn* the mistakes she/he made the previous week and to struggle through the learning of the unprepared new pieces—and the cycle repeats itself.

Because it is much easier for practicing students to "do" something rather than to "undo" something, it is highly desirable for teachers to prevent errors in new pieces. Systematic presentation is one key to error prevention. The following teaching strategies usually would be involved in such a systematic presentation:

* Lead students to find measures and sections that are the same, similar or different.

* Let students try selected easier measures.

* Guide students to find the more difficult parts.

* Incorporate eurhythmic activities, including tapping and counting to feel the rhythms.

- Teach practice procedures that reduce the difficulties to manageable tasks, such as tapping and counting the rhythm, and practicing hands or voices separately.

- Examine the musical and interpretive aspects of the piece, such as dynamics, articulation and mood.

This organized study saves time and prepares students for productive and successful practice at home. The home practice assignment can direct the student to employ various practice techniques:

- tap and count selected measures or sections before playing

- count aloud while playing

- practice hands separately to check the notes and fingering

- practice in sections, starting with those that are most difficult

- practice selected parts in specific and creative ways

Teachers can also prepare students for new pieces by assigning only the troublesome parts before assigning the entire piece. Specific questions and practice techniques for those sections should be part of the assignment. After a week or two, when students are assigned the piece as a whole, they will discover that the piece is almost fully learned. With this systematic approach, students can learn longer and more difficult pieces in a shorter period of time.

To facilitate systematic presentation, a worksheet can be prepared for pieces using questions and activities such as the following:

- Do you see mostly skips (3rds) or steps (2nds)? _____ Play all the skips. Play all the measures with skips.

- What intervals do you see that are larger than a 3rd? _____ Name and play the measures with large intervals.

- Which fingers always play the black keys? _____ Play all the black keys. Play all the measures with black keys.

- How many F-sharps do you find? _____ Play all the measures with F-sharps.

- Which measures are alike? _____ Play the measures that are alike.

- Which measures have the same interval pattern but start on different notes? _____ Play the interval pattern starting on any note you like. Say the intervals as you play.

- Which measure(s) has a five-finger pattern? _____ Play the five-finger pattern.

- Which measures have broken chords? _____ Play the notes of each broken chord at the same time to form a blocked chord.

- Which measures in the LH are like measures in the RH? _____ Play the LH part of that measure and then play the RH part of the similar measure.

- What five-finger pattern is found in these measures? _____ Play the five-finger pattern, then play each measure that has the five-finger pattern.

- Which measures have chords? _____ Play the chords broken, moving from bottom to top and back down, while saying the note names. Do the same while saying the finger numbers.

APPLYING PRINCIPLES OF DISCOVERY LEARNING AND SYSTEMATIC PRESENTATION

The following types of activities can be used to apply discovery learning and systematic presentation to a newly assigned piece. (Note: All of the steps below would not necessarily be completed in one lesson.) Similar strategies can be used to prepare students for learning pieces at any level. See example 2.3 following these nine steps.

1. The teacher asks the student to listen to the piece without watching the music and decide whether the cowboy's pony is galloping, walking or trotting. This helps the student discover the character and appropriate tempo for the piece.

2. The teacher plays measure 1, asking the student to watch the music. The student then plays it.

3. The student is asked to look at the entire piece and find all the measures with the same LH pattern as m. 1. The student then plays one of those measures.

4. The student is asked to look at the last two measures of the piece and describe the RH. The student should discover the tie and then play the last two measures hands together, while counting aloud.

5. The teacher asks the student to find LH measures that are similar, but not identical, to m. 1 (for example, mm. 6 and 8). The student plays mm. 6 or 8, then plays m. 1 for comparison.

6. The teacher asks the student to tap and count mm. 3 and 4 with both hands, then play and count those measures.

7. The teacher asks the student to compare mm. 5 and 7. Then the student determines the beginning RH finger number for each measure and writes it on the music or circles it. The student then plays mm. 5 and 7.

8. The teacher asks the student to identify the RH interval from the last note of m. 5 to the first note of m. 6, and the RH interval from the last note of m. 7 to the first note of m. 8. The student plays RH mm. 5 and 6, then RH mm. 7 and 8. Finally, the student plays each pair of measures hands together.

9. The teacher plays mm. 11–13 and asks the student to imagine what is happening with the pony at the end of the piece, and how this relates to the term *ritardando* and the decrescendo.

Example 2.3 "A Cowboy's Song," pp. 30-31 from *Alfred's Basic Piano Library*, Lesson Book 1B, by Palmer, Manus and Lethco

CORRECTION OF ERRORS

Regardless of careful preparation and systematic presentation, errors will still occur. Teaching students to evaluate their playing and correct errors is a process that is learned in the lesson. Often when a student makes a mistake, teachers instinctively correct the error rather than leading students to discover what was incorrect. When students discover their own errors, they will become more aware of what they are playing and less prone to make mistakes. This can be facilitated by asking questions, such as the following:

- Were all the notes correct?

- I heard an incorrect note in this line. Can you find it?

- I will play this measure two ways. Which way is correct? How did *you* play it?

- Is this section in a major or minor key? Did your playing sound major or minor?

- What is the interval between these two notes? What interval did you play?

- What is the key of this section? How does that affect what you play?

Pitch errors can be heard, but rhythm errors must be felt and are less likely to be detected. Activities such as the following can help correct rhythm errors:

- eurhythmic activities, including tapping and counting to feel the rhythms

- counting aloud while playing

- playing simultaneously with the teacher to hear rhythm irregularities

- listening to the teacher play or tap the written rhythm and the incorrect rhythm (played previously by the student) and identifying which is the correct rhythm

EXPERIENCE AND FOLLOW-THROUGH

Follow-through is the reinforcement of new concepts and skills that occurs in the lesson. It assures the teacher that the student understands what has been experienced and that the student will be able to apply the principles during home practice. Once it is clear that the student understands and can execute the skill, sufficient follow-through has occurred. If a piece has been presented incrementally and systematically and the student can play small segments of the piece, the student is ready for home practice.

When a new concept is introduced, teachers should provide reinforcement through activities that allow the student to experience that concept in a variety of contexts. As an example, reinforcement of a specific interval could be implemented using any or all of the following progression of steps over several weeks. The student

1. Identify the interval aurally.

2. Hear and feel the interval by playing it in various locations on the keyboard.

3. Play the interval above or below a given key.

4. Identify the interval by looking at the keyboard while the teacher plays it.

5. Identify the interval and name the notes from flash cards.

6. Writes the interval above or below any given note(s).

Follow-through is continued by experiencing material during practice at home. Practice includes consistent, accurate repetition and is necessary to acquire physical and mental facility.

GOOD LEARNING HABITS

Good learning habits that are experienced in the lesson are more likely to be applied during practice at home. If something is not experienced in the lesson, it cannot be applied during practice. For example, when accurate reading is the goal, good habits include practicing slowly, counting aloud, practicing small sections, repetition, and keeping the eyes on the page.

Students will practice more effectively and maintain good learning habits when they have a systematic and detailed assignment sheet. Initially, a series of practice steps written in the method book or on the assignment sheet is essential for all pieces. Each step should be taught to the student during the lesson. Students can learn one or two steps a week and teachers can add, modify and delete steps as students progress to higher levels.

Teachers can create a master list of various practice steps. From this list, appropriate practice steps can be chosen and assigned for each piece or activity. (To save time, teachers may provide the master list to students and simply indicate the assigned steps by number.) Ideas for a master list of practice steps follow. Teachers can create their own set of abbreviations for instructions to use on student assignment sheets.

1. Point to the notes while counting aloud.

2. Tap the rhythm hands separately (HS) while counting aloud, and hands together (HT) while saying "right," "left," or "both" to indicate which hand(s) should play.

3. Point to the music and name the notes.

4. Point to the notes and name the intervals.

5. Point to the fingering and name the finger numbers.

6. Play on the key cover while naming finger numbers.

7. Play each hand separately (HS), tapping the keys without depressing them so that the piece is played silently on the tops of the keys.

8. Play the RH alone while counting aloud, saying the finger numbers or naming the notes.

9. Play the LH alone while counting aloud, saying the finger numbers or naming the notes.

10. Find all the measures that are the same and play them.

11. Find the measures that are different from all the others and play them.

12. Play the lines that are the same.

13. Play the piece again, transposing it to a different key.

14. Play hands together (HT) in "slow motion" while counting aloud.

15. Play at performance tempo.

TRIAL AND ERROR

Some students learn best by trial and error. They use this mode of learning when they learn to walk, ride a bike or throw a ball. Although this mode of learning yields less-than-perfect results, students often find problems more fun than the solutions and gain satisfaction from conquering difficulties in their own way. Such students answer questions by guessing, and practice pieces by playing them over and over. Over emphasis on good learning habits may cause tension and reduce the joy and excitement of learning. Teachers can analyze each student's learning approach and create a learning environment that allows for mistakes and balances trial and error with thoughtful learning.

VARIED ACTIVITIES

Younger students will be more attentive during lessons when activities are gamelike, change frequently, and are sometimes away from the piano. For more advanced students, a variety of activities and learning challenges make lessons more interesting. Lessons will be more enjoyable when they include the following:

- flashcards to reinforce a variety of concepts

- theory workbooks with gamelike activities

- computer software programs for theory, ear training, music history and appreciation

- contests for achieving goals

- board and card games for drilling musical concepts and terminology

- "explorer" or "detective" worksheets to find similarities, differences and musical patterns

- stimulating group instruction

- role playing, with the student playing the role of teacher

- large-motor movement activities away from the piano

SIMULTANEOUS ACHIEVEMENT OF MULTIPLE GOALS

Activities, games and drills can make teaching more efficient if they simultaneously achieve more than one goal. Furthermore, students will learn to process multiple bits of information, as they do when learning and playing pieces. For example, the teacher can play one of two flashcards containing a series of notes and ask students which card was played (see example 2.4). When students become more proficient, they can choose from three or more cards.

Example 2.4 Sample flashcards

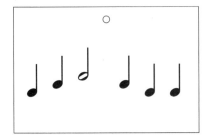 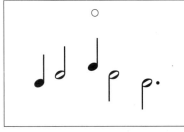 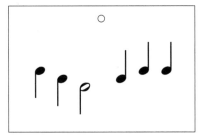

The teacher will play one of the cards by beginning on any white key and moving up or down by step. To correctly identify which card was played, students must identify pitch direction as well as note duration and stem direction (indicating which hand played). Short drills such as these can reinforce the students' knowledge of several basic elements. Students can additionally be asked to do the following:

- clap and count the rhythm on each card

- point and say the hand (right or left) that is to play each note

- point to and say the direction (up or down) of the notes

- play each example from a given starting pitch, moving stepwise up and down

In another activity that achieves multiple goals, students are asked to play an ascending 3rd in the low register of the piano with RH fingers 2 and 4. This appears to be an interval drill. However, it also reinforces distinguishing high and low sounds, right and left hands, and finger numbers. More advanced students can achieve multiple goals when they play scales in a specific rhythm pattern or with varying dynamics (such as making a *crescendo* while ascending and a *decrescendo* while descending).

INDIVIDUAL LEARNING STYLES

Each student processes information differently. Some are visual learners and may need to watch what the hands are doing, see the page, learn with flashcards and worksheets, and write the information to gain a complete understanding.

Others students learn best by hearing. They can remember what the teacher says or plays, and may need to close their eyes and listen as they play. These students may need to repeat the information aloud, talk about a technical problem and learn rhythms by saying rhymes or words.

Still other students learn by touch. They learn best from movement activities for the entire body, by manipulating objects, having activities change frequently and by handling flashcards. They also learn by repeating patterns and will benefit from closing their eyes to feel intervals, black keys or five-finger patterns.

Since teachers may not be able to exactly determine each student's learning type, and since some students may require a combination of learning styles, lessons should include activities and styles that will meet the needs of all students. For example, when learning a new interval over a period of time, all students should experience it in the following ways:

- hear it;

- see and feel it on the keyboard;

- feel it without looking at the keyboard;

- play it several times;

- listen to the teacher's explanation about it;

- describe it;

- read it;

- write it.

SOUND, FEEL, SYMBOL, NAME

Because music is aural, music learning should start with an aural experience (sound). After there is a clear aural perception of the concept, it should be experienced at the keyboard (feel) and felt with the body. Once these experiences have occurred, the sign or symbol (notation) can be recognized, and finally, a name for that symbol can be learned. For example, if the teacher plays a series of loud and soft sounds on the piano and asks the student to identify them as loud or soft, this draws on the student's previous knowledge. When students aurally understand loud and soft, they can play loud and soft sounds. Students can judge by feel and by ear whether the music is loud or soft or somewhere in between. They do not need to know either the symbol or the name to play loudly. Later, they can learn that *f* is the symbol for loud, and that the symbol is the abbreviation for the Italian word *forte*.

The correct progression of learning can be applied at any level. The elementary piece "Join the Fun" (see example 2.5) might be learned in the following way:

1. Without seeing the musical score or the teacher's hands, the student is asked to listen as the teacher plays pairs of measures. The student identifies the following pairs of RH measures as being "the same" or "different": mm. 1–2 and 5–6, mm. 3–4 and 7–8, mm. 7–8 and 15–16, mm. 9–10 and 11–12. (*sound*)

2. The student is shown the score. As the teacher plays the same pairs of measures, the student finds and plays them, and describes as much as possible (notes, intervals and five-finger pattern). (*sound, feel, symbol and name*)

3. Without seeing the musical score, the student listens and observes as the teacher plays the LH of mm. 3–4, then the student plays it back. Next, the student finds these measures on the score and plays it each time it occurs in the piece. (*sound, feel and symbol*)

4. Without showing the student the musical score, the teacher describes the contrary and parallel motion between the hands in mm. 10 and 12, and then plays those measures. The student plays each of the measures by copying the teacher. The student is then asked to find these measures on the score and play them again. (*sound, feel and symbol*)

Example 2.5 "Join the Fun," p. 13 from *Alfred's Basic Piano Library*, Lesson Book 1B, by Palmer, Manus and Lethco

The early-intermediate piece, "German Dance in D Major" by Franz Joseph Haydn, might be introduced as follows (see example 2.6):

1. Without looking at the teacher's hands or the musical score, the student listens to the teacher play the LH part of line 3 (mm. 9–12) and identifies each of the chords as "peaceful" or "restless" (or other terms that indicate relaxation and tension). (**sound**)

2. The student is asked to watch the teacher's hands and listen while the teacher plays the music a second time, and then to copy the teacher's playing, without looking at the music. (**sound and feel**)

3. The student is asked to look at the music (mm. 9 – 12) and find the chords. (**symbol**) The teacher then introduces the chords as tonic and dominant. (**name**)

4. The same procedure (listen, imitate, read) can be used to present the sequence in the RH of m. 4, beat 3, through m. 6, beat 2. The student only needs to identify that the pattern repeats itself, starting on a different note. (**sound, feel and symbol**)

Example 2.6 Haydn's "German Dance in D Major," p. 11 from *Masterpieces with Flair*, Book 1, edited by Jane Magrath

When students experience pieces aurally and physically before reading and playing them, the students' learning and technical facility will be enhanced. Examples of these experiences at the elementary level include the following:

- Listening to recordings of pieces helps students achieve an initial *aural* image.

- Hearing the teacher demonstrate passages in contrasting characters (by changing dynamics, tempo or articulation) facilitates intelligent interpretive decisions based on an *aural* experience.

- Tapping new rhythms on their body or on the piano's music stand gives students *physical* experiences before they play the rhythms on the keyboard with individual fingers.

- "Playing" music on the closed keyboard cover allows students to experience their pieces *physically* before playing them on the piano.

There are many other creative ways for teachers to build aural and physical experiences for elementary students.

SUMMARY

Piano teaching is more effective when basic principles of learning are followed. These principles include the following:

- Students comprehend more quickly when new concepts are related to something they already know.

- Students are more likely to remember information they discover for themselves and are better able to apply the information in different contexts.

- Discovery learning can be balanced with rote learning.

- Rote learning is effective for beginning students to develop a physical feel for playing. It helps students experience aspects of technique and expressive elements. It is also an effective teaching tool for technical exercises, or when using abstracts to teach a piece beyond the student's reading ability.

- Prevention of errors is achieved by the preparation of new concepts and skills and the systematic presentation of new pieces.

- Teachers should prepare students for new concepts and skills incrementally, over a period of time, prior to use in pieces.

- Systematic presentation of new pieces can help prevent ineffective practice.

- Home practice should be based on lesson experiences and should follow detailed assignments.

- Students can be guided to correct their own errors.

- During the lesson, teachers must use follow-through to ensure student comprehension. Such reinforcement helps students apply what they have learned in the lesson to home practice.

- A variety of activities and learning challenges make lessons more effective and enjoyable.

- Teaching is most efficient when a learning experience achieves several goals at once.

- Teachers should present new information in a variety of ways to meet the needs of every student, regardless of their individual learning style.

- Because music is aural by nature, learning musical elements should start with an aural experience.

- Students should experience each new concept or skill physically, immediately after its aural introduction.

- Once students understand concepts and skills aurally and through physical experience, they can learn the corresponding symbols and names.

PROJECTS FOR NEW TEACHERS

1. Choose an elementary piece, play it, and determine where students are likely to make errors. To help determine this, look for anything in the music that changes, is different or is complex. Find measures for students to compare for similarities and differences. Prepare a presentation of the piece that will help students prevent errors. Use examples 2.5 and 2.6 on pages 30–31 as models for your presentation.

2. Choose an elementary piece and prepare a systematic presentation that includes student discovery and experience. Use example 2.3 on pages 24–25 as a guide. Choose the practice steps you would assign from the list on page 27.

3. Develop a set of abbreviations for five of the fifteen practice steps on page 27 to use on student assignment sheets.

PROJECTS FOR EXPERIENCED TEACHERS

1. Choose an elementary piece and devise two gamelike activities for presenting the piece. At least one of the activities should achieve multiple goals simultaneously.

2. Describe how you would present each of these concepts using (in order) sound, feel, symbol and name:
    *   ties
    *   treble C and bass C
    *   legato
    *   interval of a 5th

3. Based on what the student already knows, describe how you would present each of the following concepts:

Concept	What the Student Already Knows
eighth notes	• what it feels like to jog • rhythm of quarter notes
quarter rests	• rhythm of quarter notes • concepts of sound and silence • what it feels like to take a rest
octave sign	• has played pieces in different registers of the piano • can find the next key with same letter name by counting eight white keys up or down • familiar with an octopus having eight "arms"
staccato	• can bounce a ball, hop or jump • has heard short sounds in everyday life • has played legato
minor five-finger pattern	• has played major five-finger patterns • understands half steps • understands finger numbers • understands "moving down" on the keyboard
loud and soft	• can speak or sing loudly and softly • has heard loud and soft sounds in everyday life • can move quickly or slowly into the piano key

Chapter 3
BEGINNING METHODS

Choosing appropriate materials is one of the most important considerations when starting a new student. Some experienced teachers, and some who have extensive pedagogical training, devise methods based on their own background and education; they write exercises and pieces or supplement with books of pieces that follow the progression of concepts and skills compatible with their teaching philosophy. Most teachers, however, rely on a body of materials that has been designed to instruct beginning students. These materials are commonly called *beginning methods* or *elementary methods*.

The function of a method book is to provide a logical progression for learning concepts and skills, and music for the practice of these elements. Choosing the appropriate method will help students move through the beginning stages with relative ease, while laying a strong foundation for future study. The student's learning style, experience with music, understanding of the keyboard, aural and physical development, reading capabilities, and rhythmic maturity are all factors to be considered when choosing a beginning method. Teachers should consider individual needs to select a method that meets the requirements of each student. The variety of beginning methods available today provides teachers with many choices.

In recent years, methods have been written for specific ages and types of students. There are methods for pre-school, average age (seven to nine years old), gifted, older and adult beginners. There are methods that emphasize the early development of strong reading skills and others that delay reading until later. Methods that delay reading place emphasis on such skills as aural development or technique and often start with singing or listening to recordings of the pieces. Methods that delay reading instruction are beyond the scope of this chapter and will not be discussed.

NOTE-READING APPROACHES

Methods that emphasize reading skills generally fall into three categories—middle C, multi-key and intervallic. Some methods are purely one of these types, while others are more eclectic, combining principles from the three approaches. Many modern note-reading methods begin with pre-staff (off-staff) reading before introducing reading on lines and spaces. (See chapter 4, page 67 for a description of pre-staff reading.)

Middle C Reading Approach

In the middle C reading approach, middle C is the first pitch taught, with the thumb of both hands sharing that key. Students find middle C easy to recognize since it is a ledger-line note between the two staves and looks different from the other notes that are written on long staff lines. Subsequent notes are learned one at a time and are visually memorized by their placement on the staff so that students feel secure about what notes to play. Mnemonic devices, such as "Every Good Boy Does Fine" for the treble clef lines, often are utilized to help students learn the placement of notes.

With middle C methods, note-reading is dependent upon individual note recognition, rather than on patterns and groupings of notes. Eye/hand coordination can be difficult since the adding of one note at a time delays recognition of patterns and groups. Keyboard topography that relates the white keys to the black ones is not emphasized. Therefore, even though students may have memorized the names of the piano keys and notes on the staff, they may lack a clear visualization of the keyboard and a solid kinesthetic feel for the relationship of piano keys to notes on the staff. Such insecurity leads to students looking at the keys to verify that the correct note was played. In some middle C methods, finger numbers are generously supplied, causing some students to read by finger number rather than by note placement on the staff.

In most middle C methods, minimal reinforcement of previously learned concepts and skills occurs as others are introduced. There is generally one piece to practice for each new concept or skill, each slightly more difficult than the previous one. Initially, students play with the hands close to the body as all notes are close to middle C. This limits the students' acquaintance with the whole keyboard. In a middle C approach, students also develop a feeling of security with the fingers on white keys only. The thumb, an awkward finger, is used from the beginning rather than the more natural technical progression of fingers four to three to two.

In most middle C methods, pieces are usually melodic, based on familiar-sounding patterns that imply tonic and dominant progressions. They use common meters and regular phrase structures. These limitations make the pieces sound similar and may not tap into the student's imagination. Keys other than C major are introduced slowly, limiting students to the sound of one tonality for an extended period of time. Scales are generally introduced early. Musical literacy through the study of theory and creative work is generally not a part of these methods. Examples of the middle C approach include:

Michael Aaron Piano Course. New York: Mills Music, Inc., 1945[1] (distributed by Alfred Publishing).

David Carr Glover Piano Library. New York: Belwin-Mills Publishing Corp., 1967/1968 (distributed by Alfred Publishing).

John W. Schaum Piano Course. New York: Belwin-Mills Publishing Corp., 1945 (distributed by Alfred Publishing).

John Thompson. *Modern Course for the Piano.* Cincinnati, OH: The Willis Music Company, 1937 (distributed by Hal Leonard).

Multi-Key Reading Approach

In the multi-key reading approach, students are taught rather quickly to play five-finger patterns in all major keys and simultaneously are given numerous short pieces to play in the various keys. Keys are introduced in groups and the groups are determined by the black- and white-key shape of the tonic triad.

- Group 1 (C, G and F major)—triads consisting of all white keys

- Group 2 (D, A and E major)—triads consisting of white, black, white keys

- Group 3 (D-flat, A-flat and E-flat major)—triads consisting of black, white, black keys

- Group 4 (F-sharp, B-flat and B major)—triads consisting of other black- and white-key relationships

---

[1] The date given for each method is the first publication date. Some methods sebsequently have published revised editions.

As long as the hand remains in the five-finger position, students read by direction and later by interval (contour), making note-reading easy. However, the reliance on patterns sometimes makes individual note identification more difficult. Again, some students may be tempted to read from finger numbers. Reliance on the five-finger pattern makes it difficult for some students to change to patterns that use other hand shapes.

The multi-key approach introduces students to the entire keyboard and helps them move flexibly around it. Students become equally comfortable in all keys, allowing them to transpose, improvise and harmonize melodies; these creative aspects of learning develop well-rounded musicians.

Current multi-key methods generally introduce rhythm concepts (such as pairs of eighth notes) quickly, requiring teachers to give more information and limiting student discovery. This early introduction of faster rhythmic values may result in uneven and imprecise rhythmic execution. Five-finger patterns allow for an early introduction to chords, thus giving the music a full sound, but also making greater physical demands on the students. The five-finger orientation typically results in predictable sounds of tonic, dominant and subdominant, with melody in one hand and chordal accompaniments in the other. The following is an example of the multi-key approach:

Robert Pace. *Music for Keyboard.* Chatham, NY: Lee Roberts Music Publications, Inc., 1961 (distributed by Hal Leonard).

Some methods follow a similar approach to multi-key methods, but introduce the keys gradually. In gradual multi-key methods, each key (or group of keys) is more thoroughly reinforced before others are introduced. The following are examples of methods using gradual multi-key approaches:

James Bastien. *Bastien Piano Basics.* San Diego, CA: Kjos West, 1976.

Keith Snell and Diane Hidy. *Piano Town.* San Diego, CA: Kjos Music Press, 2004.

Intervallic Reading Approach

The intervallic approach to reading musical notation generally begins with gradual-staff notation. The staff is introduced one line at a time, allowing students to focus on one interval at a time. The letter name of the first note is written to its left or shown on a keyboard position diagram. Note-reading is introduced by contour (direction and interval) and notes are grouped by patterns, allowing students to see the spatial relationships. Without the full staff, they are free to develop a strong sense of pulse, concentrate on counting, focus on comfortable technique and attend to sound production before having to read notes on the full staff.

When the full staff is introduced, landmark notes (most often treble G, bass F and middle C) are learned and used to read intervallic relationships and contours without relying on hand positions. Harmonic reading is also intervallic. Fluent reading skills are enhanced when each skill or concept is reinforced in various ways (including several pieces) before new ideas are introduced.

Such a systematic and gradual presentation of reading concepts does not always allow for playing familiar tunes. The lack of familiar tunes and the linear, and sometimes thin sound of the pieces may lack appeal for some students and parents. Teachers must present the pieces in imaginative ways, including playing optional duet accompaniments that may appear with the music. During the gradual introduction of the staff, students may start pieces in any octave and learn about the octave sign (*8va*), allowing them to explore the sound and feel of the entire keyboard. During the first levels, some intervallic methods introduce pieces in irregular and compound meters. Pieces are also composed to assist in a whole-arm approach to technical development. Representatives of methods using the intervallic approach include:

Frances Clark, Louise Goss and Sam Holland. *The Music Tree*. Princeton, NJ: Summy-Birchard Music, 1955 (distributed by Alfred Publishing).

Lynn Freeman Olson, Louise Bianchi and Marvin Blickenstaff. *Music Pathways*. New York: Carl Fischer, Inc., 1978.

Eclectic Reading Approaches

In recent years, beginning method series have combined reading elements from the three approaches already described. Representatives of methods using eclectic approaches include:

Dennis Alexander, Gayle Kowalchyk, E. L. Lancaster, Victoria McArthur, Martha Mier. *Alfred's Premier Piano Course*. Van Nuys, CA: Alfred Publishing Co., 2005.

Nancy and Randall Faber. *Piano Adventures*. Fort Lauderdale, FL: The FJH Music Co., 1993.

Barbara Kreader, Fred Kern, Phillip Keveren, Mona Rejino. *Hal Leonard Student Piano Library*. Milwaukee, WI: Hal Leonard Corporation, 1996.

Helen Marlais. *Succeeding at the Piano*. Fort Lauderdale, FL: The FJH Music Company, Inc., 2010.

Willard A. Palmer, Morton Manus, and Amanda Vick Lethco. *Alfred's Basic Piano Library*. Van Nuys, CA: Alfred Publishing Co., Inc., 1982.

COUNTING APPROACHES

Students who feel and experience the pulse strongly before more complex note values are introduced will have a solid foundation for rhythmic development. Note values that are multiples of the pulse (half notes, dotted half notes and whole notes) reinforce the feeling of the pulse and should be thoroughly learned before subdivisions of the pulse (eighth note, eighth-note triplets and sixteenth notes). Methods that encourage movement experiences, such as clapping or tapping, help develop a strong rhythmic foundation.

Counting Systems

Counting is the traditional method to reinforce accurate rhythm. Some methods encourage teachers to use one of four counting systems and others leave the decision to the teacher. The four most common counting systems are descriptive (nominative), numerical, metric and syllabic.

The following rhythm could be counted four ways: ♩   ♩   𝅗𝅥

Descriptive (nominative):	quarter	quarter	half - note
Numerical:	1	1	1 – 2
Metric:	1	2	3 – 4
Syllabic:	ta	ta	ta – a

Descriptive (Nominative) Counting

Descriptive counting uses rhythmically spoken note names (quarter, half note, etc.) to count. Students learn the counting and the name of the note value at the same time.

- "Quarter" for the quarter note ♩
- "Half-note" for the half note 𝅗𝅥
- "Half-note-dot" for the dotted half note 𝅗𝅥.
- "Whole-note-hold-it" (or "hold-that-whole-note") for the whole note 𝅝
- "Two eighths" for pairs of eighth notes ♪ ♪
- "Quar-ter-dot eighth" for a dotted quarter note followed by an eighth note ♩. ♪
- "Tri-pi-let" for triplets[2] ♪ ♪ ♪

Example 3.1 Sample rhythm with descriptive counting

For all notes, except the quarter note, the number of syllables used to count the note is the same as the number of beats or parts of beats. For example, "whole-note-hold-it" has four syllables for a note that gets four beats. However, the word "quarter" has two syllables and the quarter note has only one beat. To alleviate this problem some teachers use the descriptive words for all note values except the quarter note, and ask students to say "one" or "note" (both one-syllable words) for quarter notes. Other teachers promote using the word "quar-ter" because the feeling and hearing of the subdivision prepares students for eighth notes. When hands play together with different rhythm values for each, it becomes necessary for students to learn the metric counting system.

Numerical Counting

In numerical counting, the number of beats for each note value is counted, reinforcing the relationship of notes to each other while relating them to the basic pulse. In numerical counting, "1" for a quarter note is sensible because, in beginning music, the quarter note usually gets one

---

[2] Triplets and sixteenth notes are generally introduced to students in the early-intermediate level.

beat. It is easy because all the quarter notes are counted using the same number, "1". Half notes are counted "1–2"; dotted half notes, "1–2–3"; and whole notes, "1–2–3–4" (see example 3.2). "And" (or "&") is used to count eighth-note subdivisions; "e" and "a" are used to count sixteenth-note subdivisions (see example 3.3). As with descriptive counting, using numerical counting for beginners requires learning the metric counting system at a later time.

Example 3.2 Sample rhythm with numerical counting

Metric Counting

In metric counting, a musician counts the number of beats per measure successively, i.e., the number "1" always refers to beat 1 and "4" to beat 4 of the measure. A half note on beat 2 is counted "2–3" rather than "1–2" (as in numerical counting). Students know exactly where they are in the measure. As with numerical counting, "and" is used to count eighth-note subdivisions; "e" and "a" are used to count sixteenth-note subdivisions.

Example 3.3 Sample rhythms with metric counting

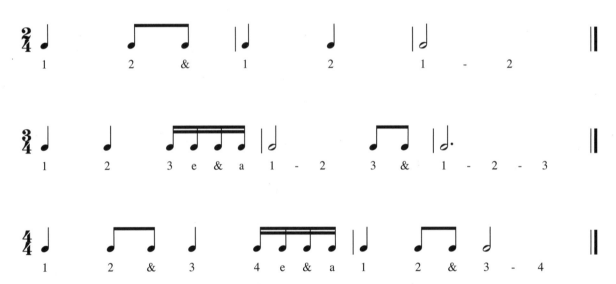

Metric counting can be confusing for some beginners who began counting numerically. For example, when a measure has four quarter notes, each note gets a different number when counted metrically ("1–2–3–4"), even though all the notes are the same length. Furthermore, when mistakes are made and it is necessary to restart in the middle of the measure, the student may have difficulty remembering the exact beat. Metric counting may also become confusing to some beginning students since it is easy to confuse rhythm-counting numbers with finger numbers. However, students who use metric counting from the beginning will not need to change counting systems.

Syllabic Counting

Syllables have been used in many cultures for learning rhythm. Some piano methods have adapted Zoltán Kodály's (1882–1967) syllabic system, which in turn is an adaptation of French rhythm syllables invented by Pierre Galin (1786–1821) in the nineteenth century. This method came to be known as the Galin-Paris-Chevé method. Unlike the other three forms of counting, syllabic counting requires students to learn an arbitrary set of syllables for the various note values. The primary advantage is that students know exactly where the beats begin, thus reinforcing a strong sense of pulse.

Since there is no meter placement (such as counting "1–2–3–4"), neutral syllables make it easier to play in irregular meters. Syllabic counting also eliminates the confusion between finger numbers and counting numbers and provides continual sounds for longer note values. Students know exactly where they are within the beat by what they are saying. It is more difficult to know the exact beat of the measure.

In one type of a syllabic counting system,

- the syllable "ta" represents the beginning of each beat. In simple meter, such as $\frac{4}{4}$, the beginning of each quarter-note beat is "ta." Likewise, in $\frac{4}{8}$ the beginning of each eighth-note beat is "ta." In compound meter, such as $\frac{6}{8}$, the beginning of each dotted quarter-note beat is also counted "ta."

- an "a" is added to the "ta" for each multiple of the beat. For example, a half note would be counted "ta-a" and a dotted half note would be "ta-a-a."

- "tay" is used for the eighth-note subdivision.

- "ty" (pronounced tee) is used for the last subdivision of triplet or sixteenth-note rhythms.

- "pi" is used for any smaller subdivision that occurs immediately after the primary beat. For example an eighth-note triplet would be counted "ta-pi-ty" and four sixteenth notes would be counted "ta-pi-tay-ty."[3]

In this syllabic counting system, the following rhythm would be counted as follows:

Example 3.4 Sample rhythm with syllabic counting

In another form of syllabic counting, the rhythmic unit and the basic rhythm pattern are counted by saying familiar words. The most familiar example of this procedure is demonstrated in Hazel Cobb's book, *Rhythm with Rhyme and Reason*.[4]

---

[3] Lynn Freeman Olson, Louise Bianchi and Marvin Blickenstaff, *Music Pathways* (New York: Carl Fischer, Inc., 1978).

[4] Hazel Cobb, *Rhythm with Rhyme and Reason: Counting Made Easy as Pie* (Mills Music, Inc., 1947).

- The quarter note is counted "pie."

- Two eighth notes are "ap-ple."

- Eighth-note triplets are "cho-co-late."

- Four sixteenths are "huck-le-ber-ry."

- Two sixteenths followed by an eighth note is "but-ter-scotch."

- An eighth note followed by two sixteenths is "goose-ber-ry."

Using this form or syllabic counting, the following rhythm would be counted:

Example 3.5 Sample rhythm with syllabic counting using words

This method of learning rhythm patterns is fun for students. Teachers can also develop their own set of words, names or geographic places for various rhythm patterns.

In both descriptive and syllabic counting, students must be careful to say the words for the longer-valued notes in rhythm and not say extra syllables faster than the pulse. For example, some students will want to say "halfnote" rather than "half - note."

Switching to Metric Counting

While metric counting is unnecessary until the two hands have to play different rhythms simultaneously, at some point, any student who uses a counting system other than metric has to learn to count metrically. Some teachers begin metric counting when eighth notes are introduced. Others begin metric counting with the introduction of time signatures.

As the student progresses, the teacher can assign both the metric counting system and the original system introduced in the early stages of learning, depending upon the rhythmic difficulty of each piece. For example, the student may be comfortable using metric counting until the dotted quarter note followed by the eighth note is introduced.

Time Signatures and Bar Lines

Most beginning methods introduce time signatures and bar lines even when a counting system other than metric is suggested, since complex rhythms without bar lines can become confusing. Without bar lines, it is also not possible for a student to develop the feel of a strong pulse on beat 1.

CHOOSING A BEGINNING METHOD

Successful teachers are familiar with a number of beginning methods to assure that educated choices are made for individual students. Judging a method by teaching it is time consuming and sometimes places the student in an experimental role. A preliminary review, using a specific set of criteria, is an excellent way to become acquainted with a wide variety of methods. Initially, three basic questions can be considered:

- Is the method systematic and logical in its presentation of concepts and skills?

- Does it provide ample reinforcement?

- Does it present a comprehensive introduction to music through piano playing?

Systematic Presentation of Concepts and Skills

The presentation of concepts and skills should be systematic and logical. For example, in many methods, beginning students learn to play pieces that use melodic 2nds only. Other intervals (3rds through 5ths) are added gradually, and larger intervals are introduced later. This is a systematic introduction to intervals. If, during the first weeks of lessons, the student has a piece that has 2nds, 3rds, and one 6th, the 6th is out of place since 6ths have not yet been presented. It is likely that the 6th would not occur again until several weeks or months later. Methods that include such out-of-order presentations are not systematic. When teachers study an unfamiliar method, they must compare each piece to the preceding one to make sure it is only incrementally more difficult. Each new concept or skill should build slowly on what the student already knows.

Ample Reinforcement

Once each new concept or skill has been introduced, students should use it in a number of pieces, or several times in the same piece, to assure mastery. For example, if a tie is presented as a new concept and practiced in a piece, but does not appear again until several other new concepts and skills have been introduced, students will probably need to relearn the concept of a tie when encountering it the second time. Likewise, when any interval is introduced, there should be several pieces in which that interval is presented with increasing complexity, variety and frequency. No other significant new concept or skill should be introduced until there has been sufficient reinforcement of the new interval.

Comprehensiveness

Methods that introduce concepts and skills in a way that help students become complete musicians are superior to those that limit their experience to repertoire and technique. Students can simultaneously experience reading, rhythm, technique, ensemble, ear development, transposition, creativity, theory, and musical performance. For example, when each new interval is introduced, students can learn to read it, fit it into a rhythmic pattern, learn the technique for playing it, and play it in a piece. However, they can also identify its sound, move it to a different place (transpose), use it as harmony as well as melody, and play it in various ways (loud, soft, short, long, fast or slow). They can hear the interval in relation to the teacher's duet part, find it in other pieces, write it, and create their own pieces with it. When a method provides this variety of experience in a single book, or through supplementary materials, the student receives a comprehensive musical education.

SPECIFIC CRITERIA FOR EVALUATING A BEGINNING METHOD

After the three primary criteria have been evaluated, teachers can further explore methods for other specific characteristics. The following series of questions can be investigated. Each question is followed by some additional considerations that will aid in evaluating a method.

Scope and Format

Is the book long enough, but not too long?	A method book must be long enough to be practical, but not so long that the student will feel discouraged from not finishing it in a timely manner.
Is the method designed for individual or group study?	Ensemble pieces, unit organization and a variety of activities in one book are characteristics of a group method.
What will the student have learned upon completion of the method?	A beginning method should include all elementary concepts and skills (see chapter 4).
Do the pages seem cluttered with superfluous material?	Method books should have more music to play than words to read. Text addressed to the parent or teacher should be limited.
Is the material presented in a clear and attractive manner?	The printing should be clear and easy to read. Any illustrations should be tasteful, colorful, simple and age-appropriate for the student.
Are the illustrations overly prominent?	Illustrations should not obscure or take precedence over the music.
What is the purpose of the illustrations?	Illustrations should match the title and sound of the pieces and appeal to the student's imagination to encourage musical playing. Some illustrations may be useful in conveying new concepts.
Is the printing the appropriate size for the targeted age level?	Methods for very young children, or those with limited sight, should have large print. As children get older, print size can become smaller.
Is the material presented in units or in a continuous format?	Units allow the teacher to organize a lesson around a small body of new information. Continuous presentation allows teachers to choose more or less material for individual students for each lesson.

Are there sufficient fingerings without being redundant?	Excessive fingerings will encourage students to read them instead of the notes.
Does the book title reflect the content?	Books with titles such as "Ten Easy Lessons" may be misleading.
Are there sufficient editorial markings, without being over edited?	Books with simple markings for dynamics, phrasing or articulation, appropriate to the student's developmental level, will encourage musical playing. Students may be unable to observe the interpretive suggestions if there are too many markings on the score.
Are the editorial markings introduced systematically?	The musical requirements suggested by the editorial markings must be consistent with the student's technical development.

The answers to many of these questions will depend upon the targeted age group. Sometimes, the foreword of the book will clearly define the age group for which the method was designed. Other times, the evaluator will need to determine the targeted age based on the format and content. When elements seem inconsistent with the targeted age group, the method loses its effectiveness. For example, the rate of progress or level of technical difficulty could indicate that the method is for students between seven and nine years old, while the illustrations and piece titles would be more appealing to a five- or six-year-old.

Keyboard Exploration

Do students explore the entire keyboard or are they restricted to one area?	Methods that limit students to playing only one section of the keyboard inhibit the students' knowledge of musical sound.
How is keyboard exploration achieved?	The entire keyboard can be utilized by playing on the black keys without the staff; using the octave sign (*8va*); playing white-key pieces in five-finger positions such as A and D minor; and using multi-key approaches to reading.
Are students required to spend too much time in one key?	When students play for a long time in one or two keys, their knowledge of musical sound and musical growth is delayed.

Reading Approach

Are the reading concepts introduced logically?	Intervals and notes must be carefully introduced in a logical order.
Is there sufficient reinforcement for each new reading concept?	There should be a minimum of two pieces that use a new concept or skill before another is introduced. Each subsequent piece can present the new concept or skill in a more complex setting.
Does contour play a role in pitch reading?	Books that present note-reading by contour, pitch patterns and rhythm groups, will help students keep their eyes on the page and become fluent readers. Fluent reading will be more difficult in methods that introduce one note at a time.
Is there sufficient time spent using pre-staff notation?	Pre-staff notation helps students focus on direction and distance, hand and finger coordination, and the pulse without having to learn notes and note names. Students should continue to read off-staff until those skills have developed.
Is the grand staff introduced gradually or all at once?	When methods move from pre-staff notation to notation on the grand staff, it can seem to students like a completely new reading system. Introducing the staff one line at a time helps some student make a smoother transition from pre-staff notation.
Once the staff is introduced, what is the basic reading approach (middle C, multi-key, intervallic, or an eclectic mixture of the three)?	Middle C methods use the full staff or clef and the first note introduced is middle C. Multi-key methods teach major five-finger patterns first. Intervallic methods start with one or two staff lines to teach the first interval and add lines as larger intervals are taught. Eclectic methods combine elements from all three approaches.
Does each new piece have a logical relationship to the previously introduced concepts and pieces?	New pieces should use only previously learned material, or introduce a new concept or skill with a simplification of previously learned material.
Do the teaching pieces have excessive fingering?	A method should provide only essential finger numbers so that students will learn to plan logical fingering. If too much fingering is given, students may become dependent on finger numbers and not read notes and contours fluently.

Are note names written in the noteheads?	Note names in noteheads help students play the correct key, even though they may have to look at their hands to play it.
If intervals are used for reading, what is the order of the interval presentation?	Seconds are most commonly introduced first, moving to 3rds, 4ths, and 5ths. Other methods introduce 3rds and 5ths first. This introduction balances the hand and introduces two intervals written either line to line or space to space.
Is transposition incorporated?	Transposing helps students read by contour. Black-key pieces can be moved to white keys and white-key pieces in a five-finger pattern can be moved to other five-finger patterns.
Are sharps and flats introduced with a definite plan?	Sharps and flats should be introduced first as indicating the next key to the right (up) or left (down). Each new sharp or flat should be sufficiently reinforced before new accidentals are presented.
Are key signatures introduced with a definite plan?	The sharps and flats in a key signature should be introduced first as accidentals marked in the score since it may be difficult to remember a key signature. The first key signatures should include only one sharp or flat and be used for several pieces before introducing a new key signature.
How is pitch reading reinforced?	A successful beginning method will include several new pieces to reinforce each new note that is introduced. Some methods also include flashcards and software to reinforce pitch reading.
Are landmark notes used?	Landmark notes help students find other notes by interval, without having to know the names of the other notes. Reading notes by relationships promotes contour reading.
What is the balance of black- and white-key use?	When a method begins with pre-staff notation on black keys, students will use black and white keys equally for a while. In multi-key methods, black and white keys are used equally.

Rhythm

Is pulse sufficiently learned before other rhythmic concepts are presented?	Quarter notes are introduced first to establish a strong sense of pulse. Introducing other rhythmic values too soon may weaken this critical foundation.
What counting system is suggested or implied?	Some methods strongly recommend a counting system and others leave the decision to the teacher. Some methods imply metric counting from the beginning by using a time signature and bar lines.
Are rhythms introduced in a logical way?	Only one new note value or rhythm pattern should be introduced at a time.
Is each new rhythm pattern sufficiently reinforced before a new one is presented?	Each new note value or rhythm pattern should be reinforced in at least two pieces before a new one is introduced.
How does the method build rhythmic understanding into the body?	The method should encourage large-motor movement (whole arm) experiences such as clapping or tapping.
Are rests introduced in a logical way and as musical silence?	Rests should be introduced in a way that encourages them to be observed and understood as silence.
When are measures and bar lines introduced?	Students should have sufficient time to develop a sense of pulse before bar lines suggest metric organization.
How is the meter signature introduced?	The meter signature should be introduced as organizing the beats into groups of equal numbers.
Is a partial meter signature used?	Some methods introduce the meter signature with a quarter-note icon below the upper number, rather than the number four. This approach can help students understand the logic of the meter signature.
Which meters are used?	Some elementary methods include only simple meters, while others include irregular and compound meters.
How is rhythm reading reinforced?	Ensemble playing, separate rhythm drills, eurhythmic activities and written drills are some of the ways a beginning method can reinforce rhythm.

Technique

Does technical development seem to be a systematic part of the method?	In some methods, each new technical requirement logically follows the previous ones and is introduced and reinforced in new pieces. In other methods, technical exercises prepare the student for the technical needs of each piece as they arise.
How is technique reinforced?	Short exercises in the method book may or may not reinforce the technical needs of the pieces. A separate technique book may be needed to prepare students for the pieces.
Does the technical development begin with a whole-arm or an individual-finger approach?	Methods that promote hands alternating with single braced fingers playing individual notes, begin to build a good hand position, a balanced hand and a whole-arm approach to technical development. Using consecutive fingers requires more finger coordination and can develop what is called a "finger technique." Unnecessary tension can result.
Do the pieces allow for equal development of both hands?	Methods that have melodies for both hands and equal numbers of notes for each hand strongly develop both hands. Mirror-patterned, parallel-motion and hand-over-hand pieces or exercises also allow both hands to develop equally.
Are technical difficulties introduced gradually?	In building piano technique, playing consecutive eighth notes and three-note chords are big steps. In some methods, they may be introduced before students have mastered easier technical skills.
Are exercises emphasized more than the pieces of music?	Students are motivated when a method places more emphasis on pieces and less emphasis on exercises.
How are five-finger patterns introduced?	Five-finger patterns are a natural outgrowth of a method that introduces multi-key or position note-reading. In other methods, five-finger patterns may be delayed.
How soon are chords introduced?	For young students, three-note chords should be delayed until the hand can play them without tension.

When and how are scales introduced?	Scales are sometimes introduced as tetrachords and sometimes as full scales complete with thumb turns. Tetrachords allow beginning students to see the full scale under the hands.
When are articulations introduced?	Non-legato is the most natural articulation to produce and usually the first articulation used in a method. Staccato and legato are other articulations that are introduced in elementary methods.
Does the method introduce all of the basic motions and coordination needed to prepare for intermediate-level repertoire?	An elementary method should present the basic motions used to play the piano. For example, fingers can move laterally to contract and extend the position of the hand. Hands can change position, alternate hand over hand, or play together in parallel or contrary motion. Thumbs can move under the hand and fingers can move over the thumb.
Does the method encourage a technique that is conducive to a musical sound?	When methods emphasize the use of the whole arm, a good piano sound can be produced.
How is the development of fingers 1 and 5 achieved?	Blocked 5ths allow fingers 1 and 5 to develop in a way that supports the arm weight.
Is the transposition of technical exercises encouraged?	Playing pieces and exercises in different keys expands technical development.
Is the use of the damper pedal taught?	Simple pedaling is appropriate for elementary students. It is best to delay complicated or syncopated (legato) pedaling until the intermediate levels.
Are chromatic figures introduced?	Short chromatic figures increase the mobility of the thumb and create new interesting sounds.

Technical development is an integral part of most well-designed methods. Pieces are chosen to present and reinforce specific physical skills in a systematic and incremental way. In some methods, the technical exercises prepare for future needs, while in others, the technical exercises seem to follow their own independent order without a logical relationship to the pieces surrounding them.

Musical Content

Was the music originally composed for the method?	Originally composed pieces are often written to support the reading, rhythmic and technical philosophies of the authors.
Is there a sufficient number of familiar pieces? Do the originally composed pieces sound somewhat familiar to most students?	Students like to play familiar-sounding pieces.
How many of the pieces are simplified versions of masterworks?	Simplified versions of masterworks appeal to students who may recognize the music or who feel as though they are playing important music.
Are titles appropriate for the targeted age level?	Pieces with overly juvenile titles, generic titles (such as *Sonatina*), or titles that would appeal to adults, will not appeal to average-age beginners. Titles like *Skateboard, Computer Game* or *Playing Soccer* will appeal to the imagination of today's average-age beginner.
Is the music appealing to the average student?	The musical taste of students is not as developed as that of teachers; therefore, in some methods the music wisely has been composed to appeal to students' tastes.
Is the music linear in nature or does it emphasize full sounds?	Linear melodies teach phrasing, but students generally like pieces with full sounds.
Are the musical sounds predictable?	Overuse of tonic and dominant harmonies creates pieces that sound alike.
Are contemporary musical sounds explored?	The method books should contain a few pieces that explore contemporary idioms (including dissonance). If these pieces also have imaginative titles that match their sound, students' musical tastes will be expanded.
Are pieces included that are easy to memorize?	Pieces with familiar patterns, patterns that repeat, and limited musical material will help motivate students to memorize.
Are the titles of the pieces chosen for a purpose?	Titles that match the musical content of the pieces will stimulate the imagination, promote expressive playing, and gradually expand a student's musical taste.

Aural Development

Do the pieces include lyrics?	Lyrics encourage singing and phrasing.
Are there enough pieces in the students' singing range?	Students are more likely to sing if the melody is in their singing range.
Does the method book encourage students to listen and make judgments about what they hear in the pieces and in their own playing?	Listening activities help students avoid errors and correct mistakes in their playing.
Are ear-training skills developed in a systematic way?	Listening activities should relate to the pieces the students are playing. A systematic ear-training program develops those listening skills.

When methods provide ways for students to develop their aural skills, they will make fewer mistakes, be able to correct the mistakes they make, and learn to listen critically to their playing.

Development of Musical Playing

Are there student/teacher duets?	Teacher duet parts promote musical playing.
Are the interpretive markings appropriate for the targeted age and level?	A few simple interpretive markings will promote musical playing.
How are musical elements, such as articulations or dynamics, introduced?	Articulations and dynamics should be introduced gradually and in a systematic way based on what the student already knows.

When methods make it easy to play musically from the very first lessons, learning will be satisfying. Moreover, students will grow as musicians and communicate more effectively to their listeners.

Creativity

Are students given the opportunity to apply new concepts and skills in creative activities such as improvisation?	Supplementary creative activities promote expressiveness and musicality. When such activities are related to new concepts and skills, they reinforce student learning.
Are students encouraged to make up melodies?	Playing "Questions and Answers" (antecedent and consequent phrases), adding pitches to given rhythm patterns, adding notes to words, or adding rhythm to a series of pitches are some of the ways to assist students in creating melodies.
Are students provided the opportunity to harmonize melodies?	Elementary students can initially harmonize melodies with tonic and dominant pitches, then blocked or broken 5ths and 6ths, and finally, tonic and dominant chords.

Students will understand concepts thoroughly when they create their own music from the musical ideas they are learning. Being able to express themselves musically through creative activities helps students grow as musicians.

Musicianship

What patterns are emphasized?	Five-finger patterns, scales, intervals, blocked chords and broken chords are some of the patterns elementary-level students learn to recognize.
How and when do students experience key or tonality?	In multi-key methods, students understand the concept of key and tonality from the very beginning.
Is there a written theory program?	Some methods have supplementary theory books that are correlated to the lesson books.
Is there a keyboard theory program?	Students can use exercises to play the theory concepts they are learning. In some methods, theory concepts are learned through studying the pieces.

Will students gain a thorough understanding of the structure of pieces?	A method with a strong theory program will build musical understanding that includes music structure.
Are theoretical concepts applied to pieces?	In some methods, the theory exercises are not related to the teaching pieces.

Students who learn about the music they play will become musically literate. If this information is related to their study pieces, they will learn and memorize them more easily.

Application of Learning Principles

Is the text sufficiently clear to enable students to gain independence from the teacher?	Methods that have written questions on the page will help students become independent learners.
Does the method provide challenge without discouragement?	Some methods include pieces that students can learn easily on their own. Methods that move too fast may discourage students.
Is the unfamiliar approached from the familiar?	New knowledge should build on what the student has already learned.
Will the pace of the method meet individual needs?	Slowly paced methods meet the needs of some students by introducing and providing much reinforcement for one concept at a time. Faster-paced methods are better for other students. They introduce many concepts and skills quickly and without much reinforcement.

Successful authors of beginning methods have observed principles of learning, leading students to learn efficiently. A good method will move at an appropriate pace for a particular age group and student type and will include activities that facilitate learning.

Supplementary Materials

Are audio recordings, orchestrated accompaniments, and theory or ear-training computer software available for the method series?	Supplementary materials enhance and make learning more enjoyable, assuring that no essential information has been omitted.
Are there flashcards?	Flashcards make learning gamelike and can be taken home by the student for daily drills.
Will students need supplementary books for reinforcement and a comprehensive education?	In some methods, all activities that assure comprehensive learning are included in the core method books. When methods move quickly from one concept or skill to the next without reinforcement, or introduce concepts and skills through teaching pieces only, students will need additional books. When a method includes several books for each level, it can be assumed that a comprehensive education relies on the use of several books.

METHODS FOR SPECIAL AGE GROUPS

Methods designed for students other than average-age beginners must meet additional criteria. Methods developed for the adult beginner should consider the following:

- The method should appeal to a student's intellect. Adult students can understand abstract concepts and ideas more quickly and more easily than children. Therefore, more text and more exploration of the musical content (theory) can be included.

- The presentation and format of the books must be appropriate for adults. Adults (with the exception of some older adults) can usually read average-sized print. The titles of the pieces must not sound childish.

- Some adults will have more highly developed coordination than children due to maturation and developed skills, such as typing and sports activities. A method that makes more technical demands is appropriate for those adults. Other adults will find finger and hand coordination as difficult as children do. The method will need to be chosen after the teacher has analyzed the student's physical coordination.

- Whenever possible, the method should include familiar tunes, especially those that were popular when the student was young.

- Opportunities for playing by ear and harmonizing familiar melodies are important for some adults.

+ Adult students have preconceived expectations and goals. These often are much higher than those of children and vary widely from student to student. The method should be chosen to support those expectations.

+ Methods that allow for an aesthetic experience in a short time are essential.

+ Adults are often willing to work hard some of the time, but they also want to enjoy themselves while making music. Successful adult methods provide enjoyable music and enable positive learning experiences.

For further discussion of teaching adult students, see chapter 11, pages 300–319. Methods and materials for preschool beginners should also meet certain criteria. (Refer to pages 296–297 in chapter 10 for a listing of such criteria.)

TEACHING WITH OR WITHOUT PRINTED METHODS

Some teachers use one method exclusively for all students, while others use different methods for different students. Some develop their own beginning curriculum without using a published method, while others combine several methods. Each of these approaches has advantages and disadvantages that teachers should consider carefully when selecting the most suitable plan(s) for their students.

Teaching with One Method Exclusively

Teachers who have learned about one method and use it exclusively have the advantage of knowing that method well. They know the pedagogical strengths of each piece and can compensate for weaknesses. As a result, they spend less time preparing for lessons. However, to avoid gaps in student development, teachers must be cognizant of the deficiencies of the method and prepare other supplementary materials. Teaching one method exclusively can make the teaching predictable, sterile and boring. Furthermore, the unique needs of individual students may not be met.

Teaching Different Students With Different Methods

The needs of individual students are best met when teachers use methods that are designed for specific student types or if the teacher chooses a method that seems best for a particular student. When teachers choose to use a variety of methods, they must take time to become familiar with each and develop appropriate lesson plans. If teachers are familiar with a number of methods, they will be able to substitute different materials at ease when a student needs a change. However, it is difficult for teachers to know all methods equally well.

Developing a Curriculum Combining More Than One Method

Teachers who are conversant with a variety of methods can develop a curriculum that integrates materials from several of them. Combining methods that are significantly different from one another broadens the musical education and helps to eliminate weaknesses that might occur from using one method alone. Both *Music Pathways* and *The Music Tree*, for example, introduce pitch reading by interval from landmarks. To combine these methods would be redundant. It is more logical to integrate one of these methods with the significantly different *Alfred's Basic Piano Library*, which introduces note-reading using positions, finger numbers, and note names in noteheads. Developing such an integrated curriculum takes time and careful planning.

Teaching Without a Published Method

Some teachers develop their own approach to teaching beginners without using a published method. They choose from a variety of beginning books and use pieces to reinforce the concepts and skills they have introduced. This gives flexibility without having to follow the prescribed order in a method. It also allows for meeting individual student needs by choosing exactly the correct piece at the right time. Teaching without a method requires extensive teaching experience and careful planning. Moreover, it is easy to overlook important concepts and steps in the learning process.

SUMMARY

Using a beginning reading method is the most common approach to teaching beginners. Teachers must know how to choose the appropriate method for each student.

- Reading approaches of methods fall into four general categories: middle C, multi-key, intervallic, and eclectic. Each reading approach is distinctly different from the other and each has its strengths and weaknesses.

- In addition to different reading modes, individual methods differ in their approaches to rhythm, technique, aural development, creativity, musicianship, and keyboard exploration.

- Most methods encourage adhering to one of four counting methods: descriptive, numerical, metric or syllabic.

- Students should study from a method that meets their individual needs.

- Teachers can learn to observe the characteristics of a method and evaluate its effectiveness.

- Each method should meet three primary criteria: systematic presentation, ample reinforcement and comprehensive musical education.

- It is effective to use tailored methods for various age groups, from preschoolers to adults.

- When teachers take time to critically evaluate available methods, they will be prepared to build on the strengths of each and will be ready to fill in the gaps caused by the weaknesses.

PROJECTS FOR NEW TEACHERS

1. Evaluate the elementary-level books (usually the first three or four books) of three beginning piano methods using the following as a guide:

   a. Describe the approach to note-reading. (See pages 35–38 and 46–47)

   b. Describe the approach to counting. (See pages 38–42)

   c. Describe how the concepts and skills are presented in a systematic way. (See page 43)

   d. Describe how the concepts and skills are reinforced. (See page 43)

   e. Describe how the method develops a comprehensive music education. (See page 43)

   f. Answer the questions posed in this chapter relating to:

   - scope and format (see pages 44–45)

   - keyboard exploration (see page 45)

   - reading approach (see pages 46–47)

   - rhythm (see page 48)

   - technique (see pages 49–50)

   - musical content (see page 51)

   - aural development (see page 52)

   - development of musical playing (see page 52)

   - creativity (see page 53)

   - musicianship (see pages 53–54)

   - application of learning principles (see page 54)

   - supplementary materials (see page 55)

2. Apply the four forms of counting described on pages 38–42 to the following four rhythms:

PROJECTS FOR EXPERIENCED TEACHERS

1. Using only the core lesson books from the first level of an elementary method that you have not taught before, make a list of all the new concepts, in the order they are introduced. Choose two additional teaching ideas from familiar materials to supplement the introduction of each new concept. These may be written exercises, games, additional solos, creative activities, theory drills, technical exercises, keyboard theory, or sight-reading materials. Briefly describe each idea and how it reinforces the new concept.

2. Choose an intervallic method and an eclectic method you have never taught and combine the first lesson books for use with a beginning student. Use the intervallic method as the primary text and the eclectic method to supplement and reinforce the reading approach. Correlate the eclectic method to the intervallic method by listing when and where specific pages of the eclectic lesson books will be used with the intervallic method.

Chapter 4

TEACHING BEGINNERS
AND ELEMENTARY STUDENTS

Learning to teach is most effective if teachers start with beginners. Some new teachers, as a result of university or other advanced training, are equipped to coach musical aspects of more advanced repertoire, but may find it difficult to acquire students at this level. Beginning, elementary, and early-intermediate students are easier to obtain. Because years have passed since new teachers were themselves at those ages and levels, it is often hard for them to remember the learning process they experienced. What is now easy for them is not easy for beginners. The methods and materials they grew up with may not suit today's students. Furthermore, most teachers are likely to have been exceptional students during their early training.

CONCEPTS AND SKILLS COVERED IN EARLY INSTRUCTION

To effectively teach beginning and elementary students, teachers need to define what elementary students will study and accomplish. Elementary students can be any age from preschool through senior adults. Regardless of age, they all need to learn the same basic concepts and skills. Naturally, some students will achieve these skills more quickly than others. Students learn to apply concepts and skills by doing the following:

- hearing
- reading
- playing the piano
- writing
- analyzing

Aural Development

It is critical that beginners start with an aural image of sound and music. Learning to play simple pieces by ear assures that the student will make music and become acquainted with the keyboard before having to read staff notation. When students play without reading, they often play more rhythmically and musically. These pieces can be played using a variety of touches, dynamics and tempos. Teachers can work on posture, body use, hand and finger position; and since students are not reading the music, they can also observe these things more readily.

When students are ready to learn a piece by reading notes, they should have an aural impression of its elements before beginning to learn it. For example, before learning "Mexican Hat Dance" (see example 4.1), students should already know how melodic 3rds and 2nds sound and how quarter and half notes sound when grouped in measures containing four beats.

Example 4.1 "Mexican Hat Dance," p. 39 from *Alfred's Basic Piano Library,* Lesson Book 1A, by Palmer, Manus and Lethco

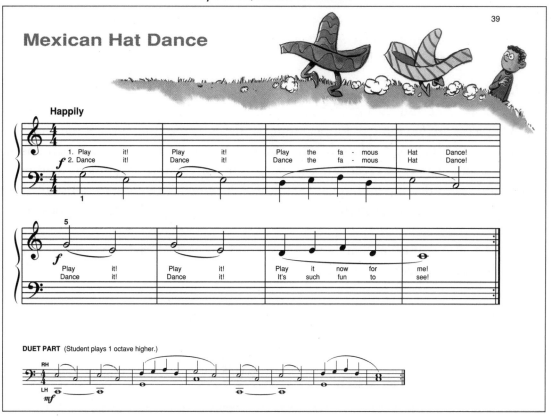

Students use their ears to help them know whether they have played everything correctly. They can ask themselves the following questions:

- Did the notes and intervals sound correct?

- Did every measure sound as if it contained four beats ($\frac{4}{4}$ meter)?

- Was the sound loud or soft?

- Did the notes sound smooth and connected or detached?

When the initial approach to learning has a strong aural emphasis, students will learn to correct their own mistakes through listening.

Some students learn to read quickly, using their ears as an aid. Others want to learn by ear only and struggle with reading music. When students lack the discipline needed to learn reading, teachers need to make the reading program as fun and imaginative for them as playing by ear. Lessons for these students include a balance between aural learning and reading. When familiar tunes are taught to these students through reading, they often play them by ear, using rhythms they have heard which may be different from those notated on the page. When teachers try to correct these different rhythms, the student and teacher can quickly become frustrated. Teachers should allow for some rhythmic discrepancies when teaching familiar tunes. It is probably best for ear-oriented students to read unfamiliar tunes so they can learn both correct notes and rhythms by reading.

Students whose ears are not as highly developed should be encouraged to play familiar tunes by ear. With the teacher playing along, they can be asked to fill in only a few missing notes or measures until they become more proficient. In addition to playing familiar tunes by ear, singing selected pieces from the lesson assignment and a systematic ear-training curriculum will enhance their musical development.

Pieces Taught by Rote

Pieces taught by rote usually intrigue aural learners and help all students use their ears. Often, such pieces are too difficult for beginning students to read, but are not too challenging technically. Good rote pieces consist of a limited number of pitch and rhythm patterns, used over and over in a variety of creative ways. Such rote pieces motivate students and provide the opportunities to develop additional technical skills while demanding the use of the ear. Learning pieces by rote helps train students to play and hear groups of notes, as opposed to one note at a time.

The first ten measures of "Rainbow Fish" (see example 4.2) can be taught by rote to a student in the first few weeks of lessons.

Example 4.2 "Rainbow Fish"(excerpt), p. 8 from *Bean Bag Zoo*, Book 1, by Catherine Rollin

The following can be demonstrated by the teacher and copied by the student.

1. The teacher demonstrates the first measure of "Rainbow Fish" and directs the student to place LH fingers 4, 3, 2 on middle C, D, E and RH fingers 2, 3, 4 on the next highest set of three black keys.

2. The teacher demonstrates the first measure, then crosses the LH over the RH and plays C and E with LH fingers 4 and 2 and directs the student to copy.

3. The teacher demonstrates mm. 1–4 and directs the student to copy.

4. The teacher demonstrates mm. 1–8, asking the student to observe that the phrase is repeated two times, with the second occurrence starting an octave lower, and directs the student to copy.

5. The teacher demonstrates mm. 9–10 and directs the student to copy.

6. The teacher demonstrates mm. 1–10 and helps the student copy.

7. The teacher plays the mm. 1–10, holding the damper pedal down throughout, and helps the student copy.

The teacher can use the following abstract to remind the student what to play when practicing "Rainbow Fish." During the lesson the teacher helps the student understand how to use the abstract (see example 4.3).

Example 4.3 Abstract version of "Rainbow Fish" (mm. 1–8)

			Repeat Both	Cross over $\frac{E}{C}$ **8**:(6 beats)
		Repeat Both	*(even higher)*	LH $\frac{2}{4}$
	3 Black Keys	*(higher)*		
	RH 2 3 4			
C D E				
LH 4 3 2				

Repeat all of line one, starting from bass C.

Rhythm Concepts and Rhythmic Development

Elementary students learn and apply the following rhythm concepts:

- pulse

- quarter notes and multiples of the pulse (half, dotted half and whole notes) and their rests

- subdivisions of the pulse (eighth notes) and their rests (A few elementary methods introduce eighth-note triplets and sixteenth notes.)

- $\frac{3}{4}$ and $\frac{4}{4}$ meters and time signatures (Some elementary methods also introduce $\frac{2}{4}$, $\frac{3}{8}$, and $\frac{6}{8}$ meters and even irregular meters such as $\frac{5}{4}$.)

- ties

- common rhythm patterns including those with pairs of eighth notes or a dotted quarter note followed by eighth note

- same/different rhythm patterns

- incomplete measures and upbeats

- tempo markings and tempo changes

- duration (length) of notes

The first rhythms that are studied should be limited to those including only the pulse (quarter notes)[1] and notes that last twice as long (half notes). The pulse is the most important rhythmic unit to be felt. As soon as students clearly understand, feel and play the pulse comfortably, they will be able to learn other multiples and subdivisions of the pulse. Subdivisions are technically more difficult to control; therefore, study and performance of them should be delayed until more physical coordination is developed.

Rhythmic errors, including uneven or unsteady tempos, are often the result of slow reading or inadequate technical readiness. It may be difficult for students to read note direction and intervals, coordinate two hands (even if the hands never play together), keep a steady beat, and play the correct rhythm. A student may understand the rhythm and know how to play it, but complicated note patterns may make it difficult to play the correct notes on time. Conversely, if the student is concentrating on the rhythm, note errors may occur. Therefore, the root of the problem must be addressed, instead of treating the symptom (the inaccurate rhythm). When teachers help students prepare for spots that are more difficult to read or play, rhythmic problems are less likely to occur. In addition to selecting music that motivates students, teachers can also select teaching pieces that focus either on a new rhythm or new notes (but not both). Students are better able to focus their attention on new rhythm and note-reading elements if other difficulties in the music are minimal.

---

[1] While other note values can be considered the pulse, or several different note values can be simultaneously felt and heard as the pulse, in early learning it is the quarter note that represents the pulse.

Building Rhythm into the Body

Tapping the rhythm of each piece when first approaching it helps students feel and hear the rhythm. Tapping, while saying "right," "left," or "both," to indicate which hand is playing, will aid in feeling the hand coordination of the piece. Tapping a third time while counting aloud makes learning even easier. If students have had music classes that included rhythm games and movement activities, learning the rhythm of pieces will be easier.

Counting

Counting aloud is a learned habit that must be established from the beginning. The earlier the counting habit is established, the easier it will become. Students should be able to count the music aloud with ease while playing from the beginning to the end of a piece. When students stop counting, it is a clue that they are experiencing some kind of difficulty. Teachers will want to determine the problem and assist students until it becomes easy. Counting aloud will aid students in playing correct rhythms, but it does not ensure that their playing will have a natural rhythmic feel.

Counting aloud has benefits besides rhythmic precision and stability. It usually slows students to a speed where they can coordinate position shifts more accurately and concentrate better, thus making fewer mistakes.

Rests

When rests are introduced, they should be understood and felt as silence. By making a silent motion with the hands for each rest during the tapping of pieces, the value of the rest will be felt in the body as an integral part of the rhythmic fabric.

Notation for rests can be confusing. The visually unique symbol for the quarter rest is easy, but half and whole rests look similar. An easy way to help students distinguish between half- and whole-rest notation is to suggest that the half rest is lighter in weight (only two beats) and therefore can sit, balance or float on top of the third staff line. The whole rest is heavier (more than two beats) and, therefore, fell down from or hangs below the fourth staff line. Whole rests should be taught as a rest for the whole measure, not a rest equal to the duration of a whole note.

Pitch Concepts and Reading Development

Elementary students learn and apply the following pitch and reading concepts:

- higher and lower

- all music notes on the grand staff and ledger-line notes between the clefs (Some elementary methods include ledger-line notes, extending the note-reading to the C's two octaves above and below middle C.)

- half steps and whole steps

- major and minor five-finger patterns, triads and melodies

- patterns within a five-finger position, including repeated, contrary, imitative and sequential patterns

- sharps, flats and naturals

- harmonic and melodic intervals from 2nds through octaves (Naming the quality of intervals is generally introduced later.)

- tonic, dominant and subdominant chords in root position and close position (**V**6/5 and **IV**6/4) in selected keys

- selected scales

Higher and Lower

Helping students relate what they know about high and low sounds to high and low on the piano will aid those who may be confused about these concepts. Asking them to play high sounds (or low sounds), or play sounds moving higher (or lower), and reinforcing those ideas by relating higher to the right and lower to the left (both starting with the letter "L"), will quickly help them experience what has been heard.

Music Alphabet and Key Names

Teachers can make several sets of cards with each letter of the musical alphabet (A through G) written on one side. The cards are shuffled and given to students to quickly arrange, in order, both forward and backward. For added fun, the cards can be arranged on the floor to resemble a snake. By the end of several weeks, students should be able to recite the musical alphabet forward and backward quickly. As a next step, students could be asked to recite it, skipping every other letter.

Finding all sets of two and three black keys introduces students to the layout of the keyboard. This can be followed by finding the white key between the two black keys (D). Teaching the key names can be completed by moving stepwise down from D to A or up from D to G. Students can then see that all the keys with the same letter name look the same all over the keyboard.

For the first few weeks, students should practice naming the keys on the piano in three ways:

- Play and name all the D's, all the A's and so on, for all the letters of the music alphabet.

- Play and name all the white keys on the entire keyboard in order from the lowest key to the highest, and then from the highest to the lowest.

- Play and name all the white keys in random order by closing the eyes, playing any key, opening the eyes, and naming and singing the note.

Learning key names can also be accomplished in gamelike activities. Teachers can spell words from the musical alphabet, like D–A–D or F–E–D, and ask students to play those words. The same words can also be used later to aid in learning notes on the staff. Teachers can assume the role of the student. The student plays keys in random order, and the teacher names the keys, sometimes incorrectly. The student must catch the teacher's mistakes. By using a variety of activities, students should be able to name any key quickly and at random.

Pre-Staff (Off-Staff) Reading

Notation without lines and spaces eliminates the confusing and complex staff lines in beginning music reading (see example 4.35 on page 110). Most modern methods begin reading with some type of off-staff notation. Teachers should choose a method with an appropriate amount of off-staff notation for the age, maturity and learning ability of the individual student. In pre-staff notation, notes with stems down are for the LH and notes with stems up are for the RH.

In many methods, students are introduced to reading by playing on black keys first. In some methods, black-key or white-key clusters encourage a whole-arm technical approach. After this brief introduction, students begin to play on individual white keys. For both black and white keys, a keyboard diagram often directs them to the correct hand placement on the keyboard for the piece. In some methods, the hands alternate, which encourages whole-arm playing that is tension free, a good tone quality, and eliminates individual finger coordination (see example 4.27 on page 104). For variety, students make octave shifts as they observe note groupings that are placed higher or lower on the page.

Using off-staff notation, consecutive notes within one hand are easily read by contour— that is, direction and interval. Later, these relationships form melodic and harmonic patterns such as intervals and broken chords. During pre-staff learning, individual notes are slightly higher and lower on the page, usually indicating stepwise motion. Note names or finger numbers in noteheads can assist students in playing the correct notes. In some methods, when white keys are introduced, students are directed where to play on the keyboard by position. When students know the position for each hand, fewer finger numbers are given. Most notes are only a 2nd apart, but melodic 3rds, 4ths, and 5ths may also be used sparingly.

Since most beginning pieces move by 2nds, students can intensify their concentration by chanting "up" or "down" as they point to the notes on the page or play the notes on the keyboard. Pointing and counting, or pointing and saying finger numbers, are also effective preliminary practice steps. Students should also *play* on the key cover while chanting the finger numbers. These learning steps should be done both in the lesson and in home practice as preparation for accurate playing.

Teachers can facilitate reading by contour and make learning gamelike by giving the student two or more flashcards that contain patterns of notes, each slightly different from the others. The teacher plays one of the patterns and the student selects the one that was played (see example 2.4 on page 28). Shorter sight-reading flashcards can be created from concepts students are learning and presented rapidly in random order, requiring a quick response by the student who plays the example beginning on any white key (see example 4.4).

It is an advantage to play only on white keys when reading pre-staff notation, since students can think the alphabet both forward and backward and play up and down the keyboard without the visual distraction of staff lines. However, changing positions and including both black and white keys allows for a greater variety of sound.

Example 4.4 Sample flashcards

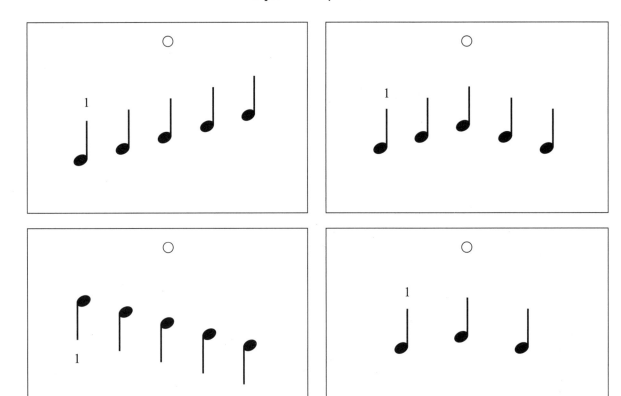

Staff Reading

When students begin to read on the staff, they can be taught to identify specific notes and can begin to read intervals by contour, recognizing that notes can be *on* lines or *in* spaces. This can be accomplished by using flashcard drills and having students write notes *on* lines and *in* spaces. Some methods introduce the staff one horizontal staff line at a time so that students can concentrate on the vertical or horizontal relationship of the notes. Seconds can be notated on a single staff line (♩♩). When the fingers skip notes (3rds), only one line is needed if the notes are on two adjacent spaces (♩♩). However, if the 3rd is on two adjacent lines, then two lines are needed (♩♩). Intervals of 4ths and 5ths can be learned in a similar way. Whether students learn to read through a gradual staff introduction or on the complete staff, they should soon begin to recognize a short series of intervals and begin to develop the skill of reading by contour (interval and direction).

On the staff, contour reading begins with interval recognition. The most frequently used intervals (2nds and 3rds) are usually introduced first and are sometimes easier to learn if the 2nds are called *steps* and the 3rds are called *skips*. (Some teachers introduce 3rds before 2nds because they believe it is technically easier to balance the hand and play legato when alternate fingers are used.) Beginning methods usually limit the reading of intervals to 2nds, 3rds, 4ths and 5ths in the early levels. Reading by contour can be facilitated by asking students to write a melody using whole notes on staff lines without clefs. The teacher might say, "Write a note on the second line from the bottom, write a note up a 2nd, write a note down a 2nd, write a note up a 3rd," etc. The students write the notes on staff paper or a dry-erase board, or place notes on the staff of a magnetic board. Students then read back the instructions that the teacher gave, using their own notation as a guide. Finally, students can play what has been written. Some of these patterns can be from pieces the student will be learning. While giving the instructions, teachers may also play the notes to add an aural component to the learning. This activity is especially effective for students who are aural learners. Hearing and speaking instructions activates their strongest learning mode.

Contour reading can also be facilitated with sight-reading flashcards (see example 4.5). Students will be able to focus precisely if these cards are notated using only one clef, rather than the grand staff. Having to observe which clef is used adds to the learning.

Example 4.5 Sample flashcards

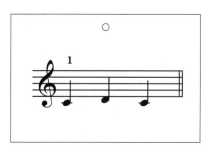 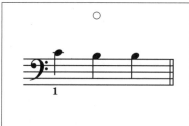 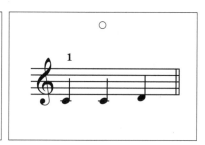

After a few weeks, the grand staff can be used and patterns from study pieces can be included. Students can play these slow, fast, counting aloud and not counting. Several can be played in any order for quick recognition and response (see example 4.6).

Example 4.6 Sample flashcards

 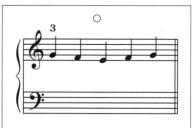 

As students progress through the elementary levels, flashcard drills can be modified to include sharps, flats and naturals. Students begin to recognize and fluently play complete five-finger patterns and broken triads (see example 4.7).

Example 4.7 Sample flashcards

  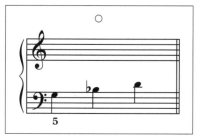

Fingerings should be associated with intervals in a systematic way. When the intervals are played within one hand, 2nds can be played by fingers 1-2, 2-3, 3-4 or 4-5; 3rds, by fingers 1-3, 2-4 or 3-5 ; 4ths, by fingers 1-4, or 2-5; and 5ths, by fingers 1-5. When students learn to associate fingerings with specific intervals, they need less fingering on the page and will be able to read music more readily. This strong tactile association of fingerings for specific intervals will assist in rapid learning at later levels, even when other fingering pairs are used for intervals. Using *Simon Says*-type games will aid in rapid learning and playing of intervals.

Simon says, "Play three harmonic (blocked) 2nds using fingers 2 and 3 of the right hand."

Simon says, "Play four melodic (broken) 3rds using fingers 2 and 4 of the left hand."

When beginners read on the grand staff, they need to know the names of the notes represented by each line and space. However, if they know a limited number of note names, they can read neighboring notes through intervallic relationships. Some methods introduce reading using hand positions to help students find their place on the keyboard (see example 4.8).

Example 4.8 Sample keyboard chart

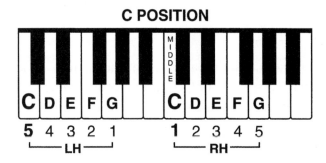

Some methods rely on a certain number of notes that are identified as *landmark* (or *guidepost)* notes. These landmark notes are chosen for logical and visually symmetrical reasons. The most common landmark notes are middle C, bass F, and treble G (see example 4.9).

Example 4.9 Common landmark notes	**Example 4.10** Reading range using landmark notes

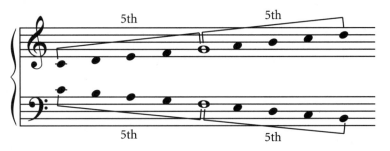

Since "F clef" is an alternative name for the bass clef and "G clef" for the treble clef, bass F and treble G are logical choices for landmarks. If students have already been introduced to the interval of a 5th, middle C can be learned, not just as a note that has a *little line* through it, but as the note that is a 5th below treble G and a 5th above bass F. Other notes can be read by interval and contour from these three landmarks. If students have been introduced to intervals from 2nds through 5ths, their reading range can be extended from treble D (fourth line) through bass B (second line) on the grand staff. (see example 4.10)

Similar landmarks can be added to expand the reading range. High G, in the first space above the treble clef, and low F, in the first space below the bass clef, are logical and symmetrical choices since they look similar on the staff (see example 4.11).

Other methods use five C's as the landmark notes, since they make a symmetrical pattern (visually speaking) on the staff (see example 4.12). This particular approach quickly develops a wide reading range that includes ledger-line notes.

Example 4.11
Additional landmark notes

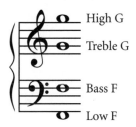

Example 4.12
Additional landmark notes

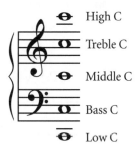

When landmarks are used to teach reading, it is imperative that the first pieces begin on these notes. Once students become familiar with these landmarks and are playing notes that move up and down from them, pieces can begin on or near landmark notes. Students will need to find the first landmark note in the piece, circle it and then relate the first note of the piece to it. If a landmark note does not appear in the piece, students should identify on the staff the position of the closest landmark note that relates to the first note of the piece. Students can be taught to go through a four-step thought process by verbalizing as follows:

1. The first note is close to landmark treble G.

2. It is higher than treble G.

3. It is up a 3rd from treble G.

4. Therefore, it is B.

These steps are essential to avoid starting a piece on an incorrect note. If students begin the piece incorrectly, the whole piece will be wrong. This approach can be presented as a *mystery* that is solved by following the *clues* to play a piece correctly.

At some point, students must learn the names of all the notes on the grand staff. Without this knowledge, they will find it difficult to locate the starting places of their pieces or find new positions used in the pieces. Sometime during the first few months of instruction, students should study note-name flashcards. Notes must be named *and* played on the keyboard. Students should work to name and play all of the notes on the grand staff, including ledger-line notes middle C, and B below and D above it. This process should be gradual, beginning with a few notes and adding additional flashcards each week until all are mastered. As students learn the notes, the speed can be gradually increased. Students should practice flashcards daily at home, as well as in the lesson.

Another effective drill is to ask students to name and play a page of notes written randomly on both clefs. Teachers can time how long it takes a student to complete the page and students can work to decrease the time over a period of a few weeks. Students can also go through their music, quickly naming and playing each note until this process is fluent.

Once note names are well learned, teachers should continue to encourage reading by patterns. Students can discover patterns, sections and measures that are similar or identical, identify melodic and harmonic intervals, and find and name major and minor five-finger patterns and triads, both blocked and broken. Furthermore, they can begin to identify simple motivic repetitions and transpositions as they start to read and perform longer patterns.

Beginning methods should introduce contour-reading skills in a systematic way. The following is one such approach to note-reading for short pieces in which the hands do not play at the same time.

- All notes move only by step, either up or down, but not both ways.

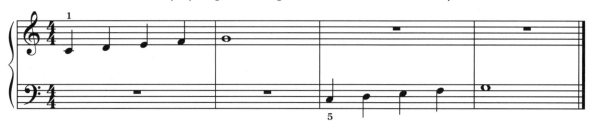

- Repeated notes are added to stepwise, single-direction motion.

- One hand goes up and the other goes down.

- ◆ Changes of direction can occur within groups of notes.

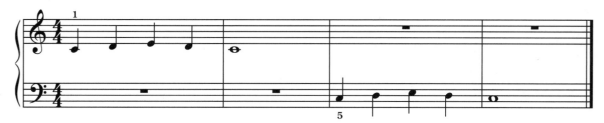

- ◆ More rhythm patterns are added to examples, using the previous skills.

- ◆ Skips go up or down, but not both, without any steps.

- ◆ Change of direction of skips occurs only between groups of notes.

- ◆ Change of direction of skips occurs within groups of notes.

- ◆ Steps, skips and repeated notes are used together.

When choosing a method, teachers should be aware of the order in which reading is presented and be alert to any steps that are missing. Such systematic order for learning to read, combined with pieces that reinforce previously learned skills in a new context, will assure facile learning.

Sharps, Flats and Naturals

In black-key pieces that use off-staff notation, it is not necessary to identify black keys by name. Likewise, major and minor five-finger patterns that use black keys can be played without introducing sharps or flats. For example, keys in the E major five-finger pattern can be identified as "E, black key, black key, A, B." It will be easier for students to practice these patterns at home if the patterns are notated in a similar way in the assignment book (for example, "D major five-finger pattern: WWBWW") showing the white- and black-key pattern, rather than writing the pattern on the staff. Later, when students begin to read sharps and flats, the black keys can be named appropriately.

When it is time to read sharps, flats and naturals, teachers should explain that a sharp can be identified as the very next key to the right (or up) and a flat as the very next key to the left (or down). This definition helps students realize that a sharp or flat can be either a white key or a black key. To help students remember whether the sharp or flat moves up or down, a simple mnemonic device can be used. When one sits on a *sharp* tack, one jumps *up* quickly. When a tire is *flat*, it goes *down*.

Students should be given pieces that use the same sharp or flat many times. If all notes that are to be sharp or flat in a given measure are not identified by a sharp or flat sign, students should circle subsequent notes or write the appropriate accidental before each note for a few weeks. Initially, it is difficult for students to remember to alter the same pitch later in the measure without the aid of the accidental. Naturals can also be logically introduced at this time. Some methods introduce natural symbols by presenting the same piece two times, once with the sharp or flat continuing through the measure and once with the natural for the second note (see example 4.13).

A simple, gamelike drill can be used to quickly identify flats, sharps and naturals. Teachers can play any black key and ask for its name, both as a sharp or as a flat. They can also play any B, C, E or F and ask for both its natural name and its sharp or flat name. For example, the teacher could play an F and ask the student to give its two names (F and E-sharp). When key signatures are first introduced, it is helpful to ask students to circle each note that is a sharp or flat, as a simple reminder.

Example 4.13 "Cafeteria," p. 58 from *The Music Tree,* Part 1, by Clark, Goss and Holland

Familiarity with Keyboard Registers

Students will have a greater sense of the keyboard and an expanded concept of the sound of the piano when they play their pieces—or parts of their pieces—in different registers of the keyboard. If they become physically comfortable moving to different registers, they will have fewer difficulties when new pieces require position changes. For pieces without changes of register, teachers can add octave shifts at musically appropriate places.

Materials used for beginning students should develop both hands equally. Each hand should be given opportunities to play melodic material and, at other times, accompanying material. Pieces with two treble clefs (or bass clefs), one for the right hand and one for the left, or pieces with both hands notated on a single staff line (see example 4.14) frequently allow the hands to share the melody and provide an additional way to expand reading skills. Developing this reading skill makes it easier to approach duets when the secondo is written in two bass clefs and the primo is written in two treble clefs.

Example 4.14 "Bass Staff," p. 66 from *The Music Tree, Time to Begin,* by Clark, Goss and Holland

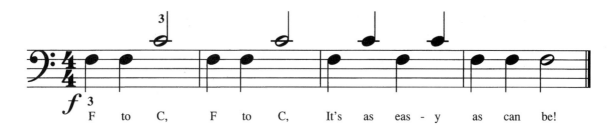

Written Finger Numbers

Students who know note names and learn to read by contour will probably not read by finger numbers or rely heavily on keyboard positions. However, those who rely on finger numbers or positions will have difficulty knowing what notes to play when pieces begin in different places on the keyboard or when positions are no longer identified. This problem can be avoided by drilling note names and encouraging intervallic reading, both in and out of positions. Finger numbers usually are needed for the following situations:

- the first note for each hand

- a change of hand position

- a hand extends out of a five-finger pattern, requiring a specific finger to play a different note

- the first note of a new line

- the top of a new page

- sharps, flats or naturals

Technical Skills

Musical playing can be encouraged from the very first lesson by emphasizing the proper physical approach to the keyboard to produce a good tone. Students can learn how the finger depresses the key and how the finger, hand and arm all work together to create that sound. Elementary students learn how to use the body correctly by developing the following:

- good posture

- natural hand and finger positions

- whole-arm motions

- a coordinated downward motion of fingers and arms

- finger independence and coordination

- hand independence and coordination

- a strong bridge (the knuckles that connect the fingers to the hand)
- fingers that rest on the keys when not in use

Elementary students develop the following technical skills:

- production of a beautiful tone at all dynamic levels
- staccato, legato and non-legato touches
- two-note slurs
- balance between melody and accompaniment
- up and down arm motions for phrasing
- smooth and free shifts of hand position (including octave shifts)
- fluency (playing continuously without hesitation)
- reaching spans of sixths, sevenths and octaves (depending on the student's hand size)
- smooth lateral motion for thumb turns and finger crossings
- crossing hands
- alternating hands techniques
- good fingering habits

Students learn these skills by playing pieces and exercises that drill the following:

- varied five-finger patterns
- blocked and broken triads
- **I, V6/5** (in complete form) and **IV6/4** chords, blocked and broken
- thumb turns and finger crossings
- easy scales and scalar passages
- repeated notes with changing fingers
- basic pedaling
- one hand legato while the other hand is staccato
- holding a note in one hand while playing shorter notes with the other hand
- hands playing together in parallel and contrary motion

A discussion of technical development for elementary-level pianists can be found in chapter 7.

Musical Concepts and Development

Elementary musical concepts overlap with previously listed technical skills in the necessity for students to develop an aural image of the sound associated with each skill. In addition, elementary students learn and are able to understand and apply the following musical concepts:

- dynamic range from *ff* to *pp*

- energetic sound

- fast and slow tempos

- steady pulse in all tempos from slow to fast

- phrases and slurs

- musically meaningful note groupings

- simple pedaling

- basic tempo markings—*allegro, allegretto, moderato, andante, adagio*

- basic music terms—*ritardando, a tempo, crescendo, diminuendo, fermata, 8va*

Rhythmic development, pitch reading and musical development are all facilitated through the learning of pieces. Many students love the challenge of being able to practice as many pieces as they like. After students are comfortable reading on the staff, they can be assigned short supplementary reading pieces at the same level of difficulty. The pieces should start in varied positions on the keyboard. Some pieces may be assigned as *tap and count only* or *name the notes only*. Others can be assigned for practice at the keyboard. It is less important that these pieces are perfected, and more important that students be given the opportunity to explore and stretch their abilities.

Teachers can assess the student's ability to apply knowledge by hearing select pieces from those that were practiced. Some of these supplementary pieces can be reassigned for more accuracy or refinement. Some might also be reassigned because the student wishes to learn them better.

Imagery

Imagery is a useful tool to encourage musical playing. Images that relate to students' everyday lives will encourage them to play more than the correct notes and rhythm. Furthermore, teachers must create interest and excitement in the imagery to help inspire students to create a musical sound.

For "The Whirlwind" (see example 4.15), the teacher can lead students to understand that a whirlwind spins smoothly and is fast and full of energy. Students can be directed to practice until the piece is legato and moderately fast with exciting crescendos and diminuendos. They can be asked to feel that the whirlwind is changing directions with each phrase of the piece. The teacher can play the piece, making the phrases clear, and ask students to spin their hands, changing the direction of the spin with each phrase. Students then practice the piece, feeling the phrases in the same way they felt them while spinning their hands. Furthermore, with the *decrescendo* and *ritardando* at the end of the piece, the music suggests that the whirlwind has lost its energy and power and, ultimately, disappears. When pieces are taken to this level of musicianship, students will begin to develop the ability to play musically and imaginatively, even when pieces do not have suggestive titles and words.

Example 4.15 "The Whirlwind," p. 37 from *Alfred's Basic Piano Library,* Lesson Book 1B, by Palmer, Manus and Lethco

Teacher Performance Demonstrations

Teacher performance demonstrations also advance musical playing. Teachers can provide a musical model by playing a student piece in two contrasting ways, asking the student which performance they prefer and why. This comparison encourages the student to listen closely, think critically, and play musically.

Teachers can also play more difficult music for students. Short, intermediate-level pieces with imaginative titles that are played musically will develop students' listening skills, ignite students' imaginations and motivate students to achieve.

Duet Accompaniments

Duet accompaniments for early-level piano solos provide opportunities for students to experience the musical qualities of the pieces more richly. When teachers play duet parts musically, students will respond subconsciously and, in turn, play more musically. Orchestrated accompaniment disks and audio recordings also provide effective musical modeling.

Dynamics

The nucleus of dynamic nuance can be introduced in the first few lessons as the student plays both loudly (*f*) and softly (*p*). Students can be directed to the correct physical motion necessary for each sound and avoid producing a loud sound by force and tension, or a soft sound with flabby fingers and arm tension.

Legato

From the beginning, many students play legato naturally and may not be aware that they are connecting the notes. When hands alternate, it is sometimes easier to produce smoothly connected notes. But when notes must be played consecutively within one hand, legato playing can be more difficult. For beginners, an overemphasis on playing legato within one hand can produce excessive tension in the body.

To play legato, students must be able to hear the difference between continuous and non-continuous sounds. Teachers can play short motives, both legato and non-legato, asking students to identify which are smooth and connected and which are disconnected. Once students can hear the difference consistently, they can begin to feel the physical motions needed to produce a legato sound.

Staccato and Non-Legato

Staccato touch adds variety, energy and excitement to playing. Just like legato, students must hear the sound and feel the correct motion to achieve staccato. Staccatos are easier to play correctly using a whole-arm motion. *Bouncing* is an excellent image for the motion and sound of staccato.

Non-legato touch is the easiest touch for many beginning students. A small space of silence separates each note and the fingers do not have to connect one note to the next. The hand, arm and finger simply move up and down. To enhance the learning of articulation, selected pieces can be practiced three times, using the three different touches—non-legato, legato and staccato.

Phrasing

Students can begin listening for musical phrases even before they can play legato. Teachers can ask students to breathe as they listen to the end of each phrase. Once students play legato, the idea of connecting notes until the end of a phrase and then allowing the music to "breathe" can be understood and mastered. Teaching students the physical motion of gently lifting the wrist forward and then releasing the finger just prior to the start of the next phrase begins to develop the technique needed for phrase endings.

Diversity of Repertoire

Elementary students should be assigned many diverse, easy pieces that expand musical understanding and ability, rather than a few harder pieces that are similar in style, content and musicality. Students will master one musical concept at a time if pieces are easier and focus on that concept. Teachers can combine and coordinate a variety of materials to avoid gaps in their students' development.

Creative and Functional Skills

Elementary students should experience the following creative and functional activities:

- improvising short pieces, using learned concepts and skills

- improvising "Questions and Answers" (antecedent and consequent phrases)

- transposing simple five-finger melodies, with simple accompaniments, to other keys

- harmonizing simple melodies with tonic and dominant pitches, chords, or open intervals such as 5ths and 6ths

- playing melodies by ear

A discussion of creative development for elementary-level students can be found in chapter 8 on pages 222–242.

Theoretical Understanding

In addition to rhythm and pitch concepts mentioned earlier in this chapter, elementary students also learn the following:

- simple forms, like A-B and A-B-A

- a few Italian terms such as *Da Capo* and *Fine*

- selected key signatures

A discussion of theoretical development for elementary-level students can be found on pages 220–222 under the heading "The Role of Music Literacy."

STARTING A BEGINNING STUDENT

The majority of students start piano study between ages 7 and 9. When children begin piano instruction during these years, it coincides with their physical development and their classroom experiences. A second-grader (typically age 7) has had experience with reading language before trying to read musical notation. Moreover, the refined physical motions required for playing the piano are best built into the nervous system while it is developing. Delaying piano lessons until age 10 or later often places students at a disadvantage when they reach the teenage years. They may not have had sufficient instruction to play music that is difficult enough to keep them interested during these often troublesome years. While preschoolers, teenagers, adults and average-age-beginners all need slightly different curricula and teaching modes, there are basic guiding principles for teaching beginners, regardless of age.

It is helpful if students receive some general musical instruction prior to piano lessons through early-childhood music programs, church choir or school music classes. Another effective alternative is a piano camp, which can be scheduled during the summer preceding formal lessons. Such a camp can meet once a week over five to six weeks or meet daily for one week. Through movement, singing, listening and games, students can be introduced to basic musical concepts and beginning pianistic skills. When regular lessons begin, the instruction can move quickly due to this previous experience.

The Interview

Planning an effective curriculum begins by interviewing the prospective student and his/her parents. The interview serves two purposes. First, it informs the teacher about what the student knows and can or cannot do. It provides important information about the learning abilities of the student and any past musical experiences. Second, it acquaints parents and the prospective student with the personality of the teacher, the teaching approach, and the business policies. An interview should offer no promises nor obligate either party.

Whether the student has had any previous instruction or not, the interview should provide the teacher with the following helpful information about the student:

- basic maturity

- knowledge of basic concepts and skills needed for piano playing

- understanding of pitch elements

- rhythm readiness

- development of the hand

- ability to learn

Basic Maturity

The interview can begin by asking the student his/her address, phone number and birth date. If students do not yet know the phone number or address, it may be an indication of their learning ability, a sign of overprotection, or the possibility that the parent does not spend time teaching these things. Throughout the interview, observation of student and parent interaction also provides clues about the child's ability to learn independently and take instruction. The child who interacts politely and obediently is likely to take instruction well from both parent and teacher. The child who talks back, is rude, acts shyly, constantly looks at the parent for answers or affirmation, or wants to do something different from the instructions given, may be more difficult to teach. The child's ability to sit still throughout the interview, pay attention and stay on task is also an indication of maturity.

Knowledge of Basic Concepts and Skills

Several activities can be used to determine a student's knowledge of basic piano-playing concepts. Short, gamelike activities can be used to determine whether the student knows right hand, left hand, finger numbers, and the musical alphabet. Directions like "put the fifth finger of the left hand on your nose" makes learning fun. The teacher can give a letter name and ask the student to recite the letter before or after it. The student can be asked to count backward from any number, one through five. Many students have played "Chopsticks," "Heart and Soul" or other pieces they have learned from a family member or friend. If the student can do this, the teacher will know that the student can learn by ear and by rote.

The following questions can be asked to determine basic knowledge about music and the keyboard:

- Do all the keys on the piano look the same? Why or why not?

- Do the black keys make a pattern? What is the pattern?

- Where are the high (or low) sounds on the piano?

- Can you make loud (or soft) sounds that go up (or down) the piano?

- Can you play some fast (slow, short, or long) sounds?

Understanding of Pitch Elements

Children can be asked to sing a familiar melody and sing back a few pitches that are within their voice range. The following activity can also aid in determining a student's level of aural readiness. The teacher plays pairs of pitches on the piano, asking the student to tell whether the pitches move from high to low or low to high. The first few pairs of pitches should be played at the extreme opposite ends of the keyboard. Gradually, the pairs of pitches are played more closely together until they are only a half step apart. The more closely the student can identify higher and lower relationships, the better the ear development.

Rhythm Readiness

Several activities can help determine rhythm readiness. The child can be asked to tap the foot and clap alternately using a steady beat. The child can clap the rhythm of a familiar song while the child and teacher sing it together.

The teacher can also clap a series of short rhythm patterns (see example 4.16), asking the student to clap them back. Each pattern should be only slightly more difficult than the previous one.

Example 4.16 Sample one-measure rhythms for interview clapbacks

If the student repeats these patterns accurately, a few longer patterns can be clapped (see example 4.17).

Example 4.17 Sample two-measure rhythms for interview clapbacks

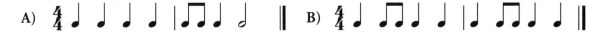

If the student has difficulty with both rhythm and pitch, the teacher may want to suggest that keyboard instruction be delayed until the student appears to be ready musically.

Some students hear pitch elements more easily than rhythm patterns, while others are rhythmically stronger. Teachers should choose a beginning method based on these factors. For example, if the student is unable to clap a steady pulse, a beginning method with greater rhythmic demands would be inappropriate.

Development of the Hand
The child can play-back some simple black-key patterns with two or three fingers, copying the teacher. The simple exercise that follows can also be used to determine the level of readiness of the hand.

1. The student makes a fist and turns the hand over onto the keyboard.

2. The fist is slowly opened until each finger touches an adjacent white key, while maintaining a good hand shape.

3. All five keys are depressed simultaneously, while still holding the hand shape.

4. Each finger is played separately several times, while keeping the other keys depressed.

This exercise can produce tension and should not be assigned for practice. However, using it in the interview can help the teacher determine whether the physical development is sufficient for piano lessons. Students who are unable to hold the hand shape or who have difficulty placing the fingers on individual white keys should perhaps delay starting piano lessons.

Ability to Learn
To determine the student's ability to learn and apply knowledge, a short beginning piece, such as "Take Off" (see example 4.18), can be presented.

Example 4.18 "Take Off," p. 4 from *The Music Tree, Time to Begin,* by Clark, Goss and Holland

The teacher shows the notation to the student and explains that one round symbol is called a note. Each time a note is seen on the page, one key is played on the piano.

The student learns the piece by responding to the following questions and directions:

- How many groups of notes are there?

- How many notes are in each group?

- Where on the page does it show you where to play on the piano? (The teacher helps the student find the keyboard icon and its corresponding location on the keyboard.)

- How do you know which hand will play? (The teacher can help the student see the RH and LH indications.)

- Play the first group of notes. (It is unnecessary for the student to play the correct rhythm at first.)

- The teacher explains that the notes get one beat. The teacher assists the student in clapping and counting the correct rhythm of the first group.

- What direction do the groups move on the page?

- Play each of the groups.

- Listen and watch my hands while I play the piece. (The teacher plays the piece with a full sound using a full-arm motion for each note, at a moderate tempo, keeping the pulse steady.)

- Now play the piece just like I did.

While students will complete these activities at different rates of speed, all of the interview activities should be completed in approximately 20 minutes. If it takes longer, the teacher may be working with a slower learner. Students able to pay attention and stay on task for the full length of the interview are mature enough to take a half-hour lesson and practice 30 minutes each day.

The interview can conclude by asking the student the following questions:

- Why do you want to take piano lessons?

- What do you want to learn to do at the piano?

- What kinds of music do you like?

- How much time do you think you can practice every day?

Parental Role During the Interview

It is important for at least one parent to participate in the interview. The teacher should provide a policy statement and information about lessons for the parent to read and a *Parent Questionnaire* to complete while the prospective student is being interviewed (see example 4.19).

The information from the questionnaire will provide additional information about the student and the home environment. If students participate in many daily extracurricular activities, watch television or play computer games excessively, it is less likely that they will do well in piano lessons. If parents are unable to help students with home practice, it may be more difficult for them to succeed. Teachers should evaluate this information to determine the likelihood of success and use this information to make decisions about accepting the student and planning the curriculum.

Teachers can also gain information from the parents' behaviors. When parents sit quietly while observing the interview, they understand that the student is being evaluated for readiness. If, however, the parent interrupts the interview, coaching the child with correct answers, it may indicate that the parent may be overprotective and more concerned with the performance of the child than with long-term learning ability. This should alert the teacher that these parents need to be educated about the learning process, the chosen method of teaching, and their role at home. Piano lessons are more successful when the parent is able to positively reinforce instruction at home.

At the end of the interview, the parent should be asked the following questions:

- Why do you want your child to take piano lessons?

- Why do you think your child is ready to take piano lessons?

- What do you want your child to learn from piano lessons?

From these questions, the teacher may find that it is the parent who wants the child to take lessons and the student is ambivalent about lessons or unwilling to practice every day. The teacher may also find that the expectations of the parent or child do not match the teacher's philosophy or goals. When this is the case, the teacher would be wise to suggest that another teacher might better meet their needs.

Example 4.19 Sample parent questionnaire

Parent Questionnaire

Name of Student _____ Age _____

Birth Date_____ Grade in School _____

Name of Mother_____

Address _____

City_____Zip_____

Home Telephone Number _____ Work Telephone Number_____

E-mail Address _____

Name of Father_____

Address _____

City_____ Zip _____

Home Telephone Number _____ Work Telephone Number_____

E-mail Address _____

Emergency Contact _____

Relationship _____ Telephone Number_____

Circle all characteristics that describe your child.

Shy   Aggressive   Talkative   Sociable   Thoughtful   Argumentative   Bossy

Whines   Talks back   Cries easily   Leader   Entertains self   Likes to read

Likes to draw and paint   Enjoys manual toys and activities   Enjoys math

Circle what most closely describes your child's learning and work habits.

Perfection-Seeking   Hurried   Meticulous   Imaginative

Number of hours your child watches TV each day _____

Number of hours your child uses the computer or other devices each day _____

List any special interests and hobbies of your child._____

List your child's other extracurricular activities. _____

What instruments do other family members play? _____

Does the family participate in other musical activities? If yes, what? _____

_____

If your child has had any previous musical instruction, please describe it. _____

_____

Describe how your child has exhibited an interest in music and the piano._____

_____

How long will your child be able to practice each day? _____

How long will you, as parent, be able to help your child practice each day? _____

Is there a piano in the home? _____

Type (keyboard, digital, acoustic) and brand_____

After the interview, the teacher should discuss the results of the interview with the parent no later than the next day. If the teacher feels the student is not ready for lessons or may be difficult to teach, he/she should speak privately with the parent. When teachers follow up the interview with a phone call on the next day, the parent(s) and child have had time for discussion and are better able to make decisions about piano lessons.

When the decision has been made to start lessons, parents should receive more information that includes guidelines about their role in piano learning. This role may include attending and observing lessons. Such participation during the beginning stages of learning makes the instruction more successful, and helps students succeed and progress more rapidly. Furthermore, parents who observe lessons can be effective home teachers, reinforcing the information in the same way the teacher originally presented it. Teachers can educate parents about effective observation:

- Parents should observe lessons quietly without interrupting. (A strong, positive relationship must develop between teachers and students.)

- Teachers should direct all instruction to the students and avoid addressing the parents.

- Parents should take notes so they can be effective home teachers.

- Parents should never instruct the student differently from the teacher, and disagreements regarding the teaching approach should be discussed privately without the student present.

Even parents who will not be home teachers should be actively involved in their children's learning.

- They should help their child read and understand the assignment.

- They should schedule practice periods.

- They should periodically check to make sure the assignment is followed and that progress is being made.

- They should make time each week to listen to the practice and performance of pieces.

COMMON PROBLEMS OF BEGINNERS

Beginning piano study includes many concepts and skills that are new to students. Students may not have used their fingers independently to any great extent, may not be able to differentiate between high and low sounds, or may not have noticed that the keyboard is organized in groups of two and three black keys. For one student, higher on the keyboard may mean playing black keys rather than keys to the right. Some may think the pointing finger is number one. Many will not know that the musical alphabet is only seven letters used over and over. Some find it difficult to see the relationship between the lines and spaces on the staff to the keys on the keyboard, while others may read finger numbers instead of noteheads to determine which note to play.

Many beginning students experience similar problems and develop the same undesirable habits. When teachers carefully prepare students for each new experience, common problems and bad habits can be avoided.

Playing Too Fast

Because children are active and tend to run rather than walk, it is understandable that beginning students often play their pieces too fast. Fast pieces sound more exciting. Counting pieces aloud during the early learning stages has a slowing influence. Students can be given the responsibility to practice a piece playing slowly until everything is accurate, and then be given permission to play it up to tempo. This can motivate them to practice slowly and carefully at first. If each day's practice includes both slow playing and up-to-tempo performances, the slow playing will become a good learning habit and a warm-up activity.

To aid with playing slowly, teachers can suggest that students play like a slow-motion movie, a turtle, or as if they are exhausted from running a 20-mile race. Teachers can help students establish the habit of pre-counting one or two measures at the appropriate playing tempo before playing the first note of a piece. This aids with setting a manageable tempo. It is also helpful for teachers to play duet accompaniments with students at slow tempos.

Pieces that require fast tempos may be easier than other pieces students are playing, so that the tempo goal can be achieved. Students should work on pieces long enough to play them at appropriate tempos successfully and accurately.

Stopping at the End of Every Measure or System

Learning to read large groups of notes is an important goal, but some students read groups of notes only measure by measure, hesitating at every bar line. Frequently, the problem can be corrected by making the student aware of it and making comparisons to other activities. For example, if one sang a familiar song and stopped at the end of every measure, the musical result would not be satisfying.

In many beginning hands-together pieces, the right hand plays the melody and the left hand adds an accompanying note or chord on the first beat of each measure. It is difficult for students to play two or three notes at once, while coordinating two hands. Such problems should be recognized as coordination difficulties rather than rhythmic misunderstandings. Hesitations can be prevented by one or all of the following successive steps:

1. Play only the first beats of each measure with both hands.

2. Play only the last beat of each measure and the first beat of the next measure.

3. Play an entire measure, plus the first beat of the next measure.

4. Play the piece at a slower tempo. (This allows students more time to think ahead and plan for the difficulties on beat 1.)

Students may also have trouble moving from one musical system or line to the next without hesitation. It is difficult to see the intervallic relationship between notes from one system to the next. A preparatory comparison of the relationship of the notes at the end of one system to the notes at the beginning of the next will usually produce more fluent playing. Students who have learned to read groups of notes and keep their eyes on the page will also find it easier to keep going when moving from one system to the next.

Playing in a Meter of Four Instead of Three

Some students initially play $\frac{3}{4}$ pieces in $\frac{4}{4}$ time. Duple meters seem more natural since our bodies are balanced and symmetrical with two arms, two legs, two ears and two eyes. Triple meter works against that sense of balance. When marching in quadruple meter, the strong beat always occurs on the same foot. When walking in triple meter, the strong beat occurs on alternate feet. This feels uncomfortable, just as triple meter feels uncomfortable to students.

For these reasons, some students tend to play triple meter incorrectly by elongating the third beat, even when they count. Preliminary movement experiences that allow students to dance to meters of three and march to meters of four will build a feeling for both. Playing familiar tunes in $\frac{3}{4}$ meter and having students clap, conduct or sing them will also help students experience and feel meters of three. If students play numerous pieces with triple meters early in their study, using the preliminary practice steps of tapping and counting, this instinct to change everything to a duple meter is avoided. The feeling for triple meter can also be enhanced by taps on beat 1 that are longer and louder than those on beats 2 and 3.

Finding Starting Keys on the Keyboard

Some students are slow to find the starting keys for pieces. They may place one hand in position, but by the time the other hand is ready, the first hand has moved out of position. Sometimes students begin to play with one hand before preparing the other hand, and the music stops while the second hand searches for its starting key.

Students should leave both hands in their lap while *thinking* about where each hand begins. The eyes locate the beginning keys or positions for both hands, and when the teacher says "go," the hands move quickly into position. All ten fingers move into position at the same time, not just the two starting fingers. If students hesitate, the routine should be repeated until the hands move quickly and securely to the starting position. Once in position, the starting fingers of both hands should *stroke* the surface of the appropriate key(s) to gain a strong tactile feel for the first note(s). When students are reading notes on the staff, they should also name the first note(s) for each hand as part of the drill.

Starting with the Wrong Hand

Students often begin a piece or phrase with the wrong hand. This can be avoided if students tap the piece while saying "right," "left," or "both" before playing it. This procedure should also be used in practice and included on the written assignment.

Depending on Note Names Written in Noteheads

Note names written in noteheads can cause some students to look at their hands frequently while playing and, thereby, impede fluent reading. Teachers can prepare students to be successful with this reading approach through a simple drill. Students place their hands in a five-finger position, playing the pattern several times while naming the notes. Then the students close their eyes while the teacher calls out the following:

1. finger numbers in any order

2. intervals (e.g., "play finger 2, up a 2nd, down a 3rd," etc.)

3. key names

Students respond by playing the correct keys. Such drills help develop a kinesthetic feel and visualization of the keyboard and facilitate an automatic response without looking at the hands.

New pieces can also be presented in this drill-like fashion. For "Snowy Day" (see example 4.20), the student places the left-hand thumb on middle C and the right-hand fourth finger on treble F. The student plays with eyes closed while the teacher calls out the following (not necessarily in the correct rhythm):

Example 4.20 "Snowy Day," p. 53 from *Alfred's Premier Piano Course,* Lesson 1A, by Alexander, Kowalchyk, Lancaster, McArthur and Mier

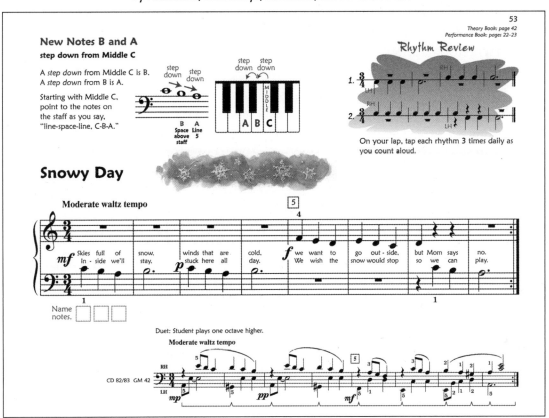

- **Finger numbers:**

"LH finger 1, 2, 3, 2, 1, 2, 3, 2. RH finger 4, 3, 2, 3, 2, 1, 2. LH finger 1, 2, 3."

- **Intervals and their direction:**

"LH finger 1, down a 2nd, down a 2nd, up a 2nd. Finger 1, down a 2nd, down a 2nd, up a 2nd. RH finger 4, down a 2nd, down a 2nd, up a 2nd, down a 2nd, down a 2nd, up a 2nd. LH finger 1, down a 2nd, down a 2nd."

If a mistake is made, the teacher can ask whether the incorrect interval sounded like a 2nd, and then have the student play the interval again. The teacher can also stop in the middle of these drills, asking the student to name what key is being played (with eyes closed).

- **Key names:**

"LH finger 1 on C, play B, play A, play B, play C, play B, play A, play B. RH finger 4 on F, play E, play D, play E, play D, play C, play D. LH finger 1 on C, play B, play A."

Through these drills, students experience pieces first without the music, so they will feel confident to practice while keeping their eyes on the page. Following the teacher's directions, students can also write the notes on staff paper, or a dry-erase board, or can place notes on the staff of a magnetic board. Students then read back the instructions that the teacher gave, using their own notation as the guide.

Playing Repeated Notes

When music includes repeated notes, students frequently move from the first key to a different key, instead of repeating. Chanting note names or "same," "up" or "down" as a preliminary practice step can prevent this problem.

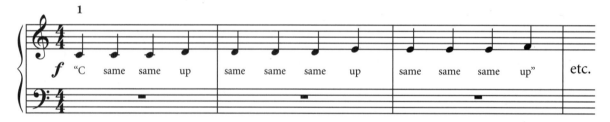

When students play the piece, they can also chant "C–C–C–D, D–D–D–E, E–E–E–F." It should be noted that it is not always possible to play and chant in rhythm. Repeated notes can also be circled by the student to call attention to them.

Reading and Playing Harmonic 2nds

Some students have trouble understanding that the two notes of a harmonic 2nd are played at the same time since they are written side by side. In some methods, the harmonic 2nd is among the first harmonic intervals students learn. Students have learned that when notes are side by side, without touching each other, they are played one after the other. The notes of harmonic intervals, with the exception of 2nds, are vertically aligned. It is effective to tell students that noteheads directly on top of each other, or touching each other, are played at the same time.

Playing After a Long Rest

Following a long rest, students may be uncertain what note to play. This situation is frequently found in beginning teaching pieces, where one hand is more active than the other (or the hands alternate) and the non-playing hand has several beats or measures of rest. This can cause students to make either a note mistake or a long pause, sometimes incorrectly interpreted by teachers as a rhythmic error. Even if the piece is written in a set five-finger position, a finger number on the first note following the rest can be an aid. Composers of beginning piano music are generally careful to write the music so there is a logical relationship between the notes before and after the rest.

Guide the student to compare the note following the rest to the note played in the same hand before the rest. This kind of comparison, before starting to play, can help prevent errors.

Keeping Eyes on the Page

Some beginning students look frequently from the music page to their hands to play the correct notes, even through this is generally unnecessary since many beginning pieces stay within one hand position. Keeping the eyes on the page is absolutely essential to fluent reading. A teacher must strive to help students develop this habit early.

One strategy is to begin a piece by asking the student to play it silently on the surface of the keys. This makes it easier for students to keep their eyes on the page and proves to them that it is possible. Silent playing aids the development of a kinesthetic sense of keyboard topography and results in performance security.

Octave or position shifts can be practiced silently over and over until the body memorizes the distance by feel. This early *ghost practicing* of octave leaps is invaluable in performing more advanced literature. Other exercises, such as five-finger patterns and scales, can also be practiced without looking at the hands. Saying the color of the keys (black or white) or the names of the notes while playing these exercises further develops this sense of keyboard topography.

Playing Numerous Notes with Both Hands

If the printed page has many notes in both hands, elementary students may feel overwhelmed and believe a piece is too difficult for them. Covering the music of one hand will often show the simplicity of the other hand. Playing each hand separately and counting aloud, while the music of the other hand is covered, make learning easier.

Holding Long Notes in One Hand

Frequently in early-level piano music, one hand is required to hold notes for the full measure, while the other hand plays faster notes, usually the melody. When the hand with the faster notes changes notes, the other hand can sympathetically lift off the key. To avoid this, students must hear and feel that they are shortening the duration of the longer note. Because the melody is easier to hear and feel, students often do not hear or feel that they are shortening the duration of the longer note, even if they might have visually observed its longer value. The following activities can help students listen and focus on longer notes:

- The teacher plays longer-valued single notes of various lengths, while the student listens and counts the number of beats.

- The teacher plays the student's piece, sometimes holding the longer notes, sometimes not, and the student identifies the correct playing.

- The student plays notes from three to ten beats long to hear the duration and to feel the sensation of holding longer notes.

- The student plays exercises such as following to develop this skill.

Observing Dynamics

Dynamic markings are the first and most common expression symbols taught in elementary music. Although beginning pieces generally include only a few dynamic markings, students do not always observe them. Dynamics result from physical motions and these motions must be practiced and built into the neuromuscular system. It is helpful for students to feel and hear the levels of loud and soft before they play a piece. While tapping the rhythm of a new piece, students can match the size and intensity of the tapping to the dynamics of the piece. Furthermore, they can play while speaking or singing the counting or note names with appropriate dynamic inflection. "Snowy Day" (see example 4.20 on page 91) might be spoken in the following way.

mf　　　　　　　　*p*　　　　*f*

C B A B　　　C B A B　　F E D E D C D C B A

Teachers should encourage students to use a variety of words to describe the sound. Pieces can be *grand, gentle, delicate, powerful,* or *rowdy,* rather than simply *loud* or *soft.* Teachers can help students hear and critically judge their playing by asking, "Did your piece sound *powerful* (or *gentle*)?" Furthermore, students are more likely to play loudly or softly if they understand the image suggested by the title of the piece. Pieces with subjects like monsters, dinosaurs, brass bands, spider webs, or secrets suggest specific dynamics.

Breaking the Phrase Line

Students often break the phrase in one hand if the other hand is required to lift. In "The Donkey" (see example 4.21), the right hand is required to play the first line legato, yet the thumb of the left hand must lift to play measure four. Beginning students usually lift both left-hand notes. In addition, the right hand often sympathetically lifts at this point, causing a break

Example 4.21 "The Donkey," p. 49 from *Alfred's Basic Piano Library,* Lesson Book 1A, by Palmer, Manus and Lethco

in the legato melody. Practicing hands separately will not correct the problem. Students must practice measures 3 and 4 (also 7 and 8) slowly, hands together, concentrating on holding the right hand while the left hand lifts. After several repetitions, the physical feel of connecting the right-hand notes will be memorized.

Executing Changes

Learning music at any level is more difficult when changes appear. Changes can involve any musical parameter or combination of parameters, such as the following:

- meter
- register
- melody (moving from one hand to the other)
- texture
- note values (slow to fast and fast to slow)
- direction of the melodic line

- starting notes and fingering for successive groups of notes

- interval size (e.g., encountering an interval larger than a 2nd after a series of 2nds)

- one hand begins playing alone after the other hand has played alone for several notes or measures

- hands playing together after hands have played separately or alternated

- note pattern (especially change within a pattern, such as when a pattern begins the same as another, but ends differently)

Any change can cause students to make mistakes. The more frequent the changes, the greater the difficulty. Teachers can prevent errors by knowing the problem areas in a piece and preparing students for them. Asking students to find similarities and differences, and play spots where changes occur, will prepare them for successful practice at home.

In "Daydreams!" (see example 4.22), measures 1 and 3 are identical, but measures 2 and 4 are not the same. It is likely that without preparation students will play measure 4 just like measure 2. Observation of the contour and preliminary practice of measures 2 and 4 will prepare students for this change. Preliminary practice on the key cover while reciting the finger numbers, and playing silently on top of the keys, are also helpful practice steps to prevent these errors from appearing.

Drills to prepare for similar places in other music can be devised and practiced in the lesson before pieces are sent home for practice. Without this preparation, students often return to the next lesson with mistakes in such places.

Example 4.22 "Daydreams!" p. 11 from *The Music Tree,* Part 1, by Clark, Goss and Holland

Repeating Learned Mistakes

Sometimes students find it difficult to correct learned mistakes. Even though the primary goal in teaching is to *prevent* mistakes, rather than *correct* them, pieces can be incorrectly learned during the early stages of study. While isolated mistakes are common to all pianists, learned mistakes result when students do not understand or forget the necessary information. Once a student kinesthetically learns a piece incorrectly, it is very difficult for him/her to unlearn it. To eliminate frustration for both the teacher and the student, it is sometimes best to drop the piece and study the same concepts and skills in another piece.

FIRST-YEAR GOALS

To achieve maximum student learning, teachers need to have a clear idea of appropriate goals for students. The primary goals of any lesson are the following:

- to make music

- to develop the skills to make that music

- to develop musical understanding

To meet these goals, the teacher devises a series of appropriate practice steps that the student experiences in the lesson, based on the student's age and experience. Along with these weekly pursuits, other goals for the first year of study include the following:

- promoting a love of music

- playing by ear and rote playing

- exploring and discovering the full keyboard and the sounds it makes (fast/slow, sound/silence, black/white keys, loud/soft, short/long, steps/skips, key names, damper pedal)

- establishing the feeling of the pulse

- singing and conducting to develop a sense of meter and phrase

- mastering fundamental knowledge in rhythm and pitch notation

- associating fingering with intervals

- using the body appropriately at the keyboard

- making a pleasing tone, both gentle and energetic

- playing selected five-finger patterns and root position triads (some teaching approaches include all major five-finger patterns)

- achieving a sense of accomplishment, measured in part by the ability to play many pieces

- identifying by ear all elements learned, including identical and similar phrases; melody and accompaniment; legato, non-legato and staccato touches; loud and soft dynamics

- visually recognizing (or matching) the music notation with what is heard

To achieve those goals, lessons at all levels should present and drill a variety of concepts, skills and experiences:

- reading, including transposition

- rhythm

- technique

- written theory

- keyboard theory, such as playing intervals, building five-finger patterns, harmonization
- aural development
- ensemble experiences
- creativity through the use of improvisation and composition
- memory development

Furthermore, beginning students should play a variety of music, including the following:

- familiar tunes and familiar-sounding pieces
- pieces that make use of the full sonority of the keyboard, have beautiful sounds, and are imaginative
- pieces that build strong technical skills and use large arm movements
- pieces with dynamic contrasts
- pieces with strong rhythmic appeal

Teachers must choose an appropriate method series that presents activities and teaching pieces in a way that meets individual needs. Most teachers use supplementary music to provide students with a comprehensive musical education. From all these materials, teachers develop lesson plans that meet the first-year goals.

LESSON PLANS AND ASSIGNMENTS

To teach effectively, it is essential to develop detailed lesson plans. Since attention spans of young children are frequently short, teachers should learn to recognize when the student is most alert in the lesson. New material can be presented during those times. A productive work period of ten minutes can be followed by five minutes of less mentally strenuous activity. Generally, the difficult things should be covered in the early part of the lesson, saving the easier items for the end of the lesson when the student is likely to be less alert.

The following lesson plan is based on the previously mentioned first-year goals and uses four books from Level 1A of *Alfred's Premier Piano Course* as the text. Goals and objectives are listed, with the Lesson Book pages that can be used to achieve the objectives. These goals and objectives are achieved through the "Suggested Materials and Activities" that follow (pp. 100–113).

While the plan may seem overly lengthy and tedious, it was written to illustrate the thinking behind effective lesson planning. More-experienced teachers devise similar lesson plans with less detail. As teaching becomes more proficient, less detail is necessary. Abbreviated lesson plans can be transferred to index cards for easy reference during a lesson.

First Week's Lesson Plan

Goals and Objectives

Developing the ear:

- establishing a steady pulse (Lesson Book, p. 6)
- clapping rhythm patterns (Lesson Book, pp. 6, 8)

Learning to use the body at the keyboard:

- sitting correctly at the piano (Lesson Book, p. 4)
- using fingers, arms and hands correctly (Lesson Book, pp. 5, 9, 11)

Exploring the keyboard:

- finding and playing groups of two and three black keys (Lesson Book, pp. 6, 10)
- playing high, low, and mid-range sounds (Lesson Book, pp. 7–11)

Preparing for reading music notation:

- learning finger numbers (Lesson Book, p. 5)
- learning about stem direction to indicate right and left hand (Lesson Book, p. 6)
- learning about quarter notes (Lesson Book, p. 6)
- learning about quarter rests (Lesson Book, p. 8)
- recognizing higher and lower notation (Lesson Book, pp. 8–11)
- learning about bar lines and measures (Lesson Book, p. 11)

Reading and learning pieces:

- learning and playing groups of two black keys (Lesson Book, pp. 7–9)
- playing with both hands in one piece (Lesson Book, p. 7)
- learning about directional notation (Lesson Book, pp. 8–9)
- learning and playing groups of three black keys (Lesson Book, pp. 10–11)

Suggested Materials and Activities

1. "How to Sit at the Piano," p. 4 from Lesson Book (see example 4.23):

    ◆ The teacher discusses the checklists on the page and demonstrates the proper sitting position.

    ◆ The student copies the sitting position.

    ◆ The teacher demonstrates items from the checklists incorrectly.

    ◆ The student identifies what is wrong with each.

Example 4.23 "How to Sit at the Piano," p. 4 from *Alfred's Premier Piano Course,* Lesson 1A, by Alexander, Kowalchyk, Lancaster, McArthur and Mier

Example 4.24 "The Secret to a Good Hand Position," p. 5 from *Alfred's Premier Piano Course,* Lesson 1A, by Alexander, Kowalchyk, Lancaster, McArthur and Mier

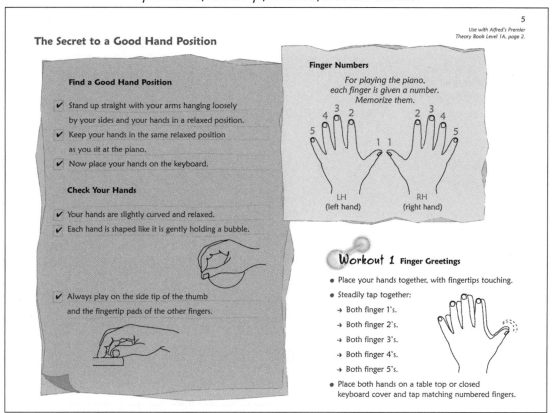

2. "The Secret to a Good Hand Position," p. 5 from Lesson Book (see example 4.24):

   • The teacher discusses the checklists on "The Secret to a Good Hand Position" and demonstrates the proper hand position.

   • The student demonstrates a good position with each hand.

   • The teacher discusses how fingers are numbered.

   • The teacher and student do "Workout 1, Finger Greetings" together.

   • The teacher plays a *Simon Says* game, asking the student to place a finger of one hand on a part of the body (e. g., "Put finger 2 of the RH on the nose," or "Put finger 3 of the LH on the ear.").

   • Theory Book, p. 2 (see example 4.25). The teacher goes through the directions on the page and assists the student in completing one example from each number to make sure he/she understands how to complete the page at home.

3. "Steady Quarter Notes," p. 6 from Lesson Book (see example 4.26):

   • The teacher introduces the quarter note and "Rhythm 1."

   • The teacher and student echo-clap (clap-back) "Rhythm 1" at different tempos.

Example 4.25 Page 2 from *Alfred's Premier Piano Course,* Theory 1A, by Alexander, Kowalchyk, Lancaster, McArthur and Mier

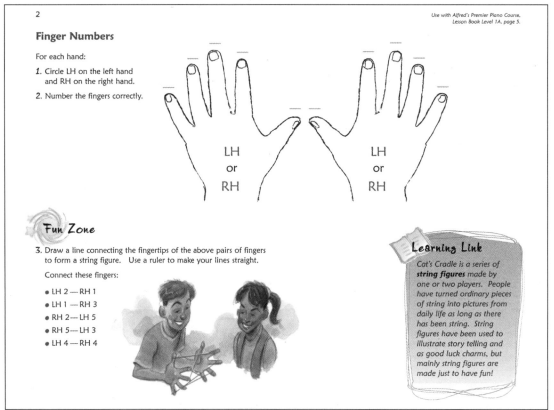

Example 4.26 "Steady Quarter Notes," p. 6 from *Alfred's Premier Piano Course,* Lesson 1A, by Alexander, Kowalchyk, Lancaster, McArthur and Mier

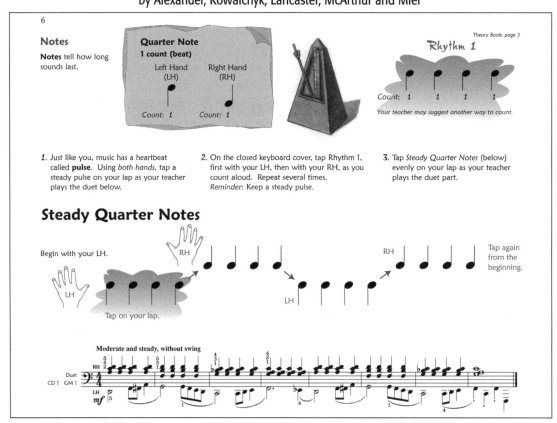

- Together, the teacher and student alternate tapping "Rhythm 1" with the LH and RH.

- The student points to the notation for "Steady Quarter Notes" while listening to the CD that accompanies the Lesson Book.

- Using the correct hands, the student taps the rhythm for "Steady Quarter Notes" with the CD.

- Using the correct hands, the student taps the rhythm for "Steady Quarter Notes" as the teacher plays the accompaniment at a slower tempo than the CD.

4. "Our Journey," p. 7 from Lesson Book (see example 4.27):

- The teacher leads the student to discover a two black-key group on the piano.

- The student plays all the groups of two black keys, from the lowest to the highest and the highest to the lowest.

- The teacher explains that notes with stems up indicate the right hand and notes with stems down indicate the left hand.

- The student taps the rhythm for "Our Journey" on his/her lap with the correct hand and counts aloud.

- The student says the words for "Our Journey" with the performance tempo on the CD.

- The student finds the keyboard diagram in the book that shows where to play the piece on the two black keys.

- The teacher explains the notation for the finger numbers, that the piece is played moderately loud, and that a double bar means the end.

- The student plays and counts the piece at a slow tempo.

- Theory Book, pp. 3–4 (see examples 4.28–4.29). The teacher goes through the directions on the page and assists the student in completing one example from each number to make sure he/she understands how to complete the page at home.

Example 4.27 "Our Journey," p. 7 from *Alfred's Premier Piano Course*, Lesson 1A, by Alexander, Kowalchyk, Lancaster, McArthur and Mier

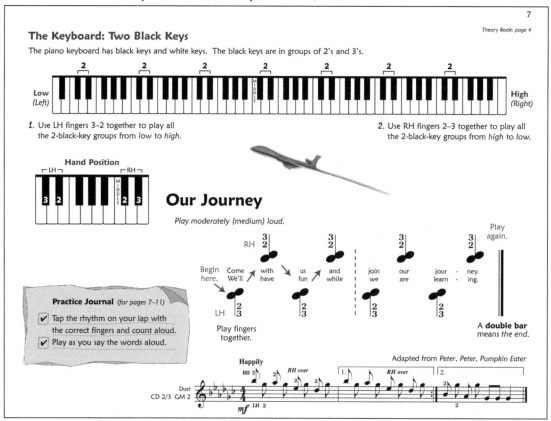

Example 4.28 Page 3 from *Alfred's Premier Piano Course*, Theory 1A, by Alexander, Kowalchyk, Lancaster, McArthur and Mier

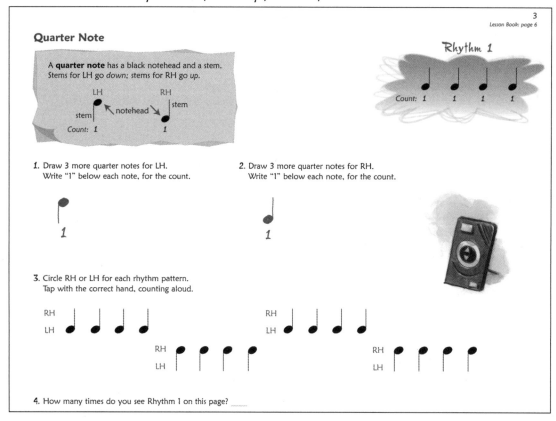

Example 4.29 Page 4 from *Alfred's Premier Piano Course,* Theory 1A,
by Alexander, Kowalchyk, Lancaster, McArthur and Mier

5. "Treasure Map," p. 8 from Lesson Book (see example 4.30):

- The teacher introduces the quarter rest and "Rhythm 2."

- The teacher and student echo-clap (clap-back) "Rhythm 2" at different tempos, using a whisper count for the rest.

- The student taps the rhythm for "Treasure Map" on the key cover (moving gracefully down for each new pattern) while counting aloud with the practice tempo on the CD.

- The student points to the notes and says the finger numbers.

- The student plays the piece on the key cover while saying the finger numbers.

- The student plays and counts the piece at a slow tempo.

- Theory Book, p. 5 (see example 4.31). The teacher goes through the directions on the page and assists the student in completing one example from each number to make sure he/she understands how to complete the page at home.

Example 4.30 "Treasure Map," p. 8 from *Alfred's Premier Piano Course,* Lesson 1A,
by Alexander, Kowalchyk, Lancaster, McArthur and Mier

Example 4.31 Page 5 from *Alfred's Premier Piano Course,* Theory 1A,
by Alexander, Kowalchyk, Lancaster, McArthur and Mier

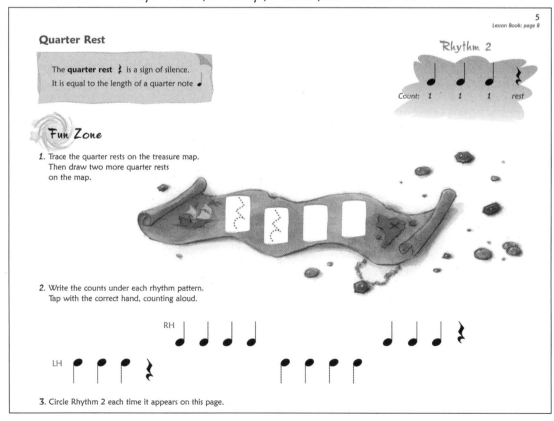

6. "Treasure Chest," p. 9 from Lesson Book (see example 4.32):

   • The teacher demonstrates "Workout 2, Piano Hands" and assists the student in experiencing the workout.

   • The student taps the rhythm for "Treasure Chest" on the key cover (moving gracefully up for each new pattern) while counting aloud with the practice tempo on the CD.

   • The student points to the notes and says the finger numbers.

   • The student plays the piece on the key cover while saying the finger numbers.

   • The student plays and counts the piece at a slow tempo.

   • Theory Book, p. 6 (see example 4.33). The teacher goes through the directions on the page and assists the student in completing one example from each number to make sure he/she understands how to complete the page at home.

Example 4.32 "Treasure Chest," p. 9 from *Alfred's Premier Piano Course*, Lesson 1A, by Alexander, Kowalchyk, Lancaster, McArthur and Mier

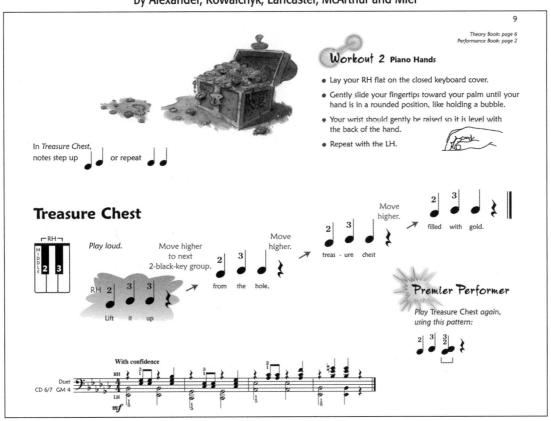

Example 4.33 Page 6 from *Alfred's Premier Piano Course*, Theory 1A, by Alexander, Kowalchyk, Lancaster, McArthur and Mier

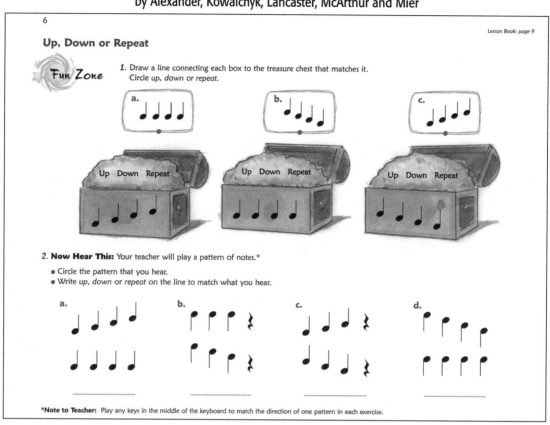

7. "Beep! Beep!" p. 2 from Performance Book (see example 4.34) optional:

- The student taps the rhythm for "Beep! Beep!" on the key cover (moving gracefully up for each new pattern) while counting aloud with the practice tempo on the CD.

- The student plays the piece on the key cover while saying the finger number for each single note.

- The student plays the piece on the piano while saying the finger number for each single note, and the teacher assists the student in discovering which fingers to use for the blocked 2nds.

- The student plays and counts the piece at a slow tempo.

Example 4.34 "Beep! Beep!" p. 2 from *Alfred's Premier Piano Course,* Performance 1A, by Alexander, Kowalchyk, Lancaster, McArthur and Mier

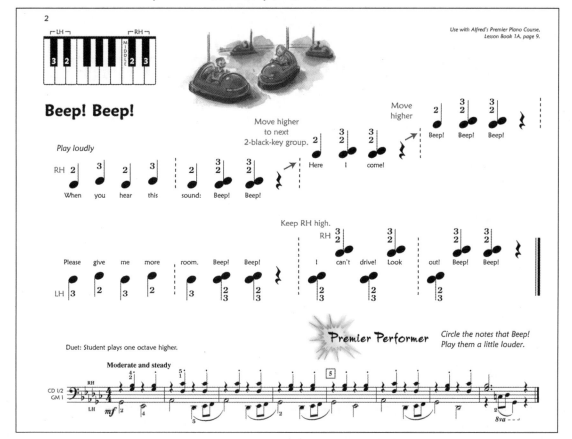

8. "Practice Carefully," p. 10 from Lesson Book (see example 4.35):

   ◆ The teacher leads the student to discover a three black-key group on the piano.

   ◆ The student plays all the groups of three black keys, from the lowest to the highest and the highest to the lowest.

   ◆ The student taps the rhythm for "Practice Carefully" on the key cover (moving gracefully down for each new pattern) while counting aloud with the practice tempo on the CD.

   ◆ The student points to the notes and says the finger numbers.

   ◆ The student plays the piece on the key cover while saying the finger numbers.

   ◆ The student plays and counts the piece at a slow tempo.

   ◆ Theory Book, p. 7 (see example 4.36). The teacher goes through the directions on the page and assists the student in completing one example from each number to make sure he/she understands how to complete the page at home.

Example 4.35 "Practice Carefully," p. 10 from *Alfred's Premier Piano Course,* Lesson 1A, by Alexander, Kowalchyk, Lancaster, McArthur and Mier

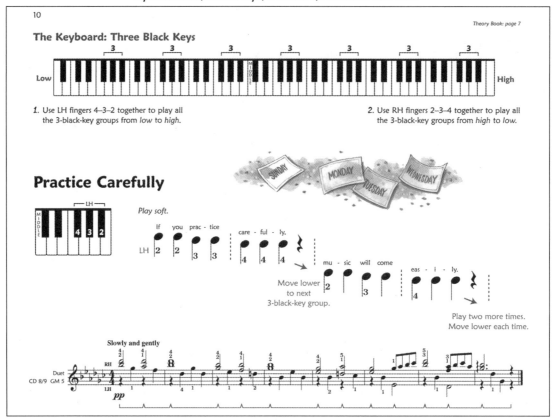

Example 4.36 Page 7 from *Alfred's Premier Piano Course,* Theory 1A, by Alexander, Kowalchyk, Lancaster, McArthur and Mier

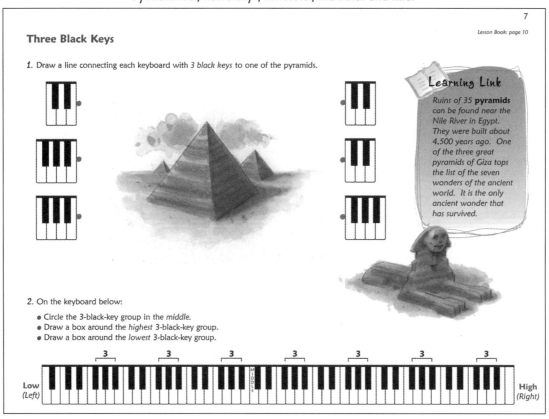

9. "It's Fun to Play!" p. 11 from Lesson Book (see example 4.37):

- The teacher demonstrates "Workout 3, Develop Strong Joints" and assists the student in experiencing the workout.

- The student demonstrates "Workout 3, Develop Strong Joints."

- The student taps the rhythm for "It's Fun to Play!" on the key cover (moving gracefully up for each new pattern) while counting aloud with the practice tempo on the CD.

- The student points to the notes and says the finger numbers.

- The student plays the piece on the key cover while saying the finger numbers.

- The student plays and counts the piece at a slow tempo.

- Theory Book, pp. 8–9 (see examples 4.38–4.39). The teacher goes through the directions on the page and assists the student in completing one example from each number to make sure he/she understands how to complete the page at home. "Now Hear This" and "Imagination Station" examples are completed in the lesson.

Example 4.37 "It's Fun to Play!" p. 11 from *Alfred's Premier Piano Course*, Lesson 1A, by Alexander, Kowalchyk, Lancaster, McArthur and Mier

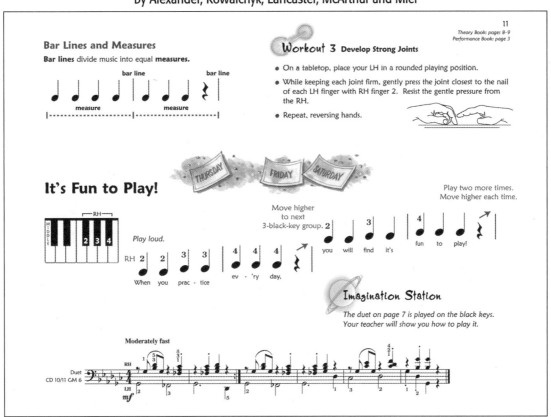

Example 4.38 Page 8 from *Alfred's Premier Piano Course*, Theory 1A, by Alexander, Kowalchyk, Lancaster, McArthur and Mier

Example 4.39 Page 9 from *Alfred's Premier Piano Course*, Theory 1A, by Alexander, Kowalchyk, Lancaster, McArthur and Mier

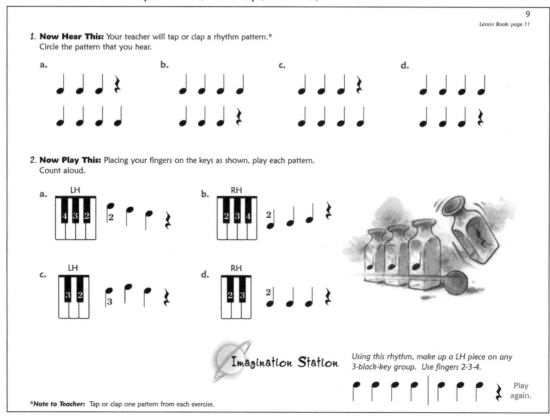

10. "Recess," p. 3 from Performance Book (see example 4.40):

    ◆ The student taps the rhythm for "Recess" with the correct hands and counts aloud.

    ◆ The student points to the notes and says the finger numbers with the practice tempo on the CD.

    ◆ The student plays the piece on the key cover while saying the finger numbers.

    ◆ The student plays the piece on the piano while saying the finger numbers.

    ◆ The student plays and counts the piece at a slow tempo.

Example 4.40 "Recess," p. 3 from *Alfred's Premier Piano Course,* Performance 1A, by Alexander, Kowalchyk, Lancaster, McArthur and Mier

11. Music Flash Cards 1–9

    ◆ The teacher reviews each card with the student, asking the questions written on the back of the card.

12. "P. J., Sara and the Incredible Music Imagination Machine," p. 24 from At-Home Book

    ◆ The teacher introduces the story and encourages the student to read it at home with his/her parents.

13. Meet with parent (At-Home Book, pp. 4, 24, 55–56):

- The teacher explains the student's assignment on p. 4 to the parent (see example 4.41).

- The teacher encourages the parent to read the story beginning on p. 24 with the student.

- The teacher explains the organization of the "Specific Practice Suggestions" on p. 55 at the back of the book and encourages the parents to do one or two ideas from these pages each day with the student.

A written assignment will assist the student in practicing at home. The teacher should make sure that the student understands how to practice each of the things on the assignment sheet that follows (see example 4.41). Both the student and parent(s) should be told that practice should occur on a daily basis.

Most, if not all, of this lesson plan and assignment can be prepared in advance. Subsequent lessons include a balance of review and new material. A teacher plans subsequent lessons on the assumption that the student will have mastered most of the new concepts, skills and pieces. However, a thorough review of recently introduced concepts and skills must precede the introduction of new material and activities. The teacher can determine a student's understanding and skill by having him/her play a portion, or all of the practice assignment. If the student demonstrates a thorough understanding by playing the assignment with a minimum number of errors, the teacher can coach musical aspects of the practiced pieces, or they can proceed to spend the majority of the lesson presenting new material and activities. However, when the student has not learned the material sufficiently, the teacher must alter the lesson plan to review material and even reassign it. Refer to chapter 7 on pages 190–195 and chapter 9 on pages 266–274 for more information about developing lesson plans.

Teachers can develop lesson plans and assignments similar to those in this chapter for any method or materials they choose to use. In addition to an assignment book, students will learn more quickly, thoroughly and independently if they have a notebook in which they write most things that they learn. The notebook can include manuscript paper as well as blank paper. They can write the musical alphabet; draw a staff and add clef signs and music notes; draw intervals; notate rhythm patterns; define symbols and other new things as they are learned. Some of the writing can be started in the lesson and completed at home. Teachers can assign specific tasks to complete in the notebook and students can feel free to write anything else they like, including pieces they have composed. For beginners, it is helpful to make specific daily assignments. The student may practice only a specific portion of the full assignment on the first day, adding other things on subsequent days of the week.

Example 4.41 A sample assignment page from *Alfred's Premier Piano Course,* At-Home 1A, by Alexander, Kowalchyk, Lancaster, McArthur and Mier

Premier Piano Course Assignment

4

TODAY'S LESSON

Day _Friday_

Date _11-11_

Time _3:45_

NEXT LESSON

Day _Friday_

Date _11-18_

Time _3:45_

Premier Piano Course Books	New Pages	Review Pages	Practice Suggestions
Lesson Book	5 - 11		For each piece in the Lesson and Performance book do the following:
Follow numbered instructions on pages 6, 7, 10, Always practice workouts on pages 5, 9, 11 each day			1) Tap the rhythm and count aloud with the Practice Tempo on the CD.
Performance Book	2 - 3		2) Play on the closed keyboard cover and say finger numbers aloud.
			3) Play and count aloud.
Theory Book	2 - 9		Complete 1 or 2 pages each day.

Other Books, Solos, Duets & Ensembles	New Pages	Review Pages	Practice Suggestions

Daily Practice Time (in minutes) *Remember to write your practice time each day.*

SUN.	MON.	TUES.	WED.	THURS.	FRI.	SAT.	TOTAL

To: Parents **From:** Teacher

Please help your child:

1. Review Flashcards
   Music Cards # _1 - 9_
   Sight-Reading Cards #
2. Listen to CD Tracks
   Lesson Book # _1, 2, 4, 6, 8, 10_
   Performance Book # _1, 3_
3. Other _Read story beginning on page 24 of At-Home Book_

To: Teacher **From:** Parents

1. My child really likes:

2. My child needs extra help with:

3. Other

SUMMARY

Effective piano teachers know how to determine student readiness for lessons, what elementary students need to learn, effective strategies to teach concepts and skills, and how to make effective lesson plans. Teachers should plan in ways that meet the needs of today's students and provide them with a comprehensive musical education.

+ Elementary students will learn specific aural, rhythm, pitch, technical, musical, creative, functional, and theoretical concepts and skills.

+ Off-staff and contour reading, landmark notes, familiarity with keyboard topography, and note identification make beginning music reading easier.

+ Knowing a systematic order for developing keyboard acquaintance, rhythm skills, aural skills, technical skills, and musical playing makes teaching more productive.

+ Drills and games for keyboard identification, note and contour reading, finger numbers, learning intervals, keeping eyes on the page, observing dynamics, finger coordination, hand coordination, and rhythmic development facilitate beginning learning.

+ Beginning students can also learn about making music through rote learning, imagery, imaginative pieces, duets with teachers, and by learning about specific musical skills, such as dynamics and articulation.

+ Ascertaining a student's readiness will help determine the best course of action for music study.

+ A comprehensive interview with beginning students and their parents gives teachers knowledge about the students' goals, their maturity, and their musical and learning skills. It helps teachers prepare individualized lessons for their students.

+ When teachers are aware of the common problems of beginners, they can learn strategies for preventing these problems.

+ Strategies for preparing for difficulties such as moving out of five-finger positions; choosing accurate fingerings; comprehending sharps, flats and naturals; and understanding meters will help teachers avoid teaching mistakes and make teaching more efficient.

PROJECTS FOR NEW TEACHERS

1. Using a beginning method book of your choice, devise a comprehensive lesson plan for a first week's lesson. Follow the model on pages 99–114. Based on the lesson plan, write a home practice assignment.

2. Develop a second lesson plan to follow the lesson plan on pages 99–114. Use the suggestions found in chapter 7 (pages 190–196) and chapter 9 (pages 266–274) as guides.

PROJECTS FOR EXPERIENCED TEACHERS

1. Choose an elementary-level piece from a beginning method series to teach to first-year students by rote. The piece should be too difficult for first-year students to read, but easy enough for them to play technically, and should provide an opportunity to develop musical playing. Develop an abstract with practice steps that will help students remember how to practice the piece (refer to examples 2.1–2.2 and 4.2–4.3). The abstract should reinforce beginning concepts that the student is learning.

2. Study several other beginning method books that you do not regularly use and find at least five pieces or activities that you could use to supplement your preferred method. Describe where and how you would use them with your preferred method series.

3. Read the section about imagery on pages 78–79. Peruse several elementary-level books and choose two pieces in which the music matches imaginative titles. Write a description of each piece, similar to the description of "Whirlwind" (example 4.15), that you can use to encourage students to play the pieces musically.

Chapter 5
TEACHING RHYTHM AND READING

The foundation of piano study for elementary students involves growth and development in three areas: 1) reading, counting and playing basic rhythms; 2) reading pitch notation on the grand staff; and 3) combining rhythms and pitches fluently on the keyboard. Before students learn to read and name these elements, they must experience them aurally and physically in many ways such as singing, chanting, playing back, clapping back and learning pieces by rote. This elementary foundation will prepare students for early-intermediate repertoire.

TEACHING RHYTHM

Rhythm is a natural part of the human experience. The heart beats in a steady pulse and humans walk with a regular gait. Rhythms are naturally tapped, clapped or drummed, many times unconsciously, as a part of daily living. Young children respond physically first to the rhythm of the music and later to the pitches. Although rhythm is experienced naturally, students must be taught to read and play rhythms. Refer to chapter 4, page 64, for a listing of elementary rhythm concepts.

Learning Rhythm with Body Movement

Teaching rhythm begins with the understanding that rhythm is felt within the body. Sound suggests movement, and as rhythm is a major contributor to that sense, rhythmic learning should begin by experiencing it through body movement. No amount of counting aloud, metronome practice, or rhythm worksheets will assure accuracy of rhythm when playing an instrument. Although all of these activities are helpful, basic rhythmic experience must take place *before* students can be expected to play rhythms accurately.

Eurhythmics, a term used by Swiss music educator Émile Jaques-Dalcroze (1865–1950) to describe movement activities in response to listening to musical sound, facilitates learning. A thorough familiarity with common rhythm patterns can be achieved through movement activities, including the following:

- walking to the beat of music to experience the pulse (quarter notes) and a steady tempo

- jogging to faster rhythmic values to feel eighth-note subdivisions

- skipping to music to feel the dotted quarter note followed by an eighth note

- walking to the beat of music and showing the strong beats with upper-body motions

- swinging the arms to the beat or conducting the beat while singing a song

- walking to the beat and singing the words of familiar songs

- singing and stepping the rhythm of familiar songs or pieces that are being learned

- clapping the pulse or the rhythm to recorded music

- clapping rhythm patterns that the teacher claps first or patterns seen in notation

- tapping the rhythm of a piece with both hands simultaneously

Developing a Sense of Pulse

A strong sense of pulse is the basis for all other rhythmic learning. For elementary students, the pulse is normally the quarter note. Later, the pulse created by a dotted quarter note or the eighth note in compound meters such as $\frac{6}{8}$ may be introduced. Rhythmic activities during the first few weeks of lessons will help assure a strong sense of pulse and a steady tempo. Students can also count aloud while experiencing activities such as the following:

- walking or marching to the beat while the teacher plays music with a strong beat

- passing a tennis-sized ball from hand to hand to the beat, while the teacher plays

- holding hands with the teacher and swinging the arms to the beat while singing songs

- tapping the beat on the body with whole-arm motions to prepare for two-hand tapping of LH and RH parts of pieces

- conducting the beat to increase student awareness of note duration

Developing a Sense for Subdivisions of the Beat

Once the body "knows" the pulse, systematic and incremental rhythmic development can occur. Rhythm values that both lengthen the beat (whole, half and dotted half notes) and subdivide it (eighth notes) can be drilled during the first months of lessons. Note values that lengthen the beat are relatively easy and can be felt as several pulses for one note. Rhythm values that subdivide the beat can be more difficult for students to comprehend. To prepare students for eighth notes (subdivisions of the beat), a sequential series of movement activities, over several weeks, would include the following:

1. The student walks to the pulse while the teacher plays quarter notes.

2. The student jogs while the teacher plays eighth notes.

3. The student walks or jogs while the teacher alternates playing quarter notes (four measures) with eighth notes (also four measures).

4. The student walks (in place or around the room) and claps two times for each step, while the teacher plays quarter notes in the LH and eighth notes in the RH.

5. The student jogs eighth notes and claps quarter notes while the teacher plays eighth notes in the LH and quarter notes in the RH.

Learning Rhythm in Patterns

As notes are combined to make short patterns, students begin to feel and hear rhythmic groups, and begin to read rhythm fluently. Short-short-long (♩ ♩ ♩) and long-short-short (♩ ♩ ♩) rhythms should be heard and experienced early in the learning progress. The rhythms of words or word groups, such as *Mis-sis-sip-pi cat-fish* (♫ ♫ ♩ ♩), can be clapped back, with the student imitating the teacher's rhythm. Initially, students can watch the teacher and imitate what they see and hear, eventually clapping back by hearing only. Students will feel the rhythms more readily if they clap-back with circular arm motions. While clap-backs can include rhythms that the student is not yet ready to read or play, the first few rhythms should have no subdivisions of the beat. Later, eighth-note subdivisions can be included.

Teachers can also play rhythms on the piano, using a single note at first, so that students can hear the rhythmic durations. Students can play back the rhythms as well, but clapping and tapping are preferable because the larger motions help students feel the rhythms internally. The first patterns should be one measure in length and in $\frac{4}{4}$ meter (see example 5.1). Each rhythm should be clapped or played at least two times before the student responds.

Example 5.1 Sample rhythms in $\frac{4}{4}$ for clap-back

When these patterns are secure, patterns in $\frac{3}{4}$ meter can be given (see example 5.2).

Example 5.2 Sample rhythms in $\frac{3}{4}$ for clap-back

If teachers want students to responsively clap a series of patterns without a break between each pattern and the student's imitation, the last beat of each pattern must be a rest so that students are alerted to when it is their turn to clap. Initially, the teacher might want to point to the student or say "clap" during the rest (see example 5.3).

Example 5.3 Sample rhythms for responsive clap-back

When students are consistently accurate with one-measure patterns, then two-measure patterns in $\frac{3}{4}$ and $\frac{4}{4}$ meter can be added.

Notating what is heard provides the link between hearing and reading. It can begin as soon as the student is reading note values and is clapping consistently and counting accurately.

Rhythm patterns, many of which can be taken from the student's repertoire, can be written on flashcards and used for various activities:

- Students choose the rhythm they hear from several similar ones.

- Students experience the rhythms by chanting or tapping them.

- Students experience a series of rhythms by improvising melodies with them, using the notes of a five-finger pattern.

As in the following exercise, a basic rhythm can be written out in advance for students to change as they hear the teacher play a slightly different rhythm.

The student sees this basic rhythm:

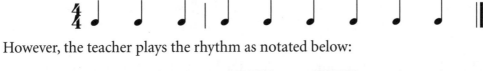

However, the teacher plays the rhythm as notated below:

The student changes the basic rhythm to match what was heard.

In addition to such independent rhythm-pattern activities, students should experience the rhythm of each new piece before playing it. Students can experience rhythms aurally, linking the ear to notation, when teachers use the following steps:

1. clap a specific, but unidentified, measure in a new piece

2. ask the student to clap it with them

3. ask the student to identify the measure in the piece

Learning the Rhythm Patterns of a Piece

Initially, some students may not understand the importance of rhythm, thinking that a piece is good enough if all the notes are correct. To demonstrate the importance of rhythm, teachers can play a familiar tune using incorrect rhythms. Conversely, students may be surprised to learn that they can identify a familiar tune just by hearing the correct rhythm alone. Once students recognize that rhythm is just as important as pitch, they are more likely to observe it. When students learn the rhythm patterns of a new piece (i.e., through tapping, clapping, or other rhythm experiences) before learning the other aspects of it, they will be able to concentrate more on the other aspects while reading the piece for the first time.

Counting

Students frequently say that they are counting *inside*, but this often results in inaccurate rhythms. Internalized counting often works when rhythms are simple, but errors will occur as rhythms become more complex. Furthermore, some students are reluctant to count while practicing.

Students can count aloud while listening to a CD recording or the teacher playing the piece. Counting with dynamics, inflection and duration can make practice more interesting and promotes musical development. Students can also be motivated to count aloud if they are given permission to cease this once they can count a piece aloud accurately and easily, or if they are only required to count during every other playing, every other day or only for pieces that are rhythmically troublesome. Most students will be motivated to improve their rhythm accuracy and fluency if the teacher regularly plays duet accompaniments with them.

Organizing the Pulses into Meters

In all standard piano literature, the pulses (or beats), are organized into groups known as measures. Elementary students learn to feel the organization of groups in $\frac{4}{4}$ and $\frac{3}{4}$ meters. Some elementary courses also introduce groups associated with $\frac{2}{4}$, $\frac{3}{8}$ and $\frac{6}{8}$ meters. Teachers can help students by playing simple pieces in various meters and having them walk to the beat and make a large upper-body motion, such as swinging the arms, on each strong beat (beat 1). Students can also conduct the meter and eventually walk to the beat at the same time. Counting pieces metrically will also help students focus on the meter. At the piano, when students accent the first beat of every measure, the result is generally choppy and unmusical. It is better to present movement activities that help students *feel* the strong beats internally. Below are other ways that students can feel and identify meters:

- from the teacher's playing

- by looking at several short, similar pieces, with the time signatures covered, and selecting the one in the meter the teacher requests

Some students are more comfortable with non-metric counting, but eventually every student has to count metrically. A natural place to begin metric counting is when the time signature is introduced, but it is unnecessary to count metrically until the hands play different rhythms at the same time. In *Alfred's Premier Piano Course*, for example, students could begin counting metrically with "Old MacDonald Had a Dog" (see example 5.4), but "Green Tea" (see example 5.5) is the first piece that requires metric counting.

Example 5.4 "Old MacDonald Had a Dog," p. 16 from *Alfred's Premier Piano Course*, Lesson 1A, by Alexander, Kowalchyk, Lancaster, McArthur and Mier

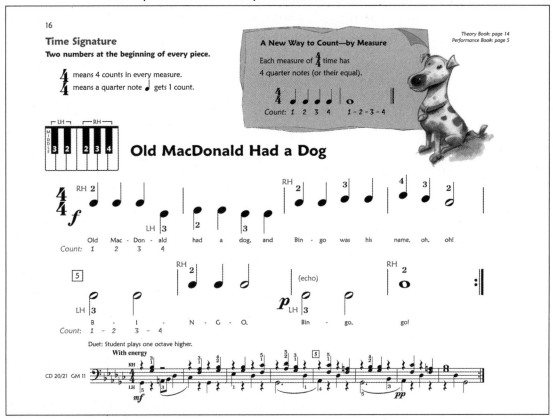

Example 5.5 "Green Tea," p. 11 from *Alfred's Premier Piano Course*, Lesson 1B, by Alexander, Kowalchyk, Lancaster, McArthur and Mier

Sequence for Learning Rhythm Patterns

Rhythm patterns should be presented through a sequence of steps over several weeks. These steps for learning a rhythm pattern provide students the opportunity to hear it, feel it, see it, write it, identify it, and, finally, play it. One sequence might have the student do some or all of the following:

1. Clap the rhythm after the teacher has tapped or clapped it (clap-back).

2. Clap or tap the rhythm from a flashcard.

3. Chant the rhythm with a rhyme.

4. Clap the rhythm and count aloud.

5. Using the rhythm, play common exercises, such as five-finger patterns.

6. Using the rhythm, improvise a melody within a five-finger pattern.

7. Write the rhythm pattern from a printed example.

8. Identify the rhythm from several notated choices, after the teacher claps it.

9. Write the rhythm pattern after hearing the teacher clap it.

10. Play pieces that use the rhythm pattern.

For example, before students play pieces using pairs of eighth notes, it is important that they clap-back numerous rhythm patterns that include eighth notes. They should count the patterns while clapping back, play them in technical exercises, improvise a melody with them, identify them from notation, and notate them after the teacher plays or claps them.

Learning About Upbeats and Incomplete Measures

Elementary students encounter pieces that begin on beats other than beat 1. These beats are known as upbeats and result in incomplete measures at the beginning (and ending) of the piece. Upbeats are preparatory beats that lead to a strong downbeat (beat 1 of the first full measure). In pieces that begin with upbeats, most other phrases in the piece will also begin with upbeats. Students can feel the difference between an upbeat and downbeat by pretending to throw a ball. The arm prepares for the throw by moving backward and snaps forward to release the ball from the hand. The preparatory motion represents the upbeat, while the throw represents the downbeat. Students can count while doing this activity. In $\frac{4}{4}$ time, they would count "4" during the preparatory motion and "1" as the ball is released from the hand. During counts 2 and 3, there would be no movement.

Conducting the meter while the teacher plays also helps students feel upbeats and downbeats, since the last beat of a measure is conducted with an upward motion and the first beat is a downward motion. To apply what they learn, initially students will need to write in metric counting for pieces using upbeats.

Learning About Rests

Rests are frequently overlooked by students, who often play the note following the rest as if it were the next beat. Furthermore, notes are often held through rests in the LH while the RH plays. These common omissions are the result of underdeveloped listening skills as well as a misunderstanding of the function of rests. The function of rests in music is to add drama and character. Rests also provide breath between phrases or melodic fragments. Contrasting textures between sections of a piece of music can be enhanced through the use of rests.

When students understand how rests support the character and overall sound of a piece, they are more likely to observe them diligently. In "Symphony Hall" (see example 5.6), rests are used to make the LH melody stand out more clearly. If students hold the harmonic 3rd in the RH of measure 4, it is more difficult to hear the next melody notes in the LH.

Example 5.6 "Symphony Hall," p. 27 from *Alfred's Premier Piano Course,* Lesson 1B, by Alexander, Kowalchyk, Lancaster, McArthur and Mier

Students may be impatient and shorten the rests. In "Leaky Faucet" (see example 5.7), the erratic dripping of a leaky faucet is simulated. If students do not observe the rests accurately, the suspense created while waiting for the faucet to drip is minimized.

Example 5.7 "Leaky Faucet," p. 59 from *The Music Tree*, Part 1, by Clark, Goss and Holland

Learning About Ties

Ties elongate a sound. Students sometimes find it difficult to observe ties that cross bar lines since no key is struck on the following downbeat. It seems unnatural not to play a key on a strong beat; therefore, students may instinctively play a note instead of observing the tie. Since the second note of the tie is notated, students are also visually stimulated to play it. Students must be able to readily identify the tie notation and feel the full duration.

Students can be prepared to observe ties in a number of ways:

- listening to the duration of both notes of the tie

- whisper-counting the beat of the second note of the tie

- shouting "hold" on the beat of the second note of the tie

- clapping the rhythm and make a silent motion for the second note of the tie

- walking to the beats as the teacher improvises, and moving only the upper part of the body (without taking a step) to the beat of the second note of the tie

Each of these techniques can also be modified and applied to teaching rests.

Learning Dotted Rhythms

Elementary students learn to read and play the dotted quarter note followed by an eighth note rhythm (♩. ♪). Students should write the rhythm and then augment it by making each note twice as long. The resulting rhythm is a dotted half note followed by a quarter (♩. ♩). From this exercise, students will understand that a dotted quarter/eighth-note rhythm has the same relationship as the dotted half-note/quarter-note rhythm and, therefore, will sound similar.

Activities using this rhythm prepare students to learn and play other dotted rhythms at more advanced levels, such as a dotted eighth note followed by a sixteenth (♪. ♬). These student activities include:

- skipping to music while the teacher plays

- clapping back rhythm patterns that include the dotted quarter note followed by an eighth note

- clapping and counting (while reading) the familiar rhythm of a quarter note tied to an eighth note, followed by another eighth note, before clapping the dotted quarter followed by an eighth note (♩ ♫ = ♩. ♪).

Observing the Duration of Note Values

Rhythm patterns and rhythmic duration are different from each other. The rhythm of a group of notes is determined by the accuracy of the initiation of each of the notes. The length of each note is its duration. The following two patterns have the same rhythm but not the same duration.

Many students play accurate rhythms but inaccurate durations. When durations are not observed, the sound suffers and the musical intent of the composer is not achieved. Students will be more likely to observe durations if they write in the counting of the longer notes. Students can be taught to keep the arm moving slightly during a longer note while holding it and moving to the next note. This small motion enables them to feel the length of the longer notes. Neglecting durations frequently occurs when hands play together. Teachers can tap or play the rhythm of one hand while the student taps or plays the other.

Durations and rests are sometimes neglected when the student's focus is drawn to some other activity. For example, when one hand has rests or notes with longer durations, the other hand may be more active and need intense concentration. The hand with the lesser activity may be neglected.

In "Symphony Hall" (see examples 5.6 and 5.8), students may cut short the value of the LH dotted half notes tied to the quarter notes. As a result, the music will sound like this:

Example 5.8 "Symphony Hall" mm. 1–5 as played inaccurately

Students will play correctly if they discover that the LH is a song. The teacher can play the LH as written and then play it again with shortened dotted half notes, and ask the student which performance sounds more like a song. The student can then sing the song, listening to and feeling the length of the dotted half notes. Finally, the student can play the LH alone, making it "sing." Students will begin to feel durations when techniques such as the following are used:

- Rhythms are clapped with larger clapping motions for longer durations and smaller clapping motions for shorter durations.

- Rhythms are stepped with smaller steps for shorter notes and longer steps for longer durations.

- Long durations, such as whole notes, are counted by saying, "Hold-that-whole-note"

- Teachers ask questions such as, "Did you hear each note last until the next one?" or, "Did you hear the dotted half note last for three beats?"

Using the Metronome

The metronome is a helpful tool, but it will not instill a rhythmic sense nor will it assure accuracy of rhythm. Some teachers use the metronome successfully with beginning students and its use becomes second nature. However, if metronome practice is assigned too early, most students become frustrated. When students are frustrated, they avoid listening to a ticking metronome, a behavior that could lead to poor listening habits in general. Recorded orchestrated accompaniments are motivating and can serve a similar purpose to metronomes.

A student must be given an opportunity to learn to use the metronome before assigning it for the practice of pieces. Initially, students should simply tap or clap and count the beat with the ticking of the metronome, followed by playing a single key with each tick. Soon they can tap or clap twice as fast or twice as slow as the ticking. When students can consistently clap or tap the rhythms of their pieces with the metronome, they can be assigned a piece below their learning level, in which the notes and rhythm are very simple and there are few, if any, subdivisions of the beat. The purpose of the assignment is not to learn the piece, but rather to learn to play the piece with the metronome.

Once these preliminary activities have been experienced, students can be assigned metronome practice for their performance repertoire. In addition, five-finger patterns can be played with the metronome, one note per tick, to develop precision, followed by two notes per tick to develop evenness. Pieces are learned quickly, and memory becomes more secure, when metronome practice starts with slow tempos and moves gradually to faster tempos.

TEACHING READING

When good reading habits are taught from the first lesson and reinforced diligently during every lesson, students learn to play new music accurately and sight-read fluently. (Refer to chapter 4 pages 65–66 for a listing of elementary reading concepts.) In addition to learning basic pitch-reading concepts, elementary students also learn to read basic rhythm patterns and to recognize similarities and differences in patterns. They develop visual and kinesthetic perceptions of the keyboard and learn to keep their eyes on the page most of the time. Furthermore, they learn to transpose and to use what they hear to assist in fluent reading.

The primary role of beginning reading is to build a memory bank of patterns and symbols that will be recognized in new surroundings (transfer of knowledge). This process is facilitated when students are assigned several pieces at the same level. These pieces should include familiar concepts and skills with a variety of keys, styles, and technical and musical requirements. Teachers should try to dedicate some time in each weekly lesson to reading games, including transposition, and to hearing the results of the daily sight-reading assignments. Most publishers of early-level piano music offer effective books for sight-reading. Many teachers keep a file of music specifically for student sight-reading. Short pieces are especially useful.

Reading Complexities

Reading music can be related to reading language. In language, there are letters that make the words, just as there are notes and symbols in music that make melodic fragments and chords. Musical phrases, made from longer melodic groupings, and harmonic progressions correspond to phrases and sentences in language. While similarities exist between language and music reading, reading keyboard music can be considered more difficult due to factors such as the following:

- There are a large variety of symbols.

- Symbols are combined in vertical and oblique patterns as well as horizontal ones.

- Different symbols and sounds have the same name. (For example, the note C has many different symbols and different sounds depending upon the octave. A quarter note will sound different depending upon the tempo and the number of counts it receives based on the time signature.)

Keyboard note-reading can be difficult due to the following elements:

- Symbols are *vertically* higher and lower on the page to represent higher and lower sounds that are *horizontally* to the right and left on the keyboard.

- Black keys are on a higher plane than white keys without a visual indication of this on the page.

- Hands and fingers move both up and down to produce the sound (up away from the keyboard and down into the keys).

- Pitch goes *up* from left to right (horizontally) on the keyboard, while pitch can also go *down* (at an angle) from left to right on the printed page.

- Keys played simultaneously are seen *horizontally* on the keyboard, but notes to be played simultaneously are seen *vertically* on the musical score.

- Finger numbers of the RH correspond to the five-note scale structure, while the LH finger numbers are reversed (finger 5 plays the first degree of the scale).

Fluency in reading can be hindered by the following:

- the student not recognizing the symbol

- the student not understanding the meaning of the symbol in the musical context

- the student failing to relate the meaning of one symbol to the next

For example, the following may cause a student's playing to falter:

- a specific note is not familiar

- a specific note may be recognized, but does not occur in the current hand position

- a specific note is not related (in the student's mind) to the previous note played

Furthermore, students make pitch errors because of the following:

- They can't hear inwardly (aurally internalize) how the music should sound.

- They don't know what the notation means.

- They don't have the technical ability to play what is seen and/or heard.

Reading Vertically

In addition to horizontal contour reading, students must also read vertically. A discussion of contour reading can be found in chapter 4 on pages 76–83. Initially, a few drills for reading words vertically will help the eyes track vertically, as well as horizontally (see example 5.9).

Example 5.9 Flashcard to exercise vertical reading

	c	h		h
a	a	a	a	a
	t	s		t

Flashcards that incorporate simple sentences written vertically on the staff can be used to drill vertical reading (see example 5.10).[1] These drills apply directly to reading vertical structures such as blocked triads.

Example 5.10 Flashcard with vertical reading on the grand staff

Vertical reading involves reading both treble and bass clefs simultaneously, and playing both hands together. Many elementary pieces alternate hands much of the time, but some pieces also begin to develop hands-together playing on beat 1 or other strong beats, on long notes, after long notes, or after rests.

As students progress into the late-elementary level, the hands will also play together in the following circumstances:

- parallel motion at the octave (same rhythm, same intervals and same direction, often with the same pitches)

- contrary motion, also called mirroring (same rhythm, same intervals in opposite direction, often played with the same fingers in both hands)

- one hand repeating the same note patterns (ostinato or drone) as an accompaniment to the other hand

- one hand playing longer note values, while the other hand plays shorter values

Modern pedagogical composers and publishers carefully consider the technical demands in creating and editing elementary piano pieces. However, teachers should isolate the spots where hands play together and help students find ways to make those spots easier to learn before students go home with the piece. Hands should be practiced together as soon as possible to encourage the reading and playing of both clefs simultaneously. When students are allowed to practice hands separately for too long a period of time, the development of the skill of reading and playing hands together is delayed.

---

[1] Sidney J. Lawrence, *A Guide to Remedial Sight Reading for the Piano Student: A Study In Corrective Teaching Procedures* (New York: Exposition Press, 1964).

Reading Notes, Rhythm and Expression Markings Simultaneously

To play fluently, note and rhythm reading must be integrated. Students may read notes correctly and know how to find them on the keyboard, but if adding rhythms confuses them, students may miss notes while trying to play the correct rhythm. Moreover, technical demands typically increase as rhythms become more complex, thus causing note errors. Initially, teachers can ask students to play only the notes without worrying about the rhythm. Conversely, the rhythm can be tapped and played on a single note only. Finally, both the notes and rhythm can be combined. Pieces that have both complex notes and rhythms should be avoided with elementary students.

In addition to notes and rhythms, students need to observe symbols of expression. This will be easier if these symbols are applied logically and sparingly. If a piece is titled "Secret," students are more likely to observe and apply the *piano* dynamic symbol (*p*). Similarly, if a piece requires staccato playing, it will be easier if all the notes of a passage are staccato, and other expressive markings are eliminated.

Developing Keyboard Orientation and Visual Perception

The notation on the page must be transferred into physical motion and sound, using eye/hand coordination. The eye reads the notation, while the brain interprets and tells the body what to do kinesthetically. When this process is operating correctly, the eye-to-brain-to-hand coordination happens instantly and the tactile sense determines whether the hand is in the correct place. If the hand is unfamiliar with the topography of the keyboard and cannot find the proper key, the fingers may play wrong notes or the student will look at the keyboard to find the correct key.

Beginning instruction should focus on helping students visualize the keyboard topography. Simple exercises can be devised. The teacher calls out directions ("G, up a 2nd, down a 3rd" for example) and students play (G-A-F), first by looking at the keyboard and then with their eyes closed.

Students can learn to play by feel (rather than looking at their hands) by following a progression of learning steps for any piece that remains in a five-finger position. While it is unlikely that teachers will apply all of these steps for any one student piece, they will, hopefully, select and apply all of these steps at some time during the early stages of a student's learning.

<u>Finger Numbers</u>

Without looking at the hands, the student reads the music and does the following:

1. chants the finger numbers for the notes

2. chants the finger numbers while "playing" his/her fingers in the air

3. chants the finger numbers while "playing" his/her fingers on the key cover

4. places the hands in the correct position on the keyboard, then chants the finger numbers while playing the notes

Intervals and Direction

Placing his/her right hand in the correct position and following the teacher's direction ("finger 2 on G, up a 2nd, down a 3rd" for example), the student does the following:

1. plays while looking at the keyboard

2. plays a second time with the eyes closed

Keeping their hands in the correct position, and reading the music, the student does the following:

1. chants the intervals and direction

2. chants (intervals and direction) and plays without looking at the hands

Note Names

While reading the music, the student chants the note names. Placing the hands in the correct position and reading the music, the student does the following:

1. keeps his/her eyes on the music and chants the note names while playing on the key cover

2. keeps his/her eyes on the music and chants the note names while playing silently on the keys

3. keeps his/her eyes on the music and chants the note names while playing the notes on the keyboard

Sometimes teachers can *dictate* what is on the page ("play finger 1, finger 5," etc. or "play finger 1, up a 2nd, up a 3rd, down a 2nd," etc.) and students play, following the dictation as they watch the music. Because the goal is to help students play securely by feeling (tactile sensations), without looking at the hands, it is not important that students completely understand or see the relationship of what the teacher is dictating to what they see on the page. After they have experienced the piece in this preliminary way, they will feel more confident about learning it by reading, without the teacher dictating.

Students can learn to understand the role of short-term kinesthetic memory as an aid to fluent reading. They can consciously apply this ability to piano playing by practicing drills, similar to those recommended by Howard Richman[3], in which the student reads and plays the following series of notes, obeying the teacher's directions.

Student reads:

---

[3] This drill is based on the work of Howard Richman. Howard Richman, *Super Sight-Reading Secrets*, 3rd edition (Reseda, CA: Sound Feelings Publications, 1986).

Teacher's directions:

1. "Look at the keyboard and play middle C with your right hand."

2. "Look at the first note. Return your hand to your lap and play the note again, keeping your eyes on the page."

3. "Return your hand to your lap while keeping your eyes on the page. Then play the next note."

4. "Keep reading and playing each new note in the same way."

When students return their hands to their laps and then play the next note without looking at their hands, they do not rely on either looking at the keyboard or the tactile sense to find the correct key. Rather, they must rely on the short-term kinesthetic memory, which helps them internally *feel* 1) the last note played, 2) the distance they traveled from the keyboard, and 3) the distance to the new key. While it is extremely helpful to find new notes from previous ones using the tactile sense, there are many times when this is not possible. Drills such as this allow the body to memorize the distance and angle of the arm needed to find specific keys. For this to be effective, the pianist must always sit with the body centered on a specific key, such as middle D, so that all other keys will always be in the same relationship to the body. The pianist will learn how far the arm and hand must always angle away from the body to find a specific key. In addition to these drills, students should practice new pieces in different octaves and study pieces that require them to move about the keyboard to build a greater sense of keyboard topography.

Keeping Eyes on the Page

To assure strong reading skills and fluent playing, students must develop the habit of keeping their eyes on the page. When students look down at their hands to find keys, they do not develop a sense of where they are on the keyboard. Furthermore, they often lose their place on the page and must find it again, making the playing slow and hesitant. Teachers can help students learn to keep their eyes on the page through several sequential activities:

1. The teacher points to each note or interval of the piece, while the student names the finger number, interval or note.

2. The student names the finger numbers, intervals or notes while pointing to the page.

3. The student points to the notes and counts the rhythm.

4. The teacher points to the notes and counts while the student plays the notes silently.

5. The teacher points to the notes as the student plays the piece for the first time.

Excessive looking at the hands often results from feeling insecure about where the hands are on the keyboard. If the teacher covers the students' hands (once the hands are in position) it will force them to play without looking at their hands. They will soon feel secure about playing the correct notes. Playing all technical exercises and performing memorized pieces with the eyes closed help build confidence in playing without looking at the hands.

Sometimes it is impossible to play relying solely on visualization or kinesthetic memory. If looking at the hands is required, teachers can draw reminders on the music to give the student permission to look down briefly. Students often keep their eyes on their hands too long, and then make mistakes because they are not looking at the score. When students must look down for position or octave changes, they should be reminded to move only the eyes, not the whole head, and move the eyes back to the page immediately after a brief glance at the hands.

Understanding the Role of the Ear

In playing any musical instrument, eye/hand coordination involves the ears, as well as the eyes and body. The eyes read the notation, the brain tells the body what to do kinesthetically, and the ears hear the sound. Once a sound is made, the ear can judge the accuracy. If the ear is undeveloped, the aural part of the process is missing and mistakes will be difficult to correct. Often, students not only look at the hands to get the correct note, but look a second time to see if they played the correct note. Learning to judge the accuracy of the notes aurally eliminates the need to look at the hands after a note is played.

Learning pieces with a combination of ear and reading is the first step toward developing the ear. It may seem contradictory to suggest that students learn music by ear when the goal is fluent reading. However, when pieces are learned by ear, students associate what is heard to what the hands do to produce the sound. Teachers can enhance what students hear inwardly by using techniques such as the following with teaching pieces (or familiar songs):

- While looking at the music, the student can sing the words with the melody of the piece while the teachers plays it. (Shy students can hum the melody or sing using "la" syllables.)

- While listening to the teacher play, the student can sing (or hum) the tune and illustrate the contour of the melody with hand motions in front of the body.

- While listening to the teacher play, the student can draw the contour of the melody on paper.

- If the student knows the melody well, he/she can play it on the piano by ear.

- The student can sing the melody with letter note names, while reading the score.

Pieces that are too difficult for the student to read can initially be taught by rote. These pieces can acquaint the student with more of the topography of the keyboard and use a greater variety of sounds than reading pieces do. When select pieces are taught in these ways, aural skills will be developed, notation will relate to what is heard and students will look at their hands less often.

Teachers can use other activities regularly to help students judge accuracy and correct their mistakes by ear. While the student looks at the score, the teacher can play the student's piece, making one mistake. The student is asked to locate the mistake and tell what the teacher played incorrectly. When students play wrong notes, teachers can say "wrong" and ask students to correct them by ear. If teachers avoid telling students how to correct errors and insist diligently that students correct errors by ear, students will learn to access the ear instead of looking at the hands to make corrections. Singing, while playing silently on the keys or on the key cover, also activates the ear. As the ear becomes a more active participant in learning, students will begin to use it automatically to help them play accurately. Inner hearing will develop, helping students *hear* what they see on the page *before* they play it and allowing them to play accurately as they read.

Learning and Playing Several Pieces Each Week

Once students are reading from the grand staff, they can be assigned several short reading pieces a week from other materials at the same level as their method series. While most of these pieces will not be perfected, beginning concepts and skills will be reinforced and applied to different contexts. Use of the method can be delayed during this period or can be used simultaneously with the supplementary books. Most students welcome the challenge and are motivated to teach themselves new pieces. Teachers can hear selected pieces or just the students' favorites, without making a lot of corrections or expecting polished playing.

As students progress, they can be assigned study pieces to be learned quickly. Some of these pieces can be retained for polishing, memorization and performance, but the majority should be reassigned only if the student is learning something valuable from the piece. For example, in one piece the student may be learning to refine staccato touch. If the student gets the staccatos exactly right, he/she will have learned something valuable, even if there is an occasional note error or incorrect dynamics. The goal of another piece may be to reinforce a specific rhythm. If the student misses a few notes but masters the rhythm, the student has learned the most important part of the piece. Correcting note or rhythm errors and reassigning every piece until it is perfect is frustrating and may not be the best use of lesson or practice time.

When practicing sight-reading, students play each piece only one or two times during the week. At the next lesson, the teacher chooses a few of these pieces to hear. Students should follow a systematic sight-reading routine that encourages good reading habits.

1. Observe the key and time signatures.

2. Look through the piece to find anything unexpected (clef changes, octave moves, accidentals).

3. Tap and count the rhythm.

4. Chant the note names of each hand separately.

5. Keep the hands quietly in the lap and imagine the fingers playing every key.

6. Play the piece silently, tapping the key surface.

7. Set a slow tempo and play while counting aloud, keeping the eyes on the page, and avoid correcting mistakes.

8. Determine if the playing was accurate; if so, then go to the next piece (if not accurate, set a slower tempo and play a second time).

Transposing as an Aid to Reading

It is helpful for students to transpose beginning pieces. Transposition requires the reader to observe interval relationships, contour, repetitions, similarities, differences and patterns. Students who observe patterns while transposing pieces usually develop analytical skills required for reading and learning new music.

At first, transposition can be experienced by having students play off-staff black-key pieces on adjacent white keys. For example, "Hand-Bells" (see example 5.11) can be played beginning on either B or A, both adjacent white keys to the starting pitch of B-flat. Rather than referring to the experience as *transposition*, it can be simply stated that the piece can begin on different keys.

Example 5.11 "Hand-Bells (Excerpt)," p.12 from *Alfred's Basic Piano Library*, Lesson Book 1A, by Palmer, Manus and Lethco

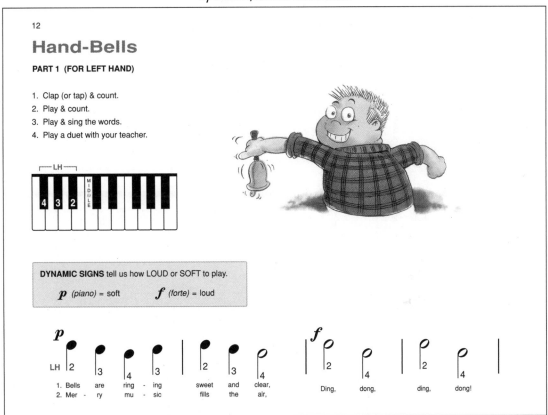

When students are reading on the staff, pieces can be similarly moved to a different place. This repositioning encourages students to read by contour (direction and interval). Teachers can help students discover familiar patterns, as well as patterns that are the same or similar.

The ear plays an important role in transposition. Students with good ears usually have little trouble transposing, but may not analyze the patterns. As a result, the transposition does not enhance reading. It is important that transposition experiences begin with analysis *before* the piece is played in the original key. Students should learn first through analysis, followed by assistance from the ear.

For "Grandpa's Clock" (see example 5.12), a teacher can help the student notice the following:

- The piece begins on the fifth degree of the five-finger pattern and descends an interval of a 5th.

- When the LH begins in m. 3, the upper note is also the fifth degree of the five-finger pattern .

- The LH consists of harmonic 2nds, 3rds, 4ths and 5ths and two melodic intervals (4th and 5th).

Example 5.12 "Grandpa's Clock," p. 10 from *Alfred's Basic Piano Library,* Lesson Book 1B, by Palmer, Manus and Lethco

- The upper note of the first line is repeated and the lower note moves by step.

- Mm. 3 and 7 are identical and mm. 4 and 8 are almost the same.

- The RH of m. 5 has the same pattern as the RH of m. 3, but starts on a different note.

- The ending has a melodic 4th and then a melodic 5th in both the RH and the LH, each starting with the fifth degree of the five-finger pattern.

Each of these observations should be experienced in a key other than C before the entire piece is transposed. These experiences help students focus on the patterns, prepare them to transpose, and aid in the learning of the piece as it is written. This kind of study also aids memorization. As students advance, transposing becomes less daunting when technical exercises are transposed regularly.

Understanding Individual Learning Styles and Their Effect on Reading Ability

Individual students learn to read music in different ways. Teachers can apply appropriate learning activities to enhance reading if they are able to determine each student's learning style as visual, aural or kinesthetic. Students who retain visual images easily usually read notation fluently and may avoid memorizing music. They will need aural activities to help them develop the ability to critique the accuracy of their playing. Students who play by ear get messages from the brain by hearing things first and sometimes avoid reading. Teachers may want to avoid teaching these students too many pieces that they recognize by ear. Students who are tactile learners learn best by feeling. They retain kinesthetic images well and may guess at what they read by applying kinesthetic patterns. These students can be asked to look at shapes and patterns in the score and imagine what they will feel like and then play them.

SUMMARY

To be able to play elementary pieces and prepare for intermediate repertoire, students must have a strong foundation in reading pitch and rhythm notation.

- Because rhythm is felt rather than heard, each rhythmic element should be experienced through body movement activities that include walking, skipping, clapping or tapping.

- The feeling of the pulse must be solidly developed before other rhythmic concepts can be learned.

- Students should learn to feel, play and count multiples of the pulse, such as half notes, before they learn about subdivisions of the pulse, such as eighth notes.

- Activities like clapping back will help students learn and feel rhythms in patterns and assist them in playing fluently.

- Tapping rhythms is superior to clapping them since using each hand individually develops a coordination similar to playing a piano.

- Teachers can find creative ways to motivate students to count aloud.

- Students learn to hear rests as silence. They can come to understand that rests provide drama and character to the music. Melodic phrases (or fragments) are frequently separated by well-placed rests.

- Duration must be recognized as a separate rhythmic element.

- When students learn to listen to the duration of notes, they will have the skill to also listen to the duration of ties.

- Elementary students can learn to use the metronome effectively if teachers present its use incrementally.

- Reading musical notation at the keyboard is more difficult for some students than reading language.

- Vertical reading, a separate skill from horizontal reading, is developed by practicing hands together.

- Successful reading of notes, rhythm and expression markings simultaneously requires incremental learning steps.

- Beginning students will learn to read notation more easily if pre-staff notation is used for a period of time.

- The following types of students are generally good music readers:

    - those who read by note relationship and contour

    - those who have a good sense of keyboard topography

    - those who can visualize the keyboard and how to play it

    - those who keep their eyes on the music

    - those who use the ear to relate what they see to what they are to play

    - those who use the ear to recognize errors

- A strong aural development program will help students read more accurately, make fewer mistakes and assist in correcting mistakes.

- When students learn many pieces that include new concepts and skills, they learn those concepts and skills thoroughly and develop strong reading skills.

- Transposition assists students in reading by relationship and contour.

- Teachers can tailor instruction to match each student's learning style.

Projects for New Teachers

1. Make a list of rhythms and rhythm patterns that students learn in the first book of a beginning piano method. Choose two of these rhythm patterns and develop a plan to introduce them and reinforce them for two subsequent weeks. The plan should include clapping or tapping the rhythm, playing it back, writing it and moving to it.

2. Using the first book of a method of your choice, develop a series of ten successive sight-reading flashcards to reinforce reading principles taught in the method.

Projects for Experienced Teachers

1. From the third level of a method, find two pieces with obvious rhythmic challenges. Define the difficulty and develop a plan for introducing each piece to prevent the student from having difficulty in practicing the assigned pieces.

2. Choose a piece for a first-year student to transpose to two different keys in subsequent lessons. Outline the steps that you would use to help the student identify the patterns needed to transpose the piece.

Chapter 6
TEACHING TECHNIQUE AND MUSICAL SOUND DEVELOPMENT

In addition to the growth and development of strong rhythm and reading skills, students must develop the physical skills for playing the piano. A solid technique allows a student to produce the needed sound and have the facility to play the music at each level of study. When good technical habits are taught from the first lesson and reinforced diligently during subsequent lessons, students learn to play comfortably and effortlessly. A facile technique and a beautiful sound are produced by using the body at the keyboard in its most natural way and using the arms, hands and fingers as a coordinated unit. Elementary students learn many technical skills. (Refer to chapter 4, pages 76–77 for a listing of elementary technical skills.)

Technique can be defined simply as "being able to do what one wants to do at the keyboard when one wants to do it." This implies that technique is not only being able to make the necessary physical moves but is also the ability to play each sound musically. Musical sound results when there is a mental image of both the physical motion and the desired sound. When the mental image is clear and the motion is made efficiently, one can produce the sound without having to spend hours mastering a particular technical difficulty. For example, unclean playing (characterized by hitting the cracks between the keys instead of depressing the key in the center) often happens when the hand is tense or if there is confusion about which key is correct. When there is a mental picture of the correct key and a kinesthetic image of what it feels like to play the pitch *before* depressing the key, the hand and fingers will usually respond and play cleanly. From the beginning of piano study, young students can be taught to imagine the desired sound and the correct motions for efficient playing.

THE NATURAL WAY TO PLAY—GOOD POSTURE

Technical goals are achieved more easily if the piano is played in a natural way. The first critical element in piano technique is the sitting position. If the posture is not correct, it is difficult to achieve other correct positions (hand, arm, and finger) and movements. Good posture is based on the natural balance and alignment of the body. Pianists should balance their weight on the two bony protuberances at the bottom of the pelvis, feel the spine all the way to the base of the skull, with the neck and head balanced on the spine. The head reaches upwards, rather than being tipped down or reaching forward. The back should be comfortably straight but not hyperextended (swayback), which creates tension in the small of the back.

Students should sit at a height that allows the forearms to be horizontal when the hands are placed on the keys. When young students cannot achieve a level forearm due to a low sitting position, they raise their arm each time a finger plays a key. They learn to play with a wrist that is too low and, as a result, excess energy is needed to play with the fingers. Sometimes students raise the wrist for every note that is played, dropping the wrist back down after each note. Such habits cause excessive tension and use unnecessary energy. Benches in the studio and at home should be at exactly the right height for each student. Casters, adjustable benches and seat cushions will help achieve this. Teachers will probably not need to place their hands under the wrist or forearms of students to raise the arms and wrists if the correct height is achieved from the beginning and adjusted as the student grows.

When students sit with the center of the body aligned with Middle D, they develop a strong sense of keyboard topography. The sitting position should be on the front half of the bench so that the body weight is distributed in a way that allows the torso to move freely from side to side, and forward and backward slightly. Movement should be from the hips, avoiding neck and waist bending. If students sit back on the bench, this freedom of upper-body movement is hindered.

The feet should be flat, resting solidly on the floor, slightly apart, and directly in front of the pedals. This allows for proper distribution of body weight and keeps the body in balance. For young students who cannot reach the floor, a footrest that allows the feet to rest comfortably and naturally can be used. These footrests come in varying sizes. Adjustable footrests with pedal extenders are also available. When footrests are not practical, students should sit back on the bench using the whole width of the bench for sitting, with the legs dangling free or ankles crossed. This sitting position for young students is a temporary, balanced solution until they have grown enough to sit forward properly.

Students should sit far enough back from the keyboard so that there is free movement of the arms in front of the body. The upper arm should be at a slight angle away from and in front of the body, as if slightly reaching for the keys. The shoulders are parallel to the keys, except when both arms move lower or higher on the keyboard. When in these positions, the shoulders are at an angle to the keys.

Students can test their own sitting distance from the keyboard by sitting on the bench, putting their hands on the keyboard and then standing up. If it is difficult to stand up while keeping the hands on the keyboard or if their legs touch the bench, they are sitting too close.

When the arm is at rest at the side of the body, the elbow is slightly bent, relaxed and free (not tight against the body or pointing outward). When lifting the arm to position the hand correctly on the keys, the elbow must rotate slightly outward and away from the body. Keeping only the slightest outward angle will avoid the upper-arm tension which results from excessive and unnatural outward angling or pointing of the elbow. When playing higher or lower on the keyboard, the whole arm should move along with the hand. If the whole arm does not move, the upper arm and elbow will stay close to the body and the forearm will move outward at an angle to the body. Instead, the whole arm should lead the hand and fingers so that the arm is centered over the finger that is playing. That movement of the arm should be initiated from the shoulder, rather than the elbow, to avoid sticking out the elbow. This motion is critical for using the fifth finger to voice high notes in the RH and low notes in the LH.

To reach keys very high and very low on the keyboard, the body should lean and roll on the hips to the right or left. The upper body should move as a unit, along with the arms, instead of sitting rigidly in one position. When both arms move to the extremities of the keyboard, the upper body should move slightly forward toward the keys to assist in the reaches. It is the hips (not the head, neck, back or waist) that initiate these forward reaches. Furthermore, straight or stiff arms should never reach for the keys at the extremes of the keyboard. When playing, the arms should be slightly bent at the elbows, similar to how the knees bend when walking. When these motions are correct, the body will not sway but will support the work of the arms and hands efficiently. Proper use of the body will help make playing the piano look effortless.

THE ROLE OF THE WHOLE ARM

Children develop large-muscle coordination before small-muscle control in the fingers. Therefore, beginning playing should start with the whole arm. Use of the whole arm precedes legato playing. Proper use of the playing mechanism (arms, hands, fingers) and the production of a beautiful tone are more important for beginning students than legato playing. Once students master the use of the arms, hands, and fingers and consistently produce a full tone, legato playing will develop naturally. Beginning single-line pieces can be played with the whole arm by playing every note of any piece with either finger two or finger three. Students should play each note in exactly the same way, incorporating the whole arm to produce a rich tone. Later, the pieces can be played with the appropriate fingering, producing a full tone using the same motions.

If students can imagine standing at the end of a bed and falling freely onto it, they will begin to feel the same sensation they need in the arm as it drops into the keys. Students can feel the arm move effortlessly by raising just the forearm, using only the biceps muscles in the front of the upper arm. When this is done correctly, the triceps muscle in the back of the upper arm will not engage. Then the wrist should be allowed to lift and the fingers and hand droop downward from the wrist.

Releasing the biceps allows the hand and arm to fall effortlessly into the lap, without engaging any additional muscles. When this is done correctly, the arm naturally rebounds slightly. On the piano, this rebound gives the performer's tone buoyancy and a ringing quality while eliminating harsh sounds when playing loudly. Students should practice this motion hands separately, and then hands together, first dropping into the lap and then dropping onto clusters of keys to develop the sensation of effortless keyboard playing. When the fingers land on the keys, the hand should look as it does when the arm is hanging limp at the side of the body.

Example 6.1 A comfortable position of the hand on the piano

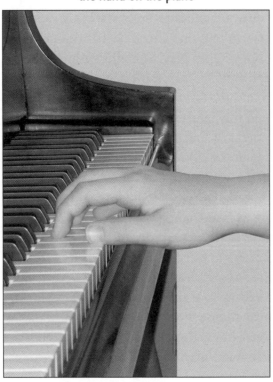

The elbow and upper arm should feel like gelatin when pushed, during both the raising and dropping of the arm. If students have trouble feeling this sensation, teachers can have students rest their arms on their laps. The teacher pulls up on the sleeve of the student's long-sleeved shirt without any help or resistance by the student, and then lets go of the sleeve allowing the arm to drop. Students easily feel the sensation they need for playing.

When students feel the forearm drop correctly, the whole arm can then be employed. The arm is lifted without engaging the shoulder or shoulder girdle (the upper back bones that connect the shoulders). The whole arm moves freely from the armpit joint without lifting or reaching with the shoulders. There is no tightening of any muscle immediately before and during the dropping; the arm should simply move upward effortlessly and then drop. These exercises will teach students to allow gravity to work.

The Use of the Arm to Play Dynamics, Articulations, and Two-Note Slurs

Loud and soft sounds are achieved by dropping the arm and finger quickly (loud) or slowly (soft). When a loud sound is required, the arm drops quickly, the key is played and the hammer hits the string with greater velocity, producing a full, rich loud tone. When the drop into the key (arm and finger) is slower and more controlled, the hammer hits the string slowly and a beautiful soft sound will result. It is impossible to play a loud sound if the finger descends into the key slowly, just as it is impossible to play a soft sound if the finger descends into the key quickly. Consequently, it is difficult to play softly and rapidly at the same time.

Students should make a loud sound without tightening the arm, hand or finger and without forcing, pushing or hitting the key. They should also make a soft sound without holding back, which results in a tightening of the upper arm. Unfortunately, loud playing is sometimes the result of force rather than speed, and of using the fingers to produce the sound without help from the arm. Using force or fingers alone will result in a harsh sound. Students should learn to drop quickly onto the keys by letting go of the tension that is holding the arm up, rather than by using force. When the arm is dropped into the keys with speed rather than force, the sound is full and rich. Students are sometimes afraid of dropping quickly and freely onto the keys for fear of playing wrong notes. Therefore, they may hold back and play with tension. If beginning students are assured that accuracy is not initially required, they will drop their hands onto the keys with greater freedom.

Some students make a soft sound by physically holding back and playing with the fingers only. This creates tension in the body and results in a thin sound, with some notes dropping out. Moving the fingers and arms together without tension produces a soft, yet full, sound. The motions for both loud and soft sounds can be experienced as follows:

+ by dropping the arm and hand into the lap while sitting away from the piano

+ by dropping the arm and finger onto a table top (from a seated position)

+ by dropping a single finger on a single piano key

+ by dropping a group of fingers on a cluster of keys

Teacher demonstrations for student viewing are critical to student comprehension.

The arm is also used to play non-legato (detached) and staccato touches and to play two-note slurs. Non-legato requires the least physical effort to execute. It is often the most natural touch for students who use the whole arm and release each key before the next one is played.

When students initially learn to play staccato, they should use the whole arm, dropping quickly and bouncing off the key. The sound of the staccato is made by releasing the key quickly. However, there is a risk of developing tension if the student perceives that the sound is made with an upward motion, by pulling away from the key. If the arm stays in the air after a staccato note is played, the body retains unnecessary tension. The arm and hand are far from the key surface and must travel farther to play the next key. The motion for staccato should be a downward, into-the-key motion—just like all other playing motions. This downward motion is followed by a quick release, with no tightening during the release.

Two-note slurs have a specific articulation, physical motion and sound. The correct sound is produced by the following:

- the physical motion of dropping and lifting

- the sound image of slightly louder to softer

- the slight shortening of the second note

Two-note slurs are played by dropping onto the first note, shifting the arm weight or rolling onto the second note, and gracefully lifting the arm off the second note. This is *one* continuous motion rather than two separate motions—drop, then lift. Teachers can draw down and up arrows on the score to remind students of the proper motion for achieving two-note slurs (see example 6.2).

Example 6.2 "Footprints" (Excerpt) by Robert Vandall
Down-up arrows to show motion of the arm for two-note slurs

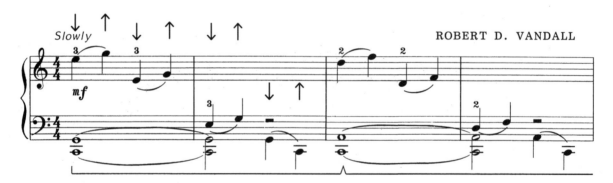

APPROPRIATE HAND AND FINGER POSITIONS

Correct hand position can be observed by looking at the position of the hand when the arms and hands are hanging naturally by the side of the body. The fingers are slightly curved and slightly contracted. The large knuckle joints, where the fingers join the hand (commonly referred to as "the bridge"), slightly protrude from the hand. When this natural hand position is raised and placed on the keyboard, the bridge will be slightly higher than the wrist. The outside of the hand is at a slight angle with the forearm. The wrist should be level and feel completely loose and flexible.

There are several other ways to help beginning students achieve a desired hand position. Students can place their hands on their knees, raising the hands without changing the position at all. Students can also place their hands flat on a table top and slowly gather the fingers up to the correct position like a spider. This exercise, when done without tension, also strengthens the finger joints so they will not collapse. Using imagery by asking students to pretend they are holding a large bubble also creates a hand position without tension.

The wrist can be raised, lowered, moved laterally (side to side) or in a complete circle, both clockwise and counter-clockwise. All of these positions and moves are used in piano playing, but the wrist should automatically return to its naturally level position as soon as possible. Wrists that stay too high, too low, or at an inward or outward angle for too long produce excessive tension.

The hand should be expanded only when necessary and return to the natural position whenever possible. Tension is produced when the hand stretches open and stays open. Students should play within a five-finger position for a sufficient amount of time until a strong hand position is secure. Students, especially those with small hands, should not be assigned pieces that will expand the hand too soon. Those who move too quickly into literature that requires an expanded hand frequently develop poor hand positions. When small hands try to reach large spans, the bridge of the hand and the joint of the thumb that connects it to the hand will collapse. Teachers should choose literature that allows the hand to develop at a natural pace.

When playing with a good hand position, fingers 2 through 5 play on the finger pad just back from the finger tip. This happens naturally when the hand is in a slightly curved and relaxed position. The thumb plays on the pad on the outside of the fingernail and it is nearly straight, without either of the two thumb joints pointing outward, collapsing inward, or touching the key surface. Particularly troublesome is the collapsing of the middle thumb joint or the excessive curving of the nail joint. Both problems can be alleviated by keeping the thumb relaxed. Teachers can help students prevent the joint closest to the thumbnail from collapsing in the following ways:

- by verbally reminding them to keep their wrists low when reaching larger spans
- by asking them to open their hand from the center of the hand
- by avoiding teaching pieces that require the student to reach or stretch

Both teachers and students must learn to recognize what the correct hand and finger positions look like and what motions are necessary to achieve them. Ultimately, students will feel the correct positions and motions kinesthetically. Exercises and pieces that encourage a natural hand position and encourage hand and fingers to move as a coordinated unit will help develop good hand and finger position. If the first pieces require independence of fingers, students may have a difficult time maintaining a good hand position. When teachers ask students to keep a good hand position and students try to do so with pieces that require individual fingers, tension can occur, playing can be more difficult, and an unpleasant sound can result. However, when students are given pieces that allow them to feel the correct motions, they will develop a good hand position, play more easily and achieve the desired sound. This applies throughout the elementary levels of study and beyond. Teachers can help students take personal responsibility by asking questions such as, "How was your hand position?" or "Did your hands feel correct?" or "Are your hands ready to play?" Revisiting short technical exercises, such as lifting and dropping, will restore the correct physical sensations.

MOVING OUT OF HAND POSITIONS

When students play pieces in set five-finger patterns for too long, they become comfortable reading only the notes in those positions and using the same fingers on the same notes. Pieces should be chosen that vary positions or allow slight moves out of a five-finger position. Students should learn to move out of initial positions in the following ways:

1) by moving to other octaves

2) by playing five-finger patterns that are neither major nor minor (e.g., modal, diminished or chromatic patterns)

3) by moving from one five-finger position to another

4) by expanding the hand position slightly (moving the thumb a 2nd or more away from the rest of the hand to play 6ths, 7ths and octaves)

5) by playing smaller intervals with different finger combinations that expand the hand (e.g., playing a 3rd with fingers 1 and 2)

6) by crossing fingers 2, 3 or 4 over the thumb or passing the thumb under fingers 2, 3 or 4

When elementary students play pieces that move to different octaves or five-finger positions, they often must make those moves quickly. These early experiences prepare students to execute jumps and leaps in later years. Quick and free movement is impeded if these moves are accompanied by tightening of the playing mechanism. As a result, accuracy is sacrificed and tension is increased. Beginning students can move smoothly, freely and without tension by practicing motions silently and feeling as though the arm is floating. It is also important for students to look where they are going on the keyboard *before* making the motion. After a few times, the motion can be accomplished by feel and without looking. Later, when they need to be made quickly, the hand can be tossed freely, as if tossing a ball. When students pretend to toss a ball, first by tightening the arm and then without the tightening, they will feel how much easier it is to toss the imaginary ball without tightening. They will soon understand how it must feel when making quick moves at the keyboard. It is more important to move correctly with freedom and be inaccurate than to be accurate with tension. Accuracy results once the correct motions are learned.

The first pieces that expand the hand from the five-finger position should be those that move the thumb away from the rest of the hand or the whole hand away from the thumb to form a 6th. As the hand expands, the bridge of the hand will flatten somewhat and the longer fingers will need to play farther back on the keys to maintain good alignment. Care must be taken that the bridge does not collapse, that the thumb and the fifth finger are played on the correct part of the finger, and that the thumb joints are neither protruding outward or collapsed. Most elementary students will be able to play broken 6ths, 7ths and octaves. Playing large, broken intervals can be facilitated by rotating the arm slightly and shifting the weight of the arm from one note to the next. Students should not reach or stretch for these large intervals, but simply open the hand slightly.

The Role and Development of the Fingers

When using individual fingers, students must feel each finger move as a unit from the bridge. The small finger muscles that supply speed are used when the fingers play from the bridge joint. Feeling the small finger muscles working and playing from the bridge joint is easier if the fingers are not overly curved.

When young students play using the finger muscles, the finger joints often collapse. This collapsing is acceptable for a short time until the fingers learn to play from the bridge joint. Later, as students are able to play from the bridge using the finger muscles in the hand, teachers can help students avoid collapsed joints. If, however, piano teaching begins with an over emphasis on curved fingers, the muscles that connect the fingers to the elbow are engaged, resulting in excessive muscular tension. This can translate into pain as the student gets older and the music becomes more technically demanding.

Playing with slightly curved fingers is efficient. This efficiency can be demonstrated by placing the hand in the air, curving the hand and fingers into a ball shape and wiggling the fingers as quickly as possible. Next, wiggle flat fingers and finally, wiggle fingers that are only slightly curved. This exercise shows that fingers wiggle more quickly and with greater ease when they are in the natural, slightly curved position.

With the proper use of fingers and arms, the bridge and the joints of the fingers will, over time, become stronger, making it easier to hold a moderate curve. To make it easier to play and to produce a good tone, the arm must be positioned behind the finger that is playing. That finger must be strong enough to support the weight of the arm. While individual use of the fingers is generally not experienced in everyday life, the finger joints strengthen naturally over the years as the hand does other tasks. For this reason, older beginners often are able to hold a firm finger shape better than younger children.

Excessive pressing on the keys after they are played sometimes causes the familiar collapsing of the nail joint. When small finger muscles are used alone (commonly called "finger technique"), it is difficult to play against the resistance of the weight of the key. The key wants to rise, pushing the finger upward. This resistance causes students to push or press the key, engaging the larger muscles that connect the fingers to the elbow. Students should not press, hit, or push the keys, but instead should simply move into the key with help from the arm.

The tone sounds before the bottom of the key is reached. Many students, even advanced ones, press the fingers all the way into the key bed and hold the keys down with excessive tension. This is especially common when playing loud chords or longer durations. Students fail to realize that once the tone is made, only a very small amount of energy is necessary to keep the key down and sustain the tone.

When students play with the whole arm, the teacher should carefully observe that they do not press on the keys. To avoid this tendency, a small amount of downward motion of the whole arm for each finger stroke assists the finger, helps avoid excessive muscular tension, and may eliminate the collapse of the nail joint. Students should move the arm and the finger together in a downward coordinated motion. The arm, hand and finger move downward to depress the keys. When the muscles are instantly released, the finger is raised by the rising of the key and is ready to play again.

The use of imagery and descriptive terms will also help students play fingers, arms, and hands with tension-free motions that are used in everyday life.

- *Swing* the finger downward into the key (to feel the finger playing from the bridge).

- *Lower* the key (to get a controlled soft sound).

- *Ride* the key like an elevator (to feel the weight of the key lifting the finger).

- *Pet*, *pat*, *caress* or *stroke* the key (to encourage soft playing without tension).

- *Tap* the key (for a soft staccato).

- *Sink* into the keys (for a full tone).

- *Fall* onto the keys (to encourage the whole-arm drop).

- *Dive* or *leap* into the keys (to encourage the use of a free arm for an energetic sound).

- *Float* to a new position (to move without tension).

- *Toss* or *flop* the hand to move quickly (to a new position without tension).

Coordination and Independence of Fingers

While the arm, hand and fingers are learning to move efficiently, finger independence, finger dexterity and coordination can also be developed using pieces and exercises. Many pieces employ patterns that require individual fingers to work independently. The patterns are usually not difficult to play, but they may be difficult to coordinate until they are built into the nervous system and stored in the memory. Because these patterns can appear randomly in music, pieces will be easier to learn once many patterns, including those listed below, are stored in the memory :

- five-finger patterns
- selected scales
- selected arpeggios

- elementary etudes
- broken chords
- finger exercises such as Hanon[1]

Developing finger coordination in a gradual and natural way helps prevent non-playing fingers from *flying* in the air. These "flying fingers" can be a common problem for beginners and result in excessive tension in the hand. Playing is efficient when the fingers remain close to the keys.

Good finger dexterity makes it easier to play legato. Once students are playing freely with a coordinated motion of hand and arm, they can be taught to play legato. Students should successfully experience legato with only two keys and then add more notes, one at a time. The coordination of lifting one finger at the exact time another finger is depressing another key can be difficult for young students. Legato playing is exactly like walking—both feet are never in the air at the same time. Students can practice "walking" with two fingers on a table top. When this motion is transferred to the keyboard, the first finger releases a small amount of weight, and the rising of the key lifts the finger as the second finger depresses another key. Feeling the transfer of arm weight from one finger to the other will reinforce the correct technique even further. Short exercises teaching legato playing can precede legato playing in pieces.

---

[1] Charles-Louis Hanon, *The Virtuoso Pianist*.

Finger Independence Aided by Five-Finger Patterns

Exercises that are carefully chosen, presented at the proper time in the right sequence, and monitored for correct physical motions assist in developing technical facility. Scales and scale-like exercises develop independence of fingers and build physical patterns into the nervous system. When students can play all five fingers on consecutive white keys with a good hand shape, other five-finger patterns can be assigned.

Students should build major five-finger patterns by ear. For practicing technique, it is not necessary to teach the construction of the five-finger patterns by discussing half and whole steps. Students whose ears are not well developed can discover the correct notes for patterns that include black keys through trial and error and teacher demonstration. The teacher can play the five-finger pattern correctly while the student plays simultaneously what he/she thinks is correct. Students soon discover the correct notes.

Minor five-finger patterns should also be taught by ear and by rote. Students can learn to describe the difference between the sounds of major or minor five-finger patterns that the teacher plays. Students can learn to play minor patterns by playing the major patterns first, and then altering them by moving the middle finger to the next key to the left. After they can move the middle finger consistently and successfully, they can play the major pattern mentally, alter it to minor mentally, and then play the minor. Once this can be done fluently, major and minor patterns can be drilled in any order.

Five-finger patterns should also be played hand over hand and will be easier if hand-over-hand blocked and broken 5ths have been experienced first. Hand-over-hand exercises help the whole arm move as a unit and help students use the body in relation to the whole keyboard, without sliding from side to side on the bench.

Five-finger patterns can be used to build a wide range of technical skills during the first years of piano lessons and can be used for more difficult technical skills in later years, even after scales have been started. Initially, the patterns should be played hands separately. Teachers should enforce good technical habits while students are playing the patterns.

- ♦ Fingers that are not playing should remain at rest on the keys and not fly into the air.

- ♦ The fingers should play from the bridge and with assistance from a slight downward motion of the arm.

- ♦ The wrist should remain level.

- ♦ Patterns should be played slowly enough that students can kinesthetically feel and visually observe the proper physical motions.

- ♦ Each pattern should be repeated several times without stopping. This repetition will build the motions into the nervous system and make the patterns automatic.

When a good hand position can be maintained (hands separately) without looking at the hands, hands can be played together.

There are many ways to practice five-finger patterns to help avoid mindless repetition, including the following:

- non-legato, staccato and legato

- one hand staccato, one hand legato

- loud and soft

- crescendo ascending, decrescendo descending

- one hand loud, one hand soft

- using a variety of rhythms, including different rhythms in each hand

- using two-note slurs

HAND INDEPENDENCE

While individual fingers are being trained to play independently, students are also learning to coordinate the two hands through repertoire. Elementary method books usually provide students with incrementally more difficult hand-coordination tasks. Pieces with frequently alternating hands prepare students to play hands together. The first pieces that include hands-together playing should only have small sections (such as cadences or endings) where hands are played together (see example 9.4 on page 268). Other appropriate pieces have the hands play together with ease in parallel or contrary motion. Students benefit from parallel playing an octave apart because they use different fingers at the same time, yet the task is easier since the notes are the same and move in the same direction (see example 6.3).

Example 6.3 "Bartók's Study," p. 7 from *Alfred's Premier Piano Course*, Lesson Book 2A, by Alexander, Kowalchyk, Lancaster, McArthur and Mier

For additional hands-together practice, students can double the melody of pieces with the other hand. Later, they can move the RH up an octave and the LH down an octave for additional coordination challenges. Contrapuntal pieces, in which the hands are totally independent, should be delayed until easier independence tasks are mastered.

PLAYING SCALES

Five-finger patterns, chords and exercises will be followed by extensive work with scales during the intermediate levels. At the late-elementary level, students should be assigned exercises that prepare for scales by learning to move the thumb under the hand (see example 6.4) and the fingers 2, 3, and 4 over the thumb.

Example 6.4 Early exercise for crossing the thumb under other fingers and crossing other fingers over the thumb

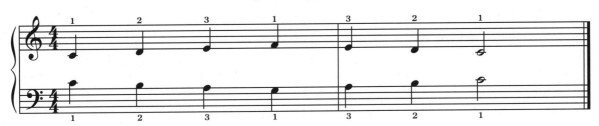

This activity also involves lateral motion of the arm and wrist. When the exercise is played with the RH, the wrist and forearm move slightly to the right to enable the thumb to play F. When the thumb moves back to C, the wrist returns to its natural straight position. When the exercise is played with the LH, the wrist and forearm move slightly to the left, then back. Care must be given to avoid the lifting of the elbow.

In some methods, scales are introduced to elementary students using tetrachords. Many teachers want students to understand the theory behind scales and introduce them in tetrachord fashion prior to learning traditional scale fingering (see example 6.5). Students are taught that each scale consists of two tetrachords separated by a whole step. In major keys, each tetrachord consists of a starting note followed by whole step, whole step, and half step.

Some teachers introduce scales by having students play all the notes in the octave with one hand using traditional fingering complete with thumb turns. When teachers teach C major first, they are teaching the scales for both technical and theoretical reasons:

◆ Students remember these notes more easily since the notes are all white keys.

◆ Many elementary pieces are in the key of C.

In this traditional approach, the C major scale is usually followed by F major and G major (one accidental). This is followed by D major and B-flat major (two accidentals).

When teachers wish to teach scales for strong technical development, they often begin with an F-sharp (G-flat), C-sharp (D-flat) or B major scale. Most often, these scales are taught to elementary students who are older. Students who learn these three scales first (usually by rote) learn the following principles of good scale fingering and good technical habits:

- Fingers 2, 3 and 4 of either hand (the longest fingers) are placed on the sets of three black keys (F-sharp, G-sharp, A-sharp) and fingers 2 and 3 are placed on the sets of two black keys (C-sharp, D-sharp). Since the black keys are farther back on the keyboard, it is logical to use the longest fingers to reach them.

- The thumb—the shortest finger—plays the two white keys of each scale, which are played to the front of the keys.

- The traditional fingering pattern of a group of three fingers followed by a group of four fingers (or vice versa) is learned easily.

Example 6.5 C major scale tetrachords, p. 24 from *Alfred's Basic Piano Library, Lesson Book 2*, by Palmer, Manus and Lethco

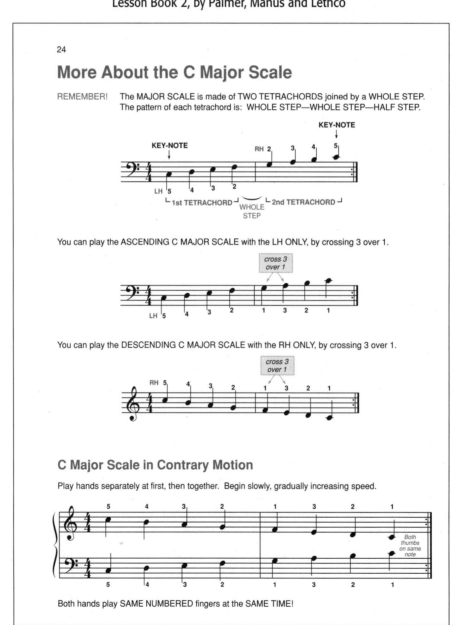

- Finger 4 is used only once per octave.

- The black keys are conveniently used as pivots for the finger turns. The thumb moves easily under the hand since the long fingers are on the higher black keys.

- The position of the hand, forward and backward on the keys, is taught by using both black and white keys.

- Both hands can be learned simultaneously since the fingering for both hands is almost the same (thumbs on white keys together; fingers 2, 3, and 4 on the sets of three black keys together; and fingers 2 and 3 on the sets of two black keys together).

The easiest way to introduce these scales is by rote using tone clusters, hands separately. Students first learn to play only the black keys in clusters (see example 6.6). Next, the thumbs on the white keys are added while the black keys are still played as clusters.

Examples 6.6 An approach to learning the B major scale

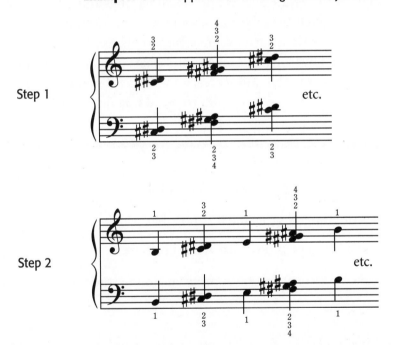

Finally, the notes are played individually, but students should continue to *think* clusters. When the scale is imagined as groups of notes, it flows smoothly, and finger and note errors are reduced. Mnemonic devices such as "two blacks, F, three blacks, C" (D-flat major) can be chanted while the scale is played. If students learn these scales for at least two octaves, the fingering habits that can be applied to all scales will begin to form automatically.

OTHER TECHNICAL SKILLS AND CONCEPTS

Fingering, the development of the left hand, the use of the damper pedal, and consecutive double-notes are skills usually learned through repertoire. Special teaching techniques assist students in learning these more difficult skills.

The Importance of Fingering

As elementary students learn to use printed fingering suggestions and appropriate fingerings for five-finger patterns, chords and scales, they develop a memory bank of fingering patterns, allowing for automatic retrieval when needed. Appropriate fingering makes playing more comfortable and solves technical problems while reducing tension. When students do not observe the written fingerings, they often play pieces with different fingerings every time. This results in several mental etchings of the same musical material, with the mind choosing, at random, a different fingering for each subsequent encounter. Because accurate playing of the piano is a physical habit and no consistent fingering habit has been established, learning of the piece is delayed. Furthermore, poor fingering habits make it more difficult to focus on musical aspects of performance.

Teachers can use several approaches to encourage good fingering or to repair poor fingering. Students can chant the finger numbers of all pieces before playing them, followed by playing while chanting the finger numbers. Teachers can ask students to write finger numbers for every note of selected pieces or "white out" the printed fingerings and ask students to supply their own. The first pieces assigned for fingering should have no options other than correct fingering. Next, students can be assigned to add fingerings to pieces similar to those they have played successfully with printed fingering. If teachers insist that students use the fingerings they have devised (good or bad), students will quickly learn the value of good fingerings. Teachers can direct students to apply the following principles when adding fingering:

- Use longer fingers on black keys (fingers 2, 3 and 4).

- Use shorter fingers on white keys (fingers 1 and 5).

- Finger as many notes as possible in one hand position.

- Use five-finger position fingering as much as possible.

- When possible, use black keys as pivots to a new position.

Since all hands are different, fingering must be appropriate to the student.

The Left Hand

Many students have difficulty playing as easily with the left hand as they do with the right hand. Left-handed pianists may have more physical strength and power in the LH, but their digital facility is often no more fluent than that of right-handed players. Much of piano music emphasizes digital facility for the RH. Generally speaking, RH parts contain more notes and require more complex finger coordination. Furthermore, the ear is more likely to listen to the higher RH melodic material and ignore the LH. When the ear listens only to the RH part, the LH part can suffer both musically and technically.

Teachers can help students develop equal facility in both hands by assigning the following:

- pieces that have equal demands (including melodic material) for both hands

- LH-alone practice for pieces and exercises before hands are played together, even when hands separately practice would not normally be assigned

- LH-alone practice two times for every one time the RH plays alone

- LH doubling (one or two octaves lower) of a dominating RH part

- many pieces and exercises with active LH parts

The Use of Damper Pedal

Young students are motivated by pieces that use the damper pedal, as the pedal allows the strings of the upper harmonics to vibrate, producing a rich sound. Such pieces sound more difficult than they are. Various early-level pieces require the student simply to depress the pedal at the beginning of the piece and lift it at the end. Several basic principles of pedaling can be learned through these early experiences with the damper pedal:

- The heel is kept on the floor while the pedal is depressed with the ball of the foot. The heel remains on the floor while the pedal is held down.

- It takes very little energy to hold the pedal down.

- It is unnecessary to push the pedal all the way to the floor (this prepares students for the various depths of pedaling at later levels).

- Depressing the pedal before the first note is played allows for a sonorous sound by opening the strings to sympathetic vibrations.

- The hands and pedal are lifted simultaneously for a clean ending to the sound.

Once the basics of pedaling are learned, students can be given simple pieces in which the pedal is added for a single section or used sparingly.[2] Pedaling is a listening skill, not a physical one, but a physical motion is needed to create the correct musical sound. Some printed pedal markings may be ambiguous, others are more precise. For first pieces using pedal, it is easier if the depressing and lifting occur simultaneously with specific notes. To develop skillful pedaling, five-finger patterns can be practiced in two-note slurs (see example 6.7), with the pedal depressed exactly with the first note and lifted exactly with the second note.

Example 6.7 Pedaling exercise using two-note slurs

Playing Chords

Young students' hands need to be sufficiently developed before they approach playing chords. A good amount of experience with five-finger patterns and finger independence should be firmly in place. When blocked chords are begun too early, the hand may become tense, with the non-playing fingers flying too far above the keyboard.

Good technique for blocked chords starts with students successfully playing broken chords and blocked 2nds, 3rds, 5ths and 6ths in comfortable ways. Three-note broken triads

---

[2] Syncopated or legato pedaling—a more advanced skill—is beyond the scope of this book.

are typically introduced first. Elementary methods often introduce the **V6/5** and **IV6/4** chords either as two-note intervals of a 6th or as three-note chords.

The three following elementary chords (**I, IV6/4** and **V6/5**) can be played at first by having students play the outside interval (blocked) and then add the middle note (see example 6.8).

Example 6.8 An early approach to playing primary chords in C major

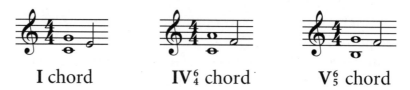

I chord   IV⁶₄ chord   V⁶₅ chord

Both the outside interval and the middle note should be played with a coordinated downward motion of the arm and fingers. Once these can be played with ease, students can begin to play all three notes simultaneously. Students should feel the whole arm dropping into the keys without tension. Exercises for these chord types should be presented several weeks prior to assigning pieces that include the chords. Broken and blocked **V6/5** and **IV6/4** chords can also be practiced hand-over-hand for variety and reinforcement.

Playing Consecutive Non-Legato Double-Notes

Some elementary pieces require students to play consecutive non-legato double notes in one hand. This is a difficult finger-independence skill. Students will be able to achieve this task by using the following succession of steps over several weeks. These steps can also be adapted for the left hand.

1. Play each blocked 3rd several times in a row with each pair of fingers (1-3, 2-4 or 3-5).

2. Play each blocked 3rd three times with a different fingering for each repetition.

3. Play the lower note of three consecutive white-key blocked 3rds with the correct fingering (1, 2, 3).

4. Play the upper note of three consecutive white-key blocked 3rds with the correct fingering (3, 4, 5).

5. Play three consecutive blocked 3rds non-legato (1-3, 2-4, 3-5).

Exercises and Etudes

Exercises and etudes (pieces that focus on one technical or musical skill) help students learn the following:

- dynamics
- articulations
- slurs
- jumps

- chords in root position and inversions
- hand crossings
- simple trill-like patterns

Short exercises and etudes for developing these skills can be found in technique books that are part of a method or printed separately.

MUSICAL SOUND DEVELOPMENT

Musical playing is closely linked to technique. Students who learn pieces only, without technical exercises, will find it difficult to play musically. To achieve the desired sounds, the body must play the keys in specific ways. A thorough technical program that places emphasis on sound production without excessive tension will help ensure musical playing. Proper technical development will aid in producing the following:

- a beautiful tone
- dynamic variety
- legato connections
- a sense of forward motion
- an energetic sound
- phrasing

- articulation and touch
- a steady pulse
- control over tempo
- note groupings
- balance

Tone Quality

A beautiful tone is the primary goal in all music-making. Sometimes, a beautiful tone in keyboard playing is described as bell-like or singing. Poor tone quality can be sluggish, superficial or harsh. Sluggish sounds are caused by a slow attack of the key and occur when notes are not released precisely or overlap with subsequent ones. When students do not use the whole arm to help the fingers when playing softly, superficial sounds are the result. This sound is often identified as "surface playing," implying that the key has not been depressed all the way to the key bed. Superficial sounds can also result from neglecting legato playing and failing to hold notes for their full duration. Harsh sounds result from attacking the key with unnecessary tension or tightness in the arms, hands or fingers. They may occur when students do not understand how to make loud sounds.

It is not simply the touch of the fingers on the keys that results in a beautiful tone, it is the combination of many elements such as the following:

- legato connections
- dynamic shape of the phrase
- attack and release of the key
- balance between the hands
- voicing within one hand
- use of the pedal

Dynamics

The use of dynamic contrast results in interesting and imaginative playing. Students must first be able to distinguish between loud and soft sounds and then learn the correct physical motions for producing a beautiful tone for both loud and soft playing (see pages 145–146). If teachers refer to loud sounds as "full" or "grand" rather than "loud," students are more likely to play with a good solid tone. Soft sounds with a full tone can be achieved by using images such as "floating" into the key or "stroking" the key. A very soft sound can be achieved if students are asked to play the passage silently on the keys first, and then play a second time "a little bit louder."

Once students know how to physically produce loud and soft sounds, they can exaggerate until the appropriate contrast is achieved. Students often think that they are playing more loudly or softly than they really are. To develop a wide range of dynamics, ask students to play a phrase "as softly as you can," then a tiny bit louder, then slightly louder, and even louder still, until they have played ten different dynamic levels. This exercise can be reversed, starting with the loudest the student can play and gradually playing the phrase until it is "as soft as possible."

In addition to the suggestions in chapter 4 on page 94, dynamic contrast and control can be achieved in several other ways:

- by counting pieces aloud with students, using loud and soft vocal levels to help them hear the levels indicated on the score

- by tapping the rhythm with students, using loud and soft taps to build appropriate physical motions

- by saying *piano* or "soft" with a soft voice and *forte* or "loud" with a loud voice, to help students think about the dynamics in pieces

- by recording or using the playback capabilities of electronic pianos or sequencers, to help students hear their own dynamics

- by playing along with students, encouraging them to play more loudly than the teacher

- by modeling dynamics, while playing duet accompaniments with students, to encourage them to play with more dynamic variety

Legato Connections and Forward Motion

The first step in learning to play legato is connecting the sound with the fingers. Beginning students may have difficulty coordinating the legato touch. This task should be delayed until the free-fall approach to the key and a good tone production are mastered (see pages 144–146). For many students, the ability to hear difference between legato and non-legato sounds is all that is needed for them to start producing the correct sound.

Students sometimes have trouble holding the first note long enough and lift it slightly before playing the next note. They should be asked to hold the note until after the second one is played, overlapping the two tones for a moment. This produces a sluggish sound, but is sometimes the only way to help students feel and hear the legato connection. Playing as though the fingers are stuck to keys with peanut butter or glue are images that can help achieve the desired sound.

In more-advanced playing, the illusion of a true legato, as is possible on wind and stringed instruments, can be created on the piano with subtle shadings of dynamics from note to note, creating a sense of forward motion. Students must understand that sound moves forward in time. They can be led to listen to the "moving" of the sound toward the next note. Listening *through* a note, not just its beginning, creates a continuous rich and full tone.

Energy

Energy is an essential element in performance. If a piece requires greater energy, it can be achieved by playing more quickly, more loudly, and/or by adding more articulation. If a piece is already loud and fast, but needs more energy to be effective, a non-legato touch might be applied. If notes are marked staccato and the tempo is fast, it may be necessary to play slightly louder, make the staccatos shorter, or increase the tempo to create the desired spirit. For a piece that requires a relaxed, peaceful, or gentle sound, a softer dynamic level, a slower tempo or a legato touch may be useful.

Phrasing

Musical phrasing can be compared to speech. In speech, the written commas and periods are reflected through pauses, breaths between word phrases, and vocal inflection. When these things are missing, the speaker sounds monotone and the listener becomes bored and ceases to listen. The same thing happens in musical performance. Unless beginnings and endings of phrases are demonstrated and the interior of the phrases shaped with subtle dynamic changes, a performance will be flat and uninteresting to the listener. Before students can do these things, they must be able to identify phrases aurally. Eurhythmic activities, like those found in chapter 8 on page 214 and in chapter 5 on pages 118–120, will help students hear and physically feel phrases.

Although students may be able to hear music phrases during special eurhythmic activities, they may not always be able to identify phrases in their own pieces. Phrase marks are not always notated for elementary pieces. To aid students in finding the phrases, either the teacher or the student can play the piece and the student can listen for the phrases. In many elementary pieces, it is relatively easy to see the phrases on the page, since they often correspond with the lines of music. In the piece "Ping-Pong" (see example 8.21 on page 229), the phrases are not marked, but each of the two lines of music is a phrase. Other indicators are also helpful. In "Ping-Pong," the parts are delineated by blocked 2nds and rests at the end of each line of music. Teachers can help students look for these and other clues that suggest ends and beginnings of phrases. When students can identify parts (phrases) by sight and/or ear, they can be taught to make the phrasing more obvious.

The words that typically accompany beginning-level pieces make sentences that match the phrases in the music. When students sing the lyrics, it helps them feel and hear the phrases. Clapping or tapping the rhythm of a piece while saying or singing the words is also an effective practice step.

To learn the correct physical motions for ending phrases, beginning students should gently lift the wrist up and forward at the end of each phrase. When lifting, the finger tip stays on the key, rolling forward on the pad of the fingertip. The finger is released toward the end of the note value, allowing the music to breathe.

The physical motion of lifting the wrist directly affects the quality of sound for the last note of the phrase. It is important that the lifting not begin until after the key has been depressed (a downward motion). If the lift begins too soon, the tone of the note will be superficial. If the release is too quick, the last note of the phrase may be accented. If the release is too soon, the sound may be choppy. Careful timing of the lifting motion, while keeping the finger on the key, results in a good sound at the end of a phrase.

Simple exercises can be devised to teach students these motions. Students can play a five-finger pattern practicing each note with the lifting motion while saying, "drop-lift, drop-lift," etc. Later, the student can play the whole five-finger pattern with the lift on the last note only—"drop, drop, drop, drop, drop-lift."

Phrasing is also aided by dynamic shaping. The first step in teaching phrase shaping is to make a simple crescendo and decrescendo for every phrase. Teachers can write crescendo and decrescendo markings in a piece for every phrase until the student begins to hear and feel those nuances naturally. Later, students can follow the rise and fall of the pitches in the melodic line and write their own dynamic markings. When this is started early, a habit will develop, and other more subtle expressive devices can be added gradually.

Teachers can also work with students to achieve appropriate vocal inflection of the words for a phrase, and then apply that inflection to playing the music. For example, in the first phrase of "Balloons" (see example 6.9), teachers can speak the phrase in a number of different ways such as:

"**Soar**ing so softly they **smooth**ly sail by."

"Soaring **so** softly **they** smoothly **sail** by."

"Soaring so **soft**ly they smoothly **sail** by."

"Soaring so **soft**ly they **smoothly** sail by."

"**Soar**ing so softly they smoothly sail **by**."

Together, the student and teacher can decide which words should be emphasized to enhance the meaning of the sentence. The first option provides the most musically satisfying inflection. The third and fourth ones might also appeal to the student. Students can then play the chosen options and decide what sounds the best. In music without words, the teacher and student together can devise sentences to match the rhythm of each phrase.

Example 6.9 "Balloons," p. 37 from *Alfred's Basic Piano Library,* Lesson Book 1A,
by Palmer, Manus and Lethco

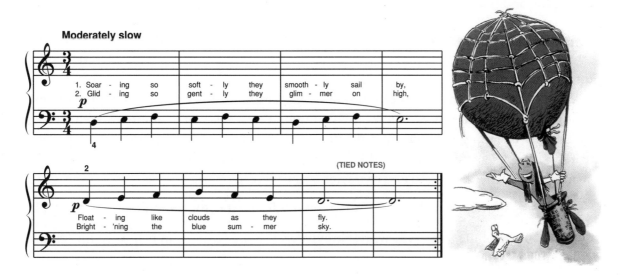

Articulation and Touch

In addition to legato, elementary students learn to play staccato, non-legato, accents and two-note slurs. It is easier to teach all articulations after students have heard them and linked them to a visual image. For example, when the teacher describes staccato as a "bouncing sound," the student has been provided with an image for both the sound and the physical motion. Imaginative titles of pieces often suggest specific articulations.

The character of a piece is enhanced when there is variety in articulation. Following are some ways in which students can hear and feel articulation:

- by moving about the room with motions that demonstrate a variety of articulations (e.g., march, tiptoe, slide)

- by practicing all articulations (staccato, legato, non-legato, two-note slurs, accents) in five-finger patterns and in scales

- by deciding which articulation sounds most appropriate in pieces or phrases when played by the teacher in a variety of ways

- by singing phrases with the appropriate articulation while keeping the character of the piece in mind

- by counting a piece with appropriate vocal articulation

- by tapping a rhythm with the appropriate articulation

- by changing the articulation of the piece to the opposite of the notated articulation, then comparing it to the desired character for the piece

Music in the style of the Classical period, with its simple phrase structure and emphasis on articulation, provides excellent opportunities for late-elementary students to achieve variety in articulation and phrasing.

Tempo and Tempo Control

Slow Playing

Children often are apt to run instead of walk. This natural instinct makes them prone to play music too quickly and out of control. This results in mistakes and interferes with musical playing. By assigning the following practice steps, teachers encourage slower tempos and greater accuracy. These, in turn, are likely to result in careful and efficient learning as well as playing that matches the mood and character of the piece.

- Setting the tempo with pre-counting can result in a starting tempo that is not too fast.

- Counting aloud, especially with subdivisions ("1 & 2 &…"), can help keep the tempo slow and steady.

- Feeling "slow motion" in the whole body by "walking as if you are tired" or "moving like a turtle" will encourage slower playing.

- Playing in "slow motion." This can be fun and result in slow playing.

- Changing the title of a piece to an opposite mood or character. This can result in slower tempos. (For example, a piece about a speedboat can be changed to a piece about a canoe or a sailboat.)

- Focusing on the hand with the longer notes will help slow the tempo.

A musically balanced diet that includes slower pieces with imaginative titles—such as slow-moving animals, balloons, clouds, falling snow, sleeping, and things that glide, float or drift—will encourage expressive, slower playing. If all pieces require fast tempos to be effective, students are unlikely to learn to play slowly.

Fast Playing

As students advance and encounter pieces that require speed, it is sometimes difficult to play up to tempo. The inability to play fast enough can be the result of faulty technique and a misunderstanding about how fast sounds are made. Moving rapidly from one note to the next requires a physical memorization of patterns achieved through slow, careful and repetitive practice. Mistakes are often made because the physical coordination and finger patterns are not solidly memorized.

As students progress into the late-elementary level and beyond, rapid horizontal arm motions become increasingly important to playing fast passages. It is more efficient to use the muscles of the arm when moving up and down the keyboard than trying to play with the fingers alone. Students will find it helpful to experience this motion by playing a glissando. In playing fast passages requiring shifts of position, students can learn to support individual fingers by moving the upper arm horizontally in such a way as to place the arm weight behind the finger that is playing.

Physical tightness also contributes to the inability to play quickly. Locking the knee joints and then trying to walk fast demonstrates how tightness impedes motion. Overemphasis on finger playing causes tension and results in tightness that inhibits quick movement. Once students learn to play scales, arpeggios and other technical exercises using coordinated finger and arm motions, they should have the ability to play quickly with freedom.

Note Groupings

Grouping notes in music is similar to the grouping of words into clauses in sentences. When children begin to read words, they pause between words without fluently connecting them into meaningful ideas. Elementary pianists often play their pieces in the same way, by pausing between notes. Most music progresses in the same way as a story. Each new note or chord has a relationship to what preceded it and each prepares for what comes next. Like grouping words into clauses, note groupings provide forward motion.

Proper grouping is achieved initially by *getting across the bar line*—by not stopping or hesitating at the end of every measure. Young students often group notes by measure because bar lines suggest this visually. One way that teachers can help discourage students from this habit is to suggest that, if a car stopped at every block, it would take a very long time to reach its destination. Students will have improved reading skills and play more fluently as a result of being trained to read music and rhythms in groups of notes (i.e., patterns, such as five-finger groups, scales, triads, chord shapes, and other common patterns), rather than note-by-note.

Balance

Balancing sound between the hands is critical for an overall beautiful sound and lays the foundation for voicing at more advanced levels. Learning to balance loud and soft sounds simultaneously is best achieved when students are assigned pieces that have melody in one hand and accompaniment in the other. Playing one hand loudly and the other hand softly can be difficult since loud and soft sounds are produced by different physical motions. This can be especially difficult when the LH has the melody. For students to develop skills in balanced playing, they can apply the following steps when learning new pieces:

1. Hands separately, play each hand at the correct dynamic level. Feel the hand with the accompaniment move slowly into the keys and the hand with the melody move quickly into the keys.

2. Hands together, play the hand with the melody at the correct dynamic level, and play the hand with the accompaniment silently.

3. Hands together, play the hand with the melody at the correct dynamic level, and play the hand with the accompaniment "so you can barely hear it," rather than silently.

4. Hands together, play the hand with the accompaniment using detached articulation, and play the hand with the melody as written. By playing the accompaniment hand in this manner or silently, that hand will feel different than the other in a way similar to when each hand is playing at a different dynamic level.

5. Hands together, play the melody as written, and block (play the chord tones together) the accompaniment notes in the other hand to reduce the frequency of notes. This helps avoid overpowering the melody with the accompaniment.

6. Hands together, concentrate on the melody, and play the accompaniment by letting the kinesthetic memory guide the fingers "on automatic."

Students should experience these steps in five-finger-pattern exercises first, and then apply them to their pieces.

SUMMARY

To be able to play elementary pieces and to prepare for intermediate repertoire, students must learn to play with technical ease.

* Students should learn to use all of the playing mechanism—the body, arms, hands and fingers—in the most natural way.

* When beginning students use the whole arm to play before they play with individual fingers, they play with less tension.

* Using the whole arm and linking the desired sound to the correct motions enable students to play loudly, softly, non-legato, staccato and two-note slurs.

- Correct hand position can be observed by looking at the hands when the arms and hands are hanging naturally by the side of the body.

- The correct hand position aids the student with appropriate finger motions.

- Students can learn what it looks and feels like to use each finger correctly.

- Playing with individual fingers involves a coordinated downward motion of the fingers and the arm.

- When students learn to feel the correct motions for various physical tasks at the keyboard, they will be able to reproduce those motions and use them with ease whenever needed.

- To avoid tension and bad physical habits, the hand should be kept in a five-finger position for a sufficient period of time.

- Chords can produce tension and, for young beginners, should be delayed until the hand has been developed adequately.

- Students can learn the foundations of basic pedaling skills during the elementary levels.

- Simple exercises and etudes help elementary students learn a variety of valuable technical skills.

- Carefully selected pieces and scales help develop hand independence.

- Scales teach both technical and theoretical principles. Tetrachords can be useful to introduce elementary students to both playing and understanding scales.

- Technical development is promoted when C-sharp, F-sharp and B major scales are taught before other keys due to the relationship of the hand to the black-key and white-key patterns.

- Learning exercises with appropriate fingerings and pieces with minimal (but essential) fingering suggestions facilitates learning and reduces technical problems.

- Systematic learning steps will help build a left hand that is strong and capable.

- Teachers can learn effective ways to teach students to produce a beautiful tone, legato touch, and phrasing.

- Students can be taught to play their pieces with energy, to play in a variety of controlled tempos, and to balance the sound of melody and accompaniment.

PROJECTS FOR NEW TEACHERS

1. Write six different rhythm patterns that elementary students can use to practice ascending and descending five-finger patterns. Use a variety of meters and arrange them in progressive order of difficulty.

2. Find five elementary pieces that expand the physical range of the hand to a 6th. Each piece should be appropriate to assign to a second-year student to add fingering.

3. From several elementary methods, select a progressive series of six elementary pieces in which the majority of the melodic material is for the left hand.

PROJECTS FOR EXPERIENCED TEACHERS

1. Peruse several elementary technique books and select a series of exercises that will help students learn to play legato during their first few months of lessons.

2. Peruse several elementary technique books and select a series of contrary-motion exercises for students. Arrange the exercises in progressive order from the most simple to the most difficult.

3. Find five elementary pieces, one for each of the following techniques, that would help students develop technically in those areas.

    ◆ octave position moves

    ◆ hand-over-hand playing

    ◆ staccato

    ◆ chordal playing

    ◆ left-hand melodic line

Chapter 7
ELEMENTARY PERFORMANCE AND STUDY REPERTOIRE

Students reinforce musical concepts, master skills, learn to play musically and have enjoyable experiences through playing pieces. Because music is central to learning, teachers can combine repertoire and other materials in a way that provides a complete learning experience. There is a wealth of available teaching material to add variety to assignments, recitals, competitions, festivals and auditions. With such diversity, it is not necessary to always assign a music book page by page or use the same material for all students. In addition, teachers are responsible for determining difficulties in pieces, teaching those pieces in ways that minimize the difficulties, devising lesson plans, and crafting assignments to promote optimal learning.

KNOWING THE TEACHING LITERATURE

In many studios, students learn and practice new concepts and skills using pieces in their method books. However, most students also need additional music for reinforcement and motivation. Teachers should be acquainted with the standard literature and other supplementary materials, and be able to choose the very best pieces from what is available.

Standard Literature

Standard literature can be found in collections of pieces by one composer and in anthologies of several different composers from one style period or from several time periods. At the elementary level, there is only a minimal amount of standard literature from past centuries. Therefore, collections of pieces by one composer often include more than one level of difficulty. Pieces in anthologies are more likely to be graded to include music by different composers at the same level of difficulty.

Baroque Period

There are only a few pieces by composers from the Baroque period that can be taught to elementary students. Even the easier pieces from the *Notebook* (Clavier-Büchlein) *for Anna Magdalena Bach* and the *Notebook for Wilhelm Friedemann Bach* may be too difficult for some students. The easiest pieces from these notebooks include the following:

• *Applicatio in C Major* (BWV 994) *Notebook for Wilhelm Friedemann Bach*	• *Chorale "Joy and Peace"* (BWV 512) *Notebook for Anna Magdalena Bach*
• *March in D Major* (BWV Anh. 122) *Notebook for Anna Magdalena Bach*	• *March in E-flat Major* (BWV Anh. 127) *Notebook for Anna Magdalena Bach*
• *Menuet in G Minor* (BWV Anh. 115) *Notebook for Anna Magdalena Bach*	• *Menuet in G Major* (BWV Anh. 114) *Notebook for Anna Magdalena Bach*
• *Musette in D Major* (BWV Anh. 126) *Notebook for Anna Magdalena Bach*	• *Polonaise in F Major* (BWV Anh. 117a) *Notebook for Anna Magdalena Bach*

A number of other Baroque composers wrote easier pieces than those that appear in the Bach notebooks. The following composers wrote a limited number of elementary-level pieces:

- Barrett, John (ca. 1676–1719)

- Clarke, Jeremiah (ca.1674–1707)

- Corelli, Arcangelo (1653–1713)

- Couperin, François (1668–1733)

- Dandrieu, Jean–François (ca. 1682–1738)

- Duncombe, William (1690–1769)

- Handel, George Frideric (1685–1759)

- Krieger, Johann (1651–1735)

- Praetorius, Michael (1571–1621)

- Purcell, Henry (1659–1695)

- Rameau, Jean–Philippe (1683–1764)

- Scarlatti, Alessandro (1660–1725)

- Scarlatti, Domenico (1685–1757)

- Telemann, Georg Philipp (1681–1767)

- Witthauer, Johann Georg (1751–1802)

Classical Period

From the Classical period, there are more pieces available that are appropriate for elementary students. Some Classical composers wrote pedagogical collections that include some pieces appropriate for today's elementary students:

- Czerny, Carl (1791–1857). *First Instruction in Piano Playing* and *100 Recreations*

- Diabelli, Anton (1781–1858). *10 Short Pieces,* Op. 125

- Hässler, Johann Wilhelm (1747–1822). *Fifty Pieces for Beginners,* Op. 38 and *Der Tonkreis*

- Mozart, Leopold (1719–1787). *The London Notebook* and small pieces written and collected into notebooks for Wolfgang and Nannerl

- Reinagle, Alexander (1756–1809). *24 Short and Easy Pieces*

- Türk, Daniel Gottlob (1750–1813). *Handstücke für Angehende Klavierspieler*

Many of these collections are no longer available in their complete forms, but some of the pieces from them are often included in anthologies for elementary students. Teachers can also find easier movements of sonatinas in sonatina collections. Other important composers from the Classical period who wrote for elementary students include the following:

- André, Johann Anton (1775–1842)
- Arnold, Samuel (1740–1802)
- Beethoven, Ludwig van (1770–1827)
- Clementi, Muzio (1752–1832)
- Haslinger, Tobias (1787–1842)
- Haydn, Franz Joseph (1732–1809)
- Hook, James (1746–1827)
- Hummel, Johann Nepomuk (1778–1837)
- Mozart, Wolfgang Amadeus (1756–1791)
- Neefe, Christian Gottlob (1748–1798)

Romantic Period

The Romantic period saw an enormous development of the mechanisms of the piano. As a result, music was composed to display the piano's virtuosic capabilities. Major composers, such as Chopin and Brahms, wrote no music for elementary students. However, the piano began to appear in homes and more people wanted to learn to play. The demand for music to teach these students resulted in new collections of pedagogical works, such as those that follow. Each of these collections contains some elementary literature. Many of these pieces can be found in anthologies of 19th-century piano music.

- Berens, Hermann (1826–1880) *50 Piano Pieces for Beginners*, Op. 70
- Beyer, Ferdinand (1803–1863) *Preparatory School*, Op. 101
- Gurlitt, Cornelius (1820–1901) *The First Lessons*, Op. 117, *Album for the Young*, Op. 140, *Little Flowers*, Op. 205, *The First Steps of the Young Pianist*, Op. 82, *Grateful Tasks*, Op. 102
- Köhler, Louis (1820–1886) *The Very Easiest Studies*, Op. 190 and *Children's Exercises and Melodies*, Op. 218
- Lynes, Frank (1858–1913) *Four Analytical Sonatinas*, Op. 39
- Oesten, Theodor (1813–1870) *Mayflowers*, Op. 61
- Schumann, Robert (1810–1856) *Album for the Young*, Op. 68
- Schytte, Ludwig (1848–1909) *25 Melodious Studies*, Op. 108
- Spindler, Fritz (1817–1905) *Sonatinas*, Op. 157
- Streabbog, Jean Louis (1835–1886) *12 Melodious Pieces*, Book 1, Op. 63

Twentieth Century

In the 20th century, Dmitri Kabalevsky (1904–1987) and Béla Bartók (1881–1945) stand out in their dedication to the composition of pedagogical pieces. Both composed a large body of advanced works for a wide variety of genres and performance mediums. In addition, they composed numerous pieces for young pianists. Bartók's six progressive volumes entitled *Mikrokosmos* provide study and performance material for elementary through advanced levels based on folk materials and contemporary styles. The two volumes, *For Children,* are another example of Bartók's pedagogical output. Kabalevsky was a master at composing appealing pieces that teach a specific skill in a simple way without sounding like etudes. Many of these pieces can be found in *24 Pieces for Children,* Op. 39 and *Children's Pieces,* Op. 27.

In addition to these two composers, others have composed interesting elementary teaching repertoire using 20th-century idioms. Some of these composers were also teachers and composed pieces expressly to meet the needs of their students.

- Finney, Ross Lee (1906–1997)
- Goedicke, Alexander (1877–1957)
- Gretchaninoff, Alexander (1864–1956)
- Kodály, Zoltán (1882–1967)
- Persichetti, Vincent (1915–1987)
- Rebikov, Vladimir (1866–1920)
- Shostakovich, Dmitri (1906–1975)
- Siegmeister, Elie (1909–1991)
- Smit, Leo (1921–1999)
- Starer, Robert (1924–2001)
- Stevens, Halsey (1908–1989)
- Tansman, Alexandre (1897–1986)
- Tcherepnin, Alexander (1899–1977)
- Toch, Ernest (1887–1964)

Pedagogical Literature

Pedagogical composers from the 20th and 21st centuries typically draw upon extensive teaching experience to compose for young students. While some have formal training in composition, others are teachers who began writing for their own students in a variety of styles, including those of other centuries. They frequently affiliate with a publisher to produce a vast library of teaching materials to meet the needs of a variety of students. Some of the more prominent at this time include the following:

Dennis Alexander (b. 1947)	Glenda Austin (b. 1951)	Melody Bober (b. 1955)
Jon George (1944–1982)	William Gillock (1917–1993)	David Carr Glover (1925–1988)
Margaret Goldston (1932–2003)	Randall Hartsell (b. 1949)	David Karp (b. 1940)
David Kraehenbuehl (1923–1997)	Martha Mier (b. 1936)	Walter and Carol Noona (b. 1932 and b. 1935)
Kevin Olson (b. 1970)	Lynn Freeman Olson (1938–1987)	John Robert Poe (1926–2004)
Catherine Rollin (b. 1952)	Wynn–Anne Rossi (b. 1956)	Robert Vandall (b. 1944)

New pedagogical music continues to be written by both well-known and new composers. Teachers can learn about what is currently available and become aware of new literature by attending conventions, perusing publishers' catalogs, reading new music reviews in professional journals, and through the internet.

Selecting and Evaluating Teaching Materials

In addition to the pieces in the method book, elementary students will learn supplementary pieces. These pieces will be assigned from the following:

- easy standard literature
- collections or anthologies of pieces by various pedagogical composers in varied music styles of the 17th through 21st centuries
- solo collections and sheet music solos by individual pedagogical composers
- collections of solo pieces that are part of a method-book series
- anthologies that include pieces at roughly the same level of difficulty, by several different composers, from one time period, or from several time periods
- collections of familiar or popular songs, hymns, folk songs, and holiday music, simplified and arranged for the elementary student
- collections of pieces for other musical mediums, such as orchestra or chamber music, simplified and arranged for solo piano

With the vast amount of music available for today's students, teachers can apply specific standards to help evaluate and select the most appropriate music for their students. There are five primary ways to measure the pedagogical value of a piece. Even though most pieces will not meet all the standards, only those pieces that meet a significant number of the following criteria should be taught:

1. Pieces should sound appealing to students so that they will want to practice and play them long after they have been learned. Students enjoy pieces that sound like music they have previously heard. Much of this music is in popular or familiar styles and may include simple arrangements of familiar classical music themes. Students like pieces that sound big, exciting and showy, and that sound harder than they are to play. These pieces may be loud, fast, use the pedal, and have several notes sounding simultaneously during part of the piece. Students also like pieces that are singable. They are less likely to enjoy pieces that are too musically complex or overly dissonant.

2. A piece should sound like its title. The notes, rhythm and expression marks should be composed in a way that musically matches the title and lyrics. Many beginning pieces include lyrics that elaborate on the title. These lyrics help develop the ear through singing. They also help students understand the concept of phrasing. Lyrics may also encourage students to play more imaginatively.

The music should be able to stand alone without the lyrics. Pieces with different titles and subject matters should not sound the same. If a piece is titled "Sailing," it should sound quiet and smooth. It is not enough to have a picture, title and lyrics about a sailboat and assume students will be able to make the piece sound like sailing.

The following two pieces are composed in ways that stir the imagination. In "The Windmill" by Margaret Goldston (see example 7.1) the soft ascending and descending arpeggiated pattern musically describes the sound and motion of a turning windmill. The LH starts the piece in the treble register of the piano, suggesting a windmill high in the air. The LH crossing over the RH even imitates the circling motion of the windmill.

"Slippery, Slimery, Slithery Snake" by Dennis Alexander (see example 7.2) is simple enough to be taught by rote to students in their first year of lessons. The long, soft, legato, scalar lines, shared between the hands, depict a long, slithering snake. The lines wind from the bass clef into the treble, depicting the snake sneaking through the grass and winding around branches. The juxtaposition of black and white key groups makes a sinister sound.

Pieces with generic titles, such as "Study," make it difficult to evoke images that encourage musical playing. While it is frequently necessary to teach studies, sonatinas or variations, these pieces must appeal musically to students to be effective teaching pieces. It is the teacher's job to make pieces interesting for students when titles are generic or not understood by students. Teachers can make pieces come alive by creating stories or adding lyrics to match the musical material. It is not always possible to find pieces that sound like their titles, but teachers should make every effort to choose methods and supplementary materials that include pieces like "The Windmill" and "Slippery, Slimery, Slithery Snake." Furthermore, teachers should avoid pieces with imaginative titles if the subject matter lacks appeal for young students. For example, pieces with titles like "Dirge" may not appeal to young piano students.

3. Pieces should be of the best quality, free of musical clichés, be surprisingly unpredictable, and have sufficient variety to keep the student and teacher interested in study and practice. Because elementary pieces often must have a limited number of notes, a few rhythmic values, a moderate tempo and minimal dynamic markings, it is sometimes

Example 7.1 "The Windmill" (Excerpt), p. 2 from *Travelin' Fingers, Book Two,* by Margaret Goldston

Example 7.2 "Slippery, Slimery, Slithery Snake" (Excerpt), p. 10 from *Animal Magic,* by Dennis Alexander

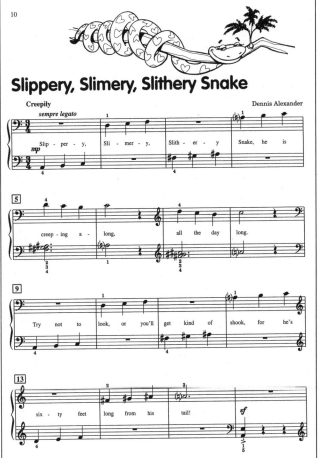

difficult to compose pieces that are imaginative and free of musical cliché. Many pieces rely on tonic, dominant and subdominant harmonies; regular meters such as $\frac{3}{4}$ and $\frac{4}{4}$; and RH melody with common LH accompaniment patterns. These can make pieces sound alike and may bore students with their predictable sounds. Teachers must be sure that chords sound complete, that dissonances have been resolved correctly and that there is a good balance between repetition and variety.

Fortunately, there are numerous pieces that display variety and demonstrate that the composer understands musical and developmental needs of students. The following are characteristics that can contribute to making pieces interesting:

- ♦ melodies divided between the hands

- ♦ melodies in the LH

- ♦ unexpected articulations, textures, notes, and harmonies

- ♦ five-finger positions that are neither major or minor

- ♦ creative accompaniment patterns

- use of the whole keyboard

- variety of phrase lengths

- unusual meters

- use of the pedal

"Wind Chimes" (see example 7.3), a piece that uses unusual scale fragments that include whole-tone patterns, provides an example of sounds that are less familiar but still appealing. The use of D-flat/F against the LH C/G ostinato presents an unusual sound. Interest is also provided by the unpredictability and variety of each phrase ending.

The first two sections (mm. 1–16) of "Lion in a Cage" (see mm. 1–14 in example 7.4) show musical quality in an economical and pedagogical way. In the A section, the tonic D minor triad in the RH alternates with an augmented sixth chord, which finally resolves to the dominant triad in m. 4. The use of the augmented sixth chord provides harmonic interest not often found in elementary pieces. In the LH of the B section (beginning at m. 9), the lion "roars" with slow submediant and tonic rolled chords in different octaves with pedal. The moves from one chord to the next in both sections are relatively easy with the RH remaining quiet.

Example 7.3 "Wind Chimes" (Excerpt), p.16 from *Diversions,* by Elvina Pearce

Example 7.4 "Lion in a Cage" (Excerpt), p.4 from *Circus Suite* by Catherine Rollin

4. The level of difficulty of the piece should be consistent throughout and appropriate for the level intended. Students will progress more successfully if each piece is the same level of difficulty throughout. It is discouraging to study a piece that has one or two measures or sections that are harder than the remainder of the piece. A familiar, intermediate-level example of such a piece is Beethoven's "Für Elise." This charming and appealing piece, so loved by students, contains two sections that are more difficult than the remainder of the piece. In the familiar A section, the hands rarely play together. Each hand plays one note at a time in continuous 16th notes. However, the B section involves hands playing together and more difficult rhythms, including 32nd notes. In the C section, the LH plays an ostinato accompaniment, while the RH plays a chordal melody, ending with a 16th-note triplet passage. Balance is also a challenge in the C section. These B and C sections are much more difficult than the A section. While early-intermediate students can play the A section with little difficulty, the B and C sections are at an intermediate to late-intermediate level.

5. Each piece should have a clear and unique pedagogical purpose. Elementary pieces should focus on only one or two technical or musical difficulties and should be chosen to meet a specific pedagogical need. Students should have a variety of pieces to learn, each of which teaches something different, as opposed to studying several pieces that drill the same concept or skill. One piece might be filled with staccatos, another might have a melody in the LH and a chordal accompaniment in the RH, and a third might feature a wide variety of rhythmic values. When a piece requires attention to the technique and sound of staccatos, it should not include other difficulties, such as balancing melody and accompaniment, or complex rhythms.

In *Etude*, (see example 7.5) the LH must project the melody over the RH's continuously repeated blocked intervals. The rhythm patterns are straightforward, consisting of only eighth, quarter and half notes. The key signature contains only one flat and there are few accidentals. Expression markings are minimal and the coordination between the hands is simple. Students are free to concentrate on what should be the goals of the piece—voicing and tonal control.

Example 7.5 "Etude" (Excerpt), p. 98 from *Essential Keyboard Repertoire*, Vol. 1, edited by Lynn Freeman Olson

In addition to the above five criteria, teachers should also consider the following when evaluating and choosing pieces for their students:

- The score should look easy to read.

- Sufficient and logical fingerings should be given.

- Whenever possible, pieces should sound harder than they actually are to play.

- Pieces that feel comfortable to play are more satisfying than those that are physically awkward.

- Pieces which include repetition, imitation and sequences are easier to learn and play.

- It is difficult to hear correct notes, rhythm, legato connections or balance between melody and accompaniment when pieces require too much pedal.

- Teachers should ask themselves whether they would like to teach the piece and which of their students would benefit from it.

A comparison of "The Chase" (see example 7.6) and "Fanfare Minuet" (see example 7.7) will show how these criteria can be applied.

"The Chase" uses two-note slurs, followed by rests, to imitate the sound and feel of galloping horses. The rising broken 4ths sound like hunting horns. Students enjoy the exciting sound and relate to the image of the hunt. They learn to play two-note slurs, broken second-inversion triads (mm. 5–6), broken root-position seventh chords in the RH (mm. 13–14), and blocked root-position seventh chords in the LH (mm. 21–22, 29–30). The rhythms are easy and repeated throughout. The rests give the hands time to reposition for the hand shapes that are slightly larger than five-finger positions. The hands play together only on strong beats and the LH has only three different chords or intervals. The piece is in the key of C major and there are no accidentals. The second half of the piece is subtly changed to provide contrast with the first half. This skilled writing allows students to concentrate on the two-note slurs, the dynamic changes and the tempo. When the piece is up-to-tempo, it will sound harder than it actually is. Most of the listed criteria are met, making this an excellent teaching piece for late-elementary students.

In "Fanfare Minuet" (see example 7.7) the opening rhythm pattern ♩ ♫♫♩, the ascending notes outlining a C major triad pattern, and the f dynamic create a fanfare sound. Such characteristics make the music exciting and sound more difficult than it actually is. The overall structure is ABA. The RH of the B section (mm. 9–16) provides contrast to the A sections. It is composed of delightful two-measure patterns that move down stepwise in a sequence of repeated blocked 3rds and a scalar pattern. The repeated two-measure pattern (mm. 9–10) teaches students about sequences and makes the piece easier to learn and memorize. In mm. 1–3, and again in mm. 17–19, the coordination between the hands is easy since the LH plays only one blocked interval on count one of each measure. In the B section (mm. 9, 11, 13, 15), the LH plays three quarter notes against the RH pattern. However, the RH repeats the same notes in each measure, making the coordination between the hands less difficult. During mm. 10, 12 and 14 the coordination is made easier by eliminating the LH on the beats where

Example 7.6 "The Chase, Op. 117, No. 15" by Cornelius Gurlitt, p. 19 from *First Favorite Classics,* Solo Book 1, by E. L. Lancaster and Kenon D. Renfrow

Example 7.7
"Fanfare Minuet" by William Duncombe, p. 40 from *Essential Keyboard Repertoire,* Vol. 1, edited by Lynn Freeman Olson

the RH notes change. Reading difficulties are also minimized by the C major key signature and the lack of accidentals.

The piece has many good features, but mm. 5–7 and mm. 21–23 make the piece unnecessarily difficult. In these measures, both hands are equally busy with note-against-note texture. In the RH of m. 7 and 23, beats 2–3 are difficult to coordinate and the required legato with fingers 5-4-3-4 adds to the difficulty. The teacher may want to teach this piece to a stronger student due to the difficulties.

DETERMINING THE DIFFICULTY OF PIECES

Teachers should choose pieces that use concepts and skills taught in beginning, elementary and late-elementary methods. Knowing what students are capable of doing at all stages of development helps teachers recognize the difficulty level of pieces. Teachers must also be able to evaluate the technical, musical, and reading characteristics of each piece.

Technical Characteristics

How many changes of hand position are there?	If there are frequent hand position changes, the piece will be more technically difficult.
How quickly must the changes of hand position be made?	If the hand-position changes are during rests or after longer notes, the piece will be easier.
How often do the hands play together?	A piece in which hands play together much of the time will be more difficult technically than if the hands alternate and play together only occasionally.
How many notes are played at once?	When many notes are played simultaneously, the piece is more difficult to read and play.
How much of the keyboard is used?	When much of the keyboard is used, the piece is more difficult.
What is the tempo requirement?	Faster pieces are usually more difficult to play than moderate or slow pieces.
How often does the thumb pass under the hand or the fingers pass over the thumb?	The more the thumb passes under the hand or the fingers cross over the thumb, the more difficult the piece.
If the pedal is required, how frequent are the changes?	The piece is more difficult if there are frequent changes of pedal.

Musical Characteristics

Are there many dynamic markings?	Pieces with a large number of dynamic markings are more difficult to read and play.
Are there many articulation markings?	The more articulation markings, the more difficult the piece is to play.
Is legato playing required?	Legato playing is more difficult than staccato or non-legato articulation.
Are there phrases that need to be shaped?	Shaping phrases requires more physical control.
Do the melody and accompaniment need to be balanced?	Playing the melody more loudly than the accompaniment can be difficult.

Reading Characteristics

How often does the direction of the melody change from going up to going down?	Changes of direction within patterns make the piece more difficult to read and play.
How many large intervals are there?	Larger intervals are more difficult to read and play than smaller intervals.
How often do the note values change?	Pieces that use only a few note values and have mostly the same note values throughout are easier to learn.
How many notes must be read at once?	The more notes there are vertically, the more difficult the music is to read.
Has the student used the pitch and/or rhythm patterns before?	A piece with familiar pitch and/or rhythm patterns is easier to read and play.
Are the pitch or rhythm patterns the same or similar throughout the piece?	A piece with a few identical or similar pitch and/or rhythm patterns is easier to learn than a piece with patterns that are all different.
How often do the pitch and/or rhythm patterns change?	When new pitch and/or rhythm patterns are introduced infrequently, the piece is easier to read and play.
How many sharps or flats are in the key signature?	The greater the number of sharps or flats in the key signature, the more difficult the piece is to learn.
How many accidentals are there?	A large number of accidentals makes a piece more difficult to read.
Are there many ledger-line notes?	The more ledger-line notes, the more difficult the reading will be.
Are there any clef changes or reading from the same clef?	Clef changes or reading from the same clef make the piece harder to read.

Some pieces may be easy to play technically, but are difficult to learn due to reading challenges. Furthermore, one passage that is more difficult than the rest of the piece complicates the learning.

By comparing the last two pieces in *Alfred's Basic Piano Library*, Lesson Book 1B, one can begin to recognize potential challenges and learn to evaluate the overall difficulty of pieces more proficiently (see examples 7.8 and 7.9).

Example 7.8 "When Our Band Goes Marching By!" p. 46 from *Alfred's Basic Piano Library,* Lesson Book 1B, by Palmer, Manus and Lethco.

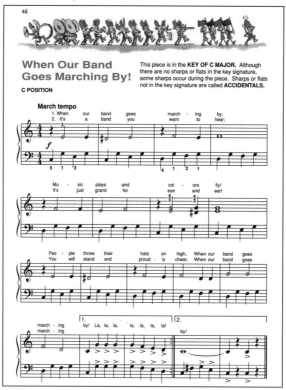

Example 7.9 "Sonatina," pp. 44–45 from *Alfred's Basic Piano Library,* Lesson Book 1B, by Palmer, Manus and Lethco.

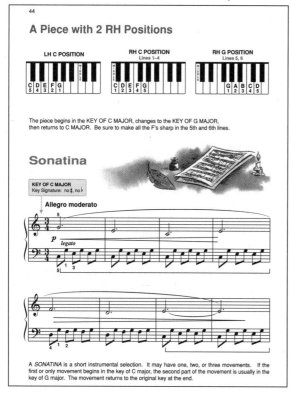

Technical Characteristics

"When Our Band Goes Marching By!"	"Sonatina"
two Alberti-bass patterns (see m. 1 and m. 3)	two Alberti-bass patterns in the A section, and RH patterns combining eighth notes and quarter notes in the B section
Hands play together once or twice per measure (often on weak beats) but play parallel quarter notes in the first ending.	hands play together on beat 1 of each measure throughout
rhythm consists of quarter and half notes	many eighth notes, combined with dotted half and quarter notes
no hand-position changes	two hand-position changes
melodic changes of direction at least every two measures	frequent melodic changes of direction throughout
note values change almost every other measure	note values change approximately once each measure in the B section
two-note harmonic intervals in one hand occur three times	two-note harmonic intervals in one hand occur four times
range is approximately 1½ octaves	range is a little more than two octaves.
March tempo	*Allegro moderato* tempo

"Sonatina" requires a relatively fast tempo, uses faster note values, has two position moves, but has relatively easy hands-together requirements. "When Our Band Goes Marching By!" requires the hands to play together frequently, often on weak beats. This creates coordination challenges, making it more technically difficult than "Sonatina".

Musical Characteristics

"When Our Band Goes Marching By!"	"Sonatina"
one dynamic marking (m. 1)	four-measure crescendos and decrescendos in the A section
accent marks (first and second ending)	no articulation marks
no pedaling	four simple pedal indications
melody in the RH and Alberti-bass accompaniment in the LH	the A section has melody in the RH with a LH Alberti-bass accompaniment; B section has two-note harmonic intervals and single-note accompaniment
non-legato touch	long legato phrases

The relatively fast tempo, the pedaling, the long crescendos and decrescendos, and the long legato melodic phrases coupled with the required balance between the melody and the accompaniment make "Sonatina" more difficult musically than "When Our Band Goes Marching By!"

Reading Characteristics

"When Our Band Goes Marching By!"	"Sonatina"
LH has continuous quarters and RH has five different two-measure rhythm patterns: (1) mm. 1–2 (2) mm. 3–4 (3) mm. 13–14 with pick-up notes (4) mm. 15–16 (5) mm. 17–18	RH has continuous dotted half notes in the A section, and two different two-measure rhythm patterns in the B section; LH has continuous eighth notes in the A section, and mostly dotted half notes in the B section
RH has five different note patterns: (1) mm. 1–2 (2) mm. 3–4 (3) mm. 7–8 (4) 12–14 (5) mm. 15–16	RH has three different two-measure note patterns in the B section: (1) mm. 17–18 (2) mm. 19–20 (3) mm. 23–24
LH has four different note patterns: (1) m. 1 (2) m. 3 (3) mm. 15–16 (4) mm. 17–18	LH has two different note patterns in the A section: (1) m. 1 (2) m. 5
C major key signature	C major key signature for the A section and G major for the B section
mostly consists of quarter notes, quarter rests and half notes	consists of dotted half, eighth and quarter notes
no clef changes	no clef changes
hands usually play together twice per measure, with three closely related two-note harmonic intervals in the RH (mm. 7–8)	hands play together on beat 1 of each measure; LH has four identical harmonic 3rds in the B section
Both hands remain in C major five-finger position throughout	C major five-finger position in the A section; RH moves up to G major five-finger position in the B section
Two accidentals—D-sharp and F-sharp	One accidental—F-natural

In "Sonatina," the key change with F-sharp in the key signature of the B section poses a reading challenge. In "When Our Band Goes Marching By!," the syncopation, reading three notes simultaneously in mm. 7 and 8, and the frequency with which students must read notes in both hands simultaneously make the reading more difficult than in "Sonatina."

In summary, the two pieces share many common characteristics. Each has some features that are easy and some that are more difficult. "Sonatina" is more difficult musically, but easier to read and only moderately difficult to play. In contrast, "When Our Band Goes Marching By!" is easier musically, but more difficult to read and play.

ORGANIZING PIECES IN THE PROPER TEACHING ORDER

When choosing pieces, it is necessary for teachers to determine the teaching order of pieces so that students can progress incrementally. Even books that have been composed for a specific level will have pieces with varying degrees of difficulty. When arranging the pieces in a teaching order, the pedagogical features of each piece should be noted for further reference. In the solo collection *Performing in Style,* Dennis Alexander composed 11 pieces in Baroque, Classical, Romantic and 20th-Century styles for late-elementary and early-intermediate students. The pieces are arranged by style period and not in teaching order. Although all five Baroque-style pieces might not be taught to one student, a teacher should know which pieces are the easiest and which are the most difficult. As an example, these five pieces are listed here in a suggested teaching order, and pedagogical features are described.

"Prelude in G Major" (see example 7.10). Each phrase of the RH (with the exception of the last phrase on each page) stays within a five-finger position and the hand position shifts are close. The LH is significantly easier than the RH, but has thumb turns and uses the entire scale. The hands generally play together only once or twice per measure. Containing staccato and legato touches, and one mordent (the easiest ornament to play), this piece is appropriate for late-elementary students.

Example 7.10 "Prelude in G Major," pp. 4–5 from *Performing in Style,* by Dennis Alexander

"**Sarabande**" (see example 7.11). The RH has scalar passagework, with fingers crossing over the thumb, and intervals up to an octave. The LH has three-note chords in root position and first inversion, some of which are rolled. There is some imitation and note-against-note texture. One turn, a more difficult ornament than a mordent, is included. This piece is therefore more difficult than the *Prelude* but is still appropriate for late-elementary students.

"**March in D Major**" (see example 7.12). Each phrase of the RH stays within a five-finger position, but the register changes between the phrases must be made quickly. The LH plays a duet with the RH part of the time and accompanies it the rest of the time. There are clef changes to consider. The texture is largely note-against-note with some of it resembling counterpoint rather than parallel motion or mirrored motion with the melody. The staccatos, *Allegro energico* tempo and the required technical precision make this piece somewhat more difficult than the previous two pieces and, therefore, appropriate for early-intermediate students.

"**Air in D Minor**" (see example 7.13). The RH melody moves in a range of an octave and a half, with thumb turns, finger crossings, large intervals and position changes. The LH has mostly blocked intervals and plays with the RH twice per measure or in note-against-note texture. This piece has trills and a turn, both of which are more difficult than mordents. The three-part texture, legato, and expressive requirements make this piece more difficult than the previous three, but still appropriate for early-intermediate students.

Example 7.11 "Sarabande," p. 3 from *Performing in Style,* by Dennis Alexander

Example 7.12 "March in D Major" (Excerpt), p. 8 from *Performing in Style,* by Dennis Alexander

"Entrée" (see example 7.14). Both hands are equally busy and require greater hand independence than the previous pieces. The hands have scalar passages, position shifts and intervals up to an octave. The *Allegro* tempo makes this piece appropriate for progressing early-intermediate students.

Example 7.13 "Air in D Minor," p. 10 from *Performing in Style*, by Dennis Alexander

Example 7.14 "Entrée" (Excerpt), p. 6 from *Performing in Style*, by Dennis Alexander

PREPARING PIECE SUMMARIES

Excellent teaching materials are no guarantee that students will learn. Conversely, the poorest of materials can come alive in the hands of creative and inspirational teachers. To assure incremental development, some teachers limit their teaching to a carefully chosen and systematically sequenced body of pieces. They know every piece in this progression and can teach it efficiently. This careful approach to selecting repertoire is admirable, but limited. Teachers should avoid confining themselves only to pieces they have studied or taught previously. However, they do need to understand the teaching features and challenges in each new piece and be able to play it.

Before teaching a piece, teachers should identify musical, reading or technical challenges and prepare a piece summary, which lists activities that provide a clear and efficient way to present the piece. By studying the score, and reading and playing the piece, teachers can identify the following:

- problems moving from one system (line) to the next

- new or unusual elements, including elements which may be new to students at the grade level of the piece

- musically or technically complex spots

- unexpected changes of register, or position, direction, texture, key, rhythm, intervals, finger or fingering

- other places where the student might hesitate

Example 7.15 "Melodic Tune," Op. 218, No. 20 by Louis Köhler, p. 6 from *Masterwork Classics,* Levels 1–2, edited by Jane Magrath

For Louis Köhler's "Melodic Tune," Op. 218, No. 20 (see example 7.15), teachers can observe the following:

- In the LH of m. 5, the note pattern changes. Students must notice the change and understand how the pattern changes.

- In the RH of m. 5, there is a change of finger for the note C. Students must make that change to prepare for the remainder of the notes in line 2.

- In the RH of m. 9, finger 3 returns to play B. This line is an exact repetition of mm. 1–4 but at a different dynamic level.

- In m. 13, the LH note pattern changes from a triad pattern to a 3rd, followed by a 2nd. Students must notice the change or understand how the pattern changes.

- In mm. 13–14, the RH note pattern is a 2nd, followed by a 3rd. Simultaneously, the LH note pattern is a 3rd, followed by a 2nd. In both hands, most of the previous patterns have been made of 3rds. Moreover, the hands play in contrary motion and use different fingers simultaneously.

Once the challenges in a piece have been identified, the teacher should develop a piece summary, similar to the following:

"Melodic Tune," Op. 218, No. 20, by Louis Köhler

- Ask the student to compare all the LH measures, then play them by grouping the notes into chords (blocking).

- Ask the student to observe the finger change for the two RH C's in m. 5, and circle the notes and finger numbers.

- Ask the student to observe the finger change for the RH B's in mm. 7 and 9, and circle the notes and finger numbers.

- Ask the student to play the RH, saying the finger numbers aloud.

- Ask the student to compare the hands of mm. 13 and 14, play each hand separately saying the intervals and then the finger numbers, and finally play the hands together.

With each new piece, a summary can be written so that each time the piece is taught, the teacher has a clear and efficient way to present it. These summaries define essential preparatory steps and assure efficient and effective lessons. They also help the teacher choose the teaching order based on the technical and musical requirements.

The following chart shows teachers how to prepare piece summaries in an easy-to-follow outline form that can become part of the lesson plan. Summaries can be written using incomplete sentences and the teacher's own shorthand to save time.

"Melodic Tune"

Measure Numbers	What to Do	Problem or Observation
All LH mm.	Compare each m. to the next by playing each m. as a blocked chord.	m. 4–5—top two notes move up m. 6–7—top two notes move down m. 12–13—bottom two notes move up m. 14–16/17—bottom two notes move down
m. 5 (RH)	Circle RH notes and finger numbers. Play.	Finger 4 changes to finger 3 for same note
mm. 7, 9 (RH)	Write finger 2 for m. 7 RH note B. Circle RH notes and finger numbers of mm. 7 and 9. Play all RH notes and say finger numbers.	Finger 2 changes to finger 3 for same note
mm. 13–14	Compare the RH to the LH. Play RH saying intervals. Play LH saying intervals. Play RH saying finger numbers. Play LH saying finger numbers. Play hands together (HT).	RH plays a 2nd to a 3rd going down. LH plays 3rd to 2nd going up.

LESSON PLANNING

Once the curriculum for a student has been outlined, the teacher can plan week-to-week lessons. Just as university professors organize lectures, ministers outline sermons, and public school teachers prepare plans that organize the day's activities, piano teachers should plan what to teach in each lesson and how it will be taught.

A good lesson is one in which learning takes place, not one in which students impress teachers by how well they practiced or how well they can play pieces. This is not to suggest that students should not practice, but valuable learning about the piano and music can take place in the lesson even when the student has not practiced. Effective lessons have four positive results:

- ◆ The student can do or understand something better than before.

- ◆ The student is led to make judgments using their ears.

- The student learns how to practice effectively at home.

- The student is motivated to practice.

Teachers must learn how to develop lesson plans based on the piece summaries and learn how to present and prepare new pieces systematically for practice at home. They also need to know how to work on the student's practiced pieces, be able to diagnose and solve problems that occur in practiced pieces, achieve musical results and, finally, craft homework assignments.

A lesson plan brings focus to the lesson and assures learning, progress and accomplishment. Teachers should not be afraid to alter the lesson plan when the student has practiced more or less than expected or has trouble with the assignment. The lesson plan provides structure so the teacher can confidently provide a valuable learning experience, regardless of the variables.

While it may not always be possible, teachers should make every effort to include the following at every lesson:

- a variety of activities that drill various aspects of music and piano learning, including technique, rhythm, keyboard and written theory (musical understanding), creative activities (such as harmonization, improvisation, and composition), musical coaching and interpretation, ensemble playing, ear-training, reading, transposition and memory

- new ideas, concepts, and skills that will be encountered in the future

- learning experiences that prepare the student for home practice

- sufficient reinforcement (follow-through) to ensure that the student understands new concepts and skills, and can apply them during practice at home

Effective lessons are easy to construct when long-term and short-term goals are clear. For example, a long-term goal in technique might be to play all major five-finger patterns, hands together, two notes to the beat, with the metronome at $\quarternote = 60$, while keeping the fingers touching the keys. Each week, the teacher prepares a lesson plan that includes incremental steps to accomplish that goal. If the student has not practiced sufficiently for the next step, the teacher can simply review the previous technical step and save the new material for the next lesson.

Teachers should keep a notebook with long-term and short-term goals, notes about each lesson, and other information about each student. For example, a notation that one student loves soccer and needs to wear glasses to read properly, provides information that is easy to forget if the teacher has a large number of students. Students may arrive at the lesson without the assignment book and music. The teacher's notebook eliminates the need to rely on the student's assignment book. Likewise, teachers should keep their own library of books for such occasions.

A weekly log, written during and after each lesson, provides the teacher with a summary of what was accomplished and with details necessary for preparing the next lesson plan. A typical teacher's log (in shorthand) might look like the following:

long nails, need to cut

B scale HS – smooth thumb

trouble ID Maj./min.

Bach Minuet near finish–
need new Baroque

Those notes tell the teacher the following about the student:

- he/she was reminded to cut the fingernails

- he/she is working hands separately (HS) on a smooth thumb motion in the B major

- he/she is having difficulty identifying (ID) the difference between major and minor scales, so aural drills are needed

- he/she needs a new Baroque piece, to be chosen prior to the next lesson

Based on the notes in the log, the teacher can prepare an effective lesson plan. The best time to plan the next lesson is soon after a lesson has ended (if possible) so that information will be fresh in the teacher's mind.

For efficiency, teachers can use their own shorthand system and devise a new lesson plan that might look like the following examples (all are followed by a descriptive explanation of the abbreviations used).

Card No. 1

1. CHECK NAILS!

2. Hear B scale HS–check thumb–
   staccato–legato–HT

3. Begin E scale – HT contrary motion

Card No. 2

4. Intro. Duncombe "Fanfare Minuet"

T. Play

S. find phrases, ID same/different

S. find triads

S. play HS/HT mm. 4-6, 7-8   RH mm. 9, 11, 13, 15

T. play select mm. (1-3, 5, 9)

Card No. 3

5. T. play maj/min SFP triads,
   melodies–S. ID maj/min

6. Bach Minuet–articulation, test memory

When the teacher glances briefly at such an abbreviated lesson plan, he/she will be reminded of the following:

- If the thumb turns of the B major scale are fluent, the student can practice the scale with a staccato articulation, hands separately (HS), and then legato, hands together (HT).

- The E major scale can be learned hands together in contrary motion.

- For the new Baroque piece, "Fanfare Minuet" (see example 7.7), the teacher (T.) plays the piece for the student and the student (S.) will find all the phrases and identify those that are the same or different; find all the broken triads; play mm. 4–6 and 7–8, hands separately and then hands together; play the RH of mm. 9, 11, 13, and 15.

- The student will identify specific measures by listening to mm. 1–3, 5, and 9 of the "Fanfare Minuet" as the teacher plays them at random.

- The student will identify as major or minor: five-finger patterns (5FP), blocked and broken triads, and fragments of major and minor melodies that the teacher plays.

- The articulation of the Bach Minuet will be coached and the memory tested.

Detailed lesson planning is essential for new and less-experienced teachers. As teachers become more experienced, less-detailed lesson plans may be used for private lessons. Detailed lesson plans for new students, beginning students, and group lessons always help make teaching more efficient.

DEVELOPING A LESSON PLAN USING ONE PIANO SOLO

Teachers can use piece summaries to devise lesson plans. Lesson plans can be developed using a body of materials (see pages 99–115 in chapter 4) or using only one piece in which all of the concepts, skills and experiences listed on pages 97–98 are included to make a balanced and holistic lesson. A lesson based on one piece can be especially productive when the student has had little practice, but needs a new piece. The sample lesson that follows includes activities that serve more than one purpose and prepare the student to practice and learn the piece at home.

For "Melodic Tune" (see example 7.15), the following 30- to 45-minute complete lesson could be planned.

Lesson Plan for "Melodic Tune," Op. 218, No. 20 by Louis Köhler

The teacher (T.) plays the LH of lines 1 and 2 and asks the student (S.) if the two lines are the same or different. ***Ear Development***

T. plays the LH of line two and asks S. to look at the LH of lines 1 and 2, and tell which line is being played. ***Ear Development, Reading***

S. plays the LH notes of m. 1 as written and then all three notes together as a chord and identifies the chord. ***Reading, Technique, Musical Understanding***

S. studies the LH of the first three lines and finds all measures that are the same. ***Musical Understanding, Reading***

S. finds the two LH measures in the first three lines that are different from the others (mm. 5–6) and plays them as written and blocked. ***Musical Understanding, Reading***

S. plays the LH of mm. 1 and 5 and compares them, telling how they are different. ***Musical Understanding, Reading***

S. writes the LH of mm. 1 and 5 as chords on manuscript paper and then writes them in the key of C major. ***Written Theory, Transposition***

S. studies the LH of mm. 1–12, plays them by memory, and then transposes them to the key of C major. ***Reading, Memory, Transposition***

T. plays the lines of the RH randomly and asks S. to tell which line was played. Lines 1 and 3 are identical, except for the dynamics. After each line is played, S. is asked to play it. ***Reading, Ear Development***

S. plays the LH of mm. 1–8 and T. works with the hand position to achieve a soft, smooth accompaniment. ***Technique, Musical Playing***

S. plays the LH of mm. 1–12 and T. plays the RH. Parts are then reversed. ***Ensemble***

S. plays the RH of mm. 1–4 and mm. 9–12, legato, following the dynamics, while singing the counting. ***Musical Playing, Rhythm***

S. compares m. 13 to m. 14 and then plays RH alone, LH alone, and HT. ***Reading, Technique***

S. plays the last two measures, HT and identifies what chord is being played. ***Reading, Musical Understanding***

S. blocks the LH of mm. 1–4 and T. improvises a melody in the G major five-finger pattern over the chords. ***Ensemble***

T. blocks the LH of mm. 1–4 and S. improvises a melody in the G major five-finger pattern over the chords. ***Creative Experience (improvisation)***

T. transposes the LH to C major and S. improvises the melody using the C major five-finger pattern. ***Transposition, Creative Experience (improvisation)***

As a result of this lesson, the student was prepared for new concepts and skills. Each drill was presented thoroughly and there was sufficient reinforcement, as a result of practice in the lesson, to ensure effective and successful practice at home. In addition, the student experienced ear development, reading, theory (keyboard and written), transposition, rhythm, technical development, musical playing, ensemble, and creative activities.

PRESENTING NEW PIECES

The lesson piece summaries and lesson plan can be used to present a new piece. A systematic presentation of a new piece includes the following:

- the teacher playing the piece to give the student a sound image (unless the student is likely to learn the piece by ear alone)

- the student playing and singing the tonic chord and five-finger pattern or scale

- the student looking at the music and describing what he/she sees

- the student marking patterns, sections, and finding measures or sections that are the same or similar

- the student observing the relationship of the RH and LH

Teachers can assist with this process by asking carefully worded questions that are short, specific, and thought provoking. Such questions might include the following:

- Did you notice any rests in the piece?

- How many pairs of eighth notes are there?

- What does this symbol mean?

- Where are the measures that are the same?

- Did you hear any staccato sounds?

- What are the things that make this piece easy?

- Do the hands ever do the same thing?

- Why is this measure more difficult?

- How would you count this measure?

- What do you think would be the best way to practice this measure?

- How would you finger this measure?

These types of questions link the aural and visual, help to prevent errors, aid in memory and aesthetic growth, and can suggest practice approaches such as the following:

- blocking

- playing in slow motion

- practicing creative exercises developed to facilitate the learning of more difficult sections

- studying, analyzing and playing short segments by memory to provide confidence for practice and learning

Finally, when returning to the sound image, musical considerations such as phrasing and dynamics can be explored.

Students learn faster when they are assigned additional pieces containing similar note and rhythm patterns and the same technical and musical demands as those explored in the lesson. Teachers can choose pieces by the same composer or pieces by various composers that share similar characteristics with the piece that was explored in the lesson. Some of these pieces can be assigned for independent learning following the procedures used in the lesson. If elementary students are learning pieces accurately, it is unnecessary to perfect and polish all of them. A select few can be reassigned as potential performance pieces while more new pieces are assigned. If elementary students are required to practice the same pieces over and over for several weeks, the joy of music-making can easily be lost.

DIAGNOSING PROBLEMS IN PIECES

Regardless of how carefully pieces are presented, problems can occur. The lesson should include time to diagnose, solve and work on problems in practiced pieces. Teachers might begin with one of several approaches:

- The student asks the teacher to help solve a problem spot.

- The teacher asks the student to play the most difficult section(s) of a piece.

- The student demonstrates how he/she practiced at home.

- The student experiences an exercise or drill to prepare for a subsequent learning task.

- The student summarizes what was learned in the previous week's practice.

Active teaching includes quickly diagnosing mistakes or problems and applying strategies for solving them. Furthermore, teachers should help students understand why mistakes are made, showing them how the diagnosis and solution were achieved. When similar mistakes are made in other pieces, teachers should assist students in diagnosing and solving the problems themselves. Only then will students learn how to solve problems independently. Simply correcting mistakes often results in the same types of mistakes returning week after week. When a student makes a mistake, the teacher can quickly decide whether a correct response was intended and then determine what might be interfering with the correct response. Mistakes are often the result of a physical problem. The following provides an example of how a teacher might deal with such a problem.

When a student misses a black-key sharp, it may be because the black key is physically difficult to reach. It might be because the black key needs to be played by a finger that would normally play a different key. If either of these issues caused the problem, the teacher can provide technical assistance, helping the student use the hands, fingers and arms more efficiently. If the mistake was not the result of a technical problem, the teacher must find out why the student missed the sharp. There are at least three nontechnical reasons why students fail to play sharps:

- The key signature or accidental was not observed.

- It was not understood that the specific note was affected by the key signature.

- The student did not aurally detect the mistake.

If the student did not observe the key signature or if the student did not realize that the specific note was affected by the key signature, the teacher must review how key signatures affect the playing of pieces. If the student does not hear that the piece sounds incorrect without the sharp, the teacher can present an aural development activity that will help the student hear when notes are correct.

In some cases, the hand that makes a mistake may not be the cause of the problem. For example, the RH may have a difficult, large leap while the LH has a progression of chords. Some of the notes of the LH chords may be missed and the teacher may erroneously assume that the student does not know the LH notes. The student may continue to focus on the difficult RH leap even after the leap is secure. Even though the student knows the correct notes of the LH, all of the attention is still focused on the RH and the LH has not yet become automatic. The problem can be corrected if focus is shifted to the LH.

A stumble may be the result of something that precedes it. For example, if a student misses the second note of a leap, simply focusing on the missed note will rarely correct it. Feeling and practicing the distance of the leap will assure an accurate playing of the second note.

WORKING ON PRACTICED PIECES

Lesson time also includes efficient work on practiced pieces. When hearing practiced pieces, teachers may gather more information by hearing selected sections, phrases or measures, instead of hearing the entire piece. Students can usually tell the teacher where they are having problems in the piece and whether they are ready to play the entire piece without stopping. Short segments can show the teacher whether the student has grasped important issues and whether the playing has improved during the previous week. Frequent and brief interactions between teacher and student reduce the learning time. When a problem is evident, it should be analyzed and worked on until the student feels confident. It is simply not enough to suggest that the student needs more practice.

When hearing a complete piece, it is best for the teacher to stop and work on problems as they occur. The focus should be on difficult parts and reducing problem spots to small, manageable tasks presented in a logical sequence. Students may not be able to change their playing instantly, so all problems may not be resolved during the lesson. The teacher's role is to work on the problems in the lesson and help students plan an effective follow-up practice procedure for the week.

When students stumble, it is most productive to repeat the phrase with specific goals for the repetitions. A specific practice procedure must be developed for each problem spot and the student should try the procedure in the lesson. New assignments must clearly reflect these goals. Repetitions should simplify the task, and the difficulty level of each subsequent repetition should increase slightly as the following series of practice steps suggests:

1. hands separately

2. hands separately, counting aloud

3. hands together, slowly

4. hands together, with a louder dynamic

5. hands together, slightly faster

Sometimes students become discouraged when they are stopped frequently. Teachers must be aware of such frustration and learn that there are times when pieces should be played straight through, regardless of problems. A positive approach is to ask students to start the lesson by playing through their best piece.

COACHING PIECES

Coaching is the process by which a piece is taken beyond notes and rhythms, focusing on interpretive elements. Through coaching, students begin to play musically and the music comes alive for both the performer and the audience. Coaching is an important part of lessons at all levels, but it should never constitute the entire lesson except in the most advanced teaching.

Because coaching is fun for the teacher, it is easy to let coaching consume a major portion of the lesson. When this occurs, conceptual learning may stop and elements of preparation and presentation may be neglected. Conversely, it is also easy for teachers to neglect coaching altogether. With some students, specifically younger ones, teachers may be satisfied with correct rhythm and notes, fearing that students will become bored and discouraged if greater demands are made. Taking pieces beyond notes and rhythm will build musical playing from the first lessons.

Coaching should also involve the discovery process. Questions such as the following lead students to think, solve problems, and discover interpretive information on their own.

- Do you think this piece will sound better played quickly or slowly?

- Does this section sound better when the RH plays more loudly or when the LH plays more loudly?

- Where do you think the phrase ends?

- What is the mood and how can you achieve that mood?

Students who have undeveloped musical tastes will need to learn what musical elements should be enhanced. Others may know the sounds they want, but need help in learning how to achieve them. Demonstrating the sound and physical motion and telling students what to do are efficient ways to achieve the desired musical result.

ASSIGNING HOMEWORK

Work on each piece should end with a summary of what has been learned and the goals for the practice week. To ensure effective practice, a detailed assignment is needed that gives the student important information specific to each piece as follows:

- how many times to play it

- what spots or sections to practice

- what practice steps to use

- what musical elements to include

- whether or not to memorize

Basic information for assignments can be written in an assignment book, with practice details written in the margins of the student's music. Each set of instructions can be dated so that students will know the goals for each week's review pieces.

It is time-consuming but effective to ask students of all levels to write notes on the music page and to write their own assignments, throughout the lesson. This process helps students remember instructions and leads to more creative assignment procedures.

The following assignment for "Melodic Tune" (see example 7.15 on page 204) reinforces what the student learned in the lesson and guides his/her practice. Such a written assignment may seem overly lengthy and tedious, but it is provided to illustrate the importance of detailed and specific assignments.

Assignment for "Melodic Tune," Op. 218, No. 20, by Louis Köhler
(See example 7.15 on page 188)

1. Play the (LH) G major triad blocked and broken.

2. mm. 1–4:
   Play the LH of mm. 1–4.
   Play and count (preferably sing) the RH—make the melody sing.
   Play and count m. 1 HT two times.
   Play and count m. 2 HT two times.
   Play and count mm. 3–4 HT two times.
   Play mm. 1–4 HT two times—make the RH louder than the LH.

3. mm. 5–8:
   Play LH of mm. 5–6.
   Play and count (preferably sing) the RH mm. 5–8—make the melody sing.
   Play and count m. 5 HT two times, watch the RH fingering.
   Play and count m. 6 HT two times.
   Play and count mm. 7–8 HT two times.
   Play mm. 5–8 HT—make the RH louder than the LH.

4. mm. 1–12:
   Play the LH of mm. 1–12—keep it smooth and follow the dynamics.
   Transpose the LH to the key of C major.
   Play mm. 1–12 HT two times—follow the dynamics and make the RH louder than the LH.

5. mm. 13–16:
   Play m. 13 RH.
   Play m. 13 LH.
   Play m. 13 HT four times.
   Play mm. 15–16 HT.
   Play mm. 13–16 HT four times.

SUMMARY

Students reinforce their understanding of musical concepts, master skills, learn to play musically, and gain enjoyment by playing piano pieces. From the wealth of pedagogical music available today, teachers can learn to select pieces that are appropriate and appealing at every level of study. They can also learn how to evaluate the difficulty of pieces, place them in an appropriate order for teaching, plan how to teach them effectively, and prepare assignments for learning them.

- To select the best music, teachers should be knowledgeable with the composers and standard pedagogical literature for all musical time periods.

- In addition to pieces found in method books, teachers will select supplementary pieces for their students from a large variety of sources.

- Pieces that are selected for study should sound appealing so that students will be motivated to practice and perform them.

- The musical content of pieces should contribute to the image implied by the title.

- Pieces should have variety, be of the best musical quality and contain elements of unpredictability.

- Each piece should have a consistent level of difficulty and a clear pedagogical purpose.

- The music score should be easy to read and include sufficient (and logical) fingering.

- Pieces that sound more difficult than they actually are, make excellent choices for students.

- Various technical and musical characteristics must be considered when evaluating the difficulty of individual pieces of music.

- The frequency and variety of both pitch and rhythm patterns; the key signature(s); and the number of accidentals, clef changes and ledger-line notes contributes to the reading difficulty of a piece.

- Teachers can arrange pieces in a proper teaching order by observing the unique characteristics and difficulties of each piece and knowing a common progression for student achievement.

- Prepared summaries that detail characteristics and difficulties of pieces help teachers develop a clear and efficient way to present and teach them.

- Lesson planning based on piece summaries (and activity summaries) assures learning, progress and accomplishment. These teacher-generated summaries include efficient ways to present the pieces or activities.

- Effective lessons include a variety of activities, reinforcement of learned concepts, and the presentation of new materials to prepare students for home practice.

- Lessons can be planned around one piece or can include several pieces and activities.

- Singing, listening, playing "questions and answers," observation and discovery are some of the creative ways pieces can be presented to students.

- Every lesson should include time to diagnose, work on, and solve problems in practiced pieces.

- A portion of every lesson should focus on the musical aspects of playing.

PROJECTS FOR NEW TEACHERS

1. Choose two pieces that are near each other in an elementary or late-elementary book of a beginning method.

   a) Describe the technical, musical and reading characteristics of each piece by using the criteria listed in this chapter on pages 180–181.

   b) Compare the difficulties and determine how each piece is more or less difficult than the other.

2. Choose three elementary pieces by different composers. Each piece should be of a different style and character. Play and evaluate the quality of each based on the five criteria listed in this chapter on pages 174–177.

   - Describe characteristics that make it sound appealing.

   - Make a list of the characteristics that the title suggests. Describe how these characteristics are portrayed in the music.

   - List characteristics that describe the quality of the music.

   - Find the most difficult places in the score. Is the difficulty level relatively consistent throughout the piece?

   - List the pedagogical purpose(s) of the piece.

3. Choose three pieces from a late-elementary book of supplementary music.

   a) List the technical, musical and reading characteristics of each piece (see pages 180–181).

   b) Based on the above characteristics, determine the teaching order for the three pieces from the easiest to the most difficult (for an example, see pages 185–187).

PROJECTS FOR EXPERIENCED TEACHERS

1. Choose one elementary piece and develop a complete 30-minute lesson plan based on it. Use the sample lesson plan on page 194 as a guide. The lesson should include activities in all the categories listed in the middle of page 191. List the category (or categories) that each activity reinforces. Prepare an assignment that will help students successfully practice the piece (for an example, see page 200).

2. Choose three late-elementary pieces from a method book.
   a) List the potential learning problems for each. Consider the following categories of potential difficulties:
      - ornamentation
      - hands-together coordination
      - the variety of rhythmic complexities
      - changes (see pages 95–96)
      - the number of notes stacked vertically
      - the frequency, distance and speed of position shifts
      - range of pitches
      - amount and variety of articulation
      - number of new concepts or skills
      - thumb turns
      - note-against-note texture
      - key changes
      - accidentals
      - clef changes
   b) For each piece, prepare a piece summary which includes a solution for each problem, similar to that found on pages 189–190.

Chapter 8
DEVELOPING MUSICALITY IN ELEMENTARY STUDENTS

Some students have an innate musical sense and naturally play musically, while others achieve only correct notes and rhythm on their own. Still others enjoy displaying their technical skills without demonstrating an interest in playing musically. For the more innate students, the teacher's job is to make them aware of their musical instincts so they can use them effectively. For those who do not play musically, it is the teacher's job to teach and develop musicality.

Even elementary students can communicate musically. A vital first step is to help students learn to produce a musical, expressive sound and to solve technical difficulties that might interfere with musical communication. It is that which lies beyond correct notes and rhythm that makes music come alive. Some pieces may not be perfected or polished to a performance level, but from the very first lesson, teachers can make sure that all pieces are played musically in some way. One piece might be reassigned for a faster tempo, another for a louder dynamic, a third made more exciting with greater variety in articulation, and still another piece may be made more musical by adding the pedal.

In addition to learning and playing repertoire pieces, there are many other experiences that contribute to musical playing. Students can become musical in their playing as follows:

- by discovering that music communicates a mood or emotion and creates a character or personality in sound

- by learning how to listen to their own playing

- by understanding the construction of the music (music literacy or theory)

- by creating their own music

- by playing in ensembles

THE ROLE OF MOOD, EMOTION AND CHARACTER

In addition to developing the technical skills necessary for producing a good sound at the piano, students must associate mood, emotion and/or character with each piece as a critical element in achieving a musical performance. A good performance tells a story or paints a picture. Teachers can coach a musical performance, giving suggestions about interpretation, musical style and expression, but students must understand mood, emotion, and character for performances to become more than programmed perfection.

In the early stages of learning, understanding the composer's musical intent begins with imagery. In "Giant Vines Growing" (see example 8.1), the first three lines move from the low register of the piano to the high register. The last line also moves from a very low C to a very high C. This movement on the keyboard represents the growing of the vine from a seed in the ground to a very tall plant. The dynamics which begin with *mp* and reach *ff* by the end of the third line characterize the large size of the plant.

When pieces are approached through the imagination, musical playing is encouraged as a result of that image.

Example 8.1 "Giant Vines Growing," p. 15 from *A Day in the Jungle*, by Jon George

Many beginning pieces are very simple so the teacher must *sell* the sound of the pieces to students. "A Secret" (see example 8.2) uses only two different notes for the whole piece and consists almost entirely of quarter notes. Students will play more musically if teachers draw from the students' experiences with secrets (from the known to the unknown). The following questions can stimulate the student's imagination and make the piece more interesting:

- Do you speak loudly or whisper when telling a secret?

- Do you get close to a person's ear when you tell a secret?

- Is it fun to tell secrets?

- To whom do you like to tell secrets?

- Do you feel special when someone tells you a secret?

Example 8.2 "A Secret," p. 14 from *The Music Tree: Time to Begin,* by Clark, Goss and Holland

This simple piece will come to life through such questions. Students might play the piece more softly and keep the fingers very close to the keys because they can imagine themselves telling or hearing a secret.

To show that they love the sound of music, no matter how simple, and to encourage that same love and excitement in students, teachers can offer enthusiastic comments about pieces:

- "I just love this piece."

- "This is my favorite piece in this book."

- "Doesn't this piece sound exciting?"

- "I think this piece sounds just like a beautiful, peaceful summer day."

It is sometimes difficult to evoke an image with pieces that have generic titles such as sonatina, variation or suite. When the title of a piece is a character/tempo indication such as *Allegro, Andante*, or *Adagio*, for example, teachers can initiate a discussion about the composer's intentions for the mood. Students are more likely to pinpoint the music's character if they develop a large repertory of descriptive words for the mood, emotion, or character. Instead of limiting the definition of *Allegro* to "lively," students can be led to use words such as joyful, bright, cheerful, excited, radiant, ecstatic, jovial, or festive. Each piece exhibits characteristics that suggest its own special descriptive word or words. Once a word is chosen, then a story might unfold. If "jovial" seems to be the best descriptive word for a piece of music with a generic title, additional words and images, such as jolly, party, dancing, or cheering, help lead students to an explicit image.

Teachers can prepare a list of descriptive nouns, adjectives and verbs, such as those that follow, to help students develop a variety of touches, interpret the dynamics, or feel the phrases.

busy	dizzy	joyful	sarcastic	spin
bustling	dragging	mocking	scampering	stroke
caress	fearsome	pet	smudge	teasing
crackle	float	powerful	snap	terrifying
crash	foggy	prancing	sneaky	tornado
cushion	grand	questioning	sparkly	warm

Here are some other ways a teacher might capture the imagination of students:

- Describe a piece as a rubber band that stretches with tension and eases back.
- Ask students to iron phrases to get the wrinkles out.
- Ask students to play as if picking up a feather, to get a delicate sound.
- Ask students to push on the key as if it were made of rubber, to get a full sound.
- Make up words or sentences for musical phrases.
- Make up a story about a piece.
- Ask students to move to a piece, as the teacher plays it.

THE ROLE OF AURAL DEVELOPMENT

The ability to listen critically to one's own playing is the single most important skill needed for creating a beautiful sound and developing musical playing. Music is *heard* and goes beyond what is seen on the page and what is physically accomplished at the keyboard.

The primary purpose of ear development is to help students listen to and judge their own playing for accuracy, musical content and quality of sound. When students hear and listen to musical elements, they are more likely to observe those things and play them accurately. Ear development promotes inner hearing, which directs physical motions, thereby teaching students to hear inwardly and play what they see. When students develop *audiation* (to hear and comprehend music in the mind[1]), they become good readers and independent learners. They then know when they are playing the correct pitches and rhythms and are able to detect their own errors. Too often, teachers focus on technical proficiency, or precision and perfection,

---

[1] Gordon Institute for Music Learning.< http://www.giml.org >

erroneously thinking that musical playing will result. When students listen, precision and perfection are positive by-products. Other advantages include the ability to create beautiful sounds, artistic playing, and the ability to learn music quickly and accurately.

Therefore, beginning a lesson with activities that "tune-up the ears" seems as logical as beginning the lesson with technical exercises or hearing a practiced piece. Such ear-training activities direct the student to hear accurately what is being learned. Systematic and regular aural experiences ensure that this skill develops in a continuous fashion.

Playing by Ear

When students play familiar songs by ear, they are learning to develop the ear in the most natural way. Students must know the melody for songs they will play by ear. When teachers assign familiar songs for student to play by ear, students need to be told the following:

- where to begin

- the first interval

- which keys they will use to play the song

At first, the easiest songs are those that can be played entirely on black keys. Later, these songs can be transposed to the white keys. Such pieces (and their starting pitches) include "Old MacDonald Had a Farm" (F-sharp), "Hot Cross Buns" (B-flat), "Mary Had a Little Lamb" (B-flat) and "The Farmer in the Dell" (C-sharp).

Next, familiar songs that stay within the five-finger position can be played by ear. These would include "When the Saints Go Marching In," "Ode to Joy" (from Beethoven's *Ninth Symphony*) and "Jingle Bells" (chorus). After students have learned the entire scale, they can play songs with a wider melodic range. Some students may not be able to play the complete song at first. These students can be asked to play only missing measures rather than the entire melody. For example, a student could be given the following as a practice assignment and asked to play the missing measures by ear (see example 8.3).

Example 8.3 An early exercise in playing by ear

Away in a Manger

James R. Murray

When students are playing pieces with simple tonic, dominant and subdominant accompaniments, they can also begin to learn to harmonize melodies by ear. Many familiar songs like "Itsy Bitsy Spider," "Merrily We Roll Along," or "London Bridge" can be harmonized with tonic and dominant. At first, students can simply harmonize with tonic and dominant single tones. Then they can play the open 5th of the tonic and move the bottom note down a half step, forming a 6th of the **V6/5** chord, or add a major 2nd below the top note of the 5th to suggest the same chord. Later, full tonic and dominant **V6/5** chords can be played.

Example 8.4 Forms of tonic and dominant for elementary harmonization

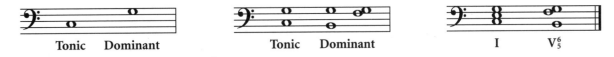

Students might first be given the melody and some harmonies and asked to complete the missing harmonies by ear (see example 8.5).

Example 8.5 An example of early harmonization

Skip to My Lou

Familiar melodies that can be harmonized with tonic, dominant and subdominant include "When the Saints Go Marching In," "Amazing Grace," and "Bingo."

Listening to the Sound

Young students who are asked, "What kind of sound do you want?" before they begin to play will learn to imagine the sound of the music through audiation. Over time, the brain will begin to develop an auditory image of the sound and a visual image of the physical motions required to make that sound on the piano. This active listening gradually results in an ease of playing since the brain has enough advance notice to tell the body the physical motions required to make that sound on the piano. The physical response to the notation also becomes more automatic. As a result, technical difficulties and physical tension are reduced. The physical response also includes the elements that make the sound musical.

Teachers who ask questions such as, "Did your playing sound loud (soft)?" or, "Did you play with the sound you wanted?" produce students who listen to their own playing using critical listening skills. Other thought-provoking questions include the following:

- Can you make your playing sound just like mine?

- How many phrases did you hear when I played? How many did you hear when you played?

- Which of these two performances sounds better? Why?

- Did your staccatos sound short and snappy?

- Did you hear the ends of the phrases?

- Did you hear the melody or the accompaniment more?

- Did your eighth notes all sound the same?

- Did you hear the sound getting louder in this line?

The same approach to listening and questioning can help students correct their own mistakes. Teachers can ask, "What interval is this?" followed by, "What interval did you play?" or "What does this rhythm sound like?" and then, "What rhythm did you play?"

Because many students may not know what constitutes an appropriate musical sound, teachers should model good musical sounds by playing regularly or by using compact disk recordings in the lessons to demonstrate the students' music. Teachers can also play a student's piece in any of a number of inappropriate ways, such as the following:

- by accenting the first beat of each measure

- by accenting the last notes of phrases

- by performing a lullaby loudly

Students can then critique the musical result.

Students can be asked to play a piece or a phrase with no dynamic change and then with exaggerated dynamics. They will hear that music is more interesting when dynamics are used. The same procedure can be used for articulations.

Ear Development Drawn from the Student's Study Pieces

Ear training is most effective when the drills are drawn from the pieces and concepts students are learning and playing. For example, in the beginning pages of *Alfred's Premier Piano Course,* Lesson Book 1A, students learn about "higher" and "lower." Two pieces that reinforce these concepts are almost identical, except that one piece goes up and the other goes down (see examples 4.30 and 4.32 on pages 106 and 107). The teacher can play one of the pieces while the student looks at the scores of both pieces (but not at the keyboard) and then tells which piece was played. This simple exercise reinforces the concept of higher and lower and prepares the student to play the pieces accurately.

Teachers can play the lines from the second page of "The Greatest Show on Earth" (see example 8.6), one at a time in any order, beginning on the first measure of each system. The students identify which line was played. Each line of music in this piece has similar characteristics but is different from the others. This requires students to listen to the playing and observe the score carefully.

Example 8.6 "The Greatest Show on Earth" (Excerpt), p. 35 from
Alfred's Basic Piano Library, Lesson Book 1B, by Palmer, Manus and Lethco

Another type of ear-development activity that uses the student's literature is an editing game. Prior to the lesson, the teacher rewrites a portion of a piece on a dry-erase board or manuscript paper, changing the piece by adding or deleting certain elements. The student follows the rewritten score while the teacher plays it several times. The first time, it is played exactly as it was rewritten. With each subsequent playing, one thing is changed. The student finds the change and corrects it in the score. Through several play-throughs, one change each time, the piece eventually returns to its original form. Changes should be basic and simple, but can increase in difficulty as the student advances.

The first four measures of "My Robot" (see example 8.7) might be rewritten to look like example 8.8.

Example 8.7 "My Robot" (mm. 1–4), p. 55 from *Alfred's Basic Piano Library,* Lesson Book 1A, by Palmer, Manus and Lethco

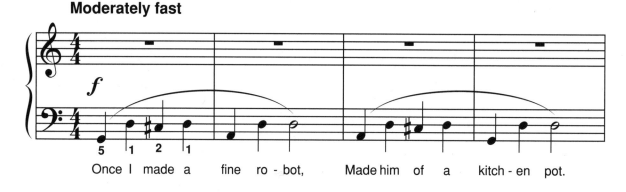

Example 8.8 Altered version of "My Robot" (mm. 1–4)

	Teacher	Student
first playing	plays as notated in the altered score	listens and follows the altered score
second playing	plays forte	changes *p* in m. 1 to *f*
third playing	plays mm. 1–2 legato	erases staccatos and writes phrase mark
fourth playing	plays mm. 3–4 legato	erases staccatos and writes phrase mark
fifth playing	plays moderately fast	changes "slowly" to "fast"
sixth playing	plays m. 4 as in the original version	changes notation to two quarter notes and a half note

As the student progresses, more sophisticated elements in the score can be altered. The first four measures of "When Our Band Goes Marching By!" (see example 8.9) might be rewritten to look like example 8.10.

Example 8.9 *"When Our Band Goes Marching By!"* (mm. 1–4), p. 46 from *Alfred's Basic Piano Library,* Lesson Book 1B, by Palmer, Manus and Lethco

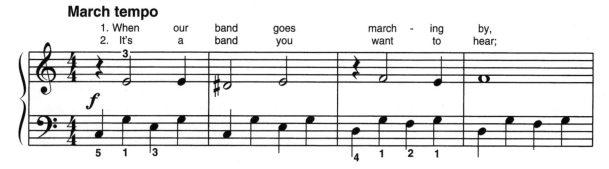

Example 8.10 Altered version of "When Our Band Goes Marching By!" (mm. 1–4)

	Teacher	Student
first playing	plays as notated in altered score	listens and follows the altered score
second playing	plays m. 4 as in the original version	changes the RH notation to a whole note (F)
third playing	plays the rhythm of m. 1 as in the original version	changes the notation to (♩ 𝅗𝅥 ♩)
fourth playing	plays the rhythm of m. 3 as in the original version	changes the notation of m. 3 to (♩ 𝅗𝅥 ♩)

Listening and Responding Physically

Using the body to express what is heard helps build music into the body and makes ear-training fun. Some simple examples for elementary students include the following:

Teacher	Student
plays music in $\frac{4}{4}$ time and accents the first beat of each measure	walks to the beat and claps on the first beat of each measure
plays a piece and changes dynamics from loud to soft at unexpected times	moves (walks, sways, jogs) making large, energetic body motions when the music is loud and small, gentle motions when the music is soft
plays music, changing from legato to staccato at unexpected times	walks with sliding steps when the music is legato and with tiptoe steps when the music is staccato
plays a series of tonic and dominant chords, changing from tonic to dominant or dominant to tonic at unexpected times	makes body motions to the chord that is heard to reflect the tension (and suspense) of the dominant chords and more relaxed motions for the tonic chords

Feeling, hearing and responding to phrases are essential parts of musical playing. Teachers can help students hear beginnings and endings of phrases and help them feel the length and shape of phrases in the following ways:

Teacher	Student
plays loud and soft phrases alternately	walks with large steps for loud phrases and small steps for soft phrases
plays ascending and descending phrases	walks forward when phrases ascend and backward when phrases descend
plays a short, familiar song, making the phrases clear	raises his/her arms at the end of each phrase
improvises music in which the phrases are relatively long and very clearly delineated	describes the shape and length of the phrases with arm motions, changing arms each time a new phrase begins
plays a piece from the student's repertoire, making beautifully shaped phrases	pulls a string out of an imaginary (or real) ball of string for each phrase

Singing

The most natural way to begin melodic ear-training is through singing. When students learn to sing their pieces, phrasing, memory and legato playing are all facilitated.

Beginning lessons may include singing familiar songs with the teacher. If some students have trouble matching the pitches of the songs, teachers can spend a portion of every lesson singing with them. The teacher can ask the student to sing any pitch and then match his/her voice to the student's. From that pitch the teacher changes the pitch one step either up or down, asking the student to copy. After several lessons, the teacher will be able to lead the student to the pitches of the songs. Students who are given this opportunity to learn to match pitch in this gradual way will likely be comfortable singing in the future.

Once students can match the pitches of the songs, they will be ready to match the teacher's pitch and can begin to sing back short melodic fragments using a single syllable such as "la." The first short melodies might be similar to the following examples.

When students' voices are able to match pitches that are used in the pieces and exercises they are playing, teachers can ask students to sing the pieces and exercises that are in the student's singing range. Singing the lyrics of pieces is a natural way to incorporate singing into the lesson and practice. In the piece "Position G" (see example 8.11), only the first line is in the young student's vocal range, but the second line could be sung two octaves higher.

Example 8.11 "Position G," p. 50 from *Alfred's Basic Piano Library,* Lesson Book 1A, by Palmer, Manus and Lethco

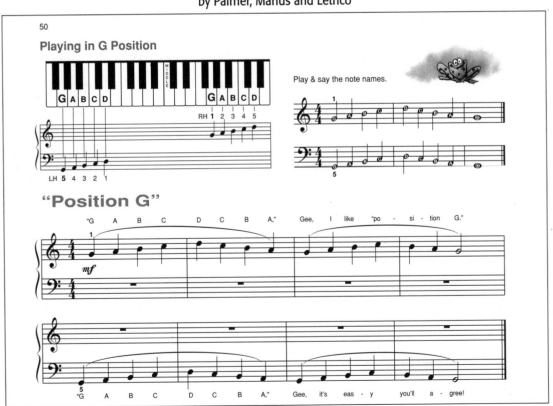

Ear-Training Drills

Ear-training drills will assure that all aspects of aural development are covered. At the elementary levels, it is difficult to extrapolate enough ear-training material from playing by ear, listening and movement activities, singing, and from the student's repertoire. Some beginning methods include ear-training books that drill concepts being studied. Ear-training activities can be devised from the methods and materials being taught.

At the elementary level, aural drills are useful for learning the following concepts:

- low and high
- loud and soft
- short and long (articulation)
- fast and slow (tempo)
- rhythm patterns
- intervals
- chords
- major and minor sounds

The teacher can select ear-training drills that will prepare for the musical ideas in the student's future repertoire. For example, a teacher might use a rhythm pattern from a future piece for a clapping drill. Teachers need to consider the following when presenting ear-training drills to students:

- Directions for a drill should state clearly what students are listening for and how they are to identify it.

- All drills should be presented a minimum of two times.

- Pitch drills should be played slowly in the middle register of the piano.

- It is important for students to experience individual intervals (and chords) through playing and listening before being asked to distinguish between them.

- To help students distinguish between pairs of intervals (or chords), they should be played both blocked and broken, as well as ascending and descending.

- A dominant chord (**V**) will be more easily recognized by ear if the 7th of the chord is included.

- Identification of specific intervals, chords, or major and minor sounds may be facilitated through imagery and descriptive words such as rough, smooth, peaceful, happy, spooky, mysterious, angry, and dark.

Teachers should stop an aural drill activity as soon as the student's accuracy falters. When such difficulties occur, teachers can assume that one or more of the following has happened:

- The teacher did not sufficiently gain the student's attention at the beginning of the activity (teachers can simply say, "listen" before each new example).

- The sequencing of the activity was incorrect.

- The activity was too complex.

- The example was presented too quickly.

- The student needed to hear the example again.

Because individual students learn in different ways, they can be allowed to respond to drills in various ways including the following:

- respond verbally to questions

- identify by name what they hear

- choose correctly from several options

- write the answer

- sing the response

- clap-back, tap-back or play-back what they hear

- move to what they hear

Categories of Aural Drills

There are several categories of ear-training drills that can be applied to a variety of musical elements. Identifying things that are the same or different; choosing the correct flashcard for what is heard; clapping, tapping or playing back what is heard; counting and rhythmic notation are some methods that can be used to promote aural development.

Same and Different

From the first lesson, teachers can play pairs of short musical ideas or clap pairs of short rhythms and ask students to tell whether the two examples sound the same or different. Students can distinguish differences in register, intervals, major and minor sounds, melodic patterns, rhythm patterns, tempos, meter, articulations, and dynamics.

Flashcards

Flashcards are a particularly useful teaching tool for various ear-training drills. Students can choose the correct card from three or four similar flashcards when the teacher presents examples for any of the following:

- dynamics

- tempos

- articulations

- note values and rhythm patterns

- intervals

- melodies

- register and melodic direction

- major and minor

- blocked (harmonic) or broken (melodic) intervals or chords

- chord progressions

- accompaniment patterns

Clap-backs, Tap-backs and Play-backs

Beginning ear-training drills for rhythm can start with clap-backs and tap-backs. See chapter 5, pages 119–121 for information on clap-backs and tap-backs.

Students can also play-back short examples that use pitch elements. Such examples can include intervals, melodies and chords. The teacher should tell the student the starting note or position and ask him/her to play-back in the same octave as heard. If teachers do not have two pianos in their studio, students can be asked to close their eyes while the teacher plays and open them for play-back starting in the octave the teacher indicates.

Melodic motives should be limited to a few beats at first and stay within a five-finger position. Initial melodies should consist entirely of quarter notes. Teachers would present such melodies over a period of weeks (using each hand), adding new melodies only when the student is able to play-back the previous ones accurately. Rhythmic accuracy should not be expected at first. After each new melody is played back accurately, the correct rhythm can also be required. Finally, dynamics and articulation can be included and required in the play-back.

Counting and Rhythmic Notation

Notating what is heard enhances reading by linking the aural and the visual. The notation of rhythms should begin with counting. When students have learned basic note values, they can count aloud while clapping back rhythms. If students have only learned to read quarter, half, dotted half and whole notes, the rhythms to be clapped and counted will be limited to those rhythmic values even though they may be able to clap rhythms with other note values (e.g., eighth notes).

After students have mastered counting aloud while clapping, they can begin notating the rhythms they hear. See page 121 for one way to encourage early rhythmic notation.

Application of Drills to Study Pieces

Aural activities related to the musical concepts studied by student should be applied to repertoire pieces. The following examples help students apply their aural knowledge to troublesome spots in their pieces.

In "Red River Valley" (see example 8.12), students are learning about tonic, subdominant and dominant chords. Students may miss LH notes unless they are able to hear the chord progression. The LH of mm. 17–32 can be written in two-measure segments on flashcards. The student listens for the different chords and arranges the cards in the correct order as the teacher plays the two-measure segments in the order of the piece. To make the game even more challenging, the teacher can play the two-measure segments in any order.

In Gurlitt's "Dance" (see example 8.13), students will learn mm. 9–12 more quickly if they realize that the melodic motive is sequenced. Teachers can play the motive from m. 9 and then play the piece and ask students to indicate when they hear the sequence. Having students first hear and identify the sequence makes them more aware of the similarities in each of these measures. Without such preparation, each measure may appear to be unique.

In "Paper Boy" (see example 8.14), students will sometimes miss the major and minor triad changes. If they first hear the teacher play the piece and are asked to identify where they hear major and minor sounds, they will be less likely to make errors when they play the piece themselves.

Example 8.12 "Red River Valley" (Excerpt), p. 41 from *Alfred's Basic Piano Library,* Lesson Book 2, by Palmer, Manus and Lethco

Example 8.13 "Dance," by Cornelius Gurlitt, p. 6 from *Everybody's Perfect Masterpieces,* Vol. 1, edited by Bigler and Lloyd-Watts

Example 8.14 "Paper Boy," p. 25 from *The Music Tree,* Part 2A, by Clark, Goss and Holland.

THE ROLE OF MUSIC LITERACY

Music literacy, which results from theoretical instruction, makes learning easier, playing more musical, and facilitates memory. A musical performance is not guaranteed, even when teachers have coached musical inflection, dynamics, phrasing and articulation. But musically literate students are likely to play more musically because they understand the structure of their music. This is similar to actors who give more convincing performances when they know the structure of the language they are speaking beyond simply saying the words in the way they have been coached.

Written theory exercises or exercises experienced through computer-assisted instruction provide important theoretical knowledge. From such theoretical instruction, students learn to identify the key of a piece; recognize scale fragments, chords, pitch and rhythm patterns; and understand how those elements relate to each other. But ultimately, theory must be related to the keyboard, the repertoire pieces, and musical interpretation.

With the teacher's guidance, students will be able to make their own interpretive and musical decisions.

- Teachers introduce pieces by helping students discover important information that may affect their musical interpretation.

- Teachers provide theory worksheets and technical exercises to reinforce the discoveries and knowledge.

- Teachers help students apply that knowledge to the interpretation and performance of pieces.

For Diabelli's "March" (see example 8.15), the discussion that follows provides sample questions that will facilitate discoveries, theory and technical exercises, and questions that lead to analysis and application to interpretation. It is unlikely that a student would complete all of the questions, discoveries or interpretive ideas for any one piece. Neither is it likely that most elementary pieces would have as many theoretical elements as this example.

Example 8.15 "March" (Primo) by Anton Diabelli, p. 23 from *Easy Classical Piano Duets for Teacher and Student,* Book 1, edited by Kowalchyk and Lancaster

Discoveries

Questions such as the following lead a student to careful observation and valuable discovery learning:

- What is the key of the piece? (**C major**)

- Find and circle all the C major five-finger patterns. (**mm. 1–2, 5–6, 17–18, and 21–22**)

- Does the C major five-finger pattern go up or down? (**Up**)

- Find and circle all the broken C major triads. (**mm. 2, 6, 18, 22**)

- Find and circle the four-note, scale-like patterns. (**mm. 9–10, 13–14**)

- What five-finger pattern could those four-note patterns belong to? (**D**) Write the name of that five-finger pattern below the measures where they occur. (At this level, students may not be able to determine that the pattern is part of the G major scale.)

- This piece has six parts, each part four measures long. Some parts are very similar. Find and label the parts using the letters A, A¹, B, B¹ (**A, A¹, B, B¹, A, A¹**)

- Find the measure that has a two-beat pattern (melodic and rhythmic) followed by the same pattern repeated on different notes. Write "S" (for sequence) above it. (**m. 3**) Find another measure that is the same. (**m. 19**)

- On what scale degree of the five-finger pattern does the sequence begin? (**4**)

Theory Worksheets and Technical Exercises

Using Diabelli's "March," students should write the following on staff paper and then play what they have written:

- the tonic five-finger pattern for the piece, both hands

- a transposition of the first two measures in another key such as G major

- a transposition of the sequence used in this piece (mm. 3, 19) in the key of G, starting on high C

Analysis and Application of Knowledge to Interpretation

The following questions can lead students to make musical decisions for Diabelli's "March:"

- Since the five-finger scale patterns move upwards, would you want to play them moving louder or moving softer? (**Louder**) Try it both ways.

- Since the patterns in measure 3 go down, would you play the second pattern softer or louder? (**Softer**) Try it both ways.

- The end of line two is different from the end of line one. Does the end of line one sound like a question or an answer? (**Question**) Does the end of line two sound like a question or an answer? (**Answer**) Will you play both the question and the answer the same way? (**No**) How can you make the end of the question sound like a question and the end of the answer sound like an answer?

♦ Are measures 9 and 10 the same? (**Yes**) Do you think m. 10 is an echo of m. 9? (**Yes**) Play m. 10 as if it were an echo. (**softer**) Play m. 10 louder than m. 9. Which way do you like the best?

♦ Why do you think the composer has marked a *crescendo* for the end of the piece? Play the last two measures with a crescendo as marked. Now, try it with a diminuendo instead. Which way sounds more like an ending of a march? (**crescendo**)

THE ROLE OF CREATIVE ACTIVITIES

The primary purpose of creative activities is to make students aware of the musical elements that create musical communication in performances. Creative activities usually take the form of composition and improvisation. All teachers, even those who do not compose or improvise, can guide students in creative experiences that provide the following benefits:

♦ stimulate the musical imagination

♦ encourage self-expression

♦ provide variety in learning

♦ help students understand specific elements in the music, including a deeper understanding of harmonic structure

♦ develop problem-solving abilities

♦ develop audiation and critical listening

Students who create their own music from the elements they are learning are more aware of those elements in repertoire. For example, beginners who make up a piece using whole notes are more likely to hold whole notes for their full value in repertoire pieces. When the imagination is linked to musical ideas in creative experiences, it is easier for students to play their repertoire with more imagination.

Improvisational experiences also aid with memorization, since both improvising and playing by memory involve playing without notation. Students who improvise regularly from the beginning of piano instruction feel comfortable with improvisation in general and experience the joy of making their own music. Some of these students may later choose to compose.

Beginning students learn new concepts and skills more easily when they experience them through improvisation. While a few beginning method books offer creative suggestions, most do not. Consequently, teachers often have to develop their own materials or assemble materials from a variety of sources for teaching creative activities. For example, the teacher might suggest that a student who is studying staccato make up a piece (at the piano) about raindrops, a hot potato, or a bouncing ball, using a limited number of pitches and rhythm values. This creative experience allows the student to focus on the sound and feel of the staccato touch, without also having to play the exact notes and rhythm of an existing piece. Furthermore, the idea that music can be related to images, both real and figurative, will begin to form in the student's mind.

Improvisation and Composition

Improvisation and composition are interrelated aspects of creativity. Improvisation is a creative experience in which musical materials are manipulated spontaneously. The result is not notated, and any repetition of the same exercise is usually different. Composition can be the notated result of an improvisation or can start in the mind and be notated immediately without any improvisational activity.

Students should be encouraged to make up pieces that they can notate, but experiences that allow total freedom often result in improvisations that are complex and beyond the student's ability to notate. It is more important for students to have creative experiences than to notate them.

Teachers can decide which activities should be notated for various forms of creative experiences. For students who show greater creative gifts, notating is an important step in the creative process. Notation and sequencing software programs for the computer can enhance the skills of students who compose.

Easy Ways to Incorporate Improvisation into the Lesson

Teachers who are not comfortable with improvisation are often reluctant to explore this form of musical expression, yet they may regularly devise simple improvisation exercises from the students' literature to aid with a technical problem. Here are other easy ways to incorporate improvisation into the lesson:

- Turn an everyday experience into an improvisation. For example, if the student has had an argument with a friend or sibling, the argument can be described on the piano through free improvisation.

- Play a portion or each phrase of a learned piece in a different octave.

- Change the dynamics or articulation of the piece to create a new character.

- Add or delete the pedal to a piece to generate a different mood.

- Change major-key sounds to minor by lowering the third scale degree, or vice versa.

- Play a short section of a piece in a different key to create a surprise.

- Add fermatas and ritardandos to a piece to create suspense and drama.

- Change rhythms to create more interest.

- Play pairs of eighth notes in a long/short rhythm to create a jazzy feel.

- Change the title of a piece and play the piece to depict the new character (for example, change the title "Gentle Breeze" to "Winter Wind").

- Improvise a short introduction and/or ending to lengthen a piece.

All creative activities need to have clear parameters and include instructions that go beyond, "make up a piece this week" or, "make up a piece about an elephant."

A creative assignment for beginners could consist of asking the student to make up a piece about a whale or hippopotamus, on the low black keys of the piano, using only quarter notes and half notes. Later, an assignment could consist of asking the student to make up a piece about clouds, using only 2nds and 5ths throughout the entire keyboard. A more advanced assignment would be for the student to make up a piece in the key of G major, with four sets of questions and answers, using all of the following note values: o 𝅝 𝅗𝅥 𝅘𝅥 𝅘𝅥𝅮

For creative assignments to be instructive, students must learn something from the experience. Teachers must be careful not to squelch a student's creativity by suggesting that the piece is wrong, odd or silly. Instead, they can make diplomatic suggestions for improving creative activities. Statements such as, "I liked how you played notes together as well as separately," followed by, "Did you think about moving your hands to other parts of the keyboard?" will open the door for expanded learning experiences.

Beginning Creative Experiences

Improvisations can be fun if they are experienced by the teacher and student (or two students) together. Early improvisational experiences using rhythms can be experienced away from the piano in ways such as the following:

- Rhythmically tapping the body or snapping the fingers in a question-and-answer fashion with the teacher are interesting ways to communicate without talking.

- Nonmusical vocal sounds, such as clicking the tongue or hissing, help students and teachers feel free about improvisation.

- Drums and other rhythm instruments expand the variety of sounds.

Some students are less inhibited when beginning improvisations on the keyboard are limited to playing without using individual fingers. Instead, they can use the whole hand, arms, elbows and fists to play a wide variety of clusters and glissandos as well as single notes. Teachers can encourage students to use the whole keyboard and the pedal.

Once short improvisations have been devised, students can lengthen pieces, creating a beginning, middle and ending. They can begin to understand structure by creating a piece that depicts a storm, which begins slowly, builds in intensity and finally subsides. Pieces in A-B-A form are a natural extension of this free form of improvisation.

Improvising with the Teacher

Improvising with the teacher as a partner helps reluctant students become comfortable with improvisation. Listening to the partner is a positive by-product of duet improvisations. Partner improvisations can be experienced in the following sequence:

1. The teacher plays a drone or an ostinato pattern on black keys in any register of the piano. The student plays a melody using black keys in another register. One partner plays half notes and the other plays quarter notes at first. Limiting the rhythmic values

frees the student to be more creative melodically. Dissonant sounds are impossible when playing only on the black keys.

2. One partner plays a drone on black keys in one register of the piano and the other creates a melody on white keys in another register.

3. Both partners improvise freely, using any black or white keys, in different registers of the keyboard.

As duet improvisations develop, they can include any musical material—single notes, clusters, chords, blocked and broken intervals and even scales. One improvisation may include only clusters or blocked intervals, for example, while others may include several different types of musical materials.

Teachers can lead students to more structure when they listen to what the students are doing and match their parts to those of the students. In one free improvisation, for example, the student may be using a particular rhythmic motive. The teacher can then incorporate that same motive into his/her part. The teacher can also suggest that the student listen to the teacher's part and try to imitate or have a "conversation" with the teacher.

These first free improvisations can be very short (four or eight measures). The teacher can help students know when to end the improvisation by suggesting that the student listen for ending "clues." For example, the teacher might stop playing momentarily, begin again, and then stop once more. Another time, the teacher might start to play more slowly. If the student listens to the teacher, he/she will feel that the music is changing in ways to suggest that the piece might be ending. After a while, students can begin to give their own cues for ending improvisations.

Body Movement and Keyboard Improvisation

Teachers can encourage keyboard improvisation by moving in various ways, asking students to match the movements with sound on the piano. For example, teachers might raise their arms above their heads and wiggle their fingers quickly. Students would likely respond by playing fast sounds, high on the piano. The teacher might move about the room with very large marching motions. Students would then respond by playing low, loud sounds that match the teacher's marching tempo. Students can play any pitches they like, varying the rhythm, register, articulation and dynamics to match the movement.

Students can learn to play music that encourages others to march, tiptoe, jog, skip, slide, stomp or move in numerous other ways. Students should experience these movements while the teacher improvises, before trying to devise their own music. Moreover, moving about the room to the teacher's playing of imaginative pieces enhances the student's creativity and ability to play performance pieces with more imagination.

Helping students devise music that simply and clearly expresses body motions leads students to understand the basic elements of music and listen to music with critical ears. At first, students can repeat a single note in a variety of ways.

For tiptoeing:

For marching:

For skipping:

At later lessons, more notes can be used.

An image, such as a trapeze artist, provides a more sophisticated vehicle for students using the body as the stimulus for an improvisation. Students can be asked to move like a trapeze artist and then try to match keyboard sounds to those motions. For example, if students mimicked a trapeze artist by swinging their arms in the same way a trapeze artist swings through the air, they could count to the motion and discover that each swing has three fast beats. Furthermore, they might discover that each swing goes up and then down. Teachers can then direct students to play in a three-beat meter, using only black keys or the notes of a specific five-finger pattern. The pitches for the first three beats should be a descending pattern and the next three beats should be an ascending pattern. Further discussion about trapeze artists swinging high in the air would help the student decide to play higher on the piano. The result might be something like the following:

In all body-inspired improvisation, students should be completely free to use any and all pitches at random to achieve the desired sound image and establish a character or mood. Some pieces can be created with one hand on black keys and one hand on white keys. Naturally, the music will not sound tonal or follow common-practice rules.

The Role of Imagery In Improvisation

Creative experiences help students apply imagination to music. Asking a student to make up a piece about an elephant can begin with a discussion of the characteristics of an elephant—massive body and foot size, small tail, large floppy ears, long trunk, and leatherlike hide. The student might comment that elephants are slow and clumsy. They find ways to portray those characteristics on the keyboard, deciding whether the piece should be loud or soft, fast or slow, hands together or alternating, played with high or low sounds, played with single notes or note clusters, or shorter or longer articulations. Furthermore, the student can determine a rhythm pattern, such as continuous dotted half notes, that defines the swinging movement of the elephant. A student might consider how to make sounds that imitate the elephant spraying water with his trunk or the sound of the elephant bellowing. Once these decisions are made, the student can create a composition of any length.

Students can bring a favorite storybook to the lesson and make up a piece to accompany the story. The story can be acted out at the piano by matching rhythm and melodic patterns to what the characters say or by creating a musical mood to match the mood of the story. Stories that have repeated phrases help students create pieces that have unity and form. For example, in the story of *Chicken-Licken,*[2] Chicken-Licken keeps repeating the phrase, "A piece of sky fell on me! I must go and tell the king." As the story is told musically, the same melodic phrase can be used every time Chicken-Licken tells someone else about the sky falling. Students can be encouraged to devise simple, unconventional notations for their pieces by drawing pictures, geometric shapes, or using different colors to represent the parts of the piece.

Short Pieces to Express One Mood

Students can improvise short pieces that express a variety of emotional states or social interactions between persons. A teacher can say, for example, "Play this five-finger pattern as if you have just won a big prize," or, "Now play the five-finger pattern as if your mother has just scolded you for something you did wrong." From these short experiences, the student can improvise short motives that reflect one of these moods. Students might play the five-finger pattern fast and loud to express joy, or slow and loud to express sadness and anger.

Improvising Melodies

When students have sufficient experience creating free improvisations, they are ready for improvisatory experiences that include key, tonality, melody, meter, and other structured musical elements.

Melodies can be made by adding the pitches of a five-finger pattern to a given rhythm pattern. Students can be encouraged to use repeated notes, articulation and dynamics. The following four-measure rhythm pattern (see example 8.16) might become an attractive melody (see example 8.17).

Example 8.16 Rhythm pattern for melodic improvisation

Example 8.17 Improvised melody based on a rhythm pattern

---

[2] *Great Children's Stories: The Classic Volland Edition,* Rand McNally, 1972.

Students can also create melodies in various ways, including the following:

◆ adding notes to words, numbers or poems

◆ changing the rhythm, meter or pitches of an existing melody

◆ adding rhythm and meter to a series of pitches

◆ making up "Questions and Answers" (antecedent and consequent phrases)

◆ improvising a melody over the teacher's accompaniment

Adding Notes to Words, Numbers or Poems

The beginning of a melody could be based on a telephone number, the rhythm of a person's name or words made from the music alphabet. Notes can be added to the rhythm of the name of a state or country or to familiar phrases such as "How are you?" and "I am fine, thank you." Poems, nursery rhymes or simple sentences created by the student or teacher are also useful. When using words or phrases, the student can tap the rhythm and then play it using notes of a five-finger pattern (see example 8.18).

Example 8.18 Melodic improvisation based on a poem

"Word" pieces can be created from words using letters of the music alphabet. For example, the start of a piece about a student's father could be made from the pitches D–A–D. Any notes from the D major or minor five-finger pattern or scale can be used for the remainder of the short piece. Rhythms, dynamics and articulations can be chosen by the student (see example 8.19).

Example 8.19 Melodic improvisation based on a word spelled from the music alphabet

A telephone number can even be a source for musical ideas. The telephone number 818-857-2221, for example, could be used to create musical motives, with each number corresponding to a scale degree (see example 8.20).

Example 8.20 Melodic improvisation based on a telephone number

The motives could then be used in creating a longer piece. The student might select the motives of measures 1 or 3 and improvise in the following manner:

- play them in different octaves

- combine them to make a two-measure motive

- play several of the notes together as chords or clusters

- use any other notes from the C major scale to create a middle section

- return to the original motive for the ending of the short piece

Students can also choose four cards from a set of note (music) flashcards and arrange them in any order to use as a motive for the beginning of a short piece.

Changing the Rhythm, Meter or Pitches of an Existing Melody

Melodies in which most of the notes are quarter notes can be varied in several ways. First, the melody can be played in double time (quarter notes become eighth notes). Afterward, some measures are played as in the original (quarter notes) and some in double time. This results in an alternation of quarters and eighths. For example, "Ping-Pong" (see example 8.21), when altered in this way, produces a very different piece (see example 8.22).

Example 8.21 "Ping-Pong," p. 9 from *Alfred's Basic Piano Library,* Lesson Book 1B, by Palmer, Manus and Lethco

Example 8.22 "Ping-Pong" with altered note values

This creative process frequently produces silly songs. Students and teachers can have fun deciding which measures should be faster and which ones should remain as written.

Changing the rhythm or meter of a melody gives it new meaning. The following familiar melody might be changed in several different ways (see example 8.23).

Example 8.23 "Blow the Man Down" melody line (Excerpt)

Students can change the meter and change one note value per measure (see example 8.24).

Example 8.24 "Blow the Man Down" in an alternative meter

Another possibility has the students changing only one pitch per measure (see example 8.25).

Example 8.25 "Blow the Man Down" with pitch substitutions

Additionally, melodic motives can be inverted, passing tones can be added, and the mode changed. Once students can alter given melodies freely, they will begin to feel comfortable creating melodies of their own.

Adding Rhythm and Meter to a Series of Pitches

Students can be provided a series of quarter-note pitches without meter or bar lines. They first play the notes as written, and then play them in $\frac{4}{4}$ or $\frac{3}{4}$ time, changing some of the quarter notes to fit the chosen meter. The following series of pitches could be arranged rhythmically in any number of ways (see examples 8.26–8.28).

Examples 8.26 Series of pitches for adding rhythm and meter

Examples 8.27 Possible melodic improvisation in $\frac{3}{4}$ meter

Examples 8.28 Possible melodic improvisation in $\frac{4}{4}$ meter

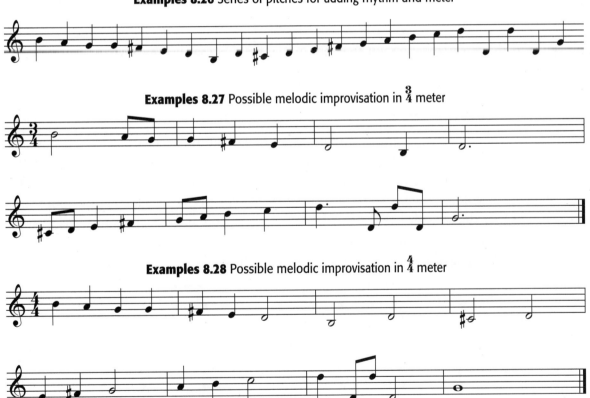

Schubert used this series of pitches in "Ecossaise" in the following way (see example 8.29):

Example 8.29 Melody from "Ecossaise in G Major," D. 145, Op. 118, No. 4" by Franz Schubert

Making Up "Questions and Answers"

The antecedent (question) and consequent (answer) phrase structure is universal in music of many style periods. It is helpful for students to narrow the choices of notes they use for their improvisation. "Questions and Answers" can be improvised as follows:

- by using black keys only

- by using black keys for the question and white keys for the answer (and vice versa)

- by using five-finger patterns

- by using triad tones

- by using non-triad tones for the question and triad tones for the answer

- by using a whole-tone scale

- by using complete scales

"Question and Answer" improvisations can begin with nonmusical questions and answers. First, the student is asked verbal questions such as, "What did you have for dinner last night?" or, "What is your favorite color?" A student might answer, "Tacos, milk and chocolate cake" or, "My favorite color is blue." Some students may need help in answering with more than one word. Once the student has answered, both the question and the answer can be restated rhythmically (see example 8.30).

Example 8.30 Rhythm pattern based on a verbal question and answer

Next, the teacher might sing a melody with the words and rhythm of the question, and the student then sings the answer. Finally, using a five-finger pattern, the teacher can play the question and the student can play the answer. The teacher should begin on the tonic note and end on any note other than tonic. The student should begin on a note of the five-finger pattern, other than the tonic, and end on the tonic (see example 8.31).

Example 8.31 Melodic improvisation based on a verbal question and answer

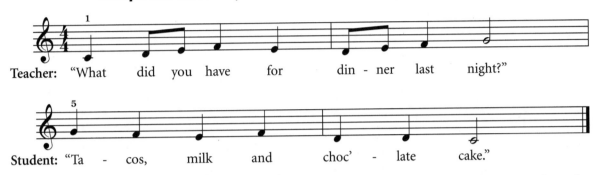

Teacher: "What did you have for din - ner last night?"

Student: "Ta - cos, milk and choc' - late cake."

Because student answers will not always match the length of the teacher's question, the question and answer phrases may not always balance at first. After students are comfortable making up rhythmic answers and playing those answers using five-finger patterns, teachers can direct the students to make their answers match the length of the questions.

When students are able to make matching answers to the teacher's questions, they can begin to make up their own "Questions and Answers." Staying within the five-finger pattern gives the student freedom to vary other elements: rhythm, dynamics, tempo, articulation, mode, and register.

Melodic improvisation helps students feel note patterns as groups. For example, when studying the broken triad as an accompaniment, it should be recognized as a unit rather than as three separate notes or two 3rds. Asking students to create "questions and answers" using broken triads helps them recognize the group of notes as a single unit.

After students are comfortable improvising melodic questions and answers, they can expand these improvisations as follows:

- by stringing several questions and answers together to make longer melodies

- by doubling the melodies at the octave with the other hand

- by accompanying the melodies with blocked 5ths, blocked triads, blocked or broken 5ths or 6ths, accompaniment patterns from triad tones, or ostinato-bass accompaniments

Experiencing "Questions and Answers" through improvisation can help students play antecedent and consequent phrases in their study pieces more musically. For example, students can identify the questions and answers and then add words to the music to reinforce the antecedent and consequent phrase structure. For the first 12 measures of Mozart's "Allegro," K. 3, the following words might be used (see example 8.32):

Example 8.32 "Allegro," K. 3 (excerpt), by W. A. Mozart, p. 62 from *Essential Keyboard Repertoire*, Vol. 1, edited by Lynn Freeman Olson (lyrics added)

Improvising Melody over the Teacher's Accompaniment

Teachers can play ostinato accompaniments in various tempos, moods and styles and ask students to improvise melodies over them. The teacher tells the student the notes on which to begin and end, then plays four measures of accompaniment. The student listens for the tempo and mood before beginning a melodic improvisation.

The first accompaniments and melodic improvisations should be on black keys. After the student can improvise freely on the black keys, the accompaniments can be in any key, with the student improvising in the five-finger pattern of that key. Teachers can make up their own ostinatos or use existing accompaniments often found in adult group piano texts. This type of improvisation activity is generally most effective with older beginners (see example 8.33).

Example 8.33 Accompaniment for black-key improvisation, p. 13 from *Alfred's Group Piano for Adults,*
Book 1 (Second Edition), by Lancaster and Renfrow

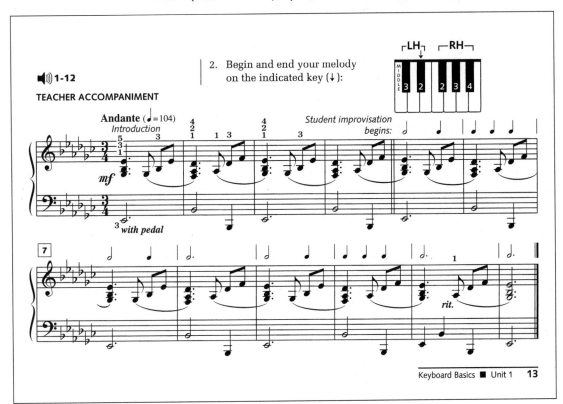

Simple accompaniments can also be created by the teacher using blocked and broken chords. The student is given a page listing the order in which the chords will be played:

$$\text{I} \quad \text{IV} \quad \text{V}_7 \quad \text{V}_7 \quad \text{I} \quad \text{V}_7 \quad \text{V}_7 \quad \text{I}$$

or

$$\text{C} \quad \text{F} \quad \text{G}_7 \quad \text{G}_7 \quad \text{C} \quad \text{G}_7 \quad \text{G}_7 \quad \text{C}$$

The student improvises a melody using only the chord tones. For this example, the teacher might play the following (see example 8.34):

Examples 8.34 Chord progression for improvising melodies

The student might play the following melody (see example 8.35):

Examples 8.35 Melodic improvisation based on a given chord progression

When students have successfully improvised using only chord tones, they can improvise using all the notes of the five-finger pattern.

After students have had experiences altering and creating melodies and improvising melodies over teacher accompaniments, they can be given simple accompaniments and asked to improvise melodies over them. Teachers can use the accompaniments from the students' repertoire. Students will learn the accompaniment first and then make up a melody using the five-finger pattern of the key of the piece. If the accompaniment has many notes, students should be instructed to limit their melody initially to one note per measure. For the accompaniment from Gurlitt's "Dance", mm. 1–8 (see example 8.13 on page 219), students might add something similar to the following simple melody (see example 8.36):

Examples 8.36 Melodic improvisation added to an existing accompaniment

Improvisations Based on Repertoire Pieces

Making up pieces based on repertoire provides variety in the lesson, encourages creativity and musical playing, and may even make the learning of the repertoire pieces more efficient.

Improvisations Made from Patterns in Actual Pieces

A simple way to begin this type of improvisation is to give the student an easy piece with four phrases of two to four measures each. The teacher and student together discover the four phrases in the piece. The student experiments by playing the phrases in several different orders. Following the experiments, the teacher and student discuss which version sounds the best.

Pieces in A-B-A form can be created by giving the student the first section (four to eight measures) of any five-finger position study piece. The student improvises a four-measure contrasting B section and then repeats the A section to finish the piece. Simple B sections can be created in many ways, including the following:

- Move both hands an octave higher and play something similar to the A section.

- Improvise a melody with the right hand alone using a different five-finger pattern.

- Play the LH alone using black keys only.

When pieces are built on a few simple patterns, students can learn the patterns by rote and then create a piece using those patterns. The actual piece can then be presented to the student with an exploration of how the composer used those patterns. In "The Bear," the LH has a broken-octave ostinato throughout, and the RH melody is based on the whole-tone scale, using three two-measure rhythm patterns (see example 8.37).

Example 8.37 *"The Bear," by Vladimir Rebikov, p. 109 from Essential Keyboard Repertoire, Vol. 1,*
edited by Lynn Freeman Olson

The teacher can show the student an F broken-octave ostinato and teach the student a whole-tone five-finger pattern from G up to D-sharp for the RH. The student can then play the LH accompaniment and improvise a whole-tone melody against it. The teacher can suggest a meter and simple rhythm pattern, or let the student decide what to play. The piece can be played in different registers and a title assigned to the finished improvisation. Afterward, the teacher can assign "The Bear" for practice. Because students will have learned the LH broken-octave technique during the improvisation, it will be easier for them to learn and play the piece.

Harmonization and Accompaniment

Students can learn to create interesting accompaniments for the melody of a piece by completing the following series of steps:

1. The teacher selects a melody that can be harmonized using tonic and dominant chords from a beginning method or folk song book.

2. The teacher and student together determine the implied harmony by first deciding which measures are comprised of notes mostly from the **I** chord and which ones have mostly notes from the **V** chord.

3. When it is unclear which chord is represented by the melody notes, the student tries both chords and decides which sounds the best.

4. The student plays only the lowest note (the root) of each of the two chords on the first beat of each measure with the LH, while playing the melody with the RH.

After students complete these steps easily, they can progress to the following:

1. Play the interval of a 5th for the **I** chord and the interval of a 6th for the **V** chord (by moving the LH fifth finger down a half step) while playing the melody.

2. Play full **I** and **V** chords (starting with **V**6/5 inversions) while playing the melody.

3. Experiment with simple accompaniment patterns that have been learned.

Because playing both the melody and accompaniment may be difficult for students to coordinate, teachers can play the piece or only the melody of the piece and students can play their chosen accompaniments. The same series of steps can be used when pieces require the **IV** chord in addition to the **I** and **V** chords.

Finishing Pieces

Another creative project could be called "Finishing Pieces."

"Space Invaders" (see example 8.38) serves as an example of one way to finish pieces. Together, the teacher and student can discover the following characteristics :

- The LH has an ostinato of two blocked 5ths that are a half step apart.

- The time signature is $\frac{4}{4}$ (common time).

- The ostinato rhythm of the LH is a half note followed by two quarter notes.

- The quarter notes of the LH are staccato.

- The RH has a melody made from the C major five-finger pattern.

- The predominant rhythm of the RH is quarter, two eighths, half note.

- The RH quarter and eighth notes are staccato.

After learning the first six measures of the piece, the student can complete four or more measures in a similar manner.

After students have successfully finished several pieces in the same style as the original piece, students can learn to finish pieces in ways that contrast with the opening measures.

Example 8.38 "Space Invaders" (Excerpt), by Dennis Alexander, p. 12 from *Especially for Boys*

Variations

The first four measures of many repertoire pieces can be used as the theme for variations. The basic musical information of the piece provides structure—the meter, harmony, rhythm and melody are all given. Students can manipulate those elements in various ways to create variations.

Variations can be quite simple at first:

- After a student has learned a piece, he/she can change one note per measure.

- The rhythm or melody of one measure of a learned piece can be changed.

- A rest can be substituted for a note on the same beat of every measure.

Pieces that have simple harmonies and distinctively different parts for the RH and LH lend themselves to variation. Variations might include the following:

- changing the meter (a piece can take on a completely different character when the meter is changed)

- reversing the role of the hands (for example, melody in the LH and blocked intervals in the RH)

- moving the accompanying chords to a different beat

- making a broken-interval, broken-chord or Alberti accompaniment from the implied triads

- blocking the melodic intervals

- changing the mode of the piece (for example, going from major to minor sounds)

- changing the character by altering articulations

- changing rhythm or pitches of the melody

In "Celebration!" (see example 8.39), measures 1–4 have the following characteristics:

- G major five-finger position for both hands

- continuous eighth note melody in the RH

- RH sounds like both melody and accompaniment since every other note is the same note (D)

- continuous half notes using blocked 5ths (G-D) in the LH

- LH plays alternately in the bass clef and the treble clef by crossing over the RH

- pedal is held throughout

Example 8.39 "Celebration!" (Excerpt) by Dennis Alexander, p. 18 from *Just for You,* Book 1

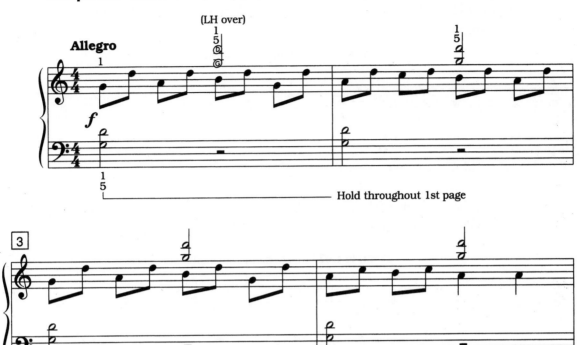

The student might create variations in one of the following ways:

◆ changing the roles of the hands (see example 8.40)

Example 8.40 "Celebration!" variation 1

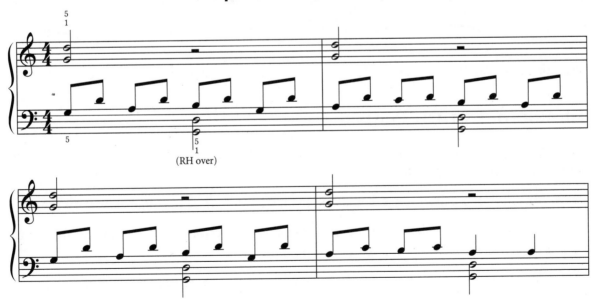

- leaving the LH in the bass clef playing whole notes and playing a single-note melody with the RH, adding some rhythmic variety, using the G major five-finger position (see example 8.41)

Example 8.41 "Celebration!" variation 2

- blocking the intervals of the RH, leaving the LH in the bass clef and breaking up the 5th to make an eighth-note ostinato (see example 8.42)

Example 8.42 "Celebration!" variation 3

Ideas for additional variations can be discovered from studying theme and variation repertoire.

THE ROLE OF ENSEMBLE PLAYING

There are several purposes for incorporating ensemble experiences as part of regular piano instruction, including the following:

- **Aural.** Intense listening is demanded from students while playing music with others.

- **Rhythm.** A steady beat must be maintained as the performers keep moving ahead in the score, regardless of mistakes or fumbles.

- **Harmony.** Elementary repertoire is enhanced by the fuller musical sound.

- **General musicianship.** Ensemble skills contribute to a student's general musicianship.

- **Social interaction.** Playing in ensembles provides social interaction for students.

Teacher Accompaniments for Student Pieces

Teacher accompaniments from method books are usually the first ensemble experiences for young students. The teacher's part must be played musically to provide a model, as most students will follow the teacher's musical inflection. To assure musical playing, teachers should practice accompaniments that are too difficult to sight-read before the student's lesson. When students experience musical playing through teacher accompaniments, they begin to play more musically on their own.

Playing duets with the teacher can enhance elementary instruction in several specific ways:

+ Students are guided toward more musical playing by the sound of the teacher's musical playing, breathing and body language.

+ Students are aided with rhythmic precision, keeping a steady tempo and pedaling.

+ Students hear a complete musical sound (harmony).

+ A positive student and teacher relationship is enhanced.

+ Duet playing is fun.

Teachers should *not* play the accompaniment until students know their part well. The duet part may be confusing to students who are struggling with their solo parts. Playing duets in lessons helps students learn to play without hesitating or stopping, thus contributing to fluent performances. When a student makes a mistake, hesitates slightly or corrects the mistake, tempo or rhythmic instability may be the result. Teachers must decide when to adjust their playing to match the student. If, however, teachers want to encourage a steady tempo and continuous playing, they should continue to play their part in tempo. Depending on the goal, either approach may be appropriate.

After these initial duet performances, teachers should be enthusiastic with students about the experience, saying how much fun it is to play music together and how beautiful the piece sounds. This enthusiasm motivates students to practice so that the duets sound even better in subsequent lessons.

Piano Duets

In addition to playing pieces with teacher accompaniments, students learn duets to play with a partner. Student duets should usually be less difficult than the student's solo music since staying together and listening to the other part are additional challenges. In some duets, the two parts are equal in difficulty; in others, one part is more difficult than the other. Naturally, the choice of which duet type to use will be determined by the level of the duet partner.

Parents who have adequate pianistic skills can make effective duet partners at home with their children. Parents who have more advanced piano skills will find it more interesting if their parts are more difficult than the student's. Parents who are only minimally proficient at the piano will do best when the duet parts are equal in difficulty. Student/parent duets provide opportunities to share special music-making times, as well as the chance to play together in recitals.

If two siblings are studying piano, duets can be a positive learning experience for both. There are sufficient opportunities for ensemble practice at home. Duets with appropriate levels for each partner are chosen. Teachers can provide guidance for their practice time to help make the experience positive. One student can start the playing, the other can count. The more-advanced sibling can be given the responsibility of adapting his/her playing to accommodate the needs of the less-advanced student.

Two students with adjacent lesson times make excellent duet partners since the music can be studied together at the lessons. More-advanced students can learn the accompaniments for elementary pieces, or they can play the more challenging part of duets with parts of unequal difficulty. Lower-level students can be challenged and inspired by the proficiency of the more-advanced student. While it is ideal to have students of equal ability as duet partners, finding times to rehearse and play can be difficult.

Other Types of Ensembles

In addition to repertoire for two or three students at one piano, there are opportunities for ensemble playing with other instruments. Easy solos for various instruments frequently have equally easy accompaniments.

If the teacher has two pianos or a digital piano laboratory, ensembles for four or eight hands at two pianos or music for several students at multiple keyboards provide fun opportunities for ensemble playing. Other ensembles are accompanied by rhythm instruments.

Some teachers' organizations sponsor multiple piano festivals (sometimes known as "monster concerts") that offer motivating performance opportunities for students. These festivals involve several students performing duets or trios simultaneously on multiple pianos. The resulting "piano orchestra" provides an opportunity to follow a conductor.

Accompaniment Disks or Recordings as Duet Partners

Accompaniment disks (General MIDI disks or compact disks) are available for some beginning piano methods and supplementary materials. This technology uses a variety of styles and instrumentations, and provides interesting accompaniments for student parts. These arrangements not only motivate students, but provide them with performance models for musical playing.

Practicing Duets and Ensembles

Ensembles should be rehearsed together once the performing partners have learned their individual parts. Students must be taught how to practice ensembles. The teacher should determine when partners are ready to practice together and work with them to establish a method for setting the tempo. When less-proficient students are given the responsibility for the tempo, they learn to establish a tempo that will help them play with confidence. During practice times, students also learn to determine which part has the melody and how to balance the parts for a musical performance.

Summary

Piano lessons should capture the interest of the elementary student and tap into the innate musical sense that lies within each individual. Teachers can use a variety of means to assist students to play musically:

- When students have an image of the piece—its mood, character or emotion— they are more likely to play musically.

- Teachers can help students make their music come alive and should be enthusiastic about the sound of the students' pieces.

- When students learn how to listen to their own playing from the very first lessons, they become more critical listeners. A systematic aural development program (ear-training) helps students learn to listen to their playing.

- Aural development is more effective if it is related to the students' pieces.

- Singing and playing by ear are the most basic forms of aural development.

- Hearing and understanding rhythms as patterns or groups encourages musical playing.

- When students see and can inwardly hear patterns of notes, their playing will be more musical.

- The study of music theory contributes to an understanding of the construction of music. Understanding the construction of music helps elementary students make interpretive decisions.

- Learning to express themselves through improvisation and composition helps students play expressively.

- Teachers can help students improvise by using a myriad of simple and short creative activities.

- Ensemble playing with teachers, parents and other students increases listening skills and contributes to musical playing.

PROJECTS FOR NEW TEACHERS

1. **Imaginative Playing**

   Select three elementary pieces with imaginative titles that suggest different images. Make a list of nonmusical characteristics for each piece, based on the titles (see pages 204–207). Find places in the music that might display the characteristics and write the characteristics at the appropriate places on the score.

2. **Ear Development**

   Select three elementary pieces and devise two ear-development activities for each. The activities should help introduce each piece by ear and prepare the students to learn it. Select appropriate aural activities from the following:

   - playing parts of the pieces for the student, to be identified on the score
   - editing
   - clap-backs
   - play-backs
   - interval identification
   - singing
   - major/minor identification
   - phrase identification
   - articulation identification
   - meter identification
   - similarities and differences
   - tempo identification
   - tonic/dominant identification
   - writing what is heard

3. **Creativity**

   Select an elementary piece that could be used for each of the following creative activities. More than one activity could be accomplished in a single piece.
   - playing each section or each phrase in a different octave
   - changing the dynamics and/or articulation
   - adding or deleting the pedal
   - playing a short section of the piece in a different key
   - changing some of the rhythms
   - changing the title of a piece for playing the piece in a new character
   - creating a new piece using the patterns of the piece
   - finishing an excerpt of a piece

PROJECTS FOR EXPERIENCED TEACHERS

1. **Imaginative Playing**

    Select three elementary pieces with imaginative titles. List three questions for each piece that will encourage students to think imaginatively about the music. Relate the questions to the image suggested by the title and characteristics in the music.

2. **Ear Development**

    Choose two elementary pieces that are each eight measures long. One should be for a first-year student; the other for a second-year student. Prepare an "editing" (altering) activity for each piece (refer to pages 211–213). Plan four changes for each piece with only one change made for each playing of the piece. Notate the edited version that the student will hear during the first playing of the piece. Then make a list of prescribed changes for each subsequent playing.

3. **Creativity**

    Describe three everyday experiences that elementary students encounter. For each experience, list suggestions for students to use to describe the experience on the piano such as the use of the whole keyboard, articulation, the pedal, tone clusters, single notes and a variety of dynamics.

Chapter 9
GROUP TEACHING

Private piano instruction is the most common mode of piano teaching. However, private lessons are the exception to most other learning activities such as school, sports, band, drama and choir. Group lessons can also be effective in piano instruction, either as an enhancement to the private lesson or as the sole mode of teaching. A group of students can be as small as two or as large as the teacher can handle. Students can be grouped homogeneously by age and/or level, or with different ages and levels in the same class. The format of the class will vary greatly, depending upon the grouping and goals for the class. Group instruction is only effective if *all* students are actively involved *all* of the time.

ADVANTAGES AND DISADVANTAGES OF GROUP AND PRIVATE INSTRUCTION

Both group and private settings for teaching have advantages and disadvantages to consider.

Advantages of Group Lessons

Group teaching gives students distinct advantages that are not possible in the private lesson. In regard to IMPROVED SKILLS:

- Group lessons develop poise and other performance skills when the student plays for others.

- Group lessons develop critical listening skills through listening to others.

- Group lessons broaden students' musical understanding by hearing and studying a greater variety of music. (This is especially true when individual students are assigned different compositions by the same composer or by different composers in the same style.)

- Group lessons develop rhythmic security and counting ability by providing an opportunity for several students to play the same pieces together or through other ensemble work.

- Group lessons provide an environment that encourages the development of functional skills.

- Group lessons develop communication skills and the ability to work in a group.

In regard to INCREASED MOTIVATION and ENTHUSIASM:

- Group lessons provide inspiration through peer performances.

- Group lessons motivate students through healthy competition.

- Group lessons provide a social outlet surrounding a common interest not normally available to private piano students.

- Group lessons promote enthusiasm and enjoyment as a result of sharing in ensemble work, rhythm drills and music games.

- Group lessons bring out the best in students through the challenge of cooperation.

- Group lessons develop supportive camaraderie.

- Group lessons provide motivation from other students as well as from the teacher.

In regards to PRACTICAL MATTERS:

- Group lessons allow a student to make up a missed lesson by attending another group at the same level on another day.

- Group lessons provide more diverse activities and expand the opportunity for creative drills and exercises, due to longer lessons.

- Group lessons allow unprepared students to benefit from the lesson.

Teaching skills are likely to improve as a result of the requirements of group instruction. In group teaching, it is essential that teachers act accordingly as follows:

- be organized

- have clear goals for every activity

- develop systematic lesson plans

- deliver information efficiently

- use lesson time effectively

- give precise explanations

- listen and respond carefully to students

- balance attention between the group and the individual

When teachers develop these skills through group teaching, they often find their private instruction techniques also improve. They become more flexible, give consistent reinforcement and learn to teach skills in a gamelike format.

In addition to advancing teaching skills, group teaching provides practical advantages. Basic concepts and skills can be presented more efficiently to several students at once without having to repeat the same material for individual students. Group lessons allow teachers to earn more income in the same amount of time, and lessons can be less expensive for the individual student. For example, if a teacher charges $40 an hour for individual instruction, but charges each of six students in a class $10 for one hour of group instruction, he/she will earn $20 more per hour. From the student's point of view, an hour of group instruction costs only one-fourth the price of a one-hour private lesson. When considering the financial advantages, however, teachers should understand that lesson and assignment preparation for groups requires more time than for individual lessons.

Disadvantages of Group Lessons

While there are many advantages to group lessons, teachers need to prepare for problems that are unique to this form of instruction.

- Small groups may not be time- and cost-efficient.

- Teachers must have enough students at approximately the same learning level and age to form an effective group.

- Students who fall behind, or move ahead more rapidly, will need to be moved to other groups or to private lessons.

- The teacher must have several groups to have the flexibility to transfer students to another class.

- Scheduling is often difficult since students have active schedules and all students at one level must be able to attend the lesson at the same time.

- When group lessons are scheduled at a different time than the private lesson, it is easy for students and parents to forget about them.

- When students have both private and group lessons, they may not prepare as well for the group lesson.

- Group teaching may make it difficult to refine students' technical development and artistic playing.

When teachers recognize these limitations, their expectations for students taught solely in a group setting can be more realistic. Teachers can find ways to minimize the problems of group instruction. Although students often find group lessons more enjoyable than private lessons, parents must frequently be educated to the value of group instruction. Parents can attend group lessons or be invited to a demonstration group lesson. Once parents see the benefits and positive results, they are likely to be more responsible for seeing that their children attend every lesson. Additionally, when students have both private and group lessons, a term tuition that is all-inclusive will generally motivate parents to remember the group lesson schedule.

Students who have both private and group lessons may take private lessons more seriously than group lessons. If teachers present group lessons as a privilege, students will look forward to them and will be better prepared for them. Students will have greater motivation to participate if they have a vested interest in the lesson. For example, if each student has a responsibility for one part of the lesson, he/she is more likely to come prepared.

Advantages of Private Lessons

There are also advantages to private lessons over group lessons:

- Lessons are easier to schedule.

- Parents understand the concept of private piano lessons.

- Teacher preparation time is less than for group lessons.

- Students may progress at their individual pace. More (or less) time can be allowed for learning a new concept or skill.

- Each student receives the undivided attention of the teacher.

- The teacher and student can develop a close rapport.

- Refined technical and musical development is possible.

- Instruction, preparation of pieces and assignments are detailed and individualized.

Private instruction is preferable when there are not enough social peers to form a group. It is also better for certain types of students:

- students with exceptional coordination and/or advanced intellectual skills

- students who practice in excess of one hour a day and who desire to play piano to the exclusion of other activities

- transfer students who need remedial work

Disadvantages of Private Lessons

Although private lessons have many advantages, teachers should be aware of the disadvantages. Some of these include the following:

- Teachers must repeat the same information many times.

- Lessons are more expensive for parents. This higher cost may result in shorter lesson times.

- Students are sometimes less motivated than those in group lessons and practice less than they should.

- There is little opportunity for camaraderie between students.

- There are few opportunities to perform for others.

- There is little opportunity for ensemble experience.

- Opportunities for developing critical listening skills are minimized.

- There is less opportunity to become acquainted with a variety of music and styles.

PREPARING TO TEACH GROUP LESSONS

Good teachers, whether group or private, share many of the same characteristics. Careful preparation ensures effective learning. It is helpful for teachers with no prior group teaching experience to observe and/or participate in effective group instruction before they begin group teaching on their own. The following are different types of teaching environments that are good entry points for beginning group teachers:

- teaching occasional master or performance classes

- conducting monthly classes dedicated to a particular type of learning, such as theory

- offering introductory summer group lessons

- teaching partner lessons

Teachers should also consider practical aspects when starting group instruction. If groups are an adjunct to private lessons, policy statements should include clear language about whether or not group lessons are mandatory. Parents should be made aware of the benefits and procedures, as well as the policies concerning fees, absences and make-ups. When teachers instruct in a home studio, they should research zoning laws to make sure they are allowed to teach more than one student simultaneously.

Generally, students should be grouped by level and by age (usually no more than one or two years apart). To help the teacher determine the best group/private curriculum and the most appropriate group for each student, the student's interview should assess the following areas:

- readiness

- maturity

- learning ability

- physical development

- rhythmic development

- aural skills

Students should be moved to a different group when they fall behind or outgrow their group. Students of different ages and levels can be grouped together for master and performance classes. Transfer students who need remedial work may benefit from having only private lessons until they are ready to join an appropriate group.

The length of group lessons varies depending on the age and level of the students, the frequency of the group lesson and the private/group lesson format. Most group lessons and partner lessons last between 45 and 60 minutes. Once-a-month groups for intermediate students can be up to 90 minutes in length.

TYPES OF GROUP LESSONS

While it would be ideal for every piano student to have both a private and a group lesson once a week, it is not always possible. With creative planning, teachers can offer quality group and private instruction for all students using a variety of formats.

- performance (master) classes

- group lessons as an adjunct to private lessons

- private/group lesson formats

  - private lessons for three weeks/group lesson during the fourth week

  - private lessons every week/group lesson every fourth week

  - both private and group lessons every week

  - private and group lessons on alternating weeks

- group lessons as the only form of instruction

  - partner lessons

  - partner/group combination lessons for groups of four students

  - group lessons every week

Performance Classes

Historically, the master class was the first mode of group teaching. In a master class, a teacher offers interpretive ideas to a performer as an audience watches. Independent teachers have applied that same mode of teaching in weekly or monthly performance classes. These classes expose students to larger amounts of repertoire and prepare them for formal performances.

In traditional master classes, the audience (other students) are generally passive learners. However, performance classes for pre-college-age students are more effective if students are active learners. Students can watch the score while the piece is performed. Following the performance, students can be asked to comment on the playing, before the teacher begins to work with the performer. Students should be encouraged to make positive comments, followed by constructive ideas. For elementary performance classes, this is most effective when each student listens for one specific element, such as the following:

- rhythm

- correct notes

- articulation

- dynamics, phrasing and other musical aspects

Since each student has a specific focus, all students can participate in the critique, not just the more outgoing ones. When students are older, the teacher can expand the auditors' involvement by including them in the actual teaching. As the teacher works with the performer, the listeners can be asked questions, such as the following:

- What do you think of the staccatos?

- Could you hear the crescendo?

- Was this performance better?

- How could it be even better?

For all levels, the master class format is effective when all participants study the score prior to the performance. Students can be asked to describe what they see on the page relating to various musical elements, including the following:

- time signature
- accidentals
- articulation
- key signature
- rests
- clef changes
- tempo terms
- dynamics
- texture
- the range of keyboard played

Teachers can lead students to make such observations by asking questions such as, "Do you see a lot of rests?" or "How much of the keyboard is used?" Based on their observations, students can be asked what kind of sounds they might expect to hear, leading to a discussion of the character or mood of the piece. At the conclusion of the performance, the teacher can ask the listeners whether that mood was effectively communicated in the performance. This format allows all the students to learn, not just the performer.

For example, if one student is playing "A Little Piece (*Stückchen*)" (see example 9.1), the other students might make the following observations:

- The piece is in $\frac{4}{4}$ (c) time.

- The left hand has eighth notes and the right hand has quarter notes.

- Half notes are the only other note value.

- There are many slur markings.

- The piece has a moderate tempo.

- The piece is generally quiet throughout.

- Both hands are in the treble clef throughout.

- There are two sections.

- There are four phrases in each section.

- The melody is in the right hand.

- The piece begins with an incomplete measure and all phrases begin with upbeats.

Example 9.1 "A Little Piece, Op. 68, No. 5," p.10 from *Schumann: Album for the Young,*
edited by Willard Palmer

Asking students what they would expect to hear when the piece is played might elicit the following responses:

- The piece will be gentle.

- It will sound smooth.

- It will not be fast.

- The melody will be heard in the right hand.

- The accompaniment in the left hand will be soft.

In "A Little Piece" there is a duet between the RH part and the lower LH notes. Young students are unlikely to observe this immediately. After the piece is played, this issue might be discussed.

The teacher can then ask the students to listen for these characteristics. Afterward they can critique the playing, helping the performing student play more musically. This exercise will motivate all students to prepare their performing pieces well, knowing that others will be listening critically. Moreover, students will begin to listen to their own playing with more critical ears during practice.

The informal master class setting gives students opportunities to learn how to be good performers, by approaching and sitting at the piano correctly and by acknowledging applause through bowing. Teaching these skills in the studio/master class helps prepare for more formal performances by eliminating anxiety about stage etiquette. Students can also become good audiences by learning to listen attentively.

Group Lessons as an Adjunct to Private Lessons

A group lesson that is an adjunct to the private lesson enhances it and provides an opportunity to include activities that are sometimes neglected in the private lesson. It can focus on one type of activity or be a mixture of the many types, including the following:

- performance
- music theory work
- ear-training work
- sight-reading and ensemble work
- functional skills and creative activities
- rhythmic work and movement activities

Performance

A portion of the lesson can function similarly to a performance class. One or more students play their performance pieces, while the others listen and make suggestions.

Music Theory Work

The learning of theoretical concepts is more fun if several students are learning together. A variety of flashcards, chalkboard (or dry-erase board), keyboard, and rhythm drills keep the class lively. Students can gather around one piano and take turns playing specific notes, intervals, and triads, making it unnecessary for each student to have his/her own keyboard.

Ear-Training Work

All theoretical concepts—such as intervals, five-finger patterns, triads, register, rhythm values—can be drilled aurally, with students taking turns or working in teams. Students can use ear-training work pages or books to circle or write what they hear. The papers can be traded and corrected by another student. For other ear-training activities, students can work with a partner. On the chalkboard, one partner can write what was heard and another can correct the work. For playbacks, one student can play musical examples and the partner can play back what was heard.

Sight-Reading and Ensemble Work

Group lessons offer opportunities for regular ensemble experience. When learning new solo pieces or sight-reading, some students can play the RH part while others play the LH. Parts can then be reversed during the lesson and the piece assigned for all students to learn both hands. When playing duets, half of the class can learn the primo, while the other half learns the secondo. Ensembles for three or more players also provide enjoyable learning and performing experiences.

Functional Skills and Creative Activities

Functional skills and creative activities are more effective when experienced in a group setting. Some students can play a written melody, while the others add chords to harmonize it. Students can take turns playing simple drone or ostinato accompaniments while others improvise a melody over the accompaniments. Pairs of students can create "Questions and Answers" (antecedent and consequent phrases). The group can describe the characteristics of animals, weather conditions, athletic activities, or other characters or events, while classmates experiment with ways to describe those characteristics on the piano. Then the whole class can discuss the results.

Rhythm Work and Movement Activities

Body-movement activities are most effective in a group setting. They enhance the learning of many aspects of music, especially rhythm. Walking, marching, running, skipping and other movements, such as swinging the arms and tapping or clapping the hands are all ways to incorporate movement into the learning process. As all students move, the teacher can call attention to the student with the most appropriate movement as an example for the others to copy, asking "Can you match your movement to Peter's?" To further enhance rhythmic development, students can take turns clapping, tapping or playing rhythms while others write them. Students can then correct their classmate's work. In another rhythm game, students must concentrate as clap-backs are "passed around" the group.

Private/Group Lesson Formats

The descriptions that follow focus on ways to include the previously mentioned activities in two different formats of the private/group combination:

- If the student has both a private and group lesson each week, the new concepts are presented in the group and reinforced in the private lesson.

- If the group lesson occurs less frequently than once a week, the new concepts are presented in the private lesson and reinforced in the group lesson.

Private Lessons for Three Weeks/Group Lesson During the Fourth Week

In this teaching format, students receive a weekly private lesson for three weeks followed by a group lesson during the fourth week. There are a number of issues for teachers to consider concerning this arrangement of group and private lessons, such as the following:

- Students should be given practice assignments that include additional goals to keep them practicing effectively during the week of the group lesson.

- Class activities will need reinforcement in the private lessons.

- Teachers must coordinate the lesson assignments for the private and group lessons.

- Specific assignments from the group lesson should be divided among the other three weeks' private lesson assignments so that all students are prepared for the next group lesson.

- Each student can study an ensemble piece in the private lesson and rehearse it with partner(s) during the group lesson.

- Students benefit from both group and private instruction without incurring excessive cost.

Private Lessons Every Week/Group Lesson Every Fourth Week

Teachers who prefer an emphasis on private lessons have the additional option of having a group lesson during the fourth week. Teachers should consider the following issues regarding this format:

- To accommodate all of their private and group lessons, teachers will need to balance their schedule to include some group lessons every week so that in any given week, each student will receive a private lesson and some students will receive a group lesson.

- Even with the above-mentioned scheduling, some teachers may need to reduce their total number of students.

- Private lessons are more consistent using this format than when there is no private lesson during the fourth week.

- Students must commit to attending both a private and a group lesson during one week of the month.

- Students may have difficulty scheduling two piano lessons during the fourth week along with school and other activities.

- Tuition is more expensive than when students receive three private lessons and one group lesson each month.

Both Private and Group Lessons Every Week

Although it is difficult to schedule in today's society, it would be ideal for each student to have both a private and a group lesson each week. This arrangement offers the best possible piano education for students and is especially good for first-year students. There are certain issues to consider concerning this format:

- Students benefit to a greater degree from individualized instruction and the dynamics of group instruction.

- Students must be very committed to piano lessons and be willing to come and be prepared for two lessons every week.

- Parents must be willing to pay a larger tuition.

- Teachers cannot teach as many students since they must schedule both group and private lessons for every student every week.

Private and Group Lessons on Alternating Weeks

In this format, the student receives both private and group lessons that alternate weekly. Both individualized instruction and the dynamics of group instruction are possible on a regular basis. This arrangement has unique issues such as the following:

- Students and parents must remember different lesson times for alternate weeks.

- Teachers can teach a larger number of students.

- More classes are possible at each level.

- The teacher must make assignments in the private lessons to keep students practicing effectively for the two-week period between private lessons.

- Teachers can teach some private lessons and some group lesson every week.

- Scheduling is a challenge.

Group Lessons as the Only Form of Instruction

Preschool age children and beginning adults (who are studying piano as a hobby) are frequently taught in a group-only setting. Some students from these groups continue their study with private instruction. For adult students who discontinue instruction after a short time, group lessons allow them to fulfill a lifelong dream without investing a large amount of money. Others who want to refine their skills will benefit from private instruction after group lessons have ended. While all beginning students can be started effectively in a group, some teachers feel that average-age students progress more rapidly when they have private lessons; others disagree.

There are various formats for group instruction including partner lessons, partner/group combinations, or group-only instruction.

Partner Lessons

Partner lessons include activities similar to those used with larger groups, and are the easiest way for teachers to begin group teaching. Using this type of lesson format, two compatible students of roughly the same age and ability are matched, taught together, and generally study the same material. Each student may also learn his/her own supplementary music.

Some partner lessons are structured to include some private instruction within the partner lesson time. While one student is receiving private instruction, the other works on theory and ear-training activities (sometimes using computer software). If the teacher has digital pianos, one student can work on specific activities and skills using a headset during the other student's private instruction time. In addition to having most of the benefits of group lessons, with fewer disadvantages, partner lessons include other advantages as well:

- Grouping and scheduling are easier since there are only two students and one lesson time to consider.

- Partner lessons allow time to refine technical development and to develop musical playing.

- Partner lessons involve both students in a teaching role as they teach each other, thus sharpening their listening and learning skills.

- With partner lessons, there is an increased possibility of retaining some intermediate-level students and teenagers, who might otherwise quit private lessons due to the lack of social aspects.

- With partner lessons, there is an added element of healthy competition as the result of students learning some of the same pieces or exercises.

- The students can easily become a team with the advantages of weekly ensemble playing.

- The lessons can be effective for both partners, even when one of the students has had little practice.

- The benefits of both group and private instruction occur every week, at a reasonable cost.

Partner/Group Combination Lessons for Groups of Four Students

In this group lesson combination, two students are partners and have a 15- to 30-minute partner lesson, followed by a 30-minute group lesson with another pair of students. The second pair has their 15- to 30-minute partner lesson after the group lesson. The four students study the same material during the group lesson and each pair learns additional music. The following should be considered when teaching partner/group combinations:

- Scheduling this format is tricky, as all four students in the group must be able to attend lessons on the same day and at the same time.

- The four students must be compatible and have the same ability and level of learning.

- The teacher must have carefully organized lesson plans and be able to use time wisely.

- Since the schedule is the same every week, parents and students do not have to remember two different lesson times.

- Every student gets the benefit of group instruction and a chance for more individualized attention at a reasonable cost.

- Keeping students together at the same level may be difficult since each student's pace of learning may vary.

Group Lessons Every Week

In this format, three or more students learn in a group setting as the sole form of instruction. Group teaching often occurs in a digital piano lab equipped with a keyboard for each student. Group lessons maximize the teaching time and the teacher's income. Students receive the benefits of group instruction and more instruction time for less money.

Teachers should plan many activities; however, they should not feel as though they must cover everything they have planned. Rather, they should make sure that each concept is presented in sufficient depth so that students have a clear understanding of the ideas and are able to practice effectively.

Planning Considerations for Group-Only Lessons

Group lessons will be easier to teach if logistical matters have been considered, such as the following:

- Classes should have only as many students as space and equipment permit and the individual teacher can manage.

- Classes for younger students should have fewer students than classes for older students since younger students often require more attention.

- Groups past elementary levels using only group instruction may have too few students to be economically viable.

- All students should stay together in a basic text or method series, but more or less challenging supplementary material can be assigned to individual students as needed.

Conducting the Lesson

Specific group-teaching strategies are essential for successful group lessons. These strategies include the following:

- Material, instructions and the pace of the lesson should be directed to the average student. (If lessons are directed to the slower student, other students may become restless and bored. If lessons are directed to the fastest student, the other students may become discouraged.)

- Activities should be planned so that all students, even the slower ones, can be successful some of the time.

- Measures of all pieces common to the group should be numbered to facilitate quick reference during the lesson.

- A minimum amount of time (if any) should be spent helping individual students during class time.

- Teachers should capture the attention of all the students before beginning any new activity.

- Teachers must constantly observe student behavior and response and be aware of the each student's level of understanding.

- Deviating from the lesson plan is essential when dictated by student response. As teachers become more adept in group teaching, they will be able to adjust the lesson plan quickly.

- High-energy activities alternated with quieter ones and activities at the piano alternated with activities away from the piano provide variety in the lesson and help control student behavior.

- Routinely used verbal cues help students begin and end activities together, play together and maintain a steady beat.

Keeping All Students Active During the Whole Lesson

Effective group lessons keep all students active all of the time, but individual students may have different tasks during any given activity, such as the following:

- As one student plays a piece, the others can sing along, clap or tap the rhythm, or improvise an accompaniment.

- Occasionally, an individual's technical problem can be worked on by the group, to the benefit of all.

- Each activity should involve all students at their individual level of ability and should have a variety of possible verbal or playing responses, such as the following:
  - the slower students play the easier of the two hands
  - the average students play the more difficult hand
  - the faster students play hands together

- To ensure that all students have had sufficient reinforcement, the teacher can ask, "Who wants to do it again?" If any student wishes to repeat the activity, all students would repeat the task together. Students are sometimes reluctant to ask for help unless the teacher gives them an opportunity to request it.

Classroom Management

When there are well-planned lessons, behavioral problems rarely arise. Most negative behavior can be eliminated if the teacher sets the tone at the very first lesson. The teacher can employ the following tools for effective classroom management and to help ensure successful lessons:

- Start and end lessons promptly.

- Prepare a thoroughly organized lesson plan for each class.

- Know the lesson plan and music well enough to allow for close observation of students.

- Establish class routines and rules to eliminate confusion and unruly behavior. For example, say "no playing the piano while the teacher is talking," and "raise your hand only to give responses."

- Give affirmation for a student's positive behavior to help eliminate negative behavior by others.

- Use an approach that is warm and friendly, yet businesslike in that it does not allow for nonsense.

- Project your voice and use a positive tone.

- Give simple and direct instructions.

- Insist upon eye contact and observe student behavior carefully.

Use of Lesson Time

More will be learned when lesson time is used wisely. Time can be saved by implementing the following teaching strategies:

- Have the students trade and correct their written homework assignments during the lesson time.

- Ask students to play their best-prepared or favorite pieces from the assignment.

- During individual or shared board activities, have one student complete the task while another corrects the work.

Developing Stimulating Lessons

Excitement, focused learning and healthy competition can be achieved as follows:

- Create a contest and assign points to students who succeed with various tasks.

- Divide the group into competing teams for the various activities.

EQUIPMENT, MATERIALS AND GAMES

Group lessons are most effective when a variety of equipment, materials, games and other activities are used to enhance the learning.

Equipment

The equipment needed for group teaching depends on the age and number of students in the class. One piano is sufficient for small groups. For larger groups, each student should have a keyboard. While not as effective, silent keyboards can be used successfully by skilled teachers.

Variety and interest can be added to group lessons by using additional equipment, such as the following:

- a sequencer to play General MIDI disks

- a compact disc player

- writing boards (dry-erase boards)

- a velcro® board and/or easel

♦ an overhead projector

♦ games and visual aids

♦ a video recorder and monitor

Materials

Any method book or materials can be used for group lessons if the teacher plans carefully. For groups that meet monthly, students may not use their regular weekly lesson materials and may have separate theory, ear training or other books specifically for the group. For groups that meet weekly or bi-weekly, a regular piano method or a series designed especially for group teaching may be used. Since such group piano series usually include all materials in one book, students don't have to switch from one book to another during class as they move among the various activities. These activities may include the following:

♦ solo and ensemble repertoire

♦ technique

♦ theory

♦ sight-reading and ear training

♦ rhythm drills

♦ composition and improvisation

Teachers can also find a wealth of ideas for activities in college group-piano texts.

Games

Games are an important part of group teaching for reinforcing musical concepts. A variety of board and card games can be purchased or created by the teacher. Commercially developed games that reinforce note values, musical symbols, rhythms, and note names are available from music stores, music catalogs and Internet sites. It is easy to make musical games that teach and drill important concepts patterned after familiar children's games. To reinforce key signatures, for example, a set of dominos can be altered by taping the letter name of a key to one half of each domino tile. Students match the key-name half of one tile to the correct number of dots on half of another tile; the dots represent the number of sharps or flats in the key signature (see example 9.2). An occasional group lesson can be a game lesson in which students rotate from game to game every 15 to 30 minutes.

Example 9.2 Dominos adapted for a key signature identification game

Using Digital Pianos in Group Instruction

Piano laboratories with digital pianos can be used effectively for group instruction, with one piano and headset for each student. Teaching can occur with or without headsets. The teacher's console and group-lesson controller allow the teacher (and students) to use headsets to listen to individuals, pairs or small groups. When the teacher can listen to and instruct individuals via headsets, it allows for some of the same advantages as private lessons. Much of this type of instruction occurs in colleges, but preparatory schools and some private studios also use digital instruments. Time will be saved when the lesson is organized to include a minimal number of switches from "headsets on" to "headsets off." Teachers can use a laboratory in a number of ways, such as the following:

- Using headsets, students can practice pieces and drills without disturbing others, both during class or when they arrive early for the lesson.

- Two students can each teach one new piece to the other, putting good learning habits into practice.

- Pairs of students can practice pieces together with one student playing the right hand and the other student playing the left hand. They can then switch parts, allowing them to hear the other part while playing only one hand.

- Pairs or small groups of students can practice duets or ensembles.

- Two students can sight-read or play technical exercises together. These activities help students count, play with a steady tempo using accurate rhythm, and listen for note accuracy and balance between melody and accompaniment.

- Small groups can work together to improvise ensembles. Each part of the ensemble can use a different instrument setting and each student can be assigned a different role. For example, five students might arrange their improvisation in the following manner:
  - blocked chords in treble using a string sound
  - broken chords in the middle register using a guitar sound
  - bass note of chords an octave lower using a low string sound
  - melody using a clarinet sound
  - countermelody improvised an octave higher with a flute sound

- Two students can give ear-training drills to each other, harmonize melodies, or improvise together.

- Students can take turns conducting an ensemble or ensemble improvisation, thus enhancing their listening and rhythmic abilities.

- ◆ Ensembles, repertoire pieces, sight-reading pieces or improvisations can be orchestrated with a different instrument setting for each piano.

- ◆ Practiced pieces can be played in the following ways:
  - by the whole group together
  - by smaller groups
  - by pairs or individuals
  - by individual students or groups of students taking turns playing succesive one- or two-measure segments while maintaining a steady beat
  - half of the group plays one hand, the other half plays the other hand
  - half of the group plays one line, followed by the other half playing the next line.

SCHEDULING GROUP LESSONS

Scheduling can be one of the most difficult aspects of group teaching. Students are often involved in many activities, making it difficult to find a convenient time for all students in the group. This process is easier when the teacher has a large number of students and is able to offer multiple classes at each level. Teachers can distribute an annual registration form for group lessons listing choices for group lesson times. Students cross out the times when they are not available. The teacher then assigns students to classes based on knowledge of each student's needs and abilities and on the student's preferences.

LESSON PLANS AND ASSIGNMENTS

Group teaching takes more planning than individual lessons and requires a carefully crafted lesson plan. The lesson must include a mixture of activities, both at and away from the keyboard. These activities must change quickly, keeping all students actively learning for the duration of the lesson. As in any good lesson, the material should follow a logical and progressive order. The progression from one activity to the next should be smooth, without any obvious break in the flow of the lesson. More activities than necessary should be planned, since it is far better to save some for the next lesson than to run out of activities.

Sample Lesson Plan for a Group Lesson as the Sole Form of Instruction

Following is a sample of a one-hour elementary group piano lesson using *Alfred's Basic Group Piano Course,* Book 2, Units 5 and 6[1]. For this lesson, each student needs a keyboard (digital piano lab) with a headset. Prior to this lesson, the teacher will have prepared and introduced the students to the interval of a 4th.

---

[1] Willard A. Palmer, Morton Manus, Amanda Vick Lethco, Gayle Kowalchyk, and E. L. Lancaster, *Alfred's Basic Group Piano Course,* Book 2 (Alfred Publishing Co., Inc., 1997), Units 5 and 6 on pages 55–63.

Teacher	Student
1. The teacher chooses one piece for each student to play from the previous week's assignment in the lesson book (pp. 43–54) to ascertain the success of the learning and playing. The teacher gives minimal help for problems and reassigns as needed. The teacher plays the duet part (or an accompaniment recording) for each piece that is sufficiently learned.	**At their pianos:** 1. Each student plays one piece from the assignment. All students follow the score and, afterward, comment on the playing. Students (who know their pieces well enough) play the piece a second time, with the teacher duet or the recorded accompaniment. **8 minutes**
2. The teacher discusses balance in the ensemble review piece, "If I Won Ten Million Dollars" on pp. 52–53 (see example 9.3). The piece is played several times, working on balance and ensemble.	2. Students perform the ensemble piece as a group without headsets, playing their previously assigned parts and working with the teacher's suggestions. **5 minutes**

Example 9.3 "If I Won Ten Million Dollars," pp. 52-53 from *Alfred's Basic Group Piano Course*, Book 2, by Palmer, Manus, Lethco, Kowalchyk and Lancaster

Teacher	Student
3. The teacher reviews the piece "Rockets," on page 48 (see example 9.4) and leads a discussion of how rockets move and sound. The students are asked to find places in the music that imitate a rocket's motion and sound.	3. The students might locate the ascending melodic lines in mm. 1–2 and 5–6. They also may note the changing dynamics (forte to piano) with the sound of the rocket fading away as it moves higher.
The teacher asks the students to listen to the piece. The teacher plays the piece in various way, such as the following: • legato and fast • with the second line an octave higher • with the first line loud and a diminuendo for the second line The teacher elicits from the students descriptions of how the music imitates the rocket's motion. The teacher asks the students to practice "Rockets" individually, using their headsets.	The students identify what things in the playing made the piece sound like a rocket, such as the following: • A rocket moves smoothly without any break. • The fast tempo and rising notes of the music are just like a rocket. • The rocket starts loud, but gets softer as it disappears. Students are assigned to practice the piece for another week to make their playing sound more like rockets. **10 minutes**

Example 9.4 "Rockets," p. 48 from *Alfred's Basic Group Piano Course,* Book 2

Teacher	Student
4. For review, the teacher asks each students to play 4ths up and down from specific keys.	4. Without headsets, each student does so in turn, from two different keys.
The teacher asks the students to identify 4ths by ear. The teacher plays pairs of intervals: 4ths and 2nds, then 4ths and 3rds, and finally 4ths and 5ths.	The students close their eyes and raise their hands whenever they hear a 4th.
The teacher asks individual students to write harmonic or melodic 4ths up or down from specific notes on the staff.	**At the board:** The students do so, and correct each other's work.
From a supply of approximately three cards per student, the teacher shows interval flashcards to each student in turn. Each student is given the flashcard for each correct answer.	The students, identify intervals from flashcards that include 2nds, 3rds, and 4ths on the staff. The student with the most flashcards at the end is the winner. **10 minutes**

Example 9.5 Theory page from Unit 6 of *Alfred's Basic Group Piano Course*, Book 2

Example 9.6 Sight Reading page from Unit 6 of *Alfred's Basic Group Piano Course*, Book 2

Teacher	Student
5. For written and creative work, the teacher begins with page 57, numbers 1 and 2 (see example 9.5). The teacher asks the students to complete the first example and moves about the room to check each student's work.	5. Each student completes numbers 1 and 2 (p. 57) for the first treble clef example.
The teacher introduces the practice steps for Sight Reading example 2a on page 58 (see example 9.6).	Students follow the practice steps, playing the examples using their headsets. **4 minutes**
6. On page 63 (see Example 9.7), the teacher directs the students to tap and count aloud rhythms "a" to "c."	6. The students tap and count aloud the examples as a group.
The teacher explains the directions for the bottom half of page 63 and directs the students to improvise two measures, in turn.	The students place their hands in C position and improvise two measures, in turn, without stopping. **4 minutes**

Example 9.7 Rhythm Drills and Composition/Improvisation, p. 63 from Unit 6 of *Alfred's Basic Group Piano Course*, Book 2

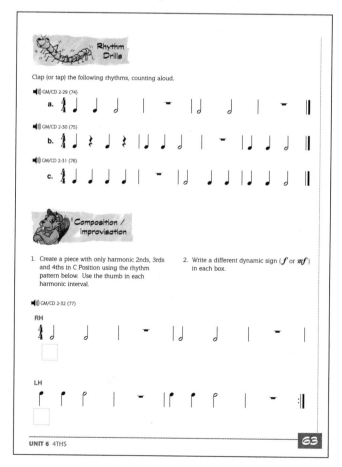

Teacher	Student
7. The teacher leads the students to find 4ths in the new piece "Play a Fourth," on page 55 (see example 9.8). The teacher leads the students to find parts of the piece that are the same or similar. The teacher taps the rhythm and counts aloud line 1 with the students. The teacher instructs students to play the first line individually with their headsets on.	**At their pianos (headsets off):** 7. The students circle all the 4ths. They trade books and correct each other's work. The students point to similar measures (mm. 1–4 and mm. 5–8). The students tap the rhythm and count line 1 with the teacher. Students play the first line individually, using headsets. **5 minutes**
8. The teacher prepares for the musical and technical requirements of future pieces by having students review the C and G major five-finger patterns by playing them. The teacher moves about the room, checking the students' posture and hand position. The teacher directs the students to place their right hands in G position and calls out the following: • finger numbers in random order (students with eyes closed) • intervals ("play G, up a 2nd, down a 2nd, up a 3rd, up a 2nd," etc.) • note names in random order ("play G, A, B, G, B, C," etc.) The teacher moves about the room, checking the students' accuracy, posture and hand position.	8. Working together with a partner (headsets on), the students play C and G major five-finger patterns up and down. • each hand separately three times • hands together three times The partners check each other's playing, posture and hand position. The students place their right hands in G position and follow the teacher's directions for the drill. **At the teacher's piano:** Individual students are asked by another student to play the C or G major five-finger patterns legato or staccato. They play loudly going up and softly going down. **10 minutes**

Teacher	Student
9. The teacher leads the students to discover and experience the various features of "Harmonic Waltz," on page 62 (see example 9.9): • the measures containing 4ths • the notes and rhythm of each hand played separately	9. The students (without headsets): • circle and play the measure with the 4ths • play and count each hand separately • play the piece as a duet, half the class playing the RH and the other half playing the LH • switch parts and play the piece again **4 minutes**

Example 9.8 "Play a Fourth," p. 55 from *Alfred's Basic Group Piano Course,* Book 2

Example 9.9 "Harmonic Waltz" and "Upside-Down Waltz," p. 62 from *Alfred's Basic Group Piano Course,* Book 2

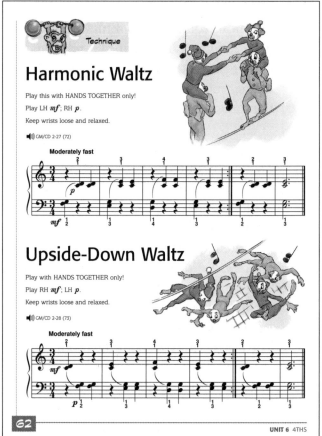

Teacher	Student
10. The teacher leads the students to compare "Upside-Down Waltz" to "Harmonic Waltz" (see example 9.9). The teacher assigns "Upside-Down Waltz" for independent practice using the same learning procedures as "Harmonic Waltz" and moves about the room assisting students.	10. The students look at "Upside-Down Waltz" and compare it to "Harmonic Waltz." The students practice "Upside-Down Waltz" independently in the lesson using headsets.　**5 minutes**

During this lesson, the students have experienced technique, theory, rhythm, expressive playing, ensemble playing, reading, keyboard topography, and aural development. Furthermore, they have been prepared for successful home practice.

It may not be possible to cover as much material in a group lesson as in a private lesson since the pace must be at a rate that all students can attain. The remaining two pieces in Unit 6 (on pages 56 and 60) can be included on the assignment as a challenge for the quicker students. A detailed and precise written assignment must be prepared in advance.

Prepared Assignment

Alfred's Basic Group Piano Course, Book 2, Unit 6 (pages 55–63)

Practice Assignment

1. "**Rockets**," page 48 (review from Unit 5) (see example 9.4)
   a. Play line 1 loud and slow; play line 1 faster.
   b. Play line 1 smoothly. Keep a steady beat.
   c. Play line 2 soft and slow; play line 2 faster.
   d. Play line two smoothly. Keep a steady beat.
   e. Play the whole piece slowly, observing the dynamics; play the whole piece faster.
   Make it sound like a rocket!
2. "**Play a Fourth**," page 55 (see example 9.8)
   a. Play mm. 1–2 and 5–6, naming finger numbers.
   b. Play mm. 1–2 and 5–6, naming the notes.
   c. Play mm. 3–4 and 7–8, naming finger numbers.
   d. Play mm. 3–4 and 7–8, naming the notes.
   e. Play the piece as written, observing the dynamics.

3. **"If I Won Ten Million Dollars,"** pages 52–53 (see example 9.3)

   a. Practice your assigned part (part 4) making sure the tempo is steady with no stops.

4. Use good practice steps and teach yourself **"Fourths are Fun!"** on page 56 and **"Old Uncle Bill"** on page 60.

5. Complete the written work on page 57 (see example 9.5).

6. Read and follow the directions on pages 58 and 63 (see examples 9.6–9.7).

7. **"Harmonic Waltz,"** page 62 (see example 9.9)

   a. Play and count each hand alone.

   b. Play and count the piece hands together.

   c. Teach yourself **"Upside-Down Waltz"** by practicing the same way you practiced **"Harmonic Waltz."**

SUMMARY

Both private and group instruction offer unique and distinctive ways to teach piano. Teachers can learn about group instruction and apply its principles to private teaching as well.

- There are advantages and disadvantages to both group instruction and private lessons.

- Group instruction can occur regularly or periodically for performance experience, theory and ear development, ensemble experience, functional skills, and creative work.

- Group lessons can supplement and reinforce the private lessons.

- Group lessons can be the primary form of instruction, with private lessons reinforcing the group lessons.

- Students can have group instruction weekly, biweekly or monthly.

- For some students, group lessons as the sole form of instruction are beneficial.

- Partner lessons, master classes, or summer "camps" are good ways to introduce teachers, students, and parents to group learning.

- Use of digital pianos can make large-group teaching even more effective.

- Teachers must determine efficient ways to group students and schedule classes.

- Materials and equipment are readily available for teachers to use for group instruction.

- Ensembles, field trips, games and competitive activities are possible during group lessons.

- Group teaching requires more planning in advance than private lessons. When teachers devise well-planned group lessons and effective assignments based on those plans, students can learn efficiently in group settings.

PROJECTS FOR NEW TEACHERS

1. Create a musical game for two or more players that teaches and drills note names or intervals. Your game may be patterned after a familiar game by modifying a deck of cards or board game, or you can create a totally new game. Write the instructions for playing the game that can be easily understood by children.

2. You have decided to incorporate monthly group lessons into your teaching schedule. Each student will receive three private lessons and one group lesson a month. Write a letter to parents introducing the benefits of this form of group instruction and how it will be implemented into your studio.

PROJECTS FOR EXPERIENCED TEACHERS

1. Plan a one-hour group lesson for first-year students that will meet monthly for the purpose of adding supplemental activities not included in the private lessons. Choose a theory book and an ear-training book to use for the class and plan the activities to correlate with a specific section of the method book the students are using. In planning the lesson, a) alternate activities at the piano with others away from the piano; b) include a game-type activity; c) alternate quieter activities with more active ones.

2. Using a group piano method series, plan a 45 minute lesson for elementary students who have only group lessons. In planning the lesson, a) follow the general format of the lesson plan in this chapter; b) alternate activities at the piano with others away from the piano; c) include a game-type activity; d) alternate quieter activities with more active ones. Write an assignment to distribute to the students following the class.

3. Using college group piano texts, find ten activities that can be used to supplement group lessons for elementary students. Choose a variety of activities to include improvisation, transposition, playing by ear, harmonization, technique, ensemble, and a game. List each activity, describe what concepts it would reinforce, and how you would use it in the lesson.

Chapter 10
TEACHING PRESCHOOLERS

Recent decades have seen an increased interest in early childhood music education. The work of 20th-century developmental psychologists supports the idea that music is a viable part of early childhood education.

- **Maria Montessori** (1870–1952) observed that children learn easily in an environment that stimulates their curiosity and imagination, and leads them to inquiry, manipulation and experience.

- **Jean Piaget** (1896–1980) believed that all children go through stages of intellectual development and must complete each developmental stage before they can move on to the next stage. Readiness for learning in each new stage of development is achieved in the previous stage.

- **Lev Vygotsky** (1896–1934) observed that play is an essential component of early learning and that the interaction of children with adults, especially parents, is essential to learning.

- **Jerome Bruner** (b. 1915) theorizes that anything can be taught to students of any age through a spiral curriculum, where general principles are presented in simple ways at first, and then with ever-increasing complexity over time. An idea must be experienced through sensing and doing; later, it can be internalized and experienced through language or symbols.

- **Howard Gardner** (b. 1943) believes that we learn in different ways (multiple intelligences). He has identified eight intelligences, of which music is one, stating that musical intelligence—sensitivity to pitch, melody and tone—emerges earlier than some other types of intelligence.

All of these ideas suggest that natural musical instincts are enhanced when music is experienced early, in age-appropriate ways. Interacting with music from an early age can enhance the child's overall development. The proliferation of preschool music programs indicates that both the musical community and parents are taking the discoveries of these psychologists and educators seriously.

ADVANTAGES OF PRESCHOOL MUSIC EXPERIENCES

The study of music and movement during the preschool years provides students with positive experiences and enhances growth in the following areas:

- patience, perseverance and commitment

- attention span and concentration

- self-awareness and respect

- self-confidence, pride and satisfaction

- give-and-take in social interaction
- sensitivity and expressiveness
- body awareness
- small- and large-motor development—specifically, balance, control and coordination
- ability to listen to instructions
- methodical learning
- vocabulary and language skills
- ability to understand abstract concepts through experience
- memory development
- ability to identify specific musical symbols
- ability to differentiate specific sound concepts related to music (high/low, loud/soft, etc.)
- vocal development
- creativity through movement and singing
- expression of everyday activities and feelings through mime and drama
- beginning keyboard skills

The piano is a perfect starting instrument for preschoolers because it allows children to easily produce attractive sounds. Additionally, these young students are less likely to have activities that interfere with home practice. Students who start music study during the preschool years establish a habit of regular practice that will carry forward into later years. Because these students have learned to make music and practice a part of their everyday life, they will be more mature musically than average-age beginners.

Piano teachers also find that there are practical considerations for teaching preschoolers. Because preschoolers learn music through interaction with their parents and teacher, parental involvement is required for effective preschool music learning. Parents who take time to share preschool music experiences will also be more likely to work successfully with their children in later years, during formal piano instruction.

Another practical advantage to teaching preschool students is that frequently they can be taught during the day, at times when most other students are not available for lessons. Teachers can increase their income by expanding the teaching days in their studios or by teaching classes in preschools or day care centers.

MUSICAL GOALS FOR TEACHING PRESCHOOLERS

The primary purposes of teaching music to young students are to foster their overall development and enhance their enjoyment of music. The goal is to create musical human beings with enhanced development through music, not necessarily to teach performance skills. The teacher provides a musical environment and musical experiences that allow the child to explore and respond. Students become musically literate and, as a result, learn music more easily in school-age years. When preschool instruction is child-centered, developmentally appropriate, concerned with the whole child, and focused on the process, the result will be a person who interacts joyously with music, rather than just a passive consumer of music.

Other goals of teaching preschoolers include raising children's musical awareness, development of their natural musicality, and enhancing their ability to do the following:

- listen

- sing tunefully

- move expressively and rhythmically

- play classroom instruments

- create self-satisfying music

After students have developed a musical vocabulary through preschool training, they are equipped to learn to read, write and perform. Reading notes and performing music on the piano before experiencing music can be compared to reading a language without understanding what the words mean.

CHARACTERISTICS OF PRESCHOOL MUSIC TEACHERS

Teaching preschoolers is different from teaching average-age beginners and elementary students. It requires unique teaching skills and special training. Not all piano teachers enjoy teaching preschoolers, but those who do can look forward to a pleasurable and positive teaching experience. Those who teach preschool music must have the following characteristics:

- knowledge of the developmental stages of children

- an understanding of the principles of learning for preschool ages

- knowledge of individual learning styles

- confidence

- sensitive communication and observation skills

- patience to provide the time and opportunity for individual musical response

- flexibility and openness to an eclectic approach

- creativity and a willingness to try new ideas

- the ability to model social and musical behaviors

- a sense of humor and the ability to smile, laugh and enjoy the children and the learning experience

- a willingness to dance, march, hop, sit on the floor and move freely

- a willingness to prepare and memorize lesson plans so that lessons progress in a smooth and natural way

ROLE OF THE TEACHER IN PRESCHOOL MUSIC

The teacher's primary roles in preschool music instruction are as follows:

- to establish a positive relationship with the child

- to be a model for the parent(s) and the child

- to provide a stimulating learning environment and a relaxed atmosphere for positive learning

- to present musical sounds and experiences using exemplary materials

- to observe the parent and child

- to educate parents about their role in their child's music learning and how they can create a musical environment in their home

- to provide parents with helpful ideas and resources for musical experiences at home

It is the teacher's job to create an environment conducive to children's exploration and learning. That environment should also be one that inspires parents as follows:

- to create a similar home environment

- to use as a model for their child's musical experiences at home

- to observe their child's behaviors and responses

- to play a supportive role

Effective teachers modify the learning experiences by observing the behavior of both the parents and the children. At times, the child may not be ready to experience music in the way that it was presented. Both teachers and parents must accept the child's natural mode of experiencing music. Teachers can use the following simple criteria for evaluating the effectiveness of their teaching of preschool children:

- Do the children seem to be interested in and enjoy the activities?

- Do the activities elicit developmentally appropriate responses?

ROLE OF THE PARENT IN PRESCHOOL MUSIC

In preschool music study, the parents' involvement is essential. Preschool children are motivated by the participation of their parents in musical experiences, with music becoming a natural part of their daily activities. Music played in the home is very influential for the child's musical development. The whole family—including siblings and grandparents—can sing, dance, and have fun with music, setting a model for music as a participatory activity in everyday life.

The primary roles of the parent(s) in preschool music are as follows:

- to attend classes and observe the teacher and the child

- to model musical behavior and experiences for the child in the class and at home

- to create a learning environment in the home

- to be supportive and encouraging to the child

Parents who participate in and support their child's inborn musical development become more active music participants. Some parents must be taught how to experience music themselves so they can become comfortable modeling for their children. In this way, the adults become students along with their children.

Musical experiences should enhance life and be an integral part of the child's entire daily routine. When getting a child ready in the morning, the mother might sing a song about brushing teeth, combing hair, or putting on shoes. The words of a song about brushing teeth provide an opportunity for the child to learn the proper way to do so. Secondarily, the pulse or rhythm of the song can be experienced with the arm while making the brushing motions.

Parents who observe and participate at the lesson learn to assist in practice at home. When the activities from the lesson are reinforced during the week, the habit of regular practice is begun. Such practice may be as simple as singing the songs. Practice sessions for preschoolers should be short, no more than 10–15 minutes long. They should be stopped if the child loses interest or the session becomes unpleasant. Several short practice sessions each day are more effective than one long session. Practice can be a positive time in which parents and children share time and bond.

CHARACTERISTICS OF PRESCHOOLERS

A knowledge of developmental characteristics for various preschool groups helps teachers know what to expect, how to plan activities and how to evaluate the effectiveness of the instruction. Expectations and musical experiences must be based on the physical, emotional, and cognitive development of the child. Age-appropriate activities promote musical growth and effective instruction.

Imitation is a natural form of learning for young children, but when learning is solely the result of mimicking, it is superficial. In addition to activities in which the children imitate, teachers should include activities that encourage and reinforce exploration, experimentation and response, all of which help children become natural musicians.

Exploration and experimentation are play for young children. It is through play that they learn best. Play is a source of pleasure; yet it is essential for progress through the various stages of emotional, physical, social, expressive and cognitive development. It should be spontaneous and active. Self-initiated play activities can often hold the students' interest longer than those initiated by the teacher. All activities can be playful, but because formal instruction cannot be self-directed, teachers should structure some activities that build conceptual growth while allowing students to explore music themselves.

Age-appropriate activities promote musical growth and effective instruction. Three-year-olds are very different from four-year-olds, and four-year-olds are different from five-year-olds. Curriculum, therefore, must be tailored to the age and maturity of the child. Since motor skills improve with increased chronological age, instruction on an instrument that requires fine-motor control (e.g., individual fingers) should be delayed until those motor skills are sufficiently developed.

Individual students in a preschool class respond in different ways. Some are active participants in activities, while others observe intently, but do not participate. This does not necessarily mean they are not listening, experiencing or interacting with the music. Students respond in developmentally appropriate ways to meet their own needs. Therefore, teachers and parents should never pressure preschool students to meet specific performance goals. Many children who never sing in class sing all the songs perfectly at home. Other children who do not respond in class or at home suddenly are able to demonstrate everything they have absorbed over several weeks or months. As children mature, they begin to respond in the class in more overt ways through movement and singing.

Musical and Developmental Characteristics

Because individual students develop at different rates in various areas, some children will respond to experiences more often found in children above or below their chronological age. Furthermore, children of different age groups will benefit from experiences using the same types of materials and activities if teachers structure them in age-appropriate ways. For example, one-year-old children enjoy hearing short chants with rhyming words. By the age of three or four, they begin to recognize songs that rhyme; by age five, they make up their own rhymes for songs.

Newborns can discriminate sounds and, at about five months, can discriminate musical sounds. While they do not respond overtly to music, they aurally collect musical sounds from the environment. They begin to make cooing sounds at two or three months. By four to six months, they reproduce sounds, discovered by chance, and repeat and modify them. Babies enjoy when the parent(s) match their sounds to create a musical conversation. The lists that follow enumerate musical and developmental characteristics of preschool students from six months to six years.

Children ages 6–18 months can be expected to have the following abilities and behaviors:

- have random responses to music
- babble, but not in imitation of the music being heard
- participate in vocal play
- reproduce sounds discovered by chance
- smile to familiar sounds
- turn their heads in the direction of music or a new sound
- sway noticeably and bounce to musical sounds

Children ages 18 months to 3 years can be expected to have the following abilities and behaviors:

- enjoy playing alone or with adults
- enjoy objects that make sounds
- avoid sharing or taking turns
- have a workable vocabulary
- have control in walking
- remember things
- enjoy the same story or song, over and over
- love rhymes
- able to maintain interest and attention for several minutes
- respond to two-step directions
- understand what the number one (1) means
- interact in directed activity
- have delayed responses to class activities
- respond to their own names
- display curiosity about the body and be able to identify various body parts
- imitate adults
- learn with individual, group and child/adult activities
- listen to stories that inspire the musical ideas of up/down, high/low, loud/soft
- play voice inflection games (voice going up for the word "up" and down for the word "down")
- chant during finger-play games
- chase, hide, and play twirling games
- learn best with an adult partner

Three-year-old children can be expected to have the following abilities and behaviors:

- communicate deliberately, using full sentences and be verbally confident
- talk incessantly to *practice* the language
- love nonsense words
- have the ability to tell stories
- listen to conversations between adults and imitate them
- listen when being reasoned with and understand simple instructions
- want approval of adults
- have a lengthening attention span and learn about patience
- begin to take turns and play cooperatively
- have a developing sense of humor

- recite simple rhymes
- like "sound-and-silence" games
- recognize printed music
- use the words "high," "low," "loud", or "soft," but may not always correctly relate the words to what is heard
- enjoy being taught chants, songs, and movement games and want them repeated over and over
- like singing or playing instruments in private
- may discontinue musical behaviors if they think someone is watching
- are able to learn when voluntary participation only is expected
- can distinguish between fast and slow
- need much encouragement and approval
- need less parental participation in the lesson than at younger ages

Four-year-old children can be expected to have the following abilities and behaviors:

- enjoy playing with other children
- are more confident, assured and better able to control emotions
- are interested in rhymes
- need attention and praise
- have acquired a vocabulary for music and movement such as, loud/soft, long/short, tiptoe, march
- respond well to directions to sing, move or play at various dynamics and tempos

Five-year-old children can be expected to have the following abilities and behaviors:

- enjoy other children during activities
- are interested in musical games with rules and enjoy structured activities
- need help in cooperating with other students
- take turns with other children
- can sing and listen to increasingly complex songs and stories
- enjoy creating sound stories (stories in which specific musical sounds can be inserted by the student or teacher)
- enjoy discovering rhyming words
- use a simple vocabulary of musical terms, such as *forte* for loud
- can utilize pictures, shapes and other symbols to represent pitch, duration, and simple musical forms
- can discuss musical concepts, such as pitch (high/low), tempo (fast/slow) and volume (loud/soft)

MUSICAL ACTIVITIES FOR PRESCHOOLERS

Preschoolers experience music through a variety of activities:

Singing Activities

- familiar and new songs of all types—rhyming, serious or silly songs, for example
- songs for daily home activities—taking a bath, having a snack, washing hands, or walking to school, for example
- songs for movement—expressive body movement or specific movements, such as jumping, skipping, and finger plays
- songs that relate to the make-believe world of children
- songs that encourage the development of particular musical elements —pulse, high/low, up/down, loud/soft, fast/slow, sound/silence, rhythm patterns, melodic patterns, repetition of words and phrases
- songs that teach the sounds of musical instruments
- improvised, spontaneous songs such as songs for the beginning and ending of class

Rhythm and Movement Activities

- moving or making hand motions to songs
- moving the body in creative ways
- experiencing rhythmic chants
- participating in dances and circle songs
- moving and dancing with the parent(s)
- moving to the beat, tempo and rhythm of music

Listening Activities and Responding to Music and Stories

- reading or listening to stories that encourage response through movement or sound
- participating in sound stories
- listening to music while resting or having a snack
- moving imaginatively to music
- expressive movement to music using props, such as scarves and hoops

Activities for Expressiveness and Creativity

- free play with sound lines and sound mats (a variety of drums, bells and shakers arranged on a mat or hung on a rope line for students to play)

- play with puppets or stuffed animals to reinforce musical *conversations* (phrases, motives)

- exploring sounds (the ticking of a clock, the jingle of keys, the honking horns of cars, the sounds animals make, etc.)

- exploring and creatively using their voices

- creating songs with the voice or with instruments

Activities Using Instruments

- exploration and use of percussion instruments

- exploration and use of homemade instruments

- exploration and use of autoharp, guitar and tone-bell instruments such as the xylophone

- exploration of the piano keyboard

- identification of instruments by sight (pictures) and sound

- pretending to play instruments

GENERAL TEACHING STRATEGIES

Preschoolers will be easier to teach if certain procedures are followed:

- Since preschool age students have short attention spans, teachers need to plan many short and varied activities of approximately three minutes in length.

- Teachers should plan special attention-getting activities for times when students' interest wanes (when students begin to wiggle, for example).

- An activity should stop when students lose interest and returned to later in the same lesson or in a subsequent lesson.

- Repetition of activities is very important. Young children forget easily and like to be able to predict what is going to happen. Therefore, repetition reviews the material and is fun for the child.

- Activities should be gamelike. For example, when naming ascending keys, the students can pretend to climb a ladder, and when naming descending keys, they can pretend to be falling leaves.

- There should be an alternation between quieter and more active activities.

- Lesson rituals and routines, rather than rules, can be established beginning with the first lesson.

- Greeting and closing songs give structure to the lesson time.

- Instructions and explanations can often be given in a musical way, such as singing "Please sit down" or "Clap my song."

- Teachers should allow extra time before and after lessons for setup and cleanup.

GENERAL MUSICIANSHIP APPROACHES FOR TEACHING MUSIC TO PRESCHOOL STUDENTS

General musicianship approaches for teaching principles of music to preschoolers tailor instruction to students from birth through age five without using a keyboard. Children are usually taught in groups. The curricula provide a holistic, well-rounded education in which students sing, listen, create, play rhythm instruments, move to music, learn about musical instruments, and learn basic musical symbols and terminology. Parents are often involved during all or part of the lessons and are encouraged to continue the activities between lessons using specific materials for home use. This approach makes music a natural and integral part of daily life and lays a strong foundation for music appreciation and future music study of any instrument.

General musicianship programs that have been specifically developed for preschool children have based their curriculum on early-childhood educational research and many of the philosophies and ideas of the following approaches to classroom music education.

The Dalcroze Approach

Swiss music educator Émile Jaques-Dalcroze (1865–1950) devised an approach to teaching that integrates movement, ear development, and improvisation to express musical ideas. This combination of movement, solfège and improvisation is known as the Jaques-Dalcroze Method. The teaching techniques combine hearing, singing, reading, and writing with physical response.

Dalcroze is best known for his movement exercises, known as *eurhythmics* (good rhythm). These activities help students develop the ability to feel, hear and invent, with the goal of converting musical knowledge into musical understanding. Through eurhythmics, the body is used as the musical instrument in a kind of rhythmic gymnastics, to express musical ideas relating to tempo, beat, duration, accents, meter, dynamics, articulation, rests, rhythmic subdivisions, rhythm patterns, phrases and form. Teachers encourage movement response by improvising on various instruments. These exercises train the body to quickly and accurately perform commands given by the brain.

Through solfège, inner hearing is developed. Hearing musical ideas both externally and internally provides the stimulus for physical response, singing, and eventually, reading and writing. Furthermore, the student learns to improvise, thus transforming these musical ideas into creative expressions through improvised body movement, vocal sounds and playing of instruments. Tapping the rhythm or walking to the beat that the teacher plays are simple applications of the Jaques-Dalcroze Method.

The Kodály Approach

Hungarian music educator and composer Zoltán Kodály (1882–1967), together with his colleagues and students, inspired, guided and developed a comprehensive system of music education, based on the following six premises:

1. All people capable of linguistic literacy are also capable of musical literacy.

2. Singing is the best foundation for musicianship.

3. Music education, to be most effective, must begin with very young children.

4. The folk songs of a child's own linguistic heritage constitute a musical *mother tongue* and should, therefore, be the vehicle for early instruction.

5. Only music of the highest artistic value should be used in teaching.

6. Music should be at the heart of the curriculum, a core subject, used as a basis for education.[1]

Example 10.1
Curwen hand symbols

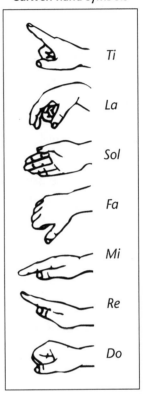

The highly developed and sequenced curriculum known as the Kodály Method is based on child-development principles, using folk songs, sung with words and with moveable-do solfège. Children learn hand signs, adapted from those developed by John Curwen (1816–1880), to facilitate the development of a tonal memory (see example 10.1).

Children also learn rhythm duration syllables, similar to those invented by Emile Chevé (1804–1864), to assist in learning rhythm patterns found in songs. Such syllables include the following:

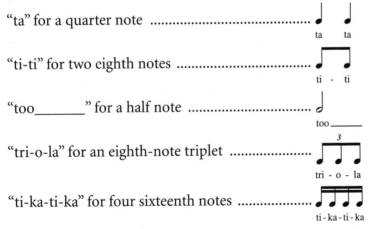

"ta" for a quarter note ....

"ti-ti" for two eighth notes ....

"too_____" for a half note ....

"tri-o-la" for an eighth-note triplet ....

"ti-ka-ti-ka" for four sixteenth notes ....

---

[1] Lois Choksy, Robert M. Abramson, Avon E. Gillespie, David Woods, Frank York, *Teaching Music in the Twenty-First Century*, 2nd edition (Upper Saddle River, NJ: Prentice Hall, Inc., 2000), p. 82.

Children are encouraged to clap, tap and move in various ways to assist in rhythmic development. They also learn to recognize rhythm patterns visually, represented by various graphic symbols,[2] and "write" them, using such symbols or sticks.

Children learn about musical form by recognizing patterns in the songs and, later, phrases and larger formal structures. Harmony begins by singing or playing tonal-center drone accompaniments. Creative teaching techniques are used to develop inner hearing and musical memory.

The Orff Approach

German composer and music educator Carl Orff (1895–1982), collaborating with others, developed a curriculum of music education known as Orff Schulwerk. Movement, the spoken voice, singing and instruments are emphasized in this approach. Free and improvised movements are used in beginning stages, followed by learning dance steps and combining the steps in folk dancing. The body is used as a percussion instrument through hand-clapping, foot-stamping, finger-snapping, and thigh-patting (*patschen*). Speech is used to teach rhythm and the voice is the first instrument to be developed. Instruments are used as an extension of voice and movement.

Students begin their music learning by experiencing environmental sounds, followed by more organized sounds. The foundation of the Orff approach combines melodic and rhythm patterns (based on speech). Students experience music elements—melody, beat, meter, tempo, and rhythm—through movement, speech, mouth sounds, nonsense words, vocal play, and by singing and by playing a variety of instruments. The exercises lead students to understand beginnings, endings, duration and patterns.

Published Orff materials provide models to encourage student improvisation, composition and movement. Teachers model and then students imitate, experiment, and create, often by working in ensembles. Specially designed Orff instruments enhance the learning. This approach is most often associated with mallet instruments tuned to the pentatonic scale and used to create ostinatos. There are also recorders, drums, wood instruments (such as wood blocks), metal instruments (such as finger cymbals), and stringed instruments (such as guitars). Students explore instruments in improvisatory ways before being introduced to notation, an example of teaching music using creativity and play.

Contemporary General Musicianship Approaches

Successful preschool music programs have been developed, which incorporate aspects of early-childhood educational research and ideas advanced by the Dalcroze, Kodaly and Orff approaches. Most established programs recommend, and some even require, short teacher-training sessions before their materials can be used. Many piano teachers teach these curricula, but other musicians and people with a musical background may teach them as well. A listing of the best-known general musicianship programs follows:

---

[2] Graphic notation includes using pictures or symbols to represent specific rhythmic values. For example, a small drawing of an animal would represent a quarter note, a medium-sized drawing of the same animal would represent a half note, and a large drawing would represent a whole note.

Harmony Road

harmonyroadmusic.com

The Harmony Road curricula include:
- *Toddler Tunes,* for ages $1^1/_2$–3, attending with a parent or caregiver
- *Music in Me* and *More Music in Me,* for ages 3–4, attending with a parent or caregiver

See page 293 for other offerings.

Kindermusik International

kindermusik.com

The Kindermusik curricula include:
- *Kindermusik Village,* for ages newborn to $1^1/_2$, attending with a parent or caregiver
- *Kindermusik Our Time,* for ages $1^1/_2$–3, attending with a parent or caregiver
- *Kindermusik Imagine That!* for ages 3–5, attending with peers for the first 30 minutes, and with a parent or caregiver for the final 15 minutes
- *Kindermusik for the Young Child,* for ages 5–7, attending with peers, with the option of parent involvement for the final 15 minutes of class
- *Kindermusik Family Time,* for families with multiple children ages newborn and up

Musikgarten

musikgarten.org

The Musikgarten curricula include:
- *Family Music for Babies,* for ages birth to $1^1/_2$, attending with a parent or caregiver
- *Family Music for Toddlers,* for ages $1^1/_2$–3, attending with a parent or caregiver
- *Cycle of Seasons,* for ages 3–5, attending with a parent or caregiver
- *Music Makers: At Home in the World,* for ages 4–7, attending with peers
- *Music Makers: Around the World,* for ages 5–8, attending with peers (includes more focus on writing and reading music)

See page 294 for other offerings.

Music Together

musictogether.com

Most classes include mixed age groups from birth to age 4. Parents are required to attend. Babies may take a special "Babies Class" for one semester as an introduction to Music Together. "Big Kids Family Music" is designed for five- and six-year-old children with their families.

Music for Young Children

myc.com

The Music for Young Children curricula include:
- *Sunrise,* for ages 2–3, attending with a parent or caregiver

See page 294 for other offerings.

EQUIPMENT AND MATERIALS FOR PRESCHOOL GENERAL MUSICIANSHIP INSTRUCTION

In general, teaching preschoolers requires special equipment and a large open space that is visually appealing to students. Learning is enhanced when various materials and equipment are used. In addition to the materials available from commercial preschool music programs, teachers can make and/or purchase other equipment from toy, music, or educational supply stores. In typical preschool music classes where a keyboard is not used, such equipment includes the following:

- rhythm instruments
- recordings and recording equipment
- art and craft materials—construction paper, newsprint, scissors, markers, crayons, pipe cleaners
- balls of various types and sizes
- bean bags
- stuffed animals and puppets
- pictures of instruments and pictures to accompany stories or music
- hula hoops
- resonator bells
- storybooks
- dramatic play props, such as colored scarves, flags or banners, balloons, bubbles, feathers
- blocks with musical symbols on them
- floor mats
- mirrors on studio walls

- rhythm charts
- flashcards
- large, laminated staff cards
- magnetic and dry-erase boards marked with a music staff and keyboard
- velcro® music boards with a music staff and supporting musical symbols.
- large table and/or floor charts of the music staff and keyboard
- round stickers, checkers, metal or rubber washers, to represent note heads for placing on staff charts and cards
- ink stamps or stickers with musical notation
- note templates for tracing
- large-sized manuscript paper

TEACHING PIANO TO PRESCHOOL STUDENTS

Since most piano teachers are interested in developing students' keyboard skills, they are more likely to favor teaching piano to preschoolers than teaching a program of general-musicianship. The curricula can focus solely on playing the piano, or the teacher can combine piano teaching with aspects of a general-musicianship approach. A preschool curriculum that focuses on learning the piano can use either a listening (playing by ear) approach or a note-reading emphasis. Some teachers teach students as young as age 3, but most preschool piano curricula are developed for four- to six-year-old children.

Piano teachers who are considering teaching piano lessons to preschool children can be assured that there are distinct advantages to teaching them. Knowing the teaching goals and the characteristics of the various age groups will help teachers decide whether to teach private or group lessons.

When teaching group lessons, it is important to group children by age, with different classes for four-year-olds, five-year-olds and six-year-olds. Since all children do not develop at the same rate and may not exactly match the developmental level of their chronological age, ages can be overlapped with one class for four- and five-year-olds and another for five- and six-year-olds. Four- and six-year-olds usually should not be taught in the same class.

Preschool students may not end up playing more advanced pieces at age 10 than students who started music instruction later. However, they will likely exhibit stronger musical skills than average-age beginners, such as the following:

- a well-developed sense of rhythmic pulse and secure rhythm skills

- greater physical ease and a full sound when playing the piano

- effective reading skills

- acute listening skills

- an innate sense of musical understanding

- security in performing for others

For teachers, improvement in their overall teaching skills is another benefit of preschool teaching. Preschool students need systematic and incremental presentations. Consequently, teachers must present ideas carefully and clearly—a skill needed for all levels of teaching. Furthermore, teachers quickly learn when their teaching is ineffective, since preschool students give recognizable signs when they do not understand.

Readiness for Preschool Piano Instruction

Piano instruction for preschool children will be easier when prospective students can demonstrate that they already understand a number of musical concepts and skills. When determining a student's readiness, teachers can consider the following abilities:

General Readiness Skills

- reads and writes his/her own name
- knows his/her right and left hand
- recognizes white keys and black keys, as well as groups of two and three black keys
- identifies high/low
- identifies up/down
- identifies numbers and music alphabet letters
- is eager to learn new things

Rhythmic Skills

- taps or walks to a steady beat and to recorded music, songs, and rhymes in triple and duple meters
- echo-claps (clap-back) easy rhythm patterns

Pitch Skills

- matches pitches and simple intervals in his/her range by singing
- echo-plays (play-back) three- or four-pitch melodic patterns
- sings songs in tune

Technique

- has the ability to move individual fingers

Lesson and Practice Readiness

- has an attention span conducive to 10 minutes of practice and 30 minutes for a lesson
- takes instruction well from the parents

Other Considerations

- shows an interest in music and piano-playing by spontaneously playing melodies on the keyboard
- has interest in the piano because older siblings or parents play an instrument
- shows maturity as a result of nursery or preschool experiences

Teachers can also use these criteria to group students into classes by their level of readiness, as well as their age. Some students already may have participated in general music classes that prepared them for more piano-specific classes. When students have not had those experiences, the teacher may want to offer a one-week readiness camp (see chapter 13, page 378). During the camp, songs, chants, and games can be used to teach students about things such as left and right, finger numbers, high and low, and the musical alphabet. Walking, marching, running, tapping and clapping activities will prepare students for rhythmic development. Activities at the keyboard can introduce black/white keys, up/down and steps/skips.

Piano Instruction Combined with a General Musicianship Approach

In this approach, students play musical games, sing and participate in movement activities, as well as play music on the piano. This lays a solid foundation for future musical study of any instrument. Listening skills are generally strong with students who have experienced piano instruction combined with general musicianship.

The piano is the primary medium for this approach, but the goal is greater than developing performing pianists. The process is often as important as the product. Students usually experience activities in the following categories:

- aural skills (including singing)

- rhythm skills

- reading notation

- keyboard acquaintance, exploration and performance

- physical aspects of playing keyboard (technique)

- music appreciation

- expressive and musical elements (including movement)

Singing and movement activities are often correlated to music that is to be played on the keyboard. Students are taught to sing songs with words, then sometimes with solfège syllables, and finally, to play the same songs on the keyboard through a combination of playing-by-ear and reading. Other keyboard pieces that are not sung first may also be taught. Parents are sometimes required to attend and participate in the lessons and in home practice.

Most published curricula have teachers' manuals and student materials for several levels. Some of the courses are designed specifically for groups, but others can be used for either group or private instruction. Examples of such curricula follow:

Harmony Road

harmonyroadmusic.com

Harmony Road has curricula for different age groups:
- *Toddler Tunes,* for ages 18 months –3 years, attending with a parent or caregiver
- *Hello Music,* for ages 3–4, attending with a parent or caregiver
- *Music in Me,* for ages 3–4, attending with a parent or caregiver
- *Musictime,* for ages 4–5, attending with a parent or caregiver
- *Harmony Road,* for ages 4^1/$_2$ –6, attending with a parent or caregiver
- *The Young Musician,* for ages 6–7, attending with a parent or caregiver
- *Keyboard Prep,* for ages 8–11

The *Harmony Road* curriculum places an emphasis on ear training, solfège singing, keyboard playing, ensemble and rhythm activities, movement, and music creativity. In addition, students work on transposition, improvisation, and composition. Students who complete the *Harmony Road, Young Musician,* and *Keyboard Prep* curricula may continue in *Keyboard Musician,* a more advanced program.

Music for Little Mozarts

musicforlittlemozarts.com

Christine H. Barden, Gayle Kowalchyk and E. L. Lancaster, *Alfred's Music for Little Mozarts,* Van Nuys, CA: Alfred Publishing Co., Inc., 1999

The *Music for Little Mozarts* series was written to provide appropriate piano instruction for four-, five- and six-year olds, while simultaneously developing listening skills. The course centers around the adventures of Beethoven Bear, Mozart Mouse and their music friends as they learn about music. A story about the music friends is contained in the Music Lesson Book at each level. The story guides students through various musical concepts while engaging their musical imaginations.

Many teachers use the Music Lesson Book and the Music Workbook for traditional private piano instruction. When the Music Discovery Book is added (either in private or group instruction), comprehensive general-musicianship activities are included. The Music Discovery Book reinforces concepts through singing, listening and movement activities. Included in the book are songs to sing for fun, motion songs to introduce musical responses to music, songs to reinforce specific rhythm patterns, and songs to aid in the development of musical expressiveness. Classical music, marches, circus music and adventure music are used for music appreciation activities. "Listen and Sing" pages include melodies for singing (using solfège or letter names) and interesting accompaniments to aid with pitch and interval study.

Music for Young Children
myc.com

Music for Young Children has curricula for different age groups:
- *Sunrise*, for ages 2–3, attending with a parent or caregiver
- *Sunshine*, for ages 3–4, attending with a parent or caregiver
- *Sunbeams*, for ages 5–6, attending with a parent or caregiver
- *Moonbeams*, for ages 7–9, attending with a parent or caregiver

Children meet in small groups, accompanied by a parent or caregiver. The development of the ear and sight-singing through the use of solfège is an integral part of the program. Each level includes listening activities and written materials to reinforce concepts introduced in the class. Performance repertoire, technique, scale and chord studies, arranging and harmonization are emphasized at the keyboard. Rhythm and keyboard ensembles are used throughout the course, and a composition unit of study is included in each level.

Musikgarten
musikgarten.org

Musikgarten offers a three-year group program that focuses on keyboard. *Music Makers: At the Keyboard*, designed for ages 6 and up, focuses on a comprehensive musicianship approach to playing the piano. The curriculum builds on songs that children know and emphasizes an aural approach to music literacy, providing a natural pathway to music reading.

Yamaha Music Education System
yamaha.com/ymes/musicschools/home.asp

Yamaha offers beginning music courses for many age groups, but the *Junior Music Course* is the cornerstone of the Yamaha Music Education System. This two-year curriculum was designed for four- and five-year-old students. Lessons are taught in groups, with parents or caregivers attending the classes. Children sing solfège, play the keyboard, sing songs, move to music, and play in both rhythm and keyboard ensembles. Typically, children hear a melody or harmony, sing it with solfège, play it on the keyboard, and then learn to read it. This, in turn, sets the stage for improvisation and composition. Music appreciation activities are also an important part of classes.

Only teachers who are sponsored by authorized Yamaha Music Schools can enter the teacher training process. After prospective teachers pass an entrance examination, they attend seminars locally and at the Yamaha Corporation headquarters in southern California.

Piano Instruction that Focuses on Listening

The most common preschool piano instruction approach with a focus on listening is the one developed by Shin'ichi Suzuki (1898–1998). In the Suzuki approach, students copy what they hear and see in the same way they learn their native language. When learning a language, young children hear their parents speaking, begin to mimic words, and then learn to express ideas in sentences. Much later, they learn a system of visual symbols for the language and learn to read and write it.

Using a similar approach, the Suzuki Talent Education System teaches strings, harp, flute and piano to preschool students, starting at about age 3. Just as a child learns language by being surrounded by those who speak it, a child learns music by being surrounded by it. This is why the Suzuki system is also known as the "mother-tongue approach."

All Suzuki students learn the same pieces, listening to recordings of the pieces they play to get the sound of them in their ears. During lessons, pieces are presented in incremental units through demonstration. The pieces are reinforced at home by the parent, through repetition and listening to the recordings. As students do not read the music initially, they are able to concentrate on technique and tone production. Mastering these skills through repetition develops a strong ear, a solid memory and an effortless technique that is built into the nervous system at an early age. After these skills have been sufficiently trained, students are taught to read the score. Since the initial teaching approach is by rote, students may not become independent learners easily and may struggle with developing reading skills.

Suzuki piano students learn pieces from a series of six repertoire books that include arrangements of folk songs and original piano repertoire. The pieces are sequenced to provide an exact order of concepts and skills. There are no instructions for the teacher or student about how to play the pieces, nor is there a teacher's manual. Teachers can learn to teach this approach by attending workshops and teacher-training courses. The Suzuki Association of the Americas maintains a list of registered teacher-trainers.

Piano Instruction that Focuses on Reading

In a preschool piano instruction program with an emphasis on reading, students are taught to read the same pitch and rhythm symbols as average-age beginners, though at a slower pace. These methods combine traditional piano instruction with age-appropriate musical experiences for preschoolers. Lessons using these methods are usually designed for private instruction, but can be used with groups. For some methods, the teacher's manuals suggest singing, body movement, improvisation, ear development and listening activities. Student lesson books, ear training books, recital books and workbooks may be available for each level.

Preschool piano methods have about twice as much reinforcement and half as much material in each book as average-age beginning methods. Illustrations and printing are larger and targeted to the younger student, and there are fewer words and directions on the page. Workbooks have more examples for each concept, and concepts are often reinforced by coloring and tracing.

Pitch reading usually begins with pre-staff notation, rather than notes on the staff. When the staff is introduced, usually one clef (and one hand) is presented at a time. Notes are often introduced one at a time and are memorized by their placement on the staff. Students may also learn steps and skips, but not larger intervals until the later levels of these courses. Each new concept or note is reinforced with more pieces than in an average-age beginner method. Color may be used to help students distinguish between the hands, for specific notes or note values.

The following are two well-known preschool reading-oriented methods:

Willard A. Palmer, Amanda Vick Lethco and Morton Manus. *Alfred's Basic Piano Library: Preparatory Course for the Young Beginner,* Van Nuys, CA: Alfred Publishing Co., Inc., 1988.

Jane Smisor Bastien, Lisa Bastien and Lori Bastien. *Bastiens' Invitation to Music.* San Diego, CA: Neil A. Kjos Music Company, 1994.

Considerations for Choosing Preschool Materials

In choosing materials for preschool keyboard instruction, teachers should consider the following:

- The approach should be appropriate for the specific preschool age and development of the student.

- Music books should have large print and uncluttered pages.

- Materials should include pictures and colorful illustrations that appeal to the student, but should not distract from the musical notation.

- Books printed in black and white should have pictures for students to color and opportunities for the placement of stickers.

- If text appears on the pages, it should not prevent students from focusing on student material.

- Titles of pieces should relate to the preschool child's world.

- Pieces should be short and easily learned. Those that introduce staff reading may be as short as four measures.

- Familiar tunes are motivating.

- Because preschoolers have not yet developed the ability to think conceptually, materials should include much repetition.

- Middle C or rote materials usually are more effective than materials that teach reading by intervals, since young students cannot yet transfer knowledge of note relationships (intervals).

- Materials should help teachers integrate rhythm and movement, singing, creating, listening and ear development, and writing activities.

- The approach should be fun and gamelike.

- The pacing must be much slower than the pace for average-age beginners.

- There should be information that explains the curriculum to parents and helps them practice with their children.

- Materials should include some or all of the following:
  - lesson books
  - keyboard floor chart
  - workbooks
  - rhythm instruments
  - recital books
  - recordings
  - ear-training books
  - flashcards

SUMMARY

Expanding teaching by including preschoolers is an option for piano teachers. Before teaching preschoolers, teachers need to realize the following:

- The primary goal for teaching music to preschoolers is to foster overall development and an enjoyment of music through musical experiences that become a part of everyday life.

- Interest in preschool learning has resulted in many preschool music programs and methods.

- The study of music during the preschool years enhances growth and development in many ways.

- Teachers need specialized tools and training to teach preschoolers. Fortunately, a vast amount of material, resources and training are available.

- One role of the teacher is to be a model for parents, so they can provide age-appropriate musical activities and a musical learning environment for their children at home.

- Musical behaviors are different for the various ages of preschool children.

- When teachers know how children respond to music at various ages, they can develop age-appropriate activities. These activities include singing, rhythm, listening, creating music and playing instruments.

- General musicianship, piano instruction and a combination of the two are the three basic approaches of teaching music to preschoolers.

- Children who experience piano instruction as preschoolers have distinct advantages over students who start at age 7 or 8.

- Piano instruction can either focus on a listening approach or a reading approach and can be taught in group or private lessons.

- Teachers should assess the readiness of students for piano instruction. If teaching in groups, divide classes according to their abilities and maturity.

- Materials specifically designed to teach piano to preschoolers make it unnecessary to use materials developed for average-age beginners.

PROJECTS FOR NEW TEACHERS

1. Find or create an age-appropriate song or game to introduce one of the following concepts to four- or five-year-olds who are studying in an approach that combines piano instruction with general musicianship:

    *   right and left hands, or right and left on the keyboard

    *   learning finger numbers, using the fingers on the keyboard, and saying these numbers forward and backward

    *   the music alphabet, and applying it to the keyboard, both forward and backward

    *   high and low, and relating them to right and left on the keyboard

    *   loud and soft, and applying them to the keyboard

    *   marching while clapping the beat

2. Choose two pieces from a preschool piano method and design a series of activities to introduce the pieces to four- or five-year-olds. The following activities should be considered:

    *   learning the words

    *   singing the words

    *   tapping the rhythm by ear (using tap-back)

    *   playing the rhythm on percussion instruments

    *   movement activities for rhythm, pulse, melody, character and dynamics

    *   playing the piece on the piano by ear

    *   tapping the rhythm from notation

    *   learning the notation

    *   playing the notes from notation

    *   "writing" the notation on a floor staff or on a magnetic board

---

Projects for Experienced Teachers

1. You would like to initiate a general musicianship preschool curriculum in your studio for students below age 4 using one of the commercial programs available on the market. Visit the websites of the following programs: *Harmony Road, Kindermusik International, Music Together, Music for Young Children* and *Musikgarten* (see page 289). Summarize the following about each program:

    *   the content of the curriculum for this age group

    *   the teacher-training requirements to teach this age group

    *   the role of the parents in each program

    Choose the program that you will implement in your studio and explain why you chose that program. In your explanation, highlight the advantages of the program you chose over the other programs.

2. Select a familiar children's story and develop it into a musical story for four-year-olds.

    *   Write musical motives (cues) for the characters or happenings, to become an integral part of the story.

    *   Suggest movements to represent each musical cue.

    Suggested stories include:

Cinderella	Peter Rabbit
Goldilocks and the Three Bears	Pinocchio
Hansel and Gretel	Rumpelstiltskin
Jack and the Beanstalk	The Three Little Pigs
The Little Red Hen	

Chapter 11

TEACHING ADULTS

Some teachers enjoy the challenges of teaching adults, while others prefer working with children. There are a number of positive aspects to teaching adults that can be very rewarding. Adult students tend to be sincerely interested in lessons and are usually intrinsically motivated. In addition to work and family responsibilities, studying piano is a commitment of time, money, energy, and effort not taken lightly. Adults who study piano are likely to acquire a deeper appreciation for music and music making, which can sometimes develop into ongoing support for musical events and the arts in general.

Teachers who teach adults find it rewarding for several other reasons:

- Teachers can interact and talk to students in an adult manner.

- Since adults can read directions and teach themselves some musical concepts, lesson time can focus on technical development, expressive playing, and reinforcement.

- Teaching can occur during hours of the day when most young students are unable to attend lessons.

- Teaching can be less stressful and more pleasurable because students progress at their own pace.

- Adult students tend to be enthusiastic and happy about their study.

- Many adult students understand that lessons are valuable for review, inspiration, and reinforcement, even when they have not practiced.

In lessons with adult students, the teacher's role is being a study partner, resource person, facilitator, and guide. Often lessons with adults are informal and more relaxed than lessons with children. The teacher should work together with adult students to set goals based on individual desires and needs. Because adults independently choose to study the piano, they may come to lessons with preconceived ideas about what they want to learn. Consequently, the focus in most adult lessons should be on enjoyment and playing music, not on a rigid curriculum. Most adults have no desire to become a concert pianist, but many times they want to play a specific piece, such as Beethoven's "Moonlight Sonata" or Pachelbel's "Canon in D." They may have a particular style of music they want to play or a certain goal they want to reach.

Although some adults study for several years, adults generally tend to study for a shorter time frame due to work schedules and lifestyle demands. This requires the teacher to be more flexible with adults than with children in terms of regular practice and lesson attendance. Since frustration with slow progress is one reason adults quit lessons, the teacher must encourage adults to be patient long enough to achieve their goals. When teachers provide repertoire and other activities that promote a feeling of success and enjoyment during the lessons, adults will study for a longer period of time. An encouraging atmosphere is also necessary, since piano playing requires deceptively challenging and potentially frustrating coordination and physical control.

Adults study piano for the following reasons:

- to ensure a meaningful and worthwhile use of leisure time
- to enjoy music and related subject matter
- to bring calmness or joy into their lives
- to reduce stress
- to grow as a person
- to develop confidence in their ability to learn and succeed
- to practice discipline
- to add structure to life in general
- to provide an outlet for creativity
- to promote positive expression of exhilarating emotions
- to develop a deeper and meaningful insight into aesthetics
- to shut out personal problems through the challenge of learning
- to improve concentration, observation, and memory
- to practice problem solving and conceptual thinking

GENERAL CHARACTERISTICS OF ADULT PIANO STUDENTS

The many categories of adult students described in detail later in this chapter include teenage beginners, collegiate non-music majors, adult piano teachers, and adults who had no previous opportunity to study. The diversity of adult students presents obstacles that differ from challenges encountered when teaching children. With this issue in mind, teachers can provide carefully planned, meaningful lessons by understanding the cognitive and physical abilities of adults, as well as their motivation, attitudes towards music, and inhibitions.

Ability to Process Information Intellectually

Many adult students come to piano lessons with the following intellectual characteristics:

- They are goal oriented.
- They have a history of education and know effective learning strategies.
- They can focus on problem solving and immediate application of knowledge.
- They want to be involved with the direction of their lessons.
- They have a lifetime of experiences to call upon to enhance their learning.
- They want to understand the reasons for what they are learning to do.
- They understand the value of perseverance.

Unlike children, adults usually have ideas about what they want to learn and how they want to learn it. Though they are not accustomed to being beginners, they usually understand concepts quickly and enjoy the process of musical discovery. They are responsive to suggestions from the teacher but want to know the rationale behind the instruction. Adults process written text easily and are very verbal, often asking questions about the music. Therefore, adults can learn more thoroughly than children and can retain long-term knowledge more easily. In general, adults have good problem-solving skills. They are able to teach some musical concepts to themselves. Many adults are self-disciplined and can plan their piano study. They can organize their practice time, pace their learning, set goals, and understand what it takes to be successful. Furthermore, they can concentrate for long periods and can complete complex activities. Consequently, teachers should communicate with adults as peers, presenting ideas differently from the way they may be expressed to children.

Because adults bring a variety of learning techniques and strategies to piano lessons from their life experience, they might not learn in the ways a teacher expects. For example, adults may want to intellectually study a piece before starting to practice it. When they begin to practice, they may tackle the most difficult spots first. Some adults do not want to play a piece for the teacher until it is well learned. Others want to play only specific sections. During lessons, some want help with only technically difficult sections, or they want the teacher to check that they are progressing correctly. Within these varying scenarios, adults use their individual learning style to control their approach, pace, practice structure, and use of lesson time. They may also decide when to drop a piece. Since lack of progress generally leads to discouragement and disinterest, they are likely to discontinue lessons if they fail to progress adequately. If lack of progress becomes apparent, teachers can take more control of the lessons.

Although adults are accomplished learners, too much responsibility and too many choices about lesson content can be confusing and frustrating. Their study can be self-directed, but it should be based on guidance, structure, and direction from the teacher. Setting goals and selecting music can be a cooperative effort. Analyzing music and evaluating the student's playing can also be collaborative. Because adults communicate well and synthesize information easily, adult lessons can become intellectual discussions that have very little to do with piano playing. Adults sometimes deflect the focus of the lesson by asking a myriad of questions, relating practice experiences, explaining problems, and raising issues beyond their current playing ability. Teachers can limit irrelevant discussions by establishing a lesson atmosphere centered on playing and music making, with social interaction kept to a minimum. During instruction, teachers can demonstrate rather than describe. They can also instruct students to show or play rather than to answer verbally.

The best sources for repertoire and other materials for adults are adult method books designed for the maturity and intellect of older beginners. Using these methods, adults can enjoy learning concepts and skills by reading the text themselves. As a result, lesson time can include other tasks, which allows more material to be covered in a shorter period.

Physical Ability That Can Impede or Enhance Piano Playing

As the piano was developed, the shape and size of the average adult body influenced the instrument's design. Decisions about the piano's physical dimensions allowed adult players to reach octaves, large chords, opposite ends of the keyboard, and the pedals. To play the piano, however, adults must not only reach the various parts of the instrument but also develop fine muscle coordination and an intellectual understanding of music. As adults begin taking lessons, they discover they lack finger, hand, and arm coordination despite having experienced other musical activities, such as singing or listening to a vast amount of music. Most likely, they have not experienced the two-hand coordination required for piano playing. Nonetheless, teachers can build upon the physical abilities adults inherently possess.

Developing mobility around the keyboard is particularly important. Technical exercises spanning a wide range of the keyboard can be used, as well as pieces requiring hand-over-hand patterns. Scales and arpeggios can be taught early on, so adults are not restricted to five-finger positions. Rote learning of exercises and pieces that improve speed and agility inspires adults and allows them to progress to more advanced repertoire in a timely manner.

To develop coordination, beginning adult students should start by only playing pieces in which (1) the hands play separately, or (2) the melody is in one hand and a simple drone-type accompaniment is in the other. Triads should be introduced early to satisfy the need for a full-sounding accompaniment. These simple pieces, with melody in one hand and chords in the other, expand finger coordination and hand independence. Although possibly daunting at first for the student, this independence is achievable. Teachers can reassure students that finger freedom can be gained as easily at the piano as at a computer keyboard.

Two other characteristics of adult students should be addressed from the beginning. The first characteristic involves finger size. Some adult students' fingers are large, making playing comfortably between the black keys difficult. These students may need to slightly exaggerate the curve of their fingers to draw their hand position more toward the outward edge of the keyboard. The second characteristic involves concentration. Adult students are able to focus intensely for long periods. While this attribute is usually positive, it can develop tension in the body counterproductive to effortless playing. Teachers should make students aware of tension whenever it is noticed during the lesson. Breaks should be encouraged during practice whenever tension is felt.

Sincere Interest in Piano Study

Unlike many children, adults make their own choice to begin taking piano lessons. In general, they know the requirements of lessons and what practicing and learning entails. Adults are serious in their desire to learn to play, and the decision to begin piano study is rarely frivolous. They want to increase their pianistic skills because they feel doing so is a worthwhile pursuit.

Adult students are usually engaged in lessons. Although their drive can be complex and can change over time, they are generally enthusiastic and self-directed learners with mature ideas about the music they are studying. They can concentrate during long lessons and can practice diligently when their schedules allow it. Their high motivation for learning is intrinsic rather than extrinsic. They understand that commitment to piano study means hard work, but they also understand that the accomplishment and proficiency gained produces positive feelings. Therefore, adults view lessons as a serious but pleasurable activity. Consequently, adult students look forward to lessons, welcome new ideas, and have dedication.

Although these characteristics are commendable, teachers and adult students may have differing goals. Teachers equate commitment to piano study with regular lesson attendance over a long period and well-prepared practiced assignments. Adult students studying piano for leisure, however, may have no intention of continuing long-term lessons. This does not dilute their commitment. Teachers must understand that some adult students wish to achieve proficiency but are not interested in developing a high level of pianistic expertise. Because adults are likely to study piano for a limited time, teachers and students should agree upon reasonable short-term goals. Teachers can make sure these goals are achieved by encouraging adults to continue study and to be patient enough to reach them.

General Interest in Music

Some adult students want to focus on gaining general music knowledge through piano lessons. For them, learning about music history and music theory is as important as playing repertoire. While many of these students want to increase their pianistic skills, they may have no interest in perfecting and polishing pieces. Although strong keyboard skills can be encouraged and developed, teachers can recognize that enjoyment and knowledge can be gained from simply making musical sounds and learning about music. Interesting and motivating lessons for these students can involve some of the following activities:

- analyzing musical structure in various genres.

- analyzing repertoire pieces.

- discussing music theory and music history texts, videos, and computer programs for self-directed study.

- discussing fiction and non-fiction books about music and the piano.

- discussing live or recorded performances the student can attend or view.

The teacher can tailor the lessons to the student's objectives. Homework assignments can be varied and include activities other than practice. If the student is learning a Beethoven sonata and a piece by Tchaikovsky, for example, reading a Beethoven biography and watching a Tchaikovsky ballet would be relevant and interesting.

Having Opinions about Repertoire and Lesson Content

Because adults have experienced more music than children, they may have strong musical preferences. They may want to learn only a specific musical style or only the music of a particular composer or period. Although teachers should be dedicated to exposing students to a broad spectrum of music, they should also be flexible. Pedagogical choices can be made after learning about each student's musical preferences.

A wealth of music is available for the many tastes of students. Adults may recognize themes from symphonies, operas, and choral works and derive satisfaction from playing accessible arrangements of them. Teachers can select pedagogically sound arrangements of these works or of other popular music, looking in particular for arrangements that have appropriate fingerings and that fit lesson plans. Learning to play by ear and read familiar songs from lead sheets are other activities that some adults enjoy. These activities develop improvisation and harmonization skills, which allow students to play music ordinarily difficult to read. Furthermore, newly composed music in popular styles, from ragtime to rock, provides opportunities for those who wish to play familiar music. Elementary and intermediate selections are appropriate for adults if the arrangements have sophisticated musical content and titles.

Many adult students want to learn to read music fluently if they did not learn to do so during their childhood. Some enjoy learning music theory or practicing technical exercises. Forcing these activities on adult students who do not enjoy them is counterproductive. They may want to explore these areas of piano study, however, if they discover that pieces are easier to play with a foundation of reading skills, technical skills, and theoretical skills.

High Expectations

Goal-oriented adult students may have specific expectations regarding how quickly they learn and the amount of material they cover. Since adults have well-developed cognitive abilities and sophisticated musical tastes, they want their playing to sound as they imagine it should. Therefore, they sometimes come to piano lessons with unrealistic expectations if they want to learn pieces beyond their abilities.

Adult students may not be aware of the patience necessary for acquiring the coordination needed to play the piano. Teachers can discuss the intricate motor skills that take time to develop, including small and large muscle coordination and hand-eye coordination rarely encountered in other activities. In addition to these skills, building the kinesthetic awareness of the keyboard necessary for fluent playing also takes time. The pace of lessons must be dictated by this motor and kinesthetic development, not by cognitive ability. Frustrations arise when adults understand pitch and rhythmic notation but are unable to "do it." High expectations conflict with the joy of making music, leaving students self-critical and discouraged.

The initial new-student interview can be used to ascertain information about the student's expectations, as well as to estimate the student's confidence in his or her ability to learn to play the piano. During the interview, new adult students can be instructed to be realistic with their goals and to accept that they might not progress as they envision. Teachers can help students establish short-term and long-term goals, including the approximate length of time and amount of practice required to reach them. Students and teachers should understand that the process of learning can be as satisfying as reaching goals. If a student expresses a desire to pursue an unrealistic goal, teachers can diplomatically guide him or her to a more appropriate task while positively encouraging and reinforcing progress. If deflecting the desire is not possible, teachers should find appropriate ways to help the student progress toward the goal.

Some adult students wish to learn advanced pieces that are too difficult. Allowing students to play these pieces may be pedagogically unsound, but wise teachers see the benefits of this type of learning. Students develop dedication and tenacity by devoting months to mastering a piece, even without the expectation of performing it for others. While some students are amenable to learning simplified versions, others insist on playing the original works. Teachers can create positive learning experiences by providing effective practice techniques and by simplifying overly difficult sections. For example, octave passages can be played as single notes, rapid decorative passages can be redistributed, and notes can be eliminated from chords. Short and easy pieces that can be learned with less intense practice provide motivation and encouragement as the more difficult piece is being learned. If a piece is still too difficult for the student after such simplifications, the teacher can suggest a similar, less challenging piece by the same composer.

Although adult students are committed to piano study, they may begin lessons with unrealistic expectations regarding how much time they can devote to practice. Adults have priorities in their lives that often interfere with regular practice and lesson attendance. Some students even abruptly discontinue lessons due to more pressing matters. Adults often require more time than young students to complete assignments, and many adults are not able to attend lessons on a weekly basis. These issues do not necessarily indicate a lack of dedication. Self-motivated students and their teachers often find that one lesson every other week works well. Others have lessons on an irregular basis, when the student feels adequately prepared and the teacher can schedule the lesson.

Lessons are positive when teachers and students have realistic expectations and when teachers are flexible with lesson cancellations or lack of practice. When practicing has been neglected, teachers can incorporate engaging activities unrelated to practice: reviewing material, teaching practice strategies, developing technique, working on aural skills, analyzing musical structure, listening to recordings, and discussing musical styles. Sight-reading and the enjoyment of lessons can be enhanced by playing duets together. When students know that lessons will always be positive learning experiences, they are less likely to cancel lessons over concerns of being ill-prepared. Additionally, teachers can assign short pieces and assignments for students who are unable to practice regularly. Permitting students to learn only one piece at a time and eliminating performance requirements are also good teaching strategies for adults with limited practice time.

Inhibitions Greater Than Young Students

Older students often have a high level of insecurity and anxiety in activities that are not part of their normal life experience. Many lack confidence because they have been away from formal education for a significant length of time. They are hesitant to participate in activities that involve perceived risk. Having listened to more music than children, they can sometimes hear the difference between amateur and professional performances. Because adults tend to expect the most from themselves, they may be self-conscious about making mistakes when they have worked hard to master simple pieces.

One way to alleviate inhibition in adult students is to instruct them in a group setting. They find encouragement when they associate with others who are enthusiastic about the piano. Group lessons create a sense of camaraderie, build confidence, and minimize embarrassment. When the group plays together, the pupils are not aware of who makes mistakes. On the other hand, some adults may be uncomfortable in the group setting, feeling that others excel beyond them. These students are more comfortable in private lessons. The new-student interview will help the teacher determine the proper lesson setting.

The challenges adult students bring to lessons call upon a teacher's sensitivity and imagination. To help students gain gratification from lessons, teachers can remind them of the reasons why they decided to study piano. In general, selected repertoire should be mastered with manageable effort and minimal stress. To be satisfying, repertoire should include pieces that use pedal, span the keyboard, or sound more difficult than they are. Pieces with few technical demands that produce minimal physical tension will encourage more practice. Pieces that demand close attention to small musical details or complex technical coordination usually are not beneficial choices. Pieces that include recorded instrumental background accompaniments provide a fuller musical sound. To help students advance without becoming overwhelmed, teachers can find appropriate music at each level that satisfies students' musical interests and abilities.

Because adult students generally have some stress in their lives, piano lessons should not add to that burden. Pieces do not need to be polished or learned to performance level. Participation in recitals, evaluations, and competitions is voluntary. Keeping the lessons friendly and free from unnecessary pressure provides an ideal environment for nurturing adults in group and private lessons.

CATEGORIES OF ADULT PIANO STUDENTS

In addition to knowing characteristics of adult students in general, teachers can familiarize themselves with characteristics of specific types of adult students since they require individualized curriculums based on their personal goals for studying piano. To help plan lessons, teachers can identify broad categories of adult students and consider how a student may fit into multiple categories. The following descriptions are arranged in order of the age group.

Students Who Continue Lessons after High School

Students who graduate from high school and wish to continue piano lessons often have the following characteristics:

- They are serious about studying piano and are dedicated.

- They understand the importance of piano study.

- They engage in piano lessons as a positive and enriching activity.

- They must balance piano lessons with other priorities in their lives.

Lessons can be adapted to take these characteristics into account. Since these students understand the benefits of piano lessons, they may be content to learn music at the same level of difficulty without advancing to more challenging repertoire. To compensate for limited practice time, short pieces and short assignments can be given over extended periods. Additionally, teachers can help these students balance piano study with other commitments by flexibly scheduling lessons.

College Students

College or university students are a unique group who may or may not be continuing lessons from high school or from earlier in their lives. College students who begin piano lessons for the first time fall into one of two groups: non-music majors who take piano as an elective, and non-piano music majors (such as violinists or singers) who must take piano to meet curriculum requirements for graduation. Although some colleges offer private lessons, beginning piano instruction is usually given in a group format. These classes typically meet two or three days per week in a digital piano laboratory. Teachers who have never taught in a digital piano laboratory will benefit from observing such classes and becoming acquainted with equipment before teaching their first classes. In addition to manuals provided by digital piano manufacturers, group piano textbooks sometimes provide useful information about how to take advantage of digital technology.

Non-music Majors

College students who are not majoring in music can take piano classes as an elective or possibly to fulfill general education requirements. Some schools offer one-semester introductory courses, while others provide classes that continue and progress through additional semesters. Other schools offer piano courses without credit through community or continuing education divisions.

Many non-music major students enroll in lessons because they have had a long-term desire to learn to play the piano but have had circumstances preventing them from previously studying. Other students who enroll in these classes have studied piano and want to continue at the university. If private lessons are not available for non-music majors, a group piano class is an alternative. Group piano classes often include students of varying skill levels. This requires teachers to be flexible and to prepare lesson plans that cover a broad scope of activities. The core of the curriculum is usually based on college-level group piano textbooks written specifically for non-music majors. These course books provide instruction in technique, theory, and repertoire and contain music appropriate for adult students, including arrangements of familiar music. In addition, they often include ensemble arrangements and material for learning to harmonize from lead sheets. Some examples of group piano textbooks written for non-music major students include the following:

Martha Hilley and Lynn Freeman Olson. *Piano for Pleasure*. 4th ed. Independence, KY: Cengage Learning, 2001.

E. L. Lancaster and Kenon D. Renfrow. *Alfred's Piano 101*, Books 1–2. Van Nuys, CA: Alfred Music, 1999.

James Lyke, Denise Edwards, Geoffrey Haydon, Ronald Chioldi, and Lee Evans. *Keyboard Fundamentals*. 6th ed. Champaign, IL: Stipes Publishing, LLC, 2012.

The varying skill levels of students must be considered when teaching a group class. When introducing a piece, some students may play hands separately while others play hands together. When the piece is assigned for practice, advanced students may be required to transpose part or all of it or to improvise over the chords used in the music. In this manner, the same repertoire can be taught to the entire class without some students feeling overwhelmed and others feeling not challenged enough. Similarly, when technique is taught in a group setting, exercises of varying difficulty can be assigned to different students within the same class. Some may be assigned five-finger patterns hands separately, while others are assigned five-finger patterns hands together or complete scales. While this teaching strategy allows the students to develop technical ability at their own pace, it also reinforces the concepts of tonality and of a tonic pitch as the students hear each other play similar patterns in the same key. Playing some technical exercises together as a group also develops a sense of a steady beat and of even rhythms. Having these informal listening opportunities is one benefit of learning in a group setting.

Non-piano Music Majors

Most college music programs have keyboard proficiency requirements for non-piano music majors. These programs provide classes that teach specific keyboard skills needed for the music major. Course requirements vary from school to school but usually range from two to four semesters of study. Sometimes the proficiency requirement can be met by successfully passing a certain number of piano classes; other schools require a separate examination. Placement tests are usually used to place students with prior piano background into an appropriate class with students who have similar skills. Instructors of these classes, however, should be prepared to simultaneously teach students of varying skill levels.

Generally, students must achieve proficiency in the following areas: repertoire, technique, keyboard harmony, transposition, harmonization, improvisation, score reading, sight-reading, and accompanying. The class curriculum is developed to incorporate these skills. Often, these piano classes correlate with theory courses to reinforce concepts presented in the theory classes. Additionally, vocalists are often required to develop basic accompanying skills and the ability to play from a choral score, while instrumentalists are often required to play from band or orchestral scores, including parts for instruments that require transposition.

The core curriculum is usually based on group piano textbooks written for college non-piano music majors. These books incrementally prepare students to develop the skills needed to pass a proficiency exam. Like textbooks for non-music majors, they are designed for adults and are arranged in chapters according to subject matter. Teachers develop their lesson plans to meet the needs of class members, rather than teaching the book page by page. Textbooks for these classes include the following:

Elmer Heerema. *Progressive Class Piano*. Van Nuys, CA: Alfred Music, 1984.

Martha Hilley and Lynn Freeman Olson. *Piano for the Developing Musician*. 6th ed. Independence, KY: Cengage Learning, 2010.

E. L. Lancaster and Kenon D. Renfrow. *Alfred's Group Piano for Adults*, Books 1–2. Van Nuys, CA: Alfred Music, 2004.

James Lyke, Tony Caramia, Reid Alexander, Geoffrey Haydon, and Ronald Chioldi. *Keyboard Musicianship*, Books 1–2. 9th ed. Champaign, IL: Stipes Publishing Company, 2009.

Elyse Mach. *Contemporary Class Piano*. 7th ed. New York, NY: Oxford University Press, 2010.

Proficiency exams often vary based on the student's major. Typical proficiency exams include the following:

- performing solo repertoire
- sight-reading
- playing major and minor scales and arpeggios
- playing chords of various qualities
- playing 7th chords and 7th-chord arpeggios
- playing modal scales
- harmonizing with primary chords, secondary chords, and secondary dominants using various accompaniment styles

- transposing melodies
- harmonizing using a two-hand accompaniment
- improvising from chord symbols
- playing common chord progressions
- playing simple modulations
- reading instrumental or vocal scores

Students Who Begin Traditional Piano Lessons as Adults

Outside the college setting, adult students can begin lessons with a private teacher for a more traditional approach that develops skills gradually. These students have the following characteristics:

- They want to realize their long-standing wish to play the piano.
- They are serious about piano study.
- They are willing to commit time and effort to lessons and practice.
- They are willing to delay instant gratification to build a strong technical and musical foundation.
- They have the potential to progress rapidly.
- They may have unrealistic expectations.

Although these students are serious about their musical goals, they might not be able to continue study for an indefinite period of time. For example, some adult students want to study piano while they have extra time over the summer and take lessons as time permits during the rest of the year. An understanding of each student's goals helps teachers develop curriculum that maximizes the given time. Methods that specialize in beginning instruction for adults in a private lesson setting include the following:

Lisa Bastien, Lori Bastien, and Jane Bastien. *Bastien Piano for Adults*, Books 1–2. San Diego, CA: Neil A. Kjos Music Co., 1999.

Nancy Faber and Randall Faber. *Adult Piano Adventures*, Books 1–2. Ann Arbor, MI: Faber Piano Adventures, 2001.

Barbara Kreader, Fred Kern, Phillip Keveren, and Mona Rejino. *Adult Piano Method*, Books 1–2. Milwaukee, WI: Hal Leonard Corporation, 2005.

Willard A. Palmer, Morton Manus, and Amanda Vick Lethco. *Alfred's Basic Adult Piano Course*: Lesson Book, Books 1–3. Van Nuys, CA: Alfred Music, 1987.

Willard A. Palmer, Morton Manus, and E. L. Lancaster. *Alfred's Basic Adult Play Piano Now!* Books 1–2. Van Nuys, CA: Alfred Music, 2000.

Adults Resuming Lessons after a Break from Piano Study

Some adults return to piano study after years of not taking lessons. These students have some or all of the following characteristics:

- They want to pursue piano study along the path they began in their younger years.

- They have forgotten much of what they learned and need remedial work.

- They sometimes have had unpleasant experiences with previous piano lessons.

- They progress rapidly as the information returns.

For those adult students at elementary or early intermediate levels, an adult method that progresses rapidly will re-acquaint the student with previously learned material. Methods that ease the student back into lessons by reviewing basic information as it appears in the music, rather than through instructional exercises or lengthy explanations, are most effective. The lessons should be positive and enjoyable to counteract any unpleasant experiences the students might have encountered during previous instruction. Students can progress at their own pace during this remedial time. Students who have had lessons only as young children will often remember previously learned information quickly. After the student has reached his or her previous level, teachers can develop a curriculum that meets individual needs.

More advanced students might have continued to play on their own. During self-study, undesirable habits might have developed and physical skills often have deteriorated. A structured technical routine, however, will return them to their previous level. Repertoire selections for these students should meet the following criteria:

- The pieces are short and at the previously achieved level.

- The pieces are longer and slightly below the previously achieved level.

- The pieces sound more difficult than they are.

- The pieces are motivating.

Although the private lesson format is best for these students, they will also benefit from performance classes with other students in which solos and duets are played. Books that review systematically are appropriate for these students and include the following:

E. L. Lancaster and Victoria McArthur. *I Used to Play Piano*. Van Nuys, CA: Alfred Music, 2004.

Wendy Stevens. *Returning to the Piano*. Milwaukee, WI: Hal Leonard Corporation, 2010.

Adults Interested in Recreational Lessons

Recreational Music Making (RMM) is a specific approach to teaching piano. The primary goal of RMM lessons is to promote enjoyment and to enhance the quality of students' lives. Adult students who want to play the piano for recreational purposes may have the following characteristics:

- They want to try lessons to see if they will like them.

- They take lessons simply for enjoyment.

- They consider piano playing a leisure activity.

- They may be interested in the social aspects of lessons.

- They may not be concerned with accuracy and precision.

- They may not be interested in developing technical skills.

Adults who take lessons for recreational purposes are often taught in groups with lessons that have realistic expectations and little pressure. Similar goals can be achieved in private or partner settings as well. Because RMM lessons are non-competitive, piano lessons can be enjoyed without stress and result in a positive effect on the student's well-being. Although individual playing is encouraged, playing by oneself in group classes is voluntary. Students are encouraged to come to every lesson, even if no practice has occurred. Although lesson plans are essential, the teacher should never feel pressured to follow them precisely and should adapt to the needs of the class.

Many RMM programs are structured for six to eight weeks, one day a week for an hour, and are taught in retail music stores, college community education classrooms, and in retirement communities. Teachers use adult piano methods and group piano textbooks, often including varied musical styles that appeal to the students. Some students elect to continue with private lessons after a group series of RMM lessons is over. Others move to the next level of recreational lessons, while some feel more comfortable repeating the same session. Repeating the first session reinforces concepts and skills and gives students the confidence to move to the next level. Varying assignments are provided to compensate for the disparity of student achievement. When a session ends, students often make decisions about the style of music and lesson content they will study during the next session.

Patterned pieces, which can be learned by rote, provide excellent repertoire for RMM students. To facilitate learning, teachers can apply the following strategies for making the pieces easier to learn:

- Teach the piece in an easy key.

- Label difficult notes with letter names.

- Teach rhythms by rote.

- Create exercises from difficult sections.

- Provide recordings of the pieces.

- Teach short sections of the selected piece each week.

RMM classes can also be taught to children or teens who prefer enjoyment over performance or who may otherwise discontinue lessons due to lack of practice time. Teachers must be willing to put students' goals and preferences ahead of their own and to work as a facilitator, giving information and suggestions. Teachers help students select appropriate learning and practice strategies and let students move at their own pace. RMM lessons provide music making opportunities for each student without the pressure of rigid goals.

Piano Teachers Who Take Lessons

Many piano teachers recognize the need to continue their own musical growth. Among these teachers are those who did not study piano beyond high school, as well as those who majored in another instrument in college. These students wish to improve their playing as a way to transform their teaching. Others want to study the pieces they teach in more depth to be able to impart that knowledge to their students. Still others want to develop specialized skills and knowledge, such as early music performance practice or jazz improvisation techniques. Since these students have busy schedules, one or two private lessons a month are often best for them. Occasional performance classes in which several similar students perform for each other are also effective.

Adult Students for Special Consideration

In addition to the broad categories of adult piano students previously described, there are groups of adult students who have special requirements. Whether these students are learning the piano for the first time or resuming lessons after a long hiatus, teachers should carefully devise lessons that fulfill their individual needs. These students include older adults, adults who play other instruments proficiently, and adults who take lessons to complete specific, short-term goals.

Older Adults

In the United States, citizens over 50 years old are becoming the largest demographic in the country. Much of this population will lead full and active lives for many years, while having more free time and discretionary income than younger generations. Testimony from these students indicates that there are many benefits for seniors who study a musical instrument. The study of music lowers anxiety levels, which in turn increases cognitive function, learning, and decision making. Studying music also appears to decrease depression and loneliness, as well as counteract physical illness. Additionally, the movements required to play the piano keep joints and ligaments flexible and strengthen the hands. For those adults suffering from physical ailments, simply concentrating on a pleasurable activity such as piano playing can decrease the awareness of pain.

Since many older students are beginners who have never had the opportunity to play the piano, embarking on this new musical journey is an exciting event for them. As a result, they are persistent and appreciative. Many of these students will especially enjoy and be motivated by music popular when they were young. Classical, well-known tunes also have appeal. The following additional strategies help older adults find success at the piano:

- Keep the learning atmosphere pressure-free and full of fun and humor.

- Encourage students to do their personal best without unreasonable expectations.

- Provide ample repetition to aid in retaining learned material.
- Allow students to learn at their own pace.
- Encourage hands-separate practice.
- Introduce chords early in the learning process.
- Set slow to moderate tempos.
- Provide individualized tasks for participation in lessons and for practice assignments.
- Provide ample encouragement and affirmation.

Some older students face physical challenges, such as poor eyesight, impaired hearing, slow reflexes, arthritis, low energy, or impaired memory. These conditions can lead to frustration, anxiety, or embarrassment. Although the rate of learning may slow down, teachers should recognize that intelligence does not diminish with age. Teachers can devise strategies to meet the needs of these students. To increase confidence and reduce or eliminate some problems unique to this age group, teachers can prepare in the following ways:

- Select music with large print and pages that are not crowded.
- Give careful, clear instruction using a deliberate speaking style.
- Be at eye level when speaking.
- Provide extra, but non-glaring, lighting.
- Suggest simple reading glasses instead of glasses with multifocal lenses, which often require a distorted head position to see the music.
- Be tolerant of less than perfect hand shape and position.
- Simplify technical tasks.

Adults Who Are Instrumentalists or Singers

Instrumentalists and singers often take piano lessons to improve their musicianship or to learn how to become better composers, songwriters, or arrangers. Singers take piano lessons to more easily learn new songs or to accompany themselves. While these musicians have knowledge and skills that facilitate their piano study, they often face unique challenges:

- They can be highly developed as musicians but are unable to apply that musicianship to piano playing.
- They might have highly developed coordination when playing their instrument but find it difficult to coordinate both hands at the piano.
- They might read only one staff fluently or might not read notated music at all.
- They can become frustrated when music is suddenly challenging to them again.

Teaching these students requires prioritizing these issues. Developing fluency reading the treble staff and the bass staff is the first priority, along with developing two-hand coordination.

Instrumentalists with more finger dexterity in one hand than the other can develop two-hand coordination using piano pieces written for one hand. After a student learns a one-hand piece, it can be played in parallel motion with the hands an octave apart. A similar approach can be used with technical exercises.

Adults Who Take Lessons for Short-Term Goals

Some adult students, including beginners and experienced players, have specific short-term goals for their piano study. Usually, these students are trying to develop skills for a functional purpose. Common goals include the following:

- to play by ear
- to read music well enough to sing in a choir
- to help their children with piano lessons
- to improve their sight-reading ability
- to improvise
- to learn specific styles

- to read chord symbols
- to play piano at church
- to accompany singers or instrumentalists
- to play chamber music
- to improve their public school teaching credentials

For these adults, the role of the teacher is to help identify goals and to provide appropriate materials and focused instruction to meet those goals in a timely manner. For example, individualized instruction for preparing to play at church may include method books and pedagogical arrangements based on traditional sacred music and praise music, lessons on embellishing hymns, techniques for accompanying congregations, and discussions about choosing appropriate music for the different parts of the worship service. Once the short-term goal is reached, the student can decide to discontinue lessons or to continue studying piano for other short-term goals or for general pianistic growth.

GENERAL STRATEGIES FOR TEACHING ADULTS

In addition to the teaching strategies mentioned earlier in this chapter, teachers can consider the following general guidelines for acclimating newly acquired adult students, for planning lessons for adult students, and for keeping adult students motivated.

When starting lessons with a new adult student who has played in the past, the following should be kept in mind:

- Determine what the student found most enjoyable and most frustrating in previous lessons.
- Make no assumptions about what has been previously learned.
- Acknowledge the student's prior learning and use that as a basis for instruction.
- Use the initial new-student interview to learn about other activities and life circumstances that could affect practice time.

To keep lesson content tailored to adult students, teachers should keep the curriculum flexible and avoid rigid standards. Lessons should be logically designed around the unique skills of the individual student, with opportunities given to the student to select repertoire and activities. Teachers can also use the following guidelines:

- Provide multiple sensory experiences during the lesson.
- Demonstrate concepts and skills when possible, rather than give lengthy explanations.
- Provide music appreciation activities related to music the students enjoy or are learning.
- Make activities interesting to promote a long attention span.
- Use verbal communication throughout the lesson.
- Incorporate written information.
- Provide worksheets for reviewing concepts such as note reading and musical terms.
- Provide a variety of pieces at one level to keep students from progressing beyond their technical capabilities.
- Limit the number of pieces the student is studying simultaneously to promote a sense of accomplishment.
- Provide familiar music and many sight-reading experiences.
- When practice has been minimal, spend lesson time solving the most critical issue.
- Focus on developing aural skills, which might have been neglected in previous instruction.

To keep adult students motivated, teachers must first ascertain what the student's goals are for taking piano lessons and assess the student's ability to reach his or her goals. The first learning experience should be as positive as possible. Then, the teacher can use the following guidelines to keep the student motivated:

- Let students take responsibility for setting relevant goals.
- Teach to meet the students' goals.
- Expect goals to be adjusted.
- Keep students informed about the objectives of each lesson.
- Assist adults in discovering their own realistic learning pace.
- Make lessons intellectually challenging.
- Structure lessons for success.
- Show admiration and respect for students' tenacity and desire to achieve goals.
- Make lessons light and full of humor.

- Show enthusiasm and love for music.

- Assure students that mistakes are normal.

- Provide honest, kind, and consistent encouragement.

- Avoid having students polish every piece.

- Establish an atmosphere of inspiration and encouragement even if practice time has been minimal.

- Encourage short periods of daily practice rather than long, infrequent sessions.

- Give regular analysis of accomplishments.

- Initiate informal playing classes or parties for adult students, during which participation and playing from memory are optional.

- Convey that performance is a way of sharing music.

- Communicate that good memories will be taken from piano lessons, even if lessons last for only a short time period.

SUMMARY

- Adult students and their teachers understand the positive benefits of piano lessons.

- Adults understand concepts and process information easily.

- With genuine interest, adult students choose to commit time and energy to piano study.

- Adult students bring a lifetime of musical experiences to piano lessons and have definite opinions about what they like.

- The physical demands of playing the piano are often as difficult for adults as they are for children.

- Adults may have unrealistic goals and expectations regarding their learning.

- Some adults are more interested in learning about music in general than learning to play the piano specifically.

- Adults are sometimes inhibited, insecure, and self-conscious about playing the piano.

- Adult students lead busy lives and have many priorities that can interfere with lesson attendance and practice time.

- Beginning adults who want traditional lessons are willing to commit time and effort to piano lessons and practice.

- Students who continue piano study after high school have changing priorities in their lives, and they may not be able to dedicate the same amount of time to practice as previously established.

- Students who play other instruments proficiently will require remedial work with clefs that they do not read, as well as a technique regimen to assist in playing music that will be satisfying to them.

- Piano teachers sometimes take lessons themselves to enhance their teaching.

- Adult students who wish to achieve specific goals through piano lessons may stop taking lessons when those goals are reached.

- Adults who return to lessons after many years away from study will generally recover their skills quickly.

- Adults who want to play the piano for recreation might study for only a limited period of time.

- Older adults gain many peripheral benefits from piano study.

- Teachers need many unique teaching skills and strategies when working with adult students.

- Beginning courses are offered at most colleges and universities for non-music majors who want to play piano.

- Most non-piano music majors are required to study piano to develop keyboard skills to supplement their musical training.

PROJECTS FOR NEW TEACHERS

1. Compare an adult-piano method designed for private instruction with a group piano textbook for college students who are non-music majors. Make a list of similarities and differences.

2. Imagine preparing for an interview with a potential adult student who studied piano as a child but did not enjoy it. Develop interview questions and activities that will reveal what the student disliked about the previous lessons, what the student hopes to gain and achieve from piano study, what kinds of music the student likes, and what information and skills the student has retained.

PROJECTS FOR EXPERIENCED TEACHERS

1. Develop a short music appreciation project for an adult piano student who has asked to learn more about opera during leisure time. Among other things, your project may include readings, listening, and attending local performances.

2. Select a familiar piece of classical music, which an adult piano student may request to play, that would be somewhat too difficult. Identify potential challenges and describe how those sections could be simplified. Select other simpler pieces that the student can study at the same time to develop the skills necessary for the more difficult piece.

Chapter 12
TEACHING POPULAR, SACRED, AND OTHER FAMILIAR MUSIC

Since students relate to music they know best, piano students benefit from experiences that incorporate familiar music into the curriculum. Young children sing folk songs or other children's songs in preschool music classes. Children and teens enjoy and listen to popular music. Adults listen to recordings of songs that were popular when they were younger. Familiar music is ubiquitous in offices and retail establishments and as background music for commercials, movies, and television programs.

Some students assume piano lessons will involve music they have experienced and heard. When familiar styles of music are omitted from piano study, students are often disappointed. Playing popular music can be especially important for some teenagers, who without the opportunity to learn and perform this music may stop taking piano lessons. Many students want to learn current songs they hear on the radio, as well as pieces in a variety of styles from previous decades. Furthermore, some want to play arrangements of sacred music, holiday music, folk songs, children's songs, and classical themes, or to learn to use lead sheets to create their own arrangements. Familiar music offers the following learning advantages:

- Parents and students are interested in music that sounds familiar.

- Students are motivated and learn pieces quickly if they are familiar with the style of the music.

- Because familiar music is often performed not exactly as written, students can enjoy the freedom of experimentation and develop skills in improvisation.

- Playing familiar songs by ear and improvising on them helps students become comfortable playing without the score, which builds confidence for playing from memory.

- Familiar music often has complex rhythms. Mastering such rhythms aids learning similar rhythms in standard literature.

- Students learn about harmony by playing familiar music from chord symbols.

Familiar music has the same compositional elements as standard repertoire—pitches, rhythm, harmony, form, motives, phrases, articulation, dynamics, and pedaling. Consequently, many skills developed from studying standard repertoire can be honed equally well by learning familiar music. Students can learn to read notes, rhythms, and fingerings accurately. They can also learn how to keep a steady tempo, improve technical skills, and play expressively. Moreover, significant personal benefits—diligence, discipline, dedication—can be achieved by studying any type of music. Studying familiar styles as part of structured piano lessons provides meaningful opportunities to learn about music in diverse ways. Teachers can incorporate familiar styles into the curriculum, as well as seek, promote, and support evaluative programs, competitions, and recitals that involve familiar styles of music. Preliminary goals of learning familiar music can include the following:

- learning arrangements, transcriptions, and simplified versions of familiar songs

- learning supplemental original pieces that use familiar styles

- sight-reading, accompanying, and embellishing hymns

- improvising in jazz styles

PLAYING POPULAR MUSIC

Historically, popular dance forms and melodies have been an important part of the teaching repertoire. Composers from different time periods arranged, transcribed, paraphrased, and composed pieces in styles that would appeal to students and home audiences. In the 18th century, simple minuets, gavottes, and other courtly dances were used by musicians for teaching purposes. In the 19th century, waltzes, marches, and polkas were popular for teaching. Today, pieces based on 20th-century, international, or regional dance styles—tangos, hoedowns, swing, boogie-woogie, rock and roll—demand a steady beat and precise rhythms, just like the dances of previous centuries. To develop lyrical playing, pieces in ballad, blues, and jazz styles require a cantabile touch, sensitive voicing, and a flexible tempo.

Popular Music Leveling and Arrangements

Teachers can find arrangements of familiar music for pianists at every level. Most elementary and intermediate methods contain arrangements of familiar songs or pieces composed in familiar styles. Additionally, there are many supplemental collections and solo sheets of arrangements of this music. Some collections group arrangements by genre, such as a book of rock songs or a book of ballads. Other collections group pieces related to a specific artist or songwriter. In any case, these pieces have been arranged with the needs and skills of developing pianists in mind. These books are likely to have the following words in their titles: *Popular, Fun, Folk, Jazz, Ragtime, Rock and Roll, Blues, Pop, Hits,* or *Movie*. The best materials have the following characteristics:

- the same level of difficulty for all pieces in one book

- no unexpected challenges in individual pieces

- pianistic arrangements

- helpful, efficient fingerings

Teachers should select pieces from these collections to meet one of the following pedagogical objectives:

- to teach a new concept or skill

- to reinforce something already learned

- to enhance the understanding and mastery of a concept or skill

- to improve reading ability

- to improve rhythmic skills

- to motivate students

Supplemental original works, written by pedagogical composers, usually are classified into the following *educational levels*:

- **early elementary (EE)**

- **elementary (E)**

- **late elementary (LE)**

- **early intermediate (EI)**

- **intermediate (I)**

- **late intermediate (LI)**

- **early advanced (EA)**

- **advanced (A)**

Pieces that are in between two levels, or collections containing pieces of different levels, are labeled using a slash (/) or the word *to*, such as *LI/EA* or *late intermediate to early advanced*.

Popular music arrangements are leveled as well. The leveling terminology is usually found on the front cover of each publication near the top of the book or solo sheet. In order of difficulty, the *pop levels* include the following: **five-finger (FF)**, **big note (BN)**, and **easy piano (EP)**.

Other terms, which are not specific to popular music, are used to describe arrangements at other levels. Popular music is also available as **pre-reading** (off-staff) arrangements and as **duet** (one piano, four hands) arrangements. Teachers can compare the leveling of popular arrangements to the leveling of original supplemental works for students. Arrangements at the five-finger level are comparable to elementary pieces; arrangements at the big note level are comparable to late elementary to early intermediate pieces; arrangements at the easy piano level are comparable to intermediate to late intermediate pieces. The following chart compares equivalent pop and educational leveling:

pop levels	educational levels
pre-reading	early elementary
five-finger	elementary
big note	late elementary to early intermediate
easy piano	intermediate to late intermediate
early advanced or advanced	early advanced to advanced

Additionally, there are popular arrangements within method books or correlated with each level of method books. Teachers can compare arrangements of a popular song at each level to decide which version is appropriate for a particular student.

Pre-reading Arrangements

Arrangements at the pre-reading level are designed for students who have had only a few weeks of study and consequently have limited skills in note reading. Melodies for the pieces usually are divided between the hands and are notated without a staff. Notes are identified by their letter names and by their higher or lower relative positions on the page. A time signature, tempo mark, barlines, dynamics, fingering, and measure numbers are included. Starting hand positions are often shown at the top of the page with a keyboard diagram, as shown in example 12.1. Most melodies remain within a single position, but some use accidentals that require movement out of the position. Students may be unfamiliar with the rhythmic notation of some of the pieces; however, they will usually play the music correctly from memory or, if not, the rhythms can be quickly learned by rote. Teacher accompaniments are usually included to create a richer musical experience.

Example 12.1 Pre-reading arrangement of "If I Only Had a Brain" (excerpt) from *Pre-Reading Book of Pop* arranged by Gayle Kowalchyk, E. L. Lancaster, and Christine H. Barden

Method Book Arrangements

Arrangements that correlate with method books reinforce concepts the student is currently learning. The arrangements are written with the same pedagogical focus as the other books in the method, while providing the enjoyment of playing familiar popular music. The pieces can be assigned concurrently with the student's lesson book, or they can be assigned as review material. Pop arrangements in method books are likely to have more helpful fingering suggestions and expressive marks than pop arrangements found elsewhere. (See example 12.2.)

Example 12.2 Method book arrangement of "Happy Birthday to You" (excerpt) from *Premier Piano Course: Pop and Movie Hits,* Book 2A, by Dennis Alexander, Gayle Kowalchyk, E. L. Lancaster, Victoria McArthur, and Martha Mier

Five-Finger Arrangements

Arrangements at the five-finger level have the melody split between the hands, often centered around middle-C position or other fixed hand position. As with pre-reading books, starting hand positions are sometimes indicated with a keyboard image marked with finger numbers. To make the arrangements more accessible, key signatures often are omitted from the solo part and accidentals are used instead. Dotted quarter notes, triplets, and 16th notes are usually avoided. Teacher accompaniments sometimes are included to create a richer musical experience. Most often, the student plays one octave higher when playing with accompaniment, as shown in example 12.3.

Example 12.3 Five-finger arrangement of "Ding-Dong! The Witch Is Dead" from *Pop and Movie Hits A to Z* (five-finger edition) arranged by Tom Gerou

Big Note Arrangements

Big note arrangements are appropriate for students at the late elementary to early intermediate levels. Lyrics are included as well as suggestions for fingering, dynamics, and articulation, as shown in example 12.4. Pedaling is sometimes indicated, although many big note arrangements are written so no pedaling is required. Big note arrangements avoid complicated hand coordination, large stretches, challenging textures, and quick position shifts. Difficult rhythms, such as 16th-note patterns and dotted rhythms, are avoided as well. Unlike five-finger arrangements, big note arrangements usually do not include duet accompaniments.

Example 12.4 Big note arrangement of "Over the Rainbow"
(excerpt) from *Pop and Movie Hits A to Z* (big note edition) arranged by Carol Matz

Easy Piano Arrangements

Easy piano arrangements are appropriate for students at the intermediate to late intermediate levels and are therefore more complex than big note arrangements. Teachers should not mistake easy piano arrangements as the *easiest* arrangements available. Pre-reading, five-finger, and big note arrangements are more accessible than easy piano arrangements. On the other hand, easy piano arrangements more closely approximate the sound of the original songs since more rhythms, chords, keys, and voicings can be incorporated than at the easier levels. Lyrics are included as well as suggestions for fingering, dynamics, and articulation. Pedaling is sometimes indicated generally, such as *with pedal* or *pedal ad lib*. Easy piano arrangements can include LH accompaniments based on blocked chords, broken chords, stride patterns, or arpeggios. These accompaniments are easier to play with knowledge of 7th chords and of chord inversions. Simple chord symbols are sometimes placed above the staff where the harmonies change, as shown in example 12.5. Eighth-note syncopation is common in easy piano arrangements, as well as simple treatments of 16th notes and triplets. Extensive octave passages, complex counterpoint, and other advanced textures are avoided.

Example 12.5 Easy piano arrangement of "Batman Theme" (excerpt) from *Top 50 Movie & TV Classics* arranged by Dan Coates

Advanced Piano Arrangements

Advanced popular arrangements can be played as effective solo pieces by students at the advanced level, especially when used for informal performances or as encore pieces. Teachers can also play them for students to demonstrate the sound of a particular rhythm or to use as music for other lesson activities. Advanced arrangements display the creativity and personality of the arranger and often include newly composed introductions, transitions, modulations, or other material. Some arrangers remain faithful to the sound of the original song, while other arrangers treat the original material quite freely. For example, an arranger may use *chord substitution* (replacing one chord with another) to re-harmonize the melody, or add embellishments to the melody itself. Since these arrangements are piano solos, lyrics are usually omitted. Some fingering, phrasing, and other interpretive suggestions are included, although less than what is included for big note or easy piano editions. Pedaling is often at the discretion of the performer. Chord symbols are usually not included since the arrangements are meant to be performed as notated and since textures may be composed linearly rather than harmonically. (See example 12.6.)

Example 12.6 Advanced arrangement of "When I Fall In Love" (excerpt) from *Popular Performer Standards* arranged by Jan Sanborn

Duet Arrangements

Popular songs are also arranged for piano duet (one piano, four hands) at various levels. These arrangements provide students with the opportunity to develop valuable ensemble skills, such as listening, rhythmic precision, and balance. Collaboratively learning a popular song with another student, a teacher, or a parent brings enjoyment into the piano lesson and is highly motivating. Such arrangements can also be used for studio recitals. Duets are usually formatted in a facing-page secondo-primo layout so students can easily read their part. (See examples 12.7 and 12.8.)

Example 12.7 Elementary duet arrangement of "The Merry Old Land of Oz" (excerpt) from *Famous & Fun Pop Duets*, Book 2, arranged by Carol Matz

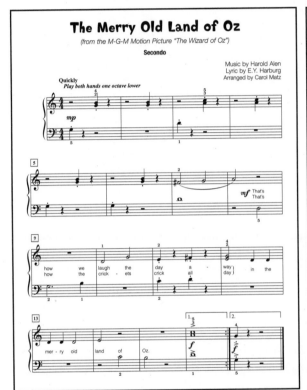

Example 12.8 Intermediate duet arrangement of "I'm in the Mood for Love" (excerpt) from *Dan Coates Popular Piano Library: Duets of Timeless Standards* arranged by Dan Coates

Graded Series of Supplementary Pop Music

In addition to pop collections of pre-reading, method book, five-finger, big note, easy piano, advanced, and duet arrangements, some graded series of pop books are designed specifically to be used as recurring piano lesson supplements for beginning through intermediate levels. Graded series are also written for Christmas music, sacred music, and jazz-style arrangements. Closer consideration is given to technical demands, reading challenges, and other required musical skills or knowledge. The books within these series are divided by educational levels, rather than pop levels. The books increase in difficulty within each series. To attain this gradual progression, levels often overlap between consecutive books. A common sequence would be as follows:

- Book 1: Early Elementary

- Book 2: Early Elementary to Elementary

- Book 3: Elementary to Late Elementary

- Book 4: Early Intermediate

- Book 5: Intermediate

The following descriptions and examples explain the characteristics of these levels.

Early Elementary

Arrangements for students at the early elementary level can be used within the first few months of piano instruction once students are reading on the staff. Pitches are limited to middle-C position (see example 12.9) or another fixed hand position. No eighth notes or dotted-quarter rhythms are used. Optional duet parts for teacher or parent add to the music-making experience.

Example 12.9 Early elementary arrangement of "Peter Cottontail" (excerpt) from *Famous & Fun Pop,* Book 1, arranged by Carol Matz

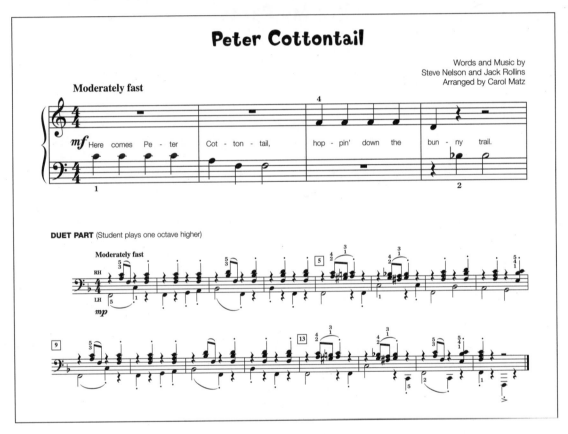

Early Elementary to Elementary

In arrangements for students at the early elementary to elementary level, more pitches are used on the grand staff than at the early elementary level, although shifting from one position to another is carefully considered by the arranger. (See example 12.10.) Some intervals and root position triads are used. No eighth notes or dotted-quarter rhythms are used. Most arrangements have optional duet parts for teacher or parent, while some are for the student alone.

Example 12.10 Elementary arrangement of "It's My Party" from
Famous & Fun Pop, Book 2, arranged by Carol Matz

Elementary to Late Elementary

Arrangements for students at the elementary to late elementary level include simple eighth-note rhythms, but dotted-quarter notes are avoided. Position shifts and accidentals are more frequent than at the earlier levels. (See example 12.11.) Some simple pedaling may be required. The selections are arranged in the most accessible keys: C, F, and G major, as well as A, E, and D minor. Optional duet parts for teacher or parent are usually not included.

Example 12.11 Late elementary arrangement of "Ding-Dong! The Witch Is Dead" (excerpt) from *Famous & Fun Pop*, Book 3, arranged by Carol Matz

Early Intermediate

Arrangements for students at the early intermediate level include eighth notes or dotted-quarter rhythms. Pitches above and below the grand staff may be included, as well as blocked 6ths. Some overlapping pedaling may be required. (See example 12.12.)

Example 12.12 Early intermediate arrangement of "The Merry Old Land of Oz" (excerpt) from *Famous & Fun Pop*, Book 4, arranged by Carol Matz

Intermediate

Arrangements for students at the intermediate level include eighth notes, dotted-quarter rhythms, triplets, compound meter, and cut time. Pitches above and below the grand staff may be included, as well as blocked 6ths and 7ths. More sophisticated pedaling is required than at the early intermediate level. Accidentals and articulations are used frequently. Coordination demands are greater than at the earlier levels. (See example 12.13.)

Example 12.13 Intermediate arrangement of "Theme from New York, New York" (excerpt) from *Famous & Fun Pop*, Book 5, arranged by Carol Matz

Other Types of Popular Sheet Music for Pianists

Piano/Vocal/Guitar Collections

Popular songs are also transcribed and arranged for piano, voice, and guitar. They are known as *piano/vocal/guitar* (PVG) arrangements, *piano/vocal/chord* (PVC) arrangements, or simply *piano/vocal* (PV) arrangements. These sheet music editions are different in appearance and content than editions for solo piano. The piano accompaniment and the vocal part are notated on separate staves, with guitar tablature and chord symbols notated above. (See example 12.14.) Tempo markings and dynamics are included; however, interpretive markings for the pianist, such as fingering, pedaling, and phrasing, are omitted. These editions are primarily designed for advanced pianists, or guitarists, who wish to accompany singers, as well as for the singers themselves.

Example 12.14 Piano/vocal/guitar arrangement of "Over the Rainbow" (excerpt) from *The Giant Book of Standards Sheet Music*

Fake Books

Fake books are large collections of melodies written on a single staff with chord symbols and lyrics. These collections, geared for jazz musicians and other improvisers, are useful for specialized teachers who teach jazz. To teach improvisation, easy piano collections can be used in place of fake books since they also include the melody line and chord symbols. Additionally, easy piano editions have the advantage of avoiding complicated chord symbols and difficult rhythms, which makes them effective teaching material for students at the intermediate level.

Learning Popular Music by Listening to Recordings

Unlike learning unfamiliar standard repertoire, students are likely to rely on their ears to help them learn arrangements of popular songs. While this enhances aural development, the students often play the pieces as they have previously heard them on recordings. Without realizing, they play the rhythms differently than written. The rhythms in popular songs are often more complex than the rhythms the students are reading and learning. The rhythms in the arrangements have necessarily been simplified, and the pieces may not sound exactly like what students have heard. Some students are satisfied with the sound of simplified arrangements; however, other students want to learn the songs as originally performed.

Two approaches can be used to deal with this issue. First, slight deviations students make to match what they have previously heard can be simply recognized as valuable, since the ear is involved in learning. Students can be allowed to play the rhythms as they have heard them. Second, if the teacher feels it would be detrimental to the student's reading skills, then careful preparatory rhythm work is essential. Before playing the piece, students should clap, play, and count the written rhythm of each hand separately, and tap and count both hands simultaneously. After students have mastered the rhythm in these ways, they can be assigned the entire piece to practice. Without this preliminary rhythm work, incorrect rhythms will be difficult to fix.

Some students will be able to play the song as they have heard it and as it is notated. These students can choose which version to play in performances. Students at the intermediate level can enhance their learning by identifying the discrepancies between written versions and recorded versions, noting the differences on the score to match what they play. Other students may be unsatisfied by the simplicity of the harmonies and textures of particular arrangements. They may want to improvise on what they have heard.

PLAYING SACRED MUSIC

Playing sacred music is another way for students to experience familiar music. There are many supplemental books of arrangements of sacred music for students at various levels. Students who wish to play sacred music can select from three types of music they may want to learn:

- hymns

- arrangements of traditional sacred music

- arrangements of contemporary Christian music

Playing Hymns

Although the main purpose of *hymnals* is to provide congregations with an extensive resource for vocal worship music throughout the church year, hymns can be studied and performed by piano students for a number of reasons. As pianists play hymns, they experience music in different keys, tempos, and styles. Hymns, however, are usually short and have harmonies often less complicated than those found in standard repertoire. Since hymn arrangements are prepared with the average church pianist or organist in mind, technical requirements are rarely overly demanding. Difficult textures, such as large chords, can usually be simplified without great effort. The compositional and notational style of many hymns—usually four separate lines written on the grand staff for sopranos, altos, tenors, and basses to sing—provides other benefits.

Benefits of Playing Four-Part Hymns

There are many pianistic and general musicianship skills that can be learned by playing four-part hymns. Four-part hymns require the pianist to continuously read four voices, divided between the hands, on two staves simultaneously. Since four-part texture is not found in music at the elementary and early intermediate levels, hymns provide an opportunity for students to learn to read music that requires both hands to play equally difficult parts simultaneously. Consequently, hymn playing can be a precursor to playing challenging four-part contrapuntal Baroque pieces. Four-part hymns often require techniques such as finger substitution, finger legato, redistribution, and legato pedaling. Sight-reading four-part hymns has far reaching benefits, including quickly developing skills such as sweeping the eyes across the staves and reading ahead. Four-part hymns also introduce the student to part writing and voice leading, which are essential concepts for understanding music composed for vocal or instrumental ensembles, as well as for compositions in general. Furthermore, hymns introduce piano students, who may have limited experience with music other than piano pieces, to a long tradition of vocal repertoire.

Embellishing Hymns for Worship Services

When students want to learn how to perform hymns to accompany congregational singing during services, they must learn to play without stopping or hesitating. They must also play with a steady tempo and with correct rhythm. Accompanying hymns requires an awareness of places where the congregation needs to take time to breathe. These spots are usually at predictable pauses (a comma, semi-colon, or period) in a hymn's text. This skill requires flexibility by the accompanist as well as careful listening. Hymn accompanists also need to be able to play a short introduction for each hymn. The introduction is often the last phrase or two of the hymn, concluded with a decisive final cadence so the congregation clearly knows when to start singing. These congregational accompanying skills transfer to other accompanying and performance situations, such as playing for solo singers or instrumentalists. After students have successfully learned a few hymns well enough so others can sing along, teachers can help them rehearse for a service, if the opportunity should arise. During a lesson, teachers can sing along without adjusting tempo as the students play the hymns.

Hymns require a full, resonant sound so congregations can hear the pitches throughout the church or other worship space. By playing hymns, students can learn to project, confidently and boldly. They can also learn to bring out the melody so the singers hear it better. Practicing this skill prepares students not only for hymn playing but also for voicing tasks in advanced repertoire.

Some students at the late intermediate level will want to learn to improvise on hymns and embellish the hymns for congregational singing. In addition to musical or creative reasons, some embellishments are also practical ways to help improve resonance. There are many devices used to embellish hymns including those in the following list.

- Playing full octave chords for the melody.

- Playing a variety of accompaniment patterns in the LH.

- Adding arpeggios with one or both hands at the ends of phrases or at the end of a hymn.

- Repeating chords in different registers for long notes.

- Playing the melody with the RH in octaves, as the LH plays the bass, tenor, and alto voices.

- Playing the bass line with the LH in octaves, as the RH plays the tenor, alto, and soprano voices, or as the RH plays full octave chords for the melody.

After being learned separately, several devices can be combined to produce an effective improvisation. Alternately, different devices can be used for each verse of the hymn, as if each repetition was a variation. Hymn improvisations can be used for *preludes* (before the service), *offertories* (during collections), and *postludes* (after the service), as well as for congregational singing. When treated as instrumental solos, they can be played more freely. For example, the melody can be used sparingly, or it can be completely omitted, while the performer improvises on the hymn's chord progressions. Despite the possible embellishments, students should not neglect the three most important considerations in accompanying congregational singing: projecting the melody, maintaining a steady tempo, and giving the music forward motion. The most common ways to achieve these essentials are doubling the melody, repeating chords in different octaves, and playing arpeggiated figures or other forward moving rhythm for long notes and for moments between phrases.

Arrangements of Traditional Sacred Music

Arrangements of hymns, gospel music, and other sacred music are most often used during weekly worship services for preludes, offertories, and postludes. They can also be used during other moments in regular worship services, such as communion, or even for special occasions, such as weddings, funerals, and holiday services. These arrangements are meant to enhance the experience of the congregation. In addition to arrangements of sacred music intended for the professional church pianist, there are many tasteful, expressive, and powerful arrangements for pianists of all levels. These pieces can be learned like other repertoire, although attention to the expressive aspects of this music is especially important. Such arrangements are available in the same levels as examples 12.1–12.6.

Playing Contemporary Christian Music

Contemporary Christian music is much different from traditional sacred music. Contemporary Christian music, also known as *praise music* or *worship music*, is based on current popular musical styles, such as alternative rock or pop ballads, although it also draws upon folk, gospel, and other traditional styles. Praise music is most often originally composed for praise bands (singers, guitarists, bass players, keyboard players, and drummers) or solo singers (vocalist and acoustic guitar, or vocalist and piano), and the musical groups who lead worship services are known as *praise bands* or *worship teams*. Consequently, piano arrangements of this genre incorporate elements such as strong rhythms, pop harmonies, and verse/chorus/bridge song structure. In many churches, this music has replaced traditional Christian music and appeals to a younger generation. Some churches offer separate contemporary and traditional services, while others use both types of music eclectically in the same service (*blended worship*).

Contemporary worship music is often performed by musicians who have not had formal training in music and who do not necessarily read music. They learn worship music most often by listening to recordings and following lead sheets. Supplemental arrangements of praise music, like supplemental arrangements of popular songs, may have simplified rhythms. They also may be written in more accessible keys than the original recordings. By using skills learned in piano lessons, such as playing by ear, harmonizing, improvising, and reading lead lines, students can learn to play this music as they wish.

Pianistic arrangements of familiar praise songs can be found in pedagogical material at all levels. Publishers offer collections with titles that delineate the style. Such arrangements are available in the same levels as examples 12.1–12.6.

PLAYING OTHER FAMILIAR MUSIC

Specific genres of music include songs instantly recognizable to most students. Holiday music—including songs for Christmas, Hanukkah, the Fourth of July, Halloween, and other holidays—is motivating and leads to rapid growth in reading and rhythm. Additionally, informal recitals can be organized around a holiday theme. Folk music and other children's songs sung in preschool and elementary school can be familiar to students and encourages them to sing while they play. This is an important component of aural development. Melodies from operas, symphonies, and ballets can also be used to teach students various skills. In addition to providing motivation, these classical themes introduce students to composers who wrote for instruments other than the piano. Holiday music, folk music, children's songs, and classical themes are interspersed throughout method books, and they are also available as collections or solo sheets at various levels. Many of these melodies can also be taught by rote or learned by ear. Jazz and jazz-style arrangements are also popular with students. Although advanced jazz playing and improvisation requires advanced technical ability and substantial experience with music theory, students at earlier levels can enjoy and benefit from graded jazzy arrangements.

Playing Familiar Melodies By Ear

Students can learn to play familiar songs *by ear* (without music). Students who have the opportunity to play by ear during elementary levels find these tasks relatively easy as they continue study. Curriculum that includes playing melodies by ear provides the following benefits:

- ability to listen to one's playing
- improved accuracy
- ability to hear and correct mistakes
- critical listening to expressive aspects of playing

- lyrical playing
- projected melodies
- greater ease and security of memorization

Routine playing-by-ear assignments can be completed in the following systematic way:

1. Students suggest some familiar melodies that they know and would like to play.

2. Teachers select appropriate songs for each student's needs.

3. Teachers provide aids to help students play the melodies by ear, including the first note and interval, the range of pitches used in the song, and some pitches for the most difficult spots.

After students are comfortable playing melodies by ear, they can begin to create their own arrangements by learning to harmonize the melodies and improvising accompaniments. These skills are sometimes introduced in method books after basic harmonic progressions are taught. Group piano books and music theory and composition books provide additional instruction in this area.

Playing Jazz

Many supplemental piano books have the term *jazz* in their titles and include pieces in the following styles: blues, boogie, country/western, Dixieland, Latin, ragtime, rock and roll, and swing. "True" jazz, different from these popular styles, is based on spontaneous expression through improvisation and requires a good ear and an extensive theory background to play it fluently and effectively. Therefore, teaching jazz in traditional piano lessons poses many challenges for the teacher and requires specialized training. Although jazz and classical music are quite different, they share many common compositional elements—notation, form, rhythm, harmony, melody, scales, chord progressions, chord inversions, accompaniments, and voicing. Many students begin traditional piano lessons and then study with a jazz specialist once they have reached the intermediate level.

Students can initially experience the sound and characteristics of jazz by reading jazz-style arrangements, which are available for all levels. While reinforcing musical concepts and technical skills appropriate for the student's level, these arrangements introduce the student to melodic embellishment, blue notes, extended harmonies (such as major 7th or minor 9th chords), ostinatos, walking bass lines, syncopations, riffs, and other devices commonly used in jazz improvisation. The jazzy arrangements in examples 12.15 and 12.16 illustrate some of these devices.

Example 12.15 "Kool Kat" (excerpt) from *Jazz-a-Little, Jazz-a-lot*, Book 3, by Catherine Rollin uses a jazzy, pizzicato-like walking bass line, syncopation, and grace notes.

Example 12.16 "Bluesy Etude" (excerpt) from *Classical Jazz, Rags & Blues*, Book 3, by Martha Mier transforms an etude by Cornelius Gurlitt using a boogie-woogie bass line and syncopated RH chords.

Some students at the advanced level can be encouraged to learn jazz-style pieces by listening to recordings and making transcriptions. Other students, who desire to play in jazz style, can be given instruction on how to experiment with their standard repertoire by adding jazz elements. For example, students can swing the eighth notes in a Baroque prelude or harmonize a slow movement of a Classical sonata with jazzy chords. These tasks will benefit students in the following ways:

- Aural acuity is improved.

- Improvisation builds confidence for playing from memory.

- Learning independence is strengthened as students make improvisational choices.

- Informal performance opportunities are likely as students will want to show off their jazz-inspired arrangements to family and friends.

These experiences are particularly empowering and motivating for adolescents.

Students who demonstrate a talent and interest in playing jazz can be referred to a jazz specialist. Jazz lessons can be taken in conjunction with traditional piano lessons, although prerequisites for jazz study include a strong sense of rhythm, a solid harmonic background, and well-developed technique. Becoming fluent at jazz improvisation requires years of practice. Students should be encouraged to listen to many recordings of jazz pianists, as well as to follow along with transcriptions if available. Although beyond the technical abilities of students at the intermediate level, these performances offer imaginative models of jazz style and provide enjoyable and inspiring listening experiences.

SUMMARY

Teachers will be more open to using familiar styles of music in their teaching when they understand the following:

- Music in familiar styles is what students know best.

- Many students assume piano lessons will be based on music they have experienced and heard.

- Students can benefit from learning from many different styles of familiar music.

- Students can learn arrangements, transcriptions, and simplified versions of familiar melodies in the same way they learn traditional styles.

- Historically, dance and folk music have been an important part of piano repertoire.

- Familiar music can be selected for its pedagogical value, as well as for its appeal.

- Familiar styles of music share common musical elements with standard repertoire, and students can learn to play familiar pieces with musicality.

- Pieces by pedagogical composers and arrangers can sound like familiar styles, and they provide excellent learning experiences.

- Teachers can help students learn notated rhythms of familiar pieces, or they can discuss the differences between the notated rhythms and the rhythms on recordings.

- Phrasing and voicing are enhanced when students sing along while playing familiar melodies.

- Students can be taught to read lead sheets and various types of chord symbols.

- Some students will want to learn how to embellish and accompany hymns.

- Some students will want to learn how to play praise music so they can play with a worship team.

- Learning about jazz increases a student's ability to improvise.

PROJECTS FOR NEW TEACHERS

1. Examine a five-finger, big note, and easy piano arrangement of a popular piece. Find an appropriate place in a method series where you could teach each.

2. Select one popular arrangement, one Christmas arrangement, and one classical arrangement from books of graded supplementary music in these styles. Find appropriate places in a method series where you can teach each arrangement.

PROJECTS FOR EXPERIENCED TEACHERS

1. Write a pre-reading or five-finger arrangement of a familiar piece that you could teach to a student. Include a teacher accompaniment.

2. Develop a series of lesson plans to prepare a student at the intermediate level to create an arrangement of "Happy Birthday to You!" by ear. List ways that the student may experiment with different accompaniment styles as harmonies.

Chapter 13
THE BUSINESS OF PIANO TEACHING

Students who complete a university music degree meet the criteria to be music professionals. However, that college experience may have done little to prepare graduates for the realities of earning a living as a piano teacher. Those new graduates who wish to teach must treat piano teaching as a business by making intelligent decisions about whom, where, what, when and how they will teach. Learning how to conduct the business aspects of piano teaching in a professional manner helps teachers earn a living, eliminates potential problems with students and parents, and results in respect for the teacher from the community.

WHOM TO TEACH

Teachers must decide what types of students they wish to teach. Most independent piano teachers teach beginners and intermediate-level students who are school age. Whether teaching private lessons only or private combined with group instruction, the lessons are usually taught after school, in the early evening, or on weekends. Lessons for adults of all levels are taught during the day or in the late evening. Some adult beginners are taught in groups, often in a digital piano laboratory. If the teacher has special training or interest in preschool-age children, private or group lessons can also often be taught during the day. Some established teachers specialize in serious intermediate to advanced students, but it takes some time to develop such a studio.

WHERE TO TEACH

The format of the lessons determines what type of teaching space is needed. Private lessons can be taught in the students' homes, the teacher's home, or a small studio space. Only one piano and a minimal amount of equipment and materials are required. If any kind of group instruction is included, more space, equipment and materials are needed. Group teaching occurs most often in a church, school, preparatory department of a university, commercial space, community arts center or music school.

Teaching in a Home Studio

A majority of teachers teach in their own homes and have convenience, flexibility and control over the teaching environment. There are many advantages to teaching in one's home:

- Teachers can allocate space in their home or create a separate, larger studio attached to the dwelling.

- Since there is no additional rent and additional utilities charges are minimal, a teacher's home may be the most economical place to teach.

- The mortgage, maintenance and utilities for the space used exclusively for teaching provide a tax deduction. This is not possible if teaching occurs in students' homes or a non-commercial space (church or school).

- Lessons can be scheduled to fit the teacher's schedule. Teaching in students' homes does not allow the same flexibility.

- Equipment and materials are at the teacher's fingertips without having to move them to a separate location.

- The teacher's personal computer(s), software, video and audio equipment can be used for instructional purposes and can be easily accessible for regular student use.

- Teachers can choose to teach as many students as they like without incurring many additional expenses.

- Teachers who have children of their own can be at home when they are there.

A home studio has some disadvantages:

- Keeping the family and business separate is a challenge since most teaching occurs during after-school hours.

- To create a professional image, the home must always be neat and clean.

- Personal and family telephone calls may intrude on the lesson. Lessons may also be interrupted by the teacher's own children.

- Family privacy and activity are compromised.

- Parents (and adult students) may not perceive the teaching to be professional in a home setting.

With careful planning, teachers can minimize some of these disadvantages. To eliminate the conflict between family and business, teachers may need to seek child care for their children. Adults, preschoolers, home-schooled students and students who can be released from school for lessons may have lessons during school hours, freeing up time for teachers to spend with their own children after school. A separate studio entrance, restroom and soundproofing materials in walls and ceilings also help separate the family from the business.

Zoning issues may add further problems for home-studio teachers. Piano teaching falls under the category of a home business. Many cities and towns have formulated ordinances for controlling home businesses to protect residential areas from unnecessary noise, odors, and excessive traffic. However, most piano teachers could not make a living without using their homes as a place of business. Ideally, ordinances would protect the right of piano teachers to teach in their homes while also protecting the neighborhood from annoyances.

Piano teachers have a responsibility to know the zoning laws in their communities and should consult an attorney about those laws. If no laws exist, teachers can become involved in a process to craft a fair and equitable ordinance so that nothing adverse will happen in the future. If possible, the local professional music teachers' association, rather than individual teachers, should become involved in the process. The cooperation of all teachers strengthens the position. The involvement of other home-based business owners adds to the number of responsible advocates.

Common zoning ordinances include a definition of a home occupation, specific conditions and standards, and the means for enforcing them. Conditions that specifically affect music teachers include, but are not limited to, these that follow (taken from ordinances for home businesses from the City of Los Angeles Municipal Code):[1]

City of Los Angeles Municipal Code
22.20.020 Home-based occupations—Regulations.

A. Home-based occupations may be established in order that a resident may carry on a business activity which is clearly incidental and subordinate to a dwelling unit in a residential zone. The establishment of a home-based occupation shall be compatible with the surrounding neighborhood and uses, and shall not adversely change the character of the dwelling unit or detract from the character of the surrounding neighborhood. Every home-based occupation shall be subject to the following standards:

1. The home-based occupation shall be demonstrably secondary and incidental to the primary dwelling unit and shall not change the character and appearance of the dwelling unit.

2. The home-based occupation shall not be conducted in any attached or unattached structure intended for the parking of automobiles.

3. The home-based occupation shall not create or cause noise, dust, vibration, odor, gas, fumes, smoke, glare, electrical interferences, hazards or nuisances. There shall be no storage or use of toxic or hazardous materials other than the types and quantities customarily found in connection with a dwelling unit, as permitted by this Title 22. No noise or sound shall be created which exceeds the levels contained in Chapter 12.08 (Noise Control) of the Los Angeles County Code.

4. There shall be only one home-based occupation per dwelling unit.

5. The use shall be conducted only by persons residing within the dwelling unit, except that no more than one person not residing on the premises may be employed, either for pay or as a volunteer, to work on the premises as part of the home-based occupation carried on in the dwelling unit. One on-site standard sized parking space shall be provided for such employee or volunteer in addition to other required parking set forth in this Title 22.

6. Signage, in any form, that indicates, advertises, or otherwise draws attention to the home-based occupation is prohibited.

7. No stock in trade, inventory or display of goods or materials shall be kept or maintained on the premises, except for incidental storage kept entirely within the dwelling unit.

8. No mechanical equipment is permitted in connection with the home-based occupation, other than light business machines, such as computers, facsimile transmitting devices and copying machines.

9. The home-based occupation shall not involve the use of commercial vehicles for delivery of materials and products to or from the premises in excess of that which is customary for a dwelling unit or which has a disruptive effect on the neighborhood. Such delivery services can include, but are not limited to, United States mail, express mail and messenger services. No tractor trailer or similar heavy duty delivery or pickup shall be permitted in connection with the home-based business.

10. Activities conducted and equipment or material used shall not change the type of construction of the residential occupancy and shall be subject to all required permits.

11. The home-based occupation shall not generate pedestrian or vehicular traffic in excess of that which is customary for a dwelling unit, or which would have a disruptive effect on the neighborhood.

12. No more than one client visit or one client vehicle per hour shall be permitted, and only from 8:00 a.m. to 8:00 p.m., Monday through Friday, in connection with the home-based occupation.

13. The home-based occupation shall cease when the use becomes detrimental to the public health, safety and welfare, or constitutes a nuisance, or when the use is in violation of any statute, ordinance, law or regulation.

---

[1] http://lacodes.lacity.org

Teachers can help their communities create a separate category for home-based educational services in the local ordinance. The ordinances for this category can be more advantageous for music teachers than those that deal with home businesses in general. They could allow for group lessons, for example. When lobbying for such an ordinance, teachers must educate lawmakers about the profession and give evidence of the advantages these educational services provide:

- The piano studio provides a safe-house for children in the neighborhood.

- Piano lessons provide a useful service that raises the level of society and offers young people a positive learning experience in their own neighborhood, without cost to the taxpayer.

- Home-based business owners work at home and do not add to traffic and pollution by commuting to work.

When piano teachers take the responsibility of being good neighbors by treating neighbors as they would like to be treated and avoiding unnecessary annoyances, problems are less likely to develop. Teachers and their clients should consider the following courtesies:

- Parents should drive safely in the teacher's neighborhood.

- Cars should be parked only in front of the teacher's house or in the teacher's driveway.

- Parents should not honk the car horn to let their child know they have arrived for them.

- Students and their siblings should not play outside during the lesson, while waiting for the lesson or while waiting to be picked up.

- Home windows should be closed when teaching.

- Recitals or other large gatherings in the home should not occur more often than the average number of social gatherings for private residences.

Teaching in Students' Homes

Some music teachers teach in students' homes. This is necessary if a teacher has no piano or lives in an apartment where teaching would be undesirable. Some teachers feel that parents who seek a teacher to come to their home are not seriously committed to piano instruction, but this may not always be true. In today's society, where both parents often work outside the home, transporting the child to the teacher's home may be difficult. There are some advantages to teaching in students' homes, such as the following:

- No student is ever late since the teacher controls the time when the lesson begins.

- Lesson materials are never accidentally left at home.

- Travel time allows the teacher to think about and prepare for the upcoming lesson.

- There is the possibility that a parent can be present for the lesson and, therefore, be better able to help the student in practice.

- The teacher becomes familiar with the student's practice instrument and can be sensitive to the home environment and practice conditions.

- The lesson is less likely to be interrupted with telephone calls for the teacher.

- Several children in one family can be efficiently taught in the home. Sometimes, all the children in the same neighborhood can have their lessons in one student's home, rotating homes on a monthly or weekly basis.

- Teachers can avoid the expense of having to rent teaching space or teach in a music school or retail setting.

- A teacher's private and professional life can be kept totally separate.

- Parents are usually willing to pay higher tuitions for the convenience of a teacher coming to their home.

Teaching in students' homes also has disadvantages:

- It is more difficult to arrange interaction between students (group/partner lessons, ensemble playing).

- Teachers may have little or no control over family pets, noisy siblings or parents, ringing doorbells and telephones.

- Teachers may have little control over the quality and maintenance of the instrument on which they teach.

- It is difficult to set up a computer lab, although the family computer or the teacher's laptop computer may be used.

- Teachers will need to travel with materials and supplies and may not have just the perfect piece or technical exercise for the right moment.

- Teachers who have children of their own are not able to be at home with them.

- The teaching schedule will be less efficient because teaching time is lost while traveling from home to home.

- In many locations, winter weather can cause travel problems.

- Traveling may make teaching appear to be more like a service industry than a teaching profession.

- There are no tax deductions for expenses related to teaching space.

It is essential that teachers establish strong policies that control the teaching environment. The teaching week should be organized so that lessons for each day are located in the same geographical area, eliminating excessive travel time. Since it is a convenience for the parents to have the teacher come to the home, teachers can charge accordingly. Transportation expenses and the value of the teacher's travel time should be calculated and added to the basic lesson fee.

Renting Teaching Space

Sometimes, a piano teacher can arrange with a church or school to rent space that is unused during prime piano-teaching hours. These institutions are used infrequently during normal teaching times and often have pianos and large spaces suitable for group teaching. Advantages to teaching in churches or schools include the following:

- Churches and schools can be less expensive (rent, utilities) than other commercial buildings.

- The clientele of the church or school is usually a good source for potential students.

- Locations near residential neighborhoods make piano lessons accessible for nearby children.

- There is usually ample parking.

- Noise is less likely to bother nearby residents.

- A teacher's private and professional life can be kept totally separate.

- Zoning problems can be avoided.

- The lesson is less likely to be interrupted with telephone calls or other home distractions for the teacher and students.

Disadvantages to teaching in churches or schools include:

- Teachers may have little control over the quality and maintenance of the piano.

- It may not be possible to set up a computer lab, although a laptop computer may be used. Even though schools and some churches have computer labs, it is not likely officials would permit their use. Location in relation to the keyboard(s) likely would not be conducive to teacher supervision.

- Teachers may need to travel with materials and supplies if they cannot be stored in the location.

- In a rented space, the teacher's time cannot be used as efficiently. Time to schedule lessons may be limited and time can be wasted when lessons are not scheduled back to back, or when lessons are canceled.

- Teachers who have children of their own are not at home with them during lesson times.

- Rental expense is incurred.

Some professional teachers open studios in commercial spaces that have the following advantages:

- They are located near residential neighborhoods.

- They have ample parking and access to public transportation.

- They are easily accessible for children.

- They will not create excessive noise for other business owners.

Renting space in a local strip mall is often a good choice for piano teachers. Teachers must have excellent business skills for choosing the right location and dealing with the public. They must have leadership abilities if they wish to hire other teachers. The following are some of the many advantages to renting commercial teaching space:

- A teacher's private and professional life can be totally separate.

- Tax advantages for the use of space are greater. In a home studio, only the space *exclusively* used for the business and all expenses related to that space can be deducted in calculating income taxes. With a commercial space, no such problem exists—all expenses can be deducted.

- There is potential for working with colleagues.

- Zoning problems are avoided.

- There is often more space available for technology-related equipment or group-teaching activities.

- A commercial setting can enhance a professional image.

- The visibility of a commercial setting may aid in student recruitment.

There are also disadvantages to teaching in a commercial studio space:

- Because overhead costs can be high, a large number of students must be maintained to meet expenses.

- When students cancel lessons, teachers may have difficulty using time as efficiently as in a home studio.

- Teachers who have children of their own are not at home with them during teaching times.

When using a rented space (and sometimes when teaching in a private residence), it is beneficial to form a partnership or small business with one or more other teachers. This can create a stimulating and supportive musical environment. The teaching space can be used continuously, making it more cost-effective. Individual teachers can teach in their areas of strength. For example, one teacher might teach preschoolers, another could teach adults, while a third could teach more advanced students. Responsibilities for group lessons can be rotated. Business records, housekeeping duties and expenses can be shared. Students have the opportunity to learn from more than one teacher and participate in programs with larger groups of piano students. The teaching staff must have the same work ethic, compatible teaching philosophies, mutual respect, and complementary teaching skills. All teachers in the partnership share expenses and profit. Information about tax benefits for partnerships and small businesses should be obtained from professional tax advisors.

Teaching for an Established Program

Established programs sometimes offer teachers opportunities for employment. These programs occur in various forms, including the following:

- private home studios
- private commercial studios
- preparatory schools at universities
- community music or arts schools
- public, private or parochial schools
- music stores

For beginning teachers, working as an employee for someone else may offer some or all of the following advantages that are not possible in other settings:

- The beginning teacher may receive advice, training, supervision, curriculum and lesson plans from the owner or director and may have the opportunity for regular interaction with other teachers.

- An established program may have a reputation that guarantees a steady supply of students for all of the teachers.

- A teaching studio and instrument will be provided.

- Other equipment (including computers), music and materials may be provided.

- All teachers in an established program often share the teaching of theory and performance classes and are able to substitute for each other in case of necessary absences.

- The owner or director of the program is responsible for all business affairs, such as collecting tuition, paying rent, purchasing materials, and scheduling lessons and recitals.

- Teachers can reap the benefits of the prestige of working with a respected institution or teacher.

- Employment benefits, such as health insurance, are sometimes provided.

As with other teaching settings, there are disadvantages to working for someone else:

- Independent teaching decisions may not be possible.

- Teachers may not be able to take students with them if they decide to leave the school, store or studio.

- The studio, store or school sometimes takes a large percentage of the tuition.

- When teaching in public, private or parochial schools, events such as assemblies and field trips may make it difficult to keep a consistent teaching schedule.

- Teachers may not be able to control certain factors, such as the length of lessons or the upkeep of instruments.

Teachers who teach in established programs work as employees or independent contractors. If the teacher is employed, income taxes, matching Social Security payments and worker's compensation taxes are deducted from the salary. Health insurance and other benefits may be provided. Employees are supplied with the materials and equipment necessary to perform their assigned tasks and the employer has the legal right to control the teaching. Independent contractors, on the other hand, receive no benefits and must arrange to pay their own taxes and benefits. The owner of the studio or school is not required to supply materials and equipment, but can specify in general terms what curriculum must be covered and what standards must be met. The independent contractor has more control over the methods used to cover the curriculum and achieve the standards.

Teachers who want to teach in an established program should prepare a resumé, showing their educational background and teaching experience. This resumé should be succinct, clearly show the teacher's strengths, and include the following:

- education

- teaching experience

- specific teaching strengths and interests

- references

A longer resumé could include the following additional information:

- professional membership(s) and activities in organizations

- a statement of teaching philosophy

- publications

- workshop and conference attendance

- a list of repertoire studied

- a list of performances

- a video or audio recording of a performance and/or a teaching demonstration

- improvisational experience

- other work experience or abilities for non-musical tasks, such as bookkeeping

- computer knowledge and experience

- community service experience

- additional references

Teaching for an established studio usually requires an interview and, sometimes, a teaching demonstration. Beginning teachers should be prepared to discuss their teaching philosophy and be able to answer questions such as the following:

- What have you learned from your students about teaching/learning?

- What are the most important things that you try to teach students?

- What are your teaching strengths?

- What would you do in an interview or a first lesson with a beginner (or a transfer student)?

- What do you need to improve most in your teaching?

Teachers should also ask questions about the teaching position, such as:

- What materials and equipment will be provided?

- Who will be responsible for curriculum?

- What are the standards and goals of the school or studio?

- What benefits will be provided?

- What is the salary?

- What are the shared responsibilities, besides the actual teaching?

- What kind of training and supervision will be available?

Because some beginning teachers will find it difficult to have enough students to teach in one setting, a combination of teaching venues may be a practical solution. For example, a teacher may teach one day a week at an established studio, two days a week at home, two days a week at a local church and one day in students' homes.

The Ideal Studio

Although it may be a number of years before a teacher can afford an ideal studio, it is practical to begin planning for that time by considering the following needs:

- a waiting area for parents and students

- a restroom for students and parents

- space for listening and computer stations
- dry-erase, chalk and bulletin boards
- climate control for acoustic instruments
- a comfortable chair and desk for the teacher
- storage for music, recordings, games, rhythm instruments
- filing cabinets for printed music and business materials
- large open space for classes that include movement
- good lighting
- metronomes
- an adjustable piano bench
- pedal extenders and adjustable footstools
- rhythm instruments
- progress charts
- flashcards
- an audio recording device
- a video recorder and monitor
- computer equipment
- music dictionaries and reference books
- a library of teaching music

Furthermore, teachers who decide to rent a commercial space or help with the planning of a music school should consider the following needs:

- a piano for each teaching room, with adjustable bench
- a second piano for each teaching room
- portable keyboards or digital pianos for group lessons

How to Acquire Students

After teachers have decided what categories of students they will teach, the kinds of lessons they will teach (group, private) and where they will teach, they must acquire students. When teachers have established a small group of students and worked with them successfully, the parents (or older students) often refer others for lessons. However, obtaining those first students is not always an easy task. Beginning teachers must consider certain factors to assure a sufficient number of students.

Studio Location

The studio should be located in an area where teachers are needed and where there is a good population base for students. Small towns and growing suburban areas often have more students than local teachers can fit into their schedules. In addition, these communities sometimes need teachers who have had more advanced training. Teachers should also consider the following when choosing a teaching location:

- Office parks and downtown areas are a source for adult students.

- A location near churches, preschools and dance studios may make it easier to acquire younger students.

- Newer residential areas usually have more children.

- School districts without music programs may have a greater demand for independent music instruction.

- A location near schools that have high-achieving students may yield students (and supportive parents) who will be more serious about piano study.

- A location near a school makes lessons convenient for children and their parents.

- A neighborhood with plenty of parking is essential.

Introducing Yourself to the Community

Teachers who want to obtain students should become known in the community as musicians, pianists and advocates for music instruction. They can participate in the area in a number of ways, including the following:

- Join the Chamber of Commerce and become acquainted with real estate agents.

- Become involved in the music program of a church or synagogue and volunteer to play for Sunday School, children's choirs, or worship services.

- Volunteer to accompany music classes and musical programs at local schools.

- Contact service organizations (e.g., Rotary International, Lions Club, Parent Teacher Association) and offer to provide musical entertainment or a lecture program about music or music education for meetings or luncheons.

- Accompany in local dance studios.

- Volunteer to teach music classes or present special programs at local preschools.

- Conduct workshops for preschool teachers to help them learn how to present musical activities.

- Volunteer to help Girl or Boy Scouts earn special music badges.

- Join the local music teachers' association or other professional music organizations and volunteer your services to help the association. List your name on the group's student/teacher referral service.

- Offer a free introductory lesson through the local Welcome Wagon agency.

- Teach introductory lessons through the local park and recreation department.

- Volunteer to play, or have students play, at a shopping mall.

- Arrange to meet the piano faculty at the local college(s) or university. If they are not familiar with your teaching, volunteer to send them a video recording that includes your performance and student lessons and performances.

- Meet other piano teachers, piano technicians, public and private school teachers, librarians, teachers' aides, church musicians and preschool teachers. Owners and sheet music buyers at local music stores are frequently asked whether they know of any available teachers.

- Accompany musicians at the local college or university.

Marketing and Advertising

Teachers can also employ marketing strategies to obtain students in the same way any new business would seek to acquire customers. Advertising in newspapers, Yellow Pages, concert programs, or on television or radio requires minimal work. However, such advertising is expensive and may not be effective for recruiting students. The World Wide Web provides coverage for little or no cost. Music Teachers National Association (mtna.org) provides its certified members an opportunity to be listed by geographical area and instrument so that parents and students can access information about them. Simple searches on the Internet will reveal numerous ways to create a presence on the web. Listings or ads in local church or synagogue newsletters, or dance-studio fliers, newsletters or programs will reach many parents with school-age children. Ads should be simple, direct and ethical, offering the most information with few words. Examples 13.1 and 13.2 provide samples of classified and display ads.

Example 13.1 Sample classified ad

Certified Piano Teacher: Master's degree; experienced; all ages and levels; holistic and enjoyable music learning; computer-assisted instruction included; references. Pine Tree neighborhood. For more information, see jmjpianolessons.com or contact by phone at 828-541-2112 or by e-mail: jmusic@aol.com

---

Example 13.2 Sample display ad

Piano Lessons

Jeanine M. Jacobson, MM
Pianist and Piano Teacher

NOW ACCEPTING STUDENTS

MM Piano Performance, University of Minnesota

Certified by Music Teachers National Association

- ◆ **Private and Group Lessons**
- ◆ **Beginners through Advanced**
- ◆ **Preschool and Classes**

- ◆ **Computer-Assisted Instruction**
- ◆ **Enjoyable Learning Experiences**
- ◆ **Recitals**

828-541-2112 ◆ jmusic@aol.com ◆ jmjpianolessons.com

A bulk mailing or fliers targeted to a select group (people with school-age children) or to the whole neighborhood will introduce teachers and their services to the local clientele. Schools, churches and organizations such as the Scouts may be able to provide teachers with mailing lists. A street-address telephone directory or public tax record can provide the names and addresses of residents in a particular neighborhood.

Fliers, business cards, brochures and letterheads should have a consistent format. They require a small investment, but present a professional image. Teachers should always carry business cards to exchange at social, professional, and business events. Business cards can also be stapled to brochures and inserted in pockets on posted fliers. Example 13.3 is a sample business card.

Example 13.3 Sample business card

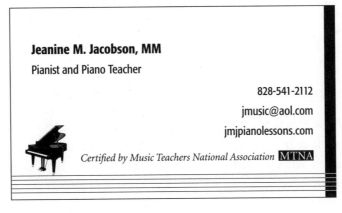

Fliers can be distributed at local schools, given to Scout leaders, left at music stores, and used in mailings. Fliers should highlight the following:

- present the teacher's strengths in the best possible light

- make clear what is unique about the teaching

- target the needs and desires of the potential clients

- provide as much information as possible, using a minimal number of words

Example 13.4 provides teachers with a sample flier.

It is best not to include tuition and fees on the flier: the costs may initially frighten away clients who are seeking lessons at a minimal tuition. Once they have an opportunity to meet the teacher and become better educated about piano lessons, they often understand the value of the lessons and are more accepting of the tuition. Furthermore, if the teacher offers a variety of lesson formats (group, partner, private, half-hour or hour lessons), the tuition will vary accordingly.

Fliers can be distributed to invite neighborhood residents to special events such as open houses and demonstration classes. Parents and prospective students could enjoy a Saturday afternoon "Piano Party" where interactive musical experiences are shared. Fliers can feature introductory recruiting programs, such as the following:

- a month of complimentary introductory group lessons to acquaint parents and children with the teacher and the teaching

- a free software program for students who enroll for a specific time

- introductory group lessons for preschoolers, creating a market of private students as these young ones get older

- a free music technology camp

- a free introductory group lesson for adults

The fliers for these events can be circulated as follows:

- given to current students' parents to distribute to friends

- given to teachers at local schools and preschools to send home with students

- distributed door to door in the neighborhood

- left on the counter at local athletic clubs

- left at the local senior citizen center

- posted on supermarket bulletin boards or in the windows of local businesses

Teachers should always ask the permission of business managers or owners to post or leave fliers. All referrals, whether by parents, music store owners, real estate agents, or other teachers, should be acknowledged with a written thank-you. Those who refer several students may be thanked with a small gift.

Example 13.4 Sample flier

Jeanine M. Jacobson, MM

Piano Teacher
Pine Tree Neighborhood

OFFERINGS

- Private and Group Lessons
- Preschool Classes
- Beginners through Advanced Students
- Lessons for Adult Students
- Lessons for School-age Children

EDUCATION AND PROFESSIONAL EXPERIENCE

- BM, Piano Performance, University of Washington
- MM, Piano Performance, University of Minnesota
- Teacher, Whitworth School of the Performance Arts
- Music Director, St. Alban's Church
- Certified by Music Teacher's National Association

TEACHING GOALS

- Develop a Lifelong Love of Music and Learning
- Develop Independent Learning Skills
- Provide a Holistic Musical Learning Experience
- Provide an Enjoyable Learning Environment
- Develop Strong Musical and Playing Skills in a Reasonable Amount of Time
- Develop Performance Poise and Security

828-541-2112 ◆ jmusic@aol.com ◆ jmjpianolessons.com

A personal website on the Internet offers teachers an opportunity to disseminate a large amount of information. Along with basic studio information for prospective students and their families, websites can provide parents and students with studio schedules, schedules of concerts in the community, and studio newsletters.

Press Releases

Newspaper press releases are a good source of free publicity. These articles are likely to be published when they feature the activities and accomplishments of local young people who are involved in unique music educational experiences. Whenever teachers have a special event for their students, enter them in competitions or evaluative programs, or have a student recital, they should send that information to the local newspaper. Articles should be concise and accompanied by an interesting picture. This kind of publicity is important even after a studio is well established. It informs the public of the accomplishments of young musicians and helps promote the entire music profession.

The Telephone Interview

Teachers should be prepared for telephone interviews with parents of prospective students or prospective adult students. Students are more likely to enroll in lessons when the teacher covers important information. When parents of potential students or potential adult students call, teachers should ask how they heard about the studio to help determine the effectiveness of their marketing strategies. Parents (and adult students) will have specific questions, but the teacher will also want to make them aware of the advantages of his/her studio and obtain basic information about the prospective student. Teachers should be prepared to discuss the following during the phone interview:

- the teacher's education and experience
- the teacher's philosophy and goals
- references to contact
- the types of lessons offered
- other studio opportunities, such as computer-assisted instruction, group lessons, competitions and recitals

Teachers should obtain the following information during the phone interview:

- contact information, including their name, address, telephone number and e-mail address
- the name and age of the student
- the musical experience of the student
- the goals of the parents and the student

Parents (and prospective adult students) frequently ask about the lesson fees. Teachers are wise to focus on what the client receives for the fee, rather than the fee itself. Teachers should encourage the person to schedule a complimentary personal interview (required for acceptance) where lesson formats, options, and the fee structure can be presented in a logical way. The free interview may include a mini-lesson, a demonstration of digital instruments, and/or an introduction to computer-assisted instructional programs.

All initial contacts (telephone or otherwise) should be followed up with a letter containing information about lessons and reinforcing what was discussed. A short, but carefully prepared video recording that shows portions of both group and private lessons and the performances of the teacher's students can also be sent after the phone call.

Teachers can also offer opportunities for parents or prospective students to observe lessons or attend a student recital. These experiences can provide additional information beyond

Example 13.5 Sample follow-up letter

JEANINE M. JACOBSON, MM
PIANO TEACHER
2000 Pine Avenue,
Sacramento, CA 98765
828-541-2112
E-mail: jmusic@aol.com
www.jmjpianolessons.com

Dear [*insert name*],

Thank you for your interest in the Jacobson Piano Studio. It was a pleasure to speak with you on the phone yesterday. Enclosed you will find more information about lessons in this studio, including a video recording of short lesson segments and student performances.

My students and their parents are excited about their musical study. I would like to offer you additional opportunities to observe piano lessons in my studio between 2:30 and 6:30 P.M. on Monday through Fridays, and between 10:00 A.M. and 4:00 P.M. on Saturdays. You and your child are welcome to attend any of my lessons.

Please call me again after you have thought more about piano lessons. At that time, we can set up a personal interview that will give us an opportunity to discuss appropriate music study for your child.

Sincerely,

Jeanine Jacobson

Jeanine Jacobson

the personal interview. Parents who are concerned about quality education for their children will welcome these opportunities. If a personal interview is not scheduled and the teacher does not receive a call from the parent within a week, a follow-up call should be made. When parents and prospective students do not schedule an interview, teachers can send them a letter similar to Example 13.5. Likewise, parents and adult students who have proceeded to schedule an interview should also receive a letter, similar to Example 13.5. In this letter, however, the teacher can confirm the date and time of the interview with the parent and/or prospective student. The last paragraph of the letter should be deleted for these students.

When parents schedule and attend an interview, they are able to observe teacher/student interaction and how effectively the teacher presents the learning material. During that interview, parents can be given the policy statement that outlines the benefits of study and gives them important information about lessons. The interview obligates neither party and is an opportunity for both to see whether lessons are advisable. The interview provides teachers with information about student readiness and musical development, and helps them plan an individualized curriculum for the student before the first lesson.

POLICIES AND POLICY STATEMENTS

The simplest way to communicate the goals and objectives of an individual's teaching is through a policy statement. Policy statements accomplish three important goals:

- They give teachers professional credibility.
- They clearly state the expectations of the teacher.
- They help avoid and solve problems.

Whenever there is a question, the policy statement can help clarify a potential misunderstanding. It includes information about the following:

- tuition (payment fees and schedules)
- lesson attendance (including information about makeup lessons, teacher absences and summer lessons)
- practice requirements
- recital and competition participation
- termination of lessons
- office hours

Tuition

The policy statement should address the following issues relating to tuition:

- cost of tuition (and any additional fees not included in the tuition)
- what is covered by the tuition (music, materials, supplies, audition fees)
- discounts or payment incentives
- collection of tuition and payment options
- late payments or nonpayment
- refund policy for missed or terminated lessons
- tuition increases (when and why it might be raised)

Payment Policies

Payment policies and billing should be conducted in a businesslike manner. Rather than collecting weekly lesson fees, professional teachers charge tuition in advance by the month, the semester, or the year. Reasons for this procedure include the following:

- Monthly or term tuitions paid in advance protect the teacher if the student suddenly discontinues lessons.
- Students commit for a specific time of the week for the entire term and that time is reserved for them.
- Unexcused absences are paid.
- An annual tuition factors in vacation time and professional enhancement.

Due to extra days in most months, some students may receive five lessons in a month, while others receive only four. Some students may have fewer lessons in some months than in others, due to holidays. Consequently, all students may not receive exactly the same number of lessons each month or each year. Parents can be reminded that they are not paying for individual lessons, but for a set number of lessons over the term. Some teachers schedule a teaching year of 40 weeks in which each student is guaranteed a minimum of 36 lessons. Students who do not miss any lessons may receive up to 40 lessons for the price of 36. With such an arrangement, teachers do not have to schedule makeup lessons for holidays, professional conference attendance, teacher illness, or for excused student absences.

Besides billing for tuition and music provided to students, teachers also charge for competition, festival and recital fees, technology lab time, music used for sight-reading, and any other materials provided to the student.

Many teachers prefer to purchase all of the music and materials, and bill the parent(s). Purchasing the students' music in advance and providing the music as part of the overall lesson fee ensures that students have the correct books in a timely manner.

Some teachers find it easier to charge a flat tuition that includes all fees and expenses. Teachers can calculate the average number and cost of books that their students use over a year's time and add that amount to the annual tuition. The fees are not itemized, but it is understood that all services and materials are included in the tuition. The tuition helps teachers pay for computer equipment, software, and a library of sight-reading and other materials, in addition to their salary. This practice eliminates the time and expense of detailed record keeping and billing.

Other teachers charge a deposit at the beginning of a term from which music and other charges (such as festival fees) are deducted. At the end of the year, parents are notified if they owe more or if they are due a refund. This requires careful record keeping and can be time-consuming.

Collecting the Tuition

After the annual tuition has been set, parents can be given the option to pay the fee by the month or by the term. The tuition is based on a year's instruction and can be divided into nine or more equal monthly payments. Both kinds of payments will have established due dates. All-inclusive fees that are paid monthly or by the term, with specific due dates, will not require billing unless the payment is late. The payment of tuition is a business arrangement between the parent and the teacher; late payments should not jeopardize the relationship between the student and the teacher. Studio policies should state clearly that chronically late payments or nonpayment will result in termination of lessons.

Discounts, Scholarships and Raising Fees

Payments made by the due dates can be rewarded with a discount. Conversely, late payments can be assessed a late fee (only with proper notification in the studio policy statement). Some teachers offer a 5–10% discount for annual or semester tuition payments made by the due date. Parents who pay by the month do not receive a discount.

Some teachers offer discounts for two or more students from the same family. When teachers offer such discounts, they are not being paid for all of their time. However, if discounts are not offered, some families may not be able to afford lessons and teachers will have to recruit other students.

A few teachers offer scholarships to students who are committed and talented, but who might not be able to take lessons without financial assistance. For both scholarships and discounts, it is sometimes better to offer an exchange of services. Housecleaning, baby-sitting, bookkeeping, teaching assistance, home maintenance or automobile repair are examples of such exchanges and should be suggested only if the services are needed by the teacher. These agreements must be entered into carefully and in a businesslike manner to avoid unpleasant results.

Fees can be raised at the beginning of each new teaching year by an amount equal (at least) to the cost of living. Announcements of the increases should be made at the end of the previous teaching year to avoid surprising families with the increased tuition at the beginning of the new teaching year.

Lesson Attendance

By having strict attendance policies, parents know that piano lessons are a serious and important educational endeavor. Such policies prevent frustration and eliminate unnecessary work for the teacher. Common policies related to lesson attendance include the following:

- Lessons missed due to illness, an accident, family emergency or vacation are excused and can be made up. An absence without notice for any other reason is considered unexcused and will not be made up.

- For lessons to be excused, the teacher must be notified 24 hours in advance. Lessons missed during family vacations can be excused if notification is given a month in advance.

- Because teachers are able to work with students who have not practiced, lessons missed because the student has not practiced are considered unexcused absences.

- More than one unexcused lesson or three excused lessons per semester can result in termination of lessons.

- Fees are not refunded or deducted for any missed lessons.

- Two makeup lessons per semester are allowed for excused absences.

- Teachers are not responsible for students who arrive early for their lessons and will not make up lesson time for students who arrive late.

Teacher Absences

Teachers may be absent from lessons due to illness, family emergency, or professional conference attendance. Some teachers consider conference attendance a vacation week, while others consider it part of professional enhancement and do not make up the lessons missed. Lessons missed due to teacher illnesses or family emergencies are generally made up. Sometimes, teachers hire a substitute teacher for absences.

Summer Lessons

Summer lessons are often necessary for teachers who must support themselves. Teachers can require that all students study a portion of the summer or make summer lessons optional. A policy statement should include information about the requirement for study during the summer.

Makeup Lessons

Information about makeup lessons should be spelled out in the policy statement for the benefit of parents and students. Makeup lessons can be handled in several ways:

- The teacher sets aside a block of time (usually on a Saturday) once a month. Students who have excused absences during that month sign up for makeup lessons during that time.

- Parents are given a list of students that includes telephone numbers and lesson times. Parents arrange to trade lesson times with another student whose lesson is no more than one day earlier or later than their child's lesson. Permission must be obtained from the parents to distribute the students' names and telephone numbers. The parent is responsible for notifying the teacher of the trade before the lesson time.

- The teacher keeps a list of students who have excused absences during the month. When another student cancels, the teacher uses that lesson time to make up a missed lesson.

- The teacher designates a week at the end of the semester in which all makeup lessons are scheduled.

Practice Requirements

Minimal practice requirements are based on student age and level. Very young students (ages 4–6) should practice approximately 30 minutes per day in separate 10- to 15-minute segments. Other beginners can usually practice 30 minutes per day in one sitting. After the first year, students often practice at least 45 minutes per day until they reach the intermediate level and above, when practice can reach an hour or more per day. These are suggested minimums based on common teacher experiences and expectations.

Policies should state how teachers will deal with inadequate practice, including the following circumstances:

- how many warnings students are allowed to receive concerning lack of practice

- when and how parents are consulted and informed of inadequate practice

- when inadequate practice is a sufficient reason for termination of lessons

Teachers can also address the needs for a quality instrument in the home and the need for an acoustic piano that is in tune and in good working order. Suggestions can be made about the location of the instrument within the home, especially in regard to its proximity to the television and other distracting elements.

Recital and Competition Participation

Most teachers require students (with the exception of students with special needs) to participate in recitals, festivals, evaluations and/or competitions. Generally, there should be a minimum participation expectation listed in the policy statement. Most teachers require students to play in all studio recitals and participate in one or more noncompetitive event outside the studio per year. Better students may participate in competitive events.

Termination of Lessons

Because most teachers expect a time and financial commitment from students for a full year, it is not necessary to guarantee that prepaid tuition payments will be refunded if a student withdraws from lessons during the year. However, some teachers make it a policy to require a one-month notification before the refund of any prepaid tuition so they have an opportunity to fill the vacant time slot.

Many teachers list the following criteria in their policy statement in regard to termination of lessons:

- inadequate practice on a continuing basis
- more than one unexcused lesson or three excused lessons per semester
- uncooperative or disruptive behavior
- repeated failure to prepare the material and achieve the goals

Sometimes, a one-month trial period, with notification of parents, precedes the termination.

Additional Policies

Other things that might be included in the policy statement include the following:

- required lesson attendance and other participation expectations for parents
- requirements and fees for additional lessons and fees for computer-assisted instruction
- the teacher's availability for office hours and parental consultation

Teachers can devise a policy statement similar to Example 13.6.

DETERMINING TUITION

Appropriate fees should be charged for piano instruction. When setting tuition, teachers should consider the following business and personal expenses:

- repairs and maintenance of equipment
- professional membership fees
- professional journals
- recital expenses
- teacher's expenses for competitions (postage, printing, travel)
- continuing education expenses
- small-business operating expenses
- paid sick leave
- paid vacations
- medical insurance
- retirement
- time spent preparing lessons
- time spent evaluating new music

Example 13.6 Sample studio policy statement

JACOBSON PIANO STUDIO~POLICY STATEMENT

ATTENDANCE: Students are required to continue lessons for a full academic year (September 1–June 15), attend all scheduled lessons and classes, and participate in an unspecified number of recitals, competitions and auditions. All students should arrive at lessons promptly, with all required materials and music.

ANNUAL CALENDAR: The calendar year includes two semesters of eighteen 45-minute weekly private lessons, four 1-hour group lessons, and an unspecified number of recitals and other events. All students are required to participate in a minimum of one event outside the studio (i.e., a competition, festival, audition) per year.

PIANO IN THE HOME: A piano in the home is required. The piano should be located in a quiet room away from the television and other distractions. An acoustic piano should be tuned at least once a year.

COMPUTER LAB: All students are required to complete ten 20-minute technology sessions per semester. Those sessions can be completed immediately before or after the private lesson or during any open time on the lab schedule.

MAKEUP LESSONS: Two makeup lessons per semester are allowed for excused absences from private lessons only. An absence due to illness, accident or family emergency is excused provided the teacher is notified at least 24 hours in advance. Lessons missed due to family vacations are excused provided notification is given a month in advance. Lessons will be made up on the fourth Saturday of each month. It is the student's responsibility to sign up for a makeup lesson time. Group lessons cannot be rescheduled.

TEACHER ABSENCES: The teacher reserves the right to miss lessons due to illness or professional commitments. The teacher can hire a substitute teacher or reschedule such lessons.

PRACTICE: Students are required to practice a minimum of five days per week and meet the minimum practice time requirement as determined by the teacher. Failure to meet the practice requirement may result in termination of lessons.

LESSON TERMINATION: Students may be asked to discontinue lessons at the end of a semester if they have had more than one unexcused absence, three excused absences, or more than four unprepared lessons. Lessons may also be terminated for unpaid tuition.

TUITION AND PAYMENT: The annual tuition is $____ ($____ per semester) and is to be paid in four equal payments of $____ due on Sept. 1, Nov. 1, Feb. 1, April 1. The tuition includes all music books, materials, and computer lab time. A 10% discount can be deducted from tuition that is postmarked by the due dates. No refunds will be made for students who terminate lessons mid-year. All students are required to make an initial deposit of $____. This deposit will be refunded or used to defray any outstanding charges at the time lessons are terminated. There will be no refunds for missed lessons. The teacher reserves the right to raise fees at the beginning of each new teaching year.

PARENT PARTICIPATION: Parents are encouraged to attend and quietly observe all lessons. The teacher reserves the right to ask the parent not to attend if the parent's presence alters the quality of the lesson. Parents are encouraged to be active participants in practice at home.

OFFICE HOURS: The teacher will be unable to discuss student progress with parents before or after the lesson since other students have lessons at those times. Parents should call or schedule an appointment with the teacher, if they have concerns or questions. The most convenient time to reach the teacher is Monday–Friday 10:00 A.M.–Noon at 828-541-2112. E-mail messages (jmusic@aol.com) are encouraged.

- time spent planning recitals

- time spent scheduling lessons

- time spent maintaining records and bookkeeping

Additionally, piano teachers should value their services and charge enough to earn a good living. These fees should be based on the following considerations:

- the economic level of the community

- the need for piano teachers in the area

- tuition charged by other piano teachers in the community

- the teacher's training and experience

- tuition charged by independent teachers in other fields (such as dance, art and academic tutoring)

- the salaries and benefits of public school teachers

- the types (group or private) and length of lessons

- personal income needed

The Economic Level of the Community

Teachers should survey the average income of families in the community. The chamber of commerce, employment and real estate offices, and census data can supply helpful information about the range of salaries in the community. The teacher may even be able to learn the median income for specific neighborhoods. Observing the types of vehicles that are driven, the median price of homes and the quality of the businesses in the community give clues to the level of affluence.

The Need for Piano Teachers in the Area

Talking to owners and managers of local music stores, church musicians, music teachers in schools and other piano teachers in the community can help determine the need for piano teachers. If the community's piano teachers have large numbers of students, long waiting lists, and offer to refer students, it is a good indication there are enough students for a new teacher.

Tuition Charged by Other Piano Teachers in the Community

If the local music teachers' organization has surveyed the lesson fees for the area, a new teacher can quickly see the range of fees, as well as the average. If there is no local association or if the association has not done such a survey, the teacher may need to poll teachers informally. Any survey should consider the educational background and teaching experience of those being surveyed.

The Teacher's Training and Experience

Teachers with a college degree in piano that included piano pedagogy training can charge more than teachers without a degree. Teachers with master's degrees and above can charge even more. Likewise, teachers who take advantage of continuing education opportunities can also factor this into their tuition charges. Practical teaching experience must also be considered. Teachers who have taught 20 students for five years can charge more than those who have taught 5 students for ten years.

Tuition Charged by Independent Teachers in Other Fields

Other independent teachers who charge for instruction include those who provide tutoring or teach gymnastics, dance, art or karate. Piano teachers should determine the average rate for these types of lessons and consider this when setting their own fees. Since most of these lessons are taught to groups, piano teachers can determine what the teacher earns per hour based on the fee paid on behalf of each child in the group, multiplied by the average number of students in a group.

The Salaries and Benefits of Public School Teachers

Piano teachers should also compare their educational preparation, teaching experience and salary to that of public school teachers. It is important to calculate not only the number of years of teaching, but the quantity of students. A public school teacher has approximately 35 student contact hours per week. A piano teacher would need to teach the same number of hours per week for the same number of years to have comparable experience. For example, if a public school teacher has taught for 10 years (35 student contact hours per week), the piano teacher who has taught an average of only 20 hours per week would need to teach approximately 15 years to receive comparable pay. Teachers should also calculate how many weeks a year they teach compared to the number of weeks the public school teacher works.

The Types and Length of Lessons

Tuition will also be determined by the kind of lessons taught and the length of those lessons. Parents and students should expect to pay more for private lessons than for group lessons. Teachers should earn approximately two times as much when they teach group lessons, since they take significantly more time to prepare. For example, when students pay $16 for 30-minute private lessons, the teacher earns $32 an hour. If a group of four students pay $8 each for a 30-minute group lesson, the teacher earns $32 for 30 minutes or $64 an hour.

Some students may have 30-minute lessons; others, 45-minute lessons; and still others, one-hour lessons. Some teachers require longer lessons for slow learners, more advanced students, and those who are practicing more. Some teachers charge proportionally more for shorter lessons than for longer lessons since preparation time for lessons of any length is approximately the same. Furthermore, shorter lessons are more difficult to teach because there is less time to cover the material. Teachers can charge 60–70% of the hourly fee for a 30-minute lesson.

Personal Income Needed

Although teachers cannot base fees totally on personal need, they must know whether teaching will provide them with a living income. A budget should be developed that reflects how much money is needed. Teachers can then determine how many hours they will have to teach to earn that income. To prepare a budget, the following must be considered:

PERSONAL EXPENSES

- food
- shelter
- utilities and phone

- car payments
- clothing
- recreation

- entertainment
- taxes, including Social Security

BENEFITS

- retirement
- sick leave

- vacation
- insurance, including personal liability

PROFESSIONAL EXPENSES

- continuing education, including concerts and conference attendance
- dues for professional organizations
- subscriptions to professional journals
- library of books and music
- financial loans on instruments
- recording equipment and computer-related technology
- recital expenses

Once a total yearly budget has been determined, that amount can be divided by the number of teaching weeks and then by the number of hours taught in a week. That figure will be the hourly tuition. If the tuition is in the average range of community independent (nonmusic) teachers and within a reasonable range of public school salaries, the teacher can earn a living by teaching piano. Example 13.7 shows how to calculate the hourly tuition, based on necessary personal income.

Example 13.7 Calculation of hourly tuition

Personal Annual Budget	Number of Teaching Weeks per Year	Number of Teaching Hours per Week	Hourly Tuition
$40,000	36 weeks	35 hours per week	$40,000 ÷ 36 weeks ÷ 35 hours=$31.75 per hour

Increasing Income

Teachers who have difficulty supporting themselves by teaching private piano lessons may supplement their income by teaching group lessons and accepting other music-related jobs, such as the following:

- working as an organist, pianist and/or choir director in churches or synagogues

- accompanying in schools for instrumental and vocal lessons, competitions, dance studios, and community theaters or choirs

- playing for weddings and funerals

- playing background music for social events such as luncheons and teas, or in restaurants and department stores

- providing musical entertainment for social and professional clubs

- working for music stores

- working for music organizations, such as symphony orchestras or opera and ballet companies

SCHEDULING

Lesson schedules will depend upon the age of students, the type and length of lessons, and the teacher's personal schedule. Teachers should determine the hours and days that they can teach and then fit students into that schedule. Lessons before school are good for students who have conflicting activities after school. Preschoolers, adults and home-schooled students can frequently be scheduled during school hours. High school students who get out of school early can have lessons in the early afternoon. Elementary and intermediate students should generally be scheduled before dinner time, with after-dinner lessons reserved for older students, adults and students whose parents work and cannot transport them to lessons at other times. Saturday lessons are also good for many students whose parents both work outside the home.

Thirty-minute lessons are common, but with such a limited time, it is difficult to provide a varied and high-quality program of study. Teachers who teach half-hour lessons may find themselves teaching extra lessons, especially to the more talented or advanced students. It is better to offer a variety of lesson lengths—30, 45 or 60 minutes. If a student wants additional instruction, he/she can choose a longer lesson time that offers more opportunities for advancement. Teachers should recommend the appropriate lesson length based on their knowledge of the student.

At the end of each teaching year, parents can enroll their children for the next year of lessons. A deposit fee should accompany the enrollment to hold a space for the student. The pre-enrollment commitment and accompanying fee help the teacher plan the new schedule, develop each student's curriculum, purchase music, update student files, and determine whether there is room for new students in the schedule. Teachers can devise an enrollment form similar to the one in Example 13.8.

Example 13.8 Sample enrollment form

JEANINE JACOBSON PIANO STUDIO
ENROLLMENT FORM FOR (*insert teaching year*)

Student Name_____

Address_____

City_____State_____ Zip _____

Telephone _____

Mother's Name_____

Address_____

Home Telephone_____Work Telephone _____

Father's Name_____

Address_____

Home Telephone_____Work Telephone _____

Emergency Contact _____

Telephone _____

To assure a place for your child for the (*insert year*) year, return this form with an enrollment fee in the amount of $50 no later than June 15, (*insert year*).

Return to:
Jeanine M. Jacobson, 200 Pine Ave., Sacramento CA 98765
Phone: 828-541-2112 E-Mail: jmusic@aol.com

The easiest way to schedule private lessons is to distribute a private-lesson time preference form before the beginning of the new teaching year. Some teachers schedule a keyboard festival night for parents and students just before lessons are to begin in the fall. Parents and students can learn about any new equipment, programs and materials in the studio and complete a lesson-time preference form during that evening. Having such a form helps teachers maximize the teaching week and schedule lessons at the times that are best for students and their families. Teachers can use a form similar to Example 13.9.

Example 13.9 Sample lesson scheduling form

JEANINE JACOBSON PIANO STUDIO
PRIVATE LESSON TIME PREFERENCE FORM

The following lesson times are available:

▶ **Monday and Wednesday**
6:00–8:00 A.M.
9:00 A.M.–12:00 Noon
1:30–5:30 P.M.
7:30–9:30 P.M.

▶ **Tuesday and Thursday**
9:00 A.M.–12:00 Noon
1:30–5:30 P.M.

▶ **Friday**
6:00–8:00 A.M.
9:00 A.M.–12:00 Noon

▶ **Saturday**
9:00 A.M. – 1:00 P.M.
1:30–5:30 P.M.

♦ 9:00 A.M.–Noon and 1:30–2:30 P.M. times are reserved for adults, preschoolers and home-schooled students.

♦ 2:30–5:00 P.M. is reserved for elementary-age students.

♦ 7:30 P.M. and later times are reserved for adults and high school students.

♦ From the available listed lesson times, list three possible lesson days and times in order of preference.

1. _____
2. _____
3. _____

List any days and times that are not possible.

_____

Student's Name _____

Telephone Number _____

_____

Return to:
Jeanine M. Jacobson, 200 Pine Ave., Sacramento CA 98765
Phone: 828-541-2112 E-Mail: jmusic@aol.com

The teacher collects the forms and assigns lesson times based on student preferences and the teaching schedule.

Group and partner lessons can be challenging to schedule. Refer to page 266 of chapter 9 for information on scheduling group lessons.

SUMMER LESSONS

Students are normally free from the demands of school and homework during the summer and can usually dedicate more time to piano study. Teachers can schedule the entire day and even consolidate their instruction into two or three days a week. Some serious students may want more than one lesson a week since they have more time to practice than during the school year. Students who have summer lessons avoid several weeks of remedial study in the fall to catch up to where they were at the end of the previous year. While there are advantages to summer lessons, regular scheduling is sometimes more difficult due to family vacations, year-round school and unpredictable summer activities. Some teachers opt for a different type of summer schedule that allows both them and students to have a rest, while still providing income for the teacher and necessary instruction for students.

Summer Camps

Camps are fun and can be scheduled for various levels during specific weeks throughout the summer. Students attend for a few hours or for the whole day for one or two weeks and experience musical activities that may be difficult to incorporate during the regular teaching year. Such activities may include ensemble music, guest performances, field trips, listening activities, games, supervised practice, and music appreciation activities. Summer camps can be based on a theme, such as the following:

- a musical style period
- jazz and popular music styles
- a musical form or genre—sonatinas, marches, dances, variations, Spanish music, etc.
- ensemble music
- sight-reading
- creative activities
- subjects—circus, animals, nature, the sea, etc.

Students from different studios can be combined, with their teachers sharing responsibilities, expenses and income.

Flexible Summer Terms

Another alternative is to offer a summer term for a specific length of time (eight or nine weeks). Students sign up for fewer lessons (six or seven) than that indicated by the term length and schedule them to accommodate summer vacations and other activities.

In general, summer is a time to enhance, explore and enjoy music together. While specific goals are still important, these goals may be more relaxed than during the regular school year. Summer pieces may be chosen that require less practice, are shorter, or are significantly different from what students normally study. Students may elect to finish a method book, reach a specific technical goal, write a composition, sight-read a specified number of pieces, or learn and play a number of ensemble pieces. Even though lessons may not be as intense as during the school year, students will be enriched and will retain much more than if they did not have summer lessons.

Introductory Classes

Summer is also a good time to offer special introductory classes for beginning students. By offering introductory lessons at reduced rates, teachers can attract more clients, many of whom will continue instruction after the introductory lessons are over. Furthermore, any beginners who have been interviewed and are starting lessons in the fall will benefit from a week of intense introduction to music fundamentals prior to the start of fall study. They get a head start without the additional pressures of school. Introductory classes also give the teacher (and parents) an opportunity to see whether the student is serious about lessons before parents make a large investment in lessons and an instrument. Eye-catching and provocative brochures or ads, like the one in Example 13.10, will intrigue potential students.

Example 13.10 Sample summer lesson brochure

Thinking About Piano Lessons?
Why Not Try?

A SPECIAL SIX-WEEK INTRODUCTORY PROGRAM

- *Classes for children*
- *Classes for adults*
- *No prior musical experience necessary*
- *Small, activity-filled classes with an emphasis on FUN*
- *No home instrument needed*
- *One-hour session each week*

June 15–July 31
JACOBSON PIANO STUDIO

828-541-2112 • jmusic@aol.com • jmjpianolessons.com

RECORD KEEPING

As business owners, piano teachers must deal with issues such as taxes, insurance, bookkeeping, investing, purchases, expenses and loans. Records (including receipts) must be kept in a convenient way. A notebook for each day of teaching can include notations about tuition payments, as well as music and materials given to students. Some teachers prefer to use a computer software program especially devised for music teachers to assist with scheduling, music inventory and financial aspects of teaching. General software programs for finance, word-processing and data bases can also be adapted for piano teachers' record keeping.

Taxes

American piano teachers, like all other workers, must pay taxes—federal and state income taxes, city business taxes, and self-employment tax (Social Security). Careful planning, good record keeping (with a separate bank account for piano teaching), and a tax advisor will keep teachers from paying unnecessary taxes. A teacher should choose a tax professional who has expertise in home-business tax law, specifically those laws that affect self-employed musicians. Because laws are complex and change frequently, it is beyond the scope of this book to give specific tax advice. However, there are basic principles to consider.

Income
Teachers need to keep careful records of income from all sources. This record keeping can be simple, but it must be updated regularly.

Expenses
Many professional expenses are deductible, thereby reducing the amount of the taxable income. Receipts should be kept for all expenses. Expenses that are deductible include, but are not limited to the following:

- a prorated portion of the house payment or rent related to the space used exclusively for teaching

- a prorated portion of real estate taxes and mortgage interest related to the space used exclusively for teaching

- all expenses (e.g., utilities, telephone, insurance, and upkeep) related to the space used exclusively for teaching

- all business expenses in a commercial studio space (e.g., rent, taxes, upkeep, utilities, telephone)

- automobile expenses for the time the vehicle is used for teaching purposes (e.g., traveling to students' homes, trips to the music store, travel to conferences and concerts)

- music, books, recordings and purchases such as metronomes, pencils, manuscript paper

- marketing expenses

- payments or investment credit on instruments and other large purchases, such as computers, software, recording equipment, video and audio equipment

- personal property taxes on studio equipment

- instrument tuning and repair

- recital expenses

- conference attendance and other continuing educational expenses

- professional association dues and professional journal subscriptions

- attorney, accountant and financial planner fees related to the studio

- concert tickets

- performance attire

- child or other dependent care during teaching time

- personal liability insurance and insurance on instruments and equipment

Insurance, Retirement and Loans

Because independent piano teachers are self-employed, they must provide their own insurance and retirement income. In addition to personal health and life insurance, piano teachers can purchase insurance to protect instruments and other expensive musical equipment. Personal liability insurance protects teachers against lawsuits that might be filed as a result of accidents in the studio. Insurance policies should also protect teachers if they transport students to musical events. Group insurance plans are available through some music teachers' associations.

It is important that teachers plan for retirement as early as possible. Investing in a retirement program over a large number of years ensures a financially secure retirement. The services of a financial planner can help teachers budget and invest for retirement.

Teachers may need to borrow money to purchase pianos, computers or other teaching aids. They can contact lending institutions to arrange for loans in the same way they arrange for automobile loans. The Small Business Administration and small-business development centers can be of assistance. Music dealers often have purchase or rental plans to assist teachers in renting or purchasing the instruments they need. It is important that teachers have established credit that shows they are able to pay their bills. A lending institution or piano retailer will require a business plan that includes the following:

- a statement of purpose

- a description of the studio

- a marketing plan

- information about local competitors

- personnel needs

- operating procedures

- equipment owned and equipment needed

- projected growth of business, including the assumptions upon which projections are based

- a profit and loss statement—sometimes a multiple-year summary

- tax returns, including gross income for the past several years

- personal financial statement

- a copy of business licenses

- a copy of resumé(s)

- evidence of teaching income, including the number of current students and tuition fees charged

- a copy of personal and business budgets

- credit history (credit cards, mortgage, car payments, etc.)

New teachers may need another responsible party to co-sign on initial loans.

COMMUNICATING WITH PARENTS

The success of piano lessons depends on the teacher, the student and the parents. It is the teacher's responsibility to educate parents in their roles as partners in the learning process. The initial interview starts this education. In addition to the interview and the policy statement, parents can be given an informational brochure that describes studio programs and outlines the responsibilities of the teacher, the parent and the student. The policy statement outlines the rules and regulations of the studio. The informational brochure communicates additional information to parents to assist them in helping their children in piano study. Example 13.11 provides a sample of an informational brochure.

Example 13.11 Sample parent information brochure

JEANINE JACOBSON PIANO STUDIO

Parent Information

PHILOSOPHY

" The primary purpose of piano lessons is to instill a love of music in each student, while teaching concepts and skills in a way that ensures success in learning to play the piano in a reasonable length of time. "

ELIGIBILITY FOR LESSONS:
The following criteria are used to determine the eligibility of the student for lessons:

- the age, maturity and interest of the student
- parental support

The criteria used to determine the eligibility of the student for continuation in the program are the following:

- attendance
- motivation and interest of student
- paid tuition
- preparation of assigned lessons

The teacher reserves the right to terminate lessons with the student if he/she feels that the student would learn better in another situation.

SCHEDULE: Every attempt will be made to schedule lessons at a convenient time for all.

PRACTICE: It is the parents' responsibility to see that their child practices. There is a direct relationship between regular practice and student success. Parents should establish a regular practice time for their child that is free from distraction, and give positive reinforcement for their child's practice. When possible, parents should help their child practice, especially at the beginning levels. If it is not possible to help directly, just being in the room while the child practices is supportive and encouraging.

- First-year students should practice no less than 30 minutes per day.
- Second- and third-year students should practice no less than 45 minutes per day.
- Students in their fourth year and above should practice no less than 60 minutes per day.
- Practicing should occur at least five days per week. If this practice requirement is not followed, it is impossible to guarantee that the student will have a successful or positive learning experience.

PREPARING STUDENTS FOR THE LESSON:
Students should come to the lessons rested and ready to work.

MUSIC, MATERIALS AND SUPPLIES: In addition to the music that is included with the tuition, each student should have a three-ring binder notebook (with pockets) and a pencil, as well as a carrying case to transport the music, notebook and other supplies.

OTHER ACTIVITIES: Group lessons and computer-assisted instruction for music theory and ear training enhance musical learning in ways that are not possible through private lessons alone. Recitals and other performance opportunities are also an important part of piano lessons. All students will participate in these activities.

PROBLEMS: Parents are encouraged to contact the teacher immediately if they perceive problems with their child's piano lessons. Waiting too long to talk to the teacher may make the problem unsolvable. It is impossible for the teacher to speak with parents immediately before or after the child's lesson since other students have lessons at those times. Please contact the teacher during office hours (Monday–Thursday 10:00 A.M.–Noon) by phone 828-541-2112 or by e-mail (jmusic@aol.com).

RESPONSIBILITIES: Piano lessons are a learning experience that requires the cooperation of the teacher, parent, and student. To ensure a level of success in each student's progress, each person involved in the process has specific responsibilities.

PARENTAL RESPONSIBILITIES

- Provide and perpetuate an enthusiastic attitude for learning.
- Provide a piano in the home that is in tune. Mr. Ralph Cate (phone 818-234-5678), a certified piano technician, is recommended.
- Provide a properly adjusted bench and adequate lighting.
- Provide a practice area and time that is free from distraction.
- See that their child arrives on time for lessons and has regular attendance.
- Participate in the interviewing process, parent meetings and conferences.
- Attend periodic group and private lessons to keep abreast of student progress.
- Assist their child in practice at home on a regular basis.
- Check the lesson assignments regularly to make sure all materials are being practiced and that the practice chart has been completed.
- Assist the child in establishing a regular practice time each day.
- Assume responsibility for makeup lessons.
- Provide encouragement and support for the child in all endeavors.
- Understand what is required of a young student (e.g., practice steps, hand positions).
- Pay tuition.
- Provide any required materials and supplies.
- Set aside time for their child to listen to special video and audio recordings.
- Listen to and, if possible, build a library of recordings for the child.
- Take the child to concerts.
- Use the public library for music-related books.
- Convey the importance of music lessons to the child when he/she may want to stop lessons.
- Keep in close contact with the teacher.

STUDENT RESPONSIBILITIES

- Attend all group and private lessons regularly and on time.
- Bring all music, including assignment book, and leave the lesson with all materials.
- Complete assignments and practice carefully on a daily basis.
- Complete the practice requirements each week.
- Participate in at least one audition or festival each year.
- Participate in all scheduled recitals and rehearsals.
- Complete required computer lab time

TEACHER RESPONSIBILITIES

- Plan a curriculum for each student and each group.
- Make a plan for each lesson.
- Write clear and detailed assignments.
- Teach systematic lessons.
- Teach the student how to practice effectively.
- Enhance student motivation
- Make sure the student understands the assignment for the week.
- Buy music and other materials.
- Communicate with parents.
- Schedule and coordinate recitals, auditions, competitions, and festivals.
- Coordinate a computer lab schedule

Additional things that might be included in the parent information brochure include a description of the benefits of piano study and a yearly studio schedule.

Regular telephone calls, teacher/parent conferences, and progress reports keep parents informed. Keeping in touch with parents via e-mail is also efficient. Teachers should meet with parents once a year and progress reports like the one in Example 13.12 should be completed at least twice a year. Parents can also be invited to attend the last lesson of each semester, so that students can demonstrate what they have learned.

Example 13.12 Sample student progress report

JEANINE JACOBSON PIANO STUDIO
PROGRESS REPORT

STUDENT_____DATE_____

	OUTSTANDING	MAKING PROGRESS	NEEDS IMPROVEMENT
Practice	☐	☐	☐
Lesson Preparation	☐	☐	☐
Attitude and Behavior in Lesson	☐	☐	☐
Technical Development	☐	☐	☐
Rhythm Development	☐	☐	☐
Sight-Reading Progress	☐	☐	☐
Theoretical Understanding	☐	☐	☐
Aural Development	☐	☐	☐
Creative Work	☐	☐	☐
Ensemble Development	☐	☐	☐
Musical Development	☐	☐	☐

TEACHER'S COMMENTS:_____

_____

TEACHER'S SIGNATURE: _____

PARENT'S COMMENTS: _____

_____

PARENT'S SIGNATURE: _____

Studio newsletters are an effective means of communicating information to parents and students. These monthly or quarterly newsletters can include the following:

- upcoming schedule changes (vacation, teacher absences, etc.)

- studio events (recitals, competitions, auditions, etc.)

- accomplishments (musical and nonmusical) of students

- informative articles for parents (practice tips, piano tuning, competitions, the benefits of music study, etc.)

- informative articles for students on interesting music-related subjects

SUMMARY

Teachers are professionals and should approach their teaching in a business-like manner. By giving thought about how to conduct a business, before beginning to teach, teachers will save time and frustration, while avoiding conflicts. To become more professional and businesslike, teachers can consider a number of issues:

- Choosing what types of students to teach (school-age children, adults and/or preschoolers) and how they will be taught (group or private lessons or a combination) will help determine where to teach.

- There are advantages and disadvantages to teaching in one's home, in student's homes, in rented spaces, as an employee for someone else, or in partnership with other teachers.

- In some municipalities, teaching in one's home may be prohibited due to zoning laws.

- When teachers choose to teach group lessons, they may need a larger space than their homes allow.

- Forming partnerships with other teachers encourages interaction with other professionals and can present a more professional image.

- Those who would like to teach for someone else in a large studio need to have a resumé and be prepared for a teaching demonstration and interview.

- Teachers can acquire students by becoming visible in their community and by using good advertising and marketing techniques.

- When teachers know how to conduct a good telephone interview, they are more likely to acquire new students.

- Teachers' policy statements protect both the teacher and the client and help to avoid conflicts.

- Professional teachers charge a tuition that is paid in advance.

- Piano teachers should charge fees that are reasonable, yet will assure them a sufficient income.

- Creative summer lesson programs will supplement the teacher's income and provide consistent and motivating instruction for their students.

- Teachers may need to find other professional employment to supplement their income.

- Teachers should know what equipment they will need and how they will finance it.

- The issues of taxes, insurance and retirement planning are important professional tasks.

- Learning how to schedule lessons efficiently will maximize the teacher's time.

- Regular communication with parents ensures that students will continue taking lessons.

PROJECTS FOR NEW TEACHERS

1. You would like to establish a studio in a specific city. To choose the most advantageous location, answer the following questions:
   - What is the average income of families in the community?
   - What types of employment are common in the community?
   - Where are the largest schools located (public, parochial and private)?
   - What types of leisure-time activities are popular with the children in the area?
   - Identify the retail music education centers in the area.
   - Identify the music schools, conservatories, preparatory schools in the area.
   - What are the local organizations that support the arts?
   - How many independent music teachers are there in the area and where do they teach?
   - What is the average fee for independent music teachers in the community?
   - What is the average salary for public school teachers in the community?
   - What are zoning requirements for home businesses or educational services?

2. You are planning to open an independent studio. Prepare the following materials:

   - a brochure about the studio to distribute to interested individuals in the community

   - a business card

   - a list of information, in the order of importance, that you would like to tell parents when they telephone requesting information about the studio

   - a studio policy statement

3. You are developing an advertising plan for a new studio. Prepare the following materials:

   - a classified ad for the newspaper

   - a display ad that can be placed in libraries, grocery stores and other public places

   - a letter of introduction that offers a music program for service organizations or Boy Scout and Girl Scout troops

4. You are applying for a teaching job with a local music school. Develop the following:

   - a professional resumé (no more than two pages in length) that highlights your qualifications

   - a list of questions that you would ask at a job interview regarding the curriculum, benefits and other information

5. Prepare a hypothetical personal budget to include the following:

   - an itemized list of personal expenses (including insurance, retirement and taxes)

   - an itemized list of professional expenses (including equipment, music, materials, and continuing education activities)

   - the amount of money that you will need to support yourself for a year

   - the fees you need to charge and the number of students you will need to achieve your financial goals

   - additional money that you may earn from other music-related jobs

PROJECTS FOR EXPERIENCED TEACHERS

1. Prepare a press release for the local newspaper on one of the following topics:

    - accomplishments of students in your studio

    - your own recent professional development activities, such as attending a workshop, convention or university course

    - a general interest article on a music topic such as practicing to learn to play a musical instrument, recent research on musical development, the importance of music education in a child's development, or guidelines for buying a piano

2. Write a newsletter to distribute to parents and students in your studio. Include the following:

    - accomplishments (both musical and nonmusical) of students in the studio

    - a calendar of upcoming studio events and musical events in the community

    - an article of interest to students in the studio

    - an article of interest to parents in the studio

3. Plan a one-week summer music camp on a specific theme for elementary or intermediate students in your studio. Develop the following materials:

    - a flier or brochure advertising the camp to parents and students

    - day-by-day lesson plans that you can use for the camp

Chapter 14
EVALUATION OF TEACHING

Since teaching is a skill, one must have a way to evaluate it and to determine whether it is producing results. When one learns to play the piano, experienced instructors guide the learning process, and thoughts and habits are developed through consistent and correct repetition during practice. Similarly, beginning teachers need the same kind of guidance, complete with consistent and correct repetition. Often, this systematic process is not available for piano teachers. They must instead rely on other means for evaluating and improving their teaching. This chapter suggests processes for such an evaluation. It is used most effectively once the teacher begins to observe or teach piano lessons.

To evaluate and improve one's teaching, one must pass through four stages:

1. Acknowledging a lack of knowledge and skills required for particular aspects of effective teaching.

2. Becoming aware of the knowledge and skills required for effective teaching.

3. Determining the steps needed to acquire the knowledge and skills necessary to be more effective, and implementing those steps.

4. Being secure in teaching, with extensive knowledge and abilities that can be drawn upon readily for each circumstance.

Teachers must find ways to work through stages 2 and 3 to evolve to the level of teaching described in stage 4.

The most common and convenient method of self-evaluation for teachers is to compare their own students' performances with those of other teachers. Competitions, festivals, auditions, recitals, master classes, and evaluations sponsored by music teachers' organizations provide opportunities for comparison and, occasionally, opinions from independent evaluators. Although this information is useful, it is limited because students who participate in these venues are usually the better students who are judged on the performance of only a few pieces, using a narrow range of criteria. Other aspects of student learning, such as sight-reading, aural development, and musical understanding, are rarely evaluated. As a result, teachers receive only minimal information about teaching effectiveness. Observing other teachers, role-playing, peer teaching, observing one's own teaching (through audio and visual recordings), and evaluation by master teachers are more useful measuring devices.

TRAITS OF EFFECTIVE TEACHING

Prior to any observation experiences, teachers should compare the traits of effective teaching to ineffective teaching. The following chart (see example 14.1) offers a comparison of some teacher and student behaviors that are the result of effective or ineffective instruction.

Example 14.1 Teacher and student behaviors

Effective Teaching	Ineffective Teaching
The student is "on task" and involved 100% of time.	The student plays while the teacher talks and doesn't follow directions.
The student is excited about learning.	The student looks bored and yawns frequently.
The student is ready for the task at hand.	The student has not been prepared and has difficulty with the task.
The student thinks and understands.	The student is confused, leading the teacher and the student to become frustrated.
The teacher knows the difference between sufficient follow-through and remaining on one task for too long.	The teacher leaves a task too soon for sufficient follow-through or stays too long on one task.
The atmosphere is nonthreatening to students.	The teacher lacks respect for the student's opinion. The student constantly wants to please the teacher, is simply compliant, or shows anxiety or fear.
The teacher lets students complete their tasks until success is achieved.	The teacher constantly stops the students.
The teacher allows the student to achieve one playing task before asking for additional requirements.	The teacher places additional requirements while the student struggles to achieve one task.
Music-making is the most important goal.	Perfection and precision are the most important goals.
The teacher lets the student discover new things, answer questions, and demonstrate mastery of the skill.	The teacher answers his/her own questions and does everything for the student.
The teacher knows the music well enough to focus on the student.	The teacher constantly looks at the musical score.
The teacher provides truthful evaluation and makes his/her expectations clear to students.	The teacher is overly kind and apologetic, often reluctant to assess the work honestly or make reasonable demands.

Effective Teaching (cont.)	Ineffective Teaching (cont.)
The teacher knows how the student is practicing and gives creative practice procedures to the student.	The teacher assigns unvaried practice techniques or gives no guidance for student practice.
The teacher coaches in a meaningful way, but not all the time.	The teacher sings along, plays in the upper register and counts for the student much of the time.
The teacher knows why mistakes were made and uses effective techniques to correct the mistakes.	The teacher simply has the student play the piece again, without clear goals for improving or correcting the mistakes.
The teacher knows when the student understands and will be able to accomplish a task.	The teacher simply asks students whether they understand or if they have any questions.
The teacher knows how to prevent errors and solve problems.	The teacher only corrects errors and assigns more practice.

ROLE-PLAYING AND PEER TEACHING

Role-playing and peer teaching provide teachers with ways to practice and improve their teaching. In role-playing, two or more teachers assume the roles of the teacher, the student(s) or parents to gain insight into solving common teaching problems. Specific problems and scenarios, such as those that follow, are acted out on the spot without prior preparation. The observers and participants critique the teacher's ability to resolve the problems or issues and offer suggestions for improvement or other potential solutions. Potential scenarios to be acted out as role-playing situations include the following:

- A student comes to the lesson without having practiced.
- The parent calls to cancel a lesson because the student has not practiced.
- A student does not like the assigned piece.
- A student doesn't speak in the lesson and is reluctant to answer questions.
- A student comes to the lesson expressing the inability to play the chords (or some other specific problem).
- A student constantly asks questions and wastes lesson time.
- A student intentionally neglects fingering.
- The key signature or accidentals are ignored.

- A student has trouble playing and counting aloud simultaneously.

- A student has trouble keeping a steady tempo.

- A student pauses at the end of every measure or at the end of every line.

- A student performance lacks phrasing or dynamic contrast.

- A student plays a practiced piece with many wrong notes.

- A student plays too fast and makes numerous mistakes.

- A student has prepared well for the lesson but plays as though he/she has practiced very little.

- A parent doesn't want to remind or force the student to practice for fear of destroying the desire to learn and play.

- A student has decided to quit lessons, but the teacher and parent(s) are seeking ways for the student to continue studying.

- A student is unmotivated and appears bored during the lesson.

- Instead of the piano, a musically talented student decides to concentrate on a particular sport and is dedicating less time to practicing the piano.

- A student is perfection-driven, but somewhat lazy.

- A student's playing does not meet the high expectations of the parent(s), even though the student already plays quite well.

In a peer-teaching model, one teacher plans and teaches a mini-lesson (15 minutes or less) to another teacher who pretends to be the student. The teacher prepares a short lesson plan consisting of one or more of the following: the presentation of a new piece, the coaching of a practiced piece or any other lesson activity, such as technical development. The teacher, the "student," and those observing critique the lesson.

OBSERVATION AND EVALUATION

While role-playing and peer-teaching experiences are valuable, observation of others' teaching and self-observation/evaluation are the best ways to evaluate one's own teaching effectiveness.

Teaching is aided by four types of observation experiences:

- observation of effective teaching

- self-observation by recording lessons (video or audio)

- self-evaluation following the lesson

- observation/evaluation by other effective teachers

Observation of Effective Teaching

Much can be learned from observing a variety of teachers—piano teachers, other music teachers, and classroom teachers. While teachers can learn by watching teachers who are less skilled, observation of effective teaching offers the best source for building knowledge and skills. Observation is essential for new teachers, but it can also enhance the skills of experienced teachers.

Observation is only effective if the observer knows specifically what to observe and follows a systematic plan. The first step in successful observation is to outline what takes place during the lesson. Those notes would include items such as the following:

- what the teacher says and does

- what the student says and does

- what materials and activities are used

- the order in which the materials and activities are presented

Notating Teaching Practices and Objectives

In a shorthand form, observers can take brief notes that detail what takes place in the lesson. It is sometimes important to notate the exact words used by the teacher, but it is not always possible to do this with extended explanations on particular topics. The first column of example 14.2 provides sample notes of a five-minute portion of a lesson. They are probably more extensive than an observing teacher would be able to write, but they provide ideas about what to observe and write. Following the lesson, the observer determines the teaching objectives for all segments of the lesson. The written objectives for the lesson segment on half and whole steps would look something like those in the second column.

Example 14.2 Sample lesson observation

Notes from an observed lesson	Objectives and strategies of the teacher as discerned by the observer
Teacher: "What is a half step?" Student: "From one key to the very next key." Teacher: "Excellent!"	When the student is expected to give precise definitions, accurate learning is ensured.
The teacher drills half steps on the keyboard using RH or LH separately—"RH finger 2 play G, up a half step, down a half step," etc. The student plays and says the names of the keys. Teacher: "You did the half steps perfectly."	The student *experiences* the half steps by playing them. The teacher is assured that the student understands. The student says the key names while playing them to reinforce the understanding of half steps and note names (e.g., G-sharp, E-flat, etc.). Reinforcement, encouragement and motivation—varied and specific to the task—are effective.

Notes from an observed lesson (cont.)	Objectives and strategies of the teacher as discerned by the observer (cont.)
Teacher: "What is a whole step?" Student: "From one key to another key, skipping one key." Teacher: "Yes. Do you always skip a white key?" Student: "No, you might skip a black or a white key." Teacher: "Well done!"	Again, when the student is expected to give precise definitions, accurate learning is ensured.
The teacher drills whole steps on the keyboard in a manner similar to the half-step drill, followed by a similar drill that mixes half steps and whole steps. Teacher: "You only missed two intervals. That was excellent."	The student *experiences* the half steps and whole steps by playing them. The teacher is assured that the student understands. The student says the key names while playing them to reinforce the understanding of half steps, whole steps and key names. Success is ensured when the student becomes comfortable with half steps and then whole steps, before mixing them. Expanding the drill to include a pattern of whole and half steps prepares the student to build five-finger patterns and, eventually, scales.
Teacher: "Let's see whether you can play patterns of half and whole steps. RH finger 1 on G, up a whole step, half step, whole step, whole step." The teacher corrects, when a mistake is made, by asking, "Was that a whole step (half step)?" Teacher: "You only mixed up two intervals. That's much better than last week."	When the teacher involves the student by asking whether it was correct, the student will become better able to find and correct his/her own mistakes during practice times at home. Students are more motivated to continue learning if they know they have improved since the last lesson.
The teacher opens the lesson book to a new piece that has a number of accidentals and asks the student to find, circle and play all the half steps. Teacher: "You found most of them, but you missed one in line 2 and two in line 3. Can you find them?" The student locates the half steps that have not been circled.	Having the student immediately find, circle and play each half step in a new piece applies what has been learned, making for a smooth transition from one lesson activity to the next. Giving the student clues for finding mistakes encourages thinking and independent learning.

Questions for Evaluating Teaching

Once the observer has outlined the lesson and determined the objectives, he/she can answer a series of questions that help to determine the effectiveness of the teaching in the following categories (see example 14.3):

- interaction between the student and the teacher

- personal qualities of the teacher

- behaviors of the student

- organization, conduct and pacing of the lesson

- content of the lesson

- teaching procedures and behaviors

- techniques used to lead the student to think and learn independently

- techniques used to develop the student's understanding of concepts and performance skills

Example 14.3
Questionnaire for evaluating teaching

Interaction between the student and the teacher:

- Was the student shy and reticent, open and responsive, or uncooperative?

- Did the student actively and willingly participate in all activities?

- Was the teacher or the student in control of the lesson?

- Did the teacher work with the student to enable learning?

- Was the lesson environment supportive and nonthreatening?

- Was there a shared sense of accomplishment?

Personal qualities of the teacher:

- Was the teacher friendly, yet businesslike?

- Was the teacher positive and enthusiastic?

- Was the teacher imaginative and creative?

- Did the teacher appear to enjoy teaching and express excitement in appropriate circumstances?

- Did the teacher appear to be comfortable and relaxed in the teaching situation?

- Did the teacher interact frequently with the student?

Questionnaire for evaluating teaching (cont.)

- Was the teacher's speaking voice clear and loud enough for the student to understand questions and explanations?

- Did the teacher use humor and make the learning enjoyable?

- Was the teacher aware of what was happening all of the time?

- Did the teacher seem to genuinely care about the student and want to help him/her learn?

- Did the teacher respond positively while observing the student's statements, facial expressions, and body language?

- Did the teacher use positive reinforcement effectively by praising hard work and good answers, as well as the student's successful performance?

Behaviors of the student:

- What was the student's most successful activity?

- What was the student's least successful activity?

- Was the student's attention always on task?

- Did the student understand the teacher's explanations and directions?

- Was the student able to play with accuracy and ease?

- For how much of the lesson was the student involved in playing and doing?

- Did the student seem proud of his/her achievement?

- Did the student feel proud and successful at the end of the lesson?

Organization, conduct and pacing of the lesson:

- Did the teacher appear to be prepared for the teaching tasks?

- Were the learning experiences sequenced logically?

- Were the most difficult tasks presented during the time the student was most able to concentrate?

- Did the teacher know when the student had learned a concept or skill and then move on to another activity?

- Were rules and routines established?

- Was there variety and balance between the types of learning experiences?

- Was the variety sufficient to keep the student actively involved and interested?

- Was there a good balance between intense and relaxed activities?

- Was a large portion of the lesson focused on one type of learning activity to the detriment of other equally important activities?

- Did the organization of material allow for smooth transitions from one activity to the next? Did some projects prepare for and lead into the next activity?

- During what percentage of the lesson time was the student playing the piano? (This should be the largest percentage of time.)

- During what percentage of the lesson time was the student actively doing learning activities that did not involve playing the piano?

- Was a large portion of the lesson time consumed with the teacher talking, or were there frequent and brief student and teacher interactions? (The teacher should talk very little and use as few words as possible.)

Content of the lesson:

- Was the lesson interesting, challenging, enjoyable and/or enlightening?

- Were appealing materials and music used?

- Was the lesson focused mostly on musical development, or on mechanical things, such as fingering, accurate note reading and precise rhythm?

- Were the teacher's objectives easy to determine?

- Was there variety in the types of skills developed—creative work, ear training, ensemble playing, harmonization, memory, musical playing, rhythm, sight-reading, technique, theory, and transposition?

- Were imaginative and creative activities included?

- How much lesson time was spent on each element, such as theory, rhythm, and ear training? Was each element presented as a separate event or integrated into the entire learning procedure?

Teaching procedures and behaviors:

- Did the teacher demonstrate an understanding of the principles of learning?

- Did the teacher evaluate the student's performance(s) accurately?

- Did the teacher quickly diagnose problems?

- Did the teacher simplify and help the student solve difficulties effectively?

- Did the teacher demonstrate the ability to prevent student errors from developing?

Questionnaire for evaluating teaching (cont.)

- Did the teacher offer solutions and strategies for breaking down problems into smaller, more manageable, tasks?

- Did the teacher use a variety of instructional techniques to achieve results?

- Did the teacher enable student exploration and problem-solving?

- Did the teacher provide frequent feedback?

- Were expectations communicated clearly?

- Was repetition used effectively?

- How often did the teacher stop the student performance(s) to work on small details?

- Was good progress made in the lesson?

- Did the teacher play for or with the student?

- Were high standards maintained?

Techniques used to lead the student to think and learn independently:

- Did the teacher help the student discover information by asking questions, rather than just providing information?

- Did the teacher formulate questions in a way that encouraged the student to think?

- Was the student allowed sufficient time to respond to questions and directions?

- Did the teacher use appropriate language for the student's age?

- Were general principles taught, as opposed to just teaching a specific piece?

- Did the student develop good learning habits?

- Did the teaching make the student more or less reliant on the teacher?

- Was the student prepared for home practice?

- Will the student be able to apply learned information to other situations?

Techniques used to develop the student's understanding of concepts and performance skills:

- Were new concepts and ideas presented clearly and with sufficient reinforcement to assure long-term understanding?

- Was there sufficient follow-through so that the student had a chance to master specific skills and feel successful?

- Was the student allowed to be involved in and experience each new idea?

Questionnaire for evaluating teaching (cont.)

- Were the various senses (aural, visual and kinesthetic) used to aid in the learning?

- Was the teacher sufficiently aware of the student's physical approach to playing?

- Were good technical habits encouraged throughout the lesson?

- Was the student guided to play with greater physical ease?

- Did the student play with rhythmic accuracy? If not, was he/she given ways to improve this accuracy?

- Were musical concepts reinforced?

- In what ways was the student encouraged to play musically?

- Were practice expectations clear?

- Did the teacher model and demonstrate effectively?

Since it may be difficult to answer all of the above questions, new teachers may want to limit each observation to one of the categories, focusing only on specific elements. For example, the teacher might focus on the organization, conduct and pacing of the lesson time. A stopwatch can be used to time segments of playing and talking to determine if there was excessive talk and whether the student played during enough of the lesson.

In addition to transcribing the lesson content, determining objectives and using questionnaires, some observations can be limited to specific teacher and/or student behaviors. For example, the teacher might want to simply observe the verbal exchange and body language of the teacher and the student. The observer would note what words the teacher and student use for specific concepts, skills, and learning tasks and how the teacher and the student relate to each other through words, facial expressions and other body motions. Another type of focused observation might involve motivation and reinforcement. The observer would note how the teacher appraises, evaluates, provides feedback, and motivates the student using positive and negative reinforcement. These focused observations help teachers concentrate on teaching issues that may be of particular interest or concern to them.

Outlining lessons, listing lesson objectives and making specific observations by answering questions help observing teachers think about how and why things are done in lessons. These perceptions help them evaluate their own teaching.

- Observation skills will become finely honed, making teachers more observant of their own teaching.

- Concentration is increased, thereby helping teachers focus more effectively in their own teaching.

- Critical thinking is developed. This ability to evaluate goals, objectives and student needs logically is essential to improving teaching skills.

- Writing the lesson observation improves the ability to write and speak succinctly. The ability to present clear explanations and write concise lesson assignments is essential in piano teaching.

Self-Observation by Recording Lessons

In addition to observations of other teachers, teachers can observe their own teaching by using audio or video recordings. Since each of these recording techniques provides unique insights, it is beneficial to use a combination of both. Audio recordings allow teachers to focus on the parts of the lesson that can be heard, without being distracted by visual images. The information gained includes the following:

- clarity of the explanations

- verbal content of the questions

- verbal responses of the students

- balance of time between playing and talking

- quality of the playing

- changes in the sounds of the student's playing

Video recordings allow teachers to focus on visual aspects of the lesson that would not be possible with an audio recording. These include items such as the following:

- student's posture

- student's and teacher's facial expressions

- student's and teacher's body language

- student's hand positions and use of body at the keyboard

- student's attention to what is happening

Established teachers can begin by recording one lesson each week. A different student can be recorded each week giving the teacher the opportunity to observe a variety of student types, levels and abilities. Preparing highly structured lesson plans and recording students without giving them advance notice will guarantee a more realistic lesson.

To evaluate improvement in teaching, it is helpful to record the same student several weeks apart and then compare the two lessons. Self-observation through recordings should continue on an irregular basis throughout a teacher's career. Use the following questionnaire (see example 14.4) to guide the evaluation of audio recordings.

Example 14.4
Evaluation of audio-recorded lessons

- What percentage of the lesson time was spent with the student playing the piano? (Time the playing segments.)

- What percentage of the lesson time was spent with the teacher talking? (Time the talking segments.) How could the same information be presented with fewer words?

- Were instructions, questions and explanations clear? How could they be improved?

- Was the teacher's vocabulary appropriate for the student?

- List any inappropriate questions or explanations and restructure each.

- Did the student exhibit trust, feeling free to question, or did he/she simply comply with instructions?

- Was the student allowed to make choices and discover new things independently?

- List statements the student was told how to do something. Should the student have been led to discover any of these things?

- List each statement that led the student to discover appropriate information.

- List each correction made during the lesson.

- List every time the student was encouraged and write the exact words used.

- List student mistakes and why they may have occurred.

- Prioritize the problems in each practiced piece. Indicate which problems were addressed in the lesson and whether positive change resulted.

Priority of problems in the piece: _____ (Title of piece)	Was the problem addressed in the lesson? (circle yes or no)		Did positive change result? (circle yes or no)	
1.	Yes	No	Yes	No
2.	Yes	No	Yes	No
3.	Yes	No	Yes	No
4.	Yes	No	Yes	No
5.	Yes	No	Yes	No

- In what way was each new piece presented to facilitate the learning of the piece during practice?

- List the things from the lesson that gave the student a sense of accomplishment.

- List questions that encouraged the student to think.

- List when and how expectations were expressed to the student.

- Did the pacing allow for as much to be accomplished as was intended? Where was time wasted?

Use the following questionnaire (see example 14.5) to guide the evaluation of video recordings.

Example 14.5
Evaluation of video-recorded lessons

Cite specific examples when answering the following questions:

- How would you describe your personality during the lesson? Use as many terms as would apply (for example, pleasant, smiling, enthusiastic, stern, friendly, outgoing, quiet).

- How do you think these personality characteristics affected the lesson and the student's behavior and responses?

- Were you aware of what was going on in the lesson at all times?

- Were you or the student having more fun? Who was more animated?

- Was there excitement about learning on your part and the student's? When and where?

- Did the student's interest wane anytime during the lesson? List the times you observed that the student was not "on task."

- What percentage of the lesson time was spent where the student was not concentrating? (Time those segments.)

- What activities were used to counteract the student's boredom?

- Were any presentations or explanations not clearly understood by the student? If yes, describe how you could have presented the same material more effectively.

- Which segments of the lesson were organized and which ones were not?

- Did the student exhibit good posture and use a good hand position throughout the lesson? If not, when were the posture and hand position not good? Were other technical problems contributing to these problems?

- Did the student leave the lesson feeling successful? What did you observe that supports your opinion?

- Did the student leave the lesson understanding all of the elements covered in the lesson? List the elements that the student clearly understood and those which might not have been understood.

- What surprised you most about the lesson?

- List several effective things about the lesson.

- Based on this video recording, list several behaviors, in order of importance, that you would like to change in your teaching.

- List several behaviors, in order of importance, that you would like to change in the student's learning and playing.

Alternative ways to use video recordings to evaluate one's teaching include the following:

- The video recording can be self-evaluated by outlining the lesson, listing objectives and answering the same questions discussed earlier in relation to observing other teachers (see pages 396–400).

- Watch the video with the sound off, observing body movement, body language, and facial expressions. (When there are no distractions from the sounds of talking and playing, it is easier to focus on the visual aspects of teacher and student behaviors.)

- Video-record lessons with the camera on the student only, to focus on student behaviors and reactions. Observe the following:

  - the student's facial expressions

  - the student's attention to the task and the teacher

  - the frequency and types of student verbal responses

  - the student's body language and posture

  - the amount of time allowed for the student to think and respond

  - the student looking at the teacher for approval

The types of student behaviors and reactions that can be observed while viewing a video recording might include the following:

anxiety	joy	simple compliance
boredom	laughter	smiling
confusion	questioning	understanding
excitement	thinking	hard work
frustration	trust	inattention

After recording and/or evaluating, the teacher should list the weaknesses in the teaching and prioritize them, listing the most critical problems first. The teacher can plan for the next lessons to include ways to eliminate the most critical problems. After the teacher has worked to eliminate weaknesses, additional recordings and evaluation can be used to verify teaching improvement. When the most critical weaknesses are remedied, the teacher can continue the same process to focus on other problems.

Self-Evaluation Following the Lesson

After several months of recording selected lessons, a simpler process can be followed. The teacher can complete an evaluation at the end of each lesson. These evaluations can be kept and used to prepare future lessons. Evaluations can also be reviewed weekly or monthly to determine strengths and weaknesses. The following (see example 14.6) provides a sample of a short evaluation form.

Example 14.6
Lesson evaluation form

Name of Student_____Date _____

1. Did the student grasp the new concepts? ☐ Yes ☐ No

2. What were the student's strongest pieces from the practiced assignment?

3. What were the student's weakest pieces from the practiced assignment?

4. Rate the student's preparation of the lesson material.
    ☐ Excellent ☐ Good ☐ Fair ☐ Poor

5. List areas in which the student needs reinforcement.

6. Was the entire lesson plan covered? ☐ Yes ☐ No
    If not, what things were omitted?

7. Did the student play musically? ☐ Yes ☐ No
    (Check areas that need work.) ☐ Dynamics ☐ Tone ☐ Touch ☐ Phrases

8. Did the student play with ease physically? ☐ Yes ☐ No
    (Check areas that need work.) ☐ Fingers ☐ Wrist ☐ Arm ☐ Posture

9. Did the student play with rhythmic accuracy? ☐ Yes ☐ No

10. Were encouragement and praise used effectively during the lesson? ☐ Yes ☐ No
    What specific words or phrases were used?

11. Rate the student/teacher interaction.
    ☐ Excellent ☐ Good ☐ Fair ☐ Poor

12. Were the presentations organized and effective? ☐ Yes ☐ No
    If not, where and how could they be improved?

13. Were student problems dealt with effectively? ☐ Yes ☐ No
    If not, where and how could they be improved?

14. What errors were corrected? How could they have been prevented?

15. Which pieces were coached for musical results? How successful was the coaching?

16. If you were the student, would you want to come back to your piano lesson next
    week? ☐ Yes ☐ No Why or why not?

As teachers become more experienced, even shorter evaluations, such as the one in example 14.7, can be completed.

Example 14.7
Lesson evaluation short form

Name of Student_____Date _____

1. What concepts and skills did the student learn that he/she did not already know?

2. What could the student do better at the end of the lesson than he/she was able to do prior to the lesson?

3. What was *actually* covered in the lesson? (Not just what was planned.)

4. What were the student's strongest areas?

5. What were the student's weakest areas?

6. How did the teaching build on the strengths and correct the weaknesses?

7. Was the lesson enjoyable?

Evaluating Group Lessons

For group lessons, each of the evaluation forms can be slightly modified. Additional questions can be included to evaluate the effectiveness of group instruction:

- Were the pace and content of the lesson directed to the average student of the group?

- Did all activities include ways for all students to be successful?

- How were the learning activities structured to meet the needs of the slower and/or less assertive students?

- Was there awareness of the behavior, response and learning of each student?

- Were all students involved during the entire lesson?

- What amount of time was spent helping individual students?

- Were high-energy activities alternated with less energetic ones?

- What specific verbal cues and class routines were used to keep the group together?

- Did the teacher use a projecting voice and a positive tone?

- Were some learning activities structured to encourage interaction between students?

Observation/Evaluation by Other Effective Teachers

While self-observation has numerous advantages, there is no substitute for an independent observer pointing out strengths and weaknesses. Regular observation by a person involved in teacher training is an invaluable aid.

Lessons that are observed should be typical lessons, and students should be informed in advance that a visitor will attend the lesson to observe the teacher, not the student. The teacher should provide the observer with a copy of the previous week's assignment sheet, a copy of the current lesson plan, and copies of the music. The observer may take notes during the lesson and conduct a discussion with the teacher following the lesson. Video-recorded lessons can also be evaluated by an independent observer, preferably with both the observer and the teacher present. The video recording can be stopped and replayed to assist the discussion of the teaching.

SUMMARY

A critical look at one's own teaching may be stressful, but it provides positive results. Teachers who take a small amount of time each week to practice evaluation skills and critique their teaching find that their teaching—and their students' learning—improve quickly. Teachers can evaluate and improve their teaching in a variety of ways:

- Role-playing and peer teaching are helpful ways to practice teaching.
- Writing critiques of observed lessons help teachers become more observant of their own teaching and think critically about goals, objectives and student needs.
- Recorded lessons give teachers specific and unique insights into their teaching.
- Simple and short evaluations of lessons can be completed on a regular basis and used to find strengths and weaknesses in one's own teaching.
- Observation by teaching specialists is the most effective form of teacher evaluation.
- Observations that look at teaching from several focused perspectives enable improvement in specific areas, including the following:
  - interaction between the teacher and student
  - personal qualities of the teacher
  - behaviors of the student
  - organization, conduct and pacing of the lesson
  - content of the lesson
  - teaching procedures and behaviors
  - techniques used to lead the student to think and learn independently
  - techniques used to develop the student's understanding of concepts and performance skills
- Teachers can use additional criteria to evaluate their group teaching.

PROJECTS FOR NEW TEACHERS

1. Observe some lessons of an experienced teacher and write detailed notes about each lesson. Write what you perceive to be the teacher's objectives and strategies. Use pages 394–395 as a guide for your notes and objectives.

2. Study the chart regarding the behaviors of effective and ineffective teaching on pages 391–392. Observe one or more lessons of an experienced teacher. As you observe, make notes about the teaching based on the behaviors described on the chart. Prepare a one-page evaluation of the teaching based on your observation and notes.

3. Audio-record some of the lessons you teach. Use the form for evaluating audio-recorded lesson on page 402 and answer as many questions as possible. Compare the evaluations, and choose and prioritize five areas that you would like to improve in your teaching. Prioritize the list in the order you would like to work on these areas.

PROJECTS FOR EXPERIENCED TEACHERS

1. Ask a friend (or fellow student) who is a piano teacher to join you in role-playing teaching projects. Choose topics based on teaching problems you may have experienced or on the suggestions listed on pages 392–393.

2. Schedule and prepare to observe a lesson taught by an effective teacher. Choose two different categories of questions from pages 396–400. Review the questions prior to the lesson. While observing the lesson, focus on the categories you have chosen and make notes related to those questions. After the lesson, answer the questions and write a one-page evaluation as to the effectiveness of the teacher in each category.

3. Using the lesson evaluation form on page 405, complete the form for several of your students. Review all of the forms and evaluate trends in your teaching. Make and prioritize a list of five areas that need work. At the end of five weeks, complete another evaluation for the same students. Compare the results to your previous evaluations.

4. Video-record some of the lessons you teach. Use the form for evaluating video-recorded lessons on page 403 and answer as many questions as possible. Compare the evaluations and choose and prioritize five areas that you would like to improve in your teaching.

Index